Shojo Beat

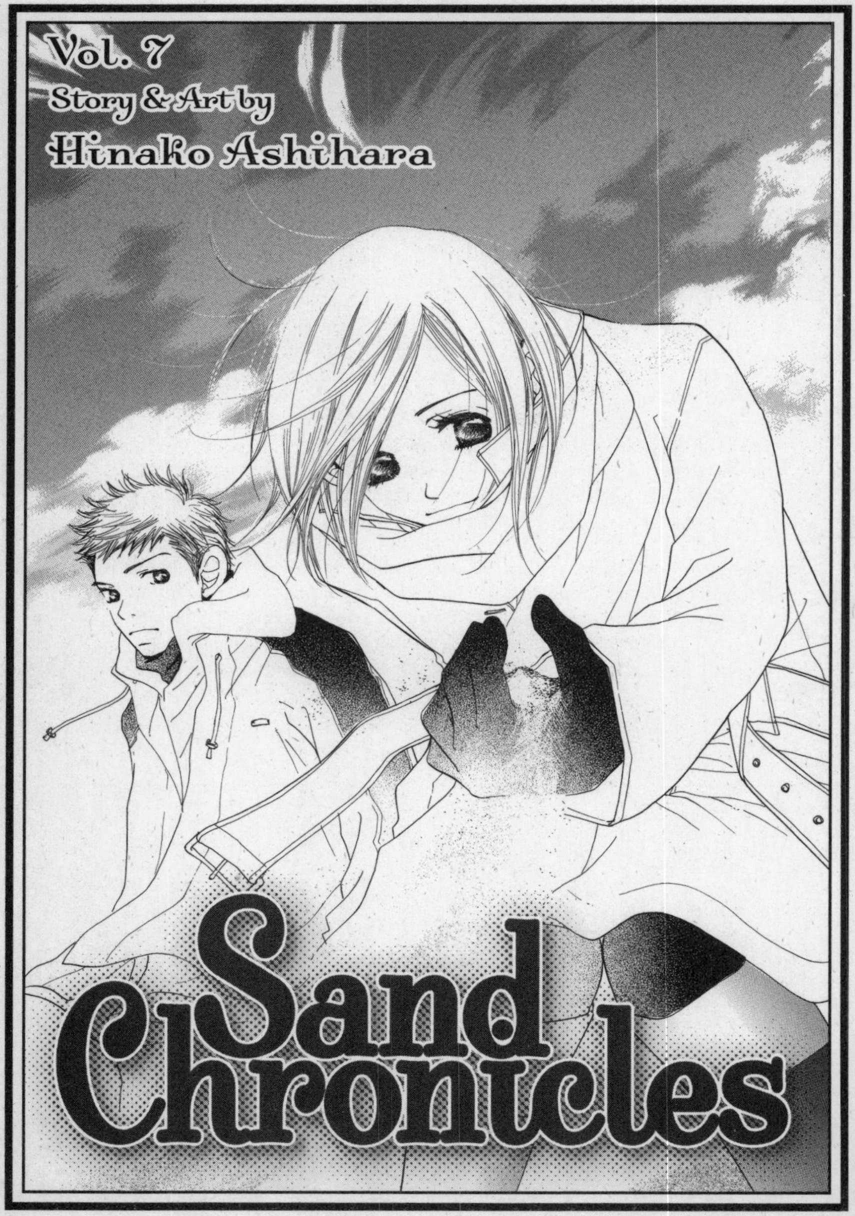
Vol. 7
Story & Art by
Hinako Ashihara
Sand Chronicles

Sand Chronicles

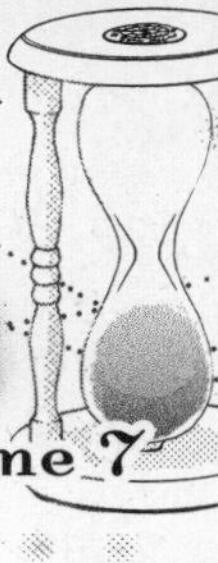

Volume 7

Contents

Story thus far...

After her parents' divorce, Ann moves to rural Shimane with her mother. When Ann's mother commits suicide, Ann's new friends, Daigo and wealthy siblings Fuji and Shika, are a great support to her. But then Ann moves back to Tokyo to live with her father...

Ann finally commits to dating Fuji. On a study trip by the seaside, they spend the night together. But Ann realizes she is still in love with Daigo. Ann's father's longtime friend Kaede has become pregnant with his child, and Ann encourages them to marry. After thinking long and hard, Ann decides to leave Fuji...and once again finds herself all alone.

Main characters

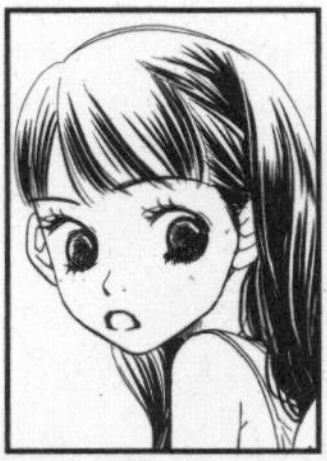

Shika Tsukishima
Shika tried to manipulate Ann into having a nervous breakdown so she could steal Daigo.

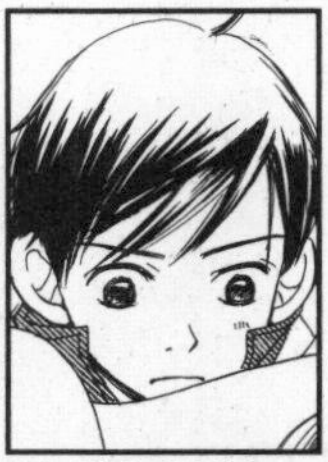

Fuji Tsukishima
It seems like no matter how many times Ann rejects him, Fuji still wants to be with her.

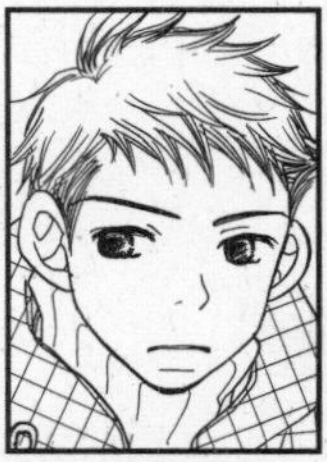

Daigo Kitamura
Daigo's friends encouraged him to date Ayumu, the girl who is tutoring him.

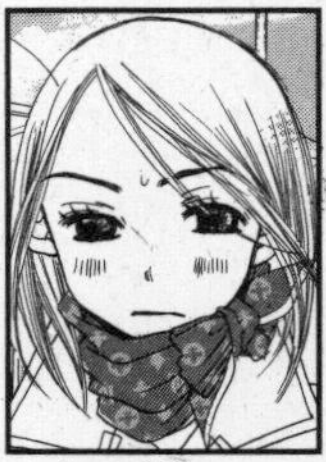

Ann Minase
Uncertain about her future, Ann decides to study Japanese literature at a junior college.

WINTER, AGE 20: SINGING SAND

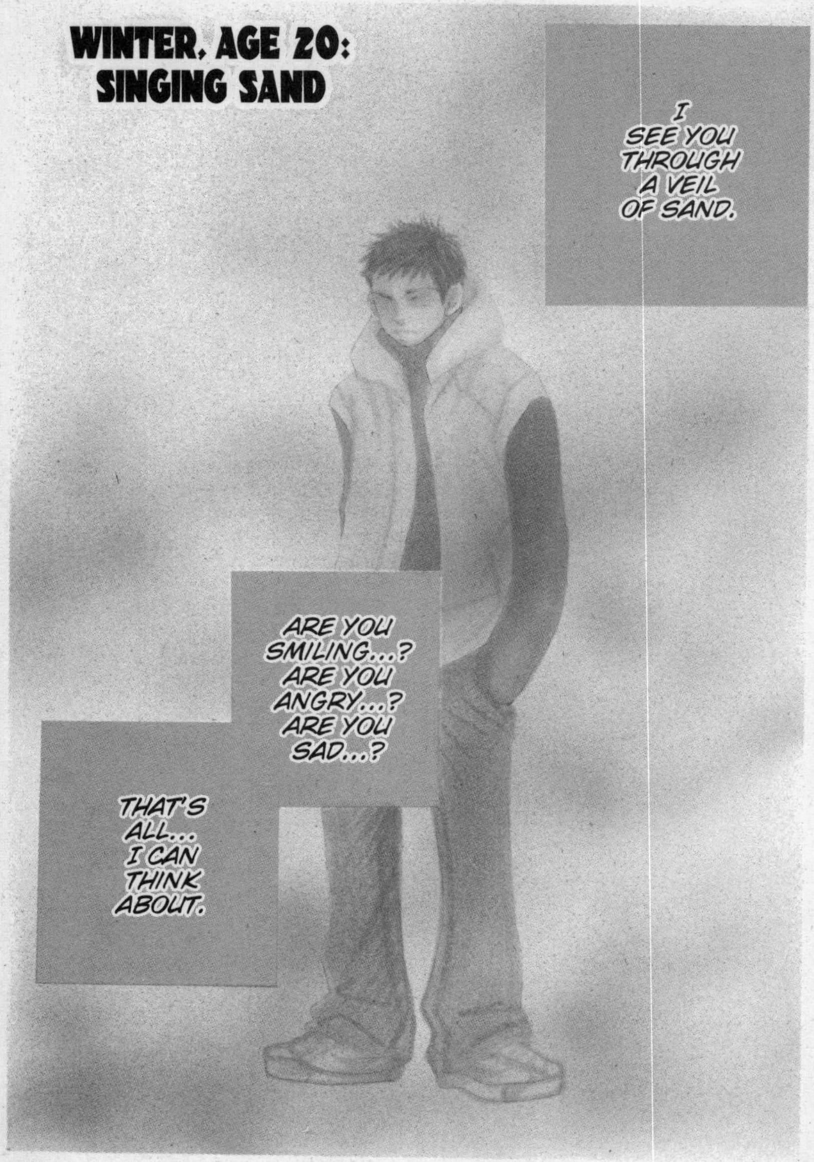
I SEE YOU THROUGH A VEIL OF SAND.
ARE YOU SMILING...? ARE YOU ANGRY...? ARE YOU SAD...?
THAT'S ALL... I CAN THINK ABOUT.

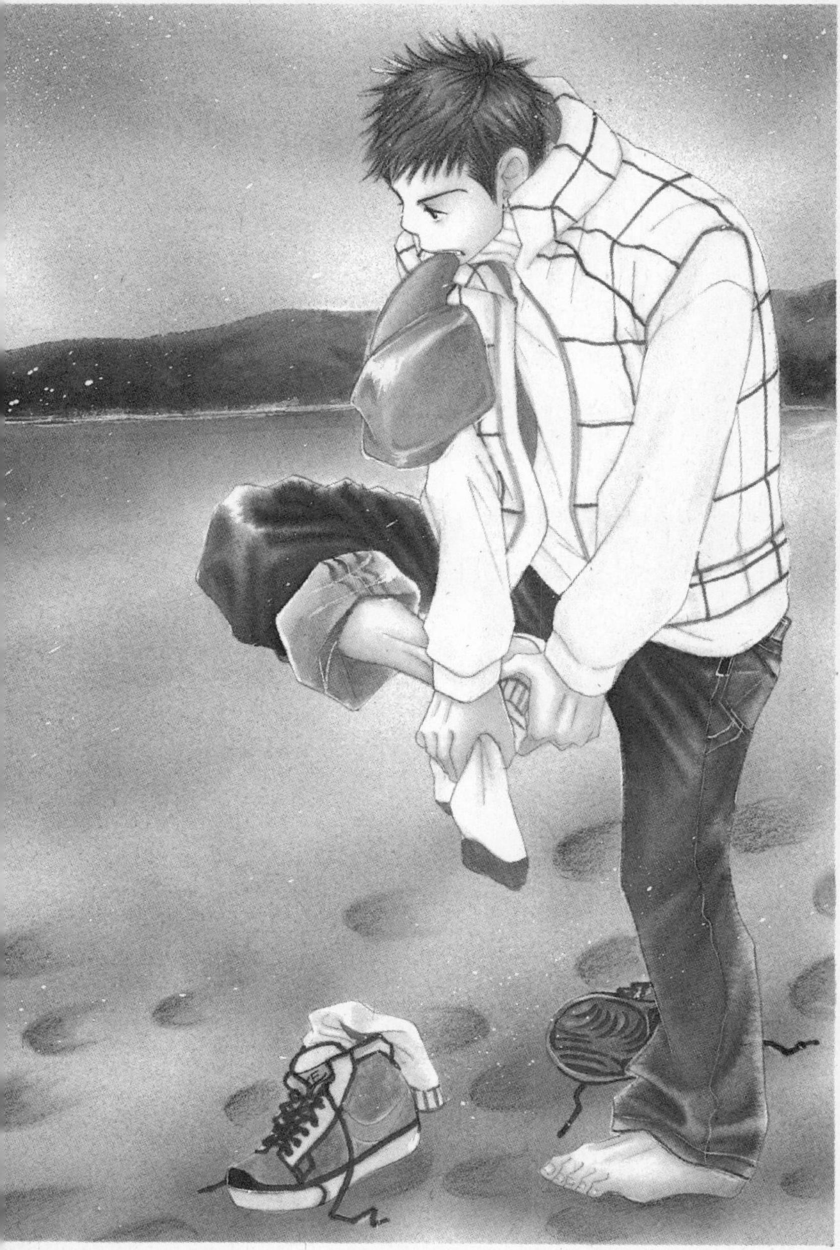

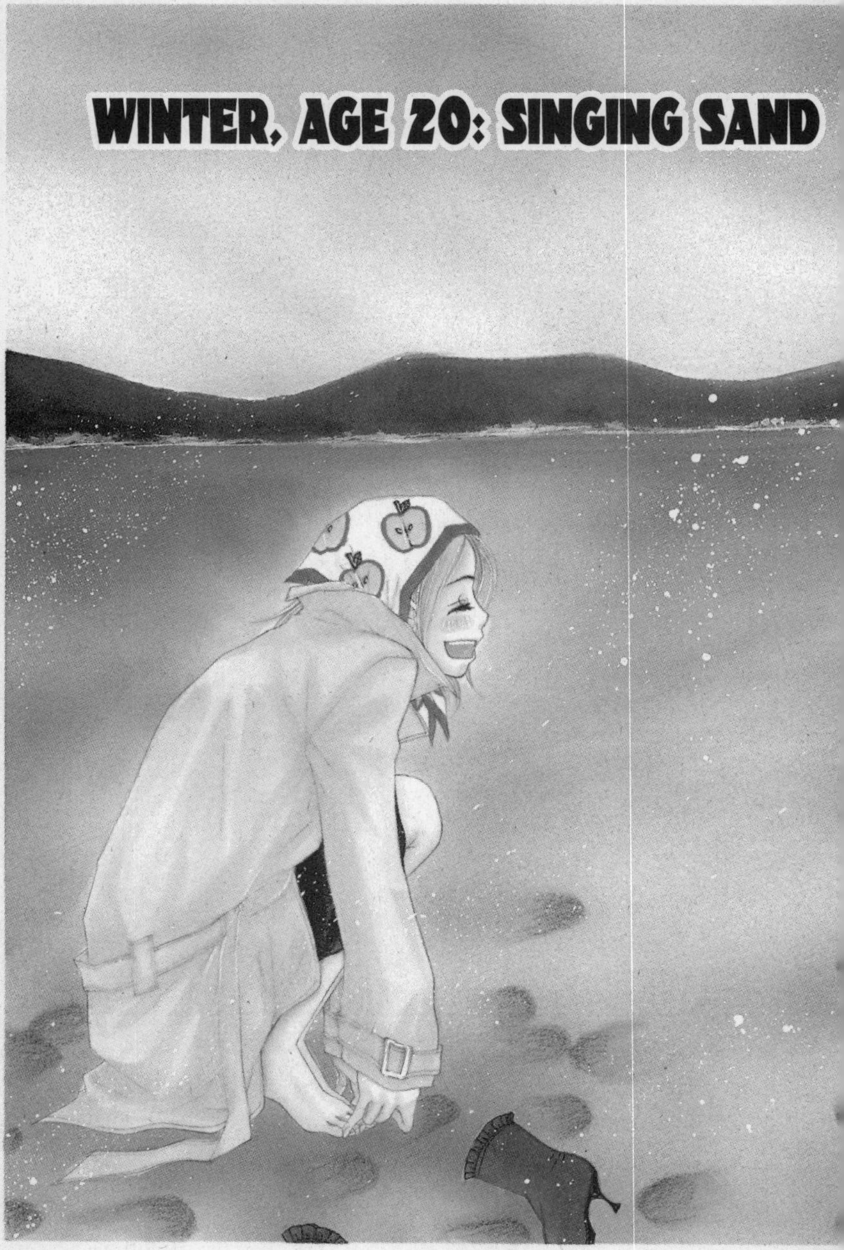
WINTER, AGE 20: SINGING SAND

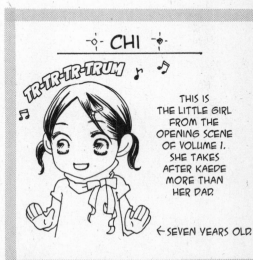

·◇· CHI ·◇·

TR-TR-TR-TRUM ♪ ♪ ♪

THIS IS
THE LITTLE GIRL
FROM THE
OPENING SCENE
OF VOLUME 1.
SHE TAKES
AFTER KAEDE
MORE THAN
HER DAD.

← SEVEN YEARS OLD.

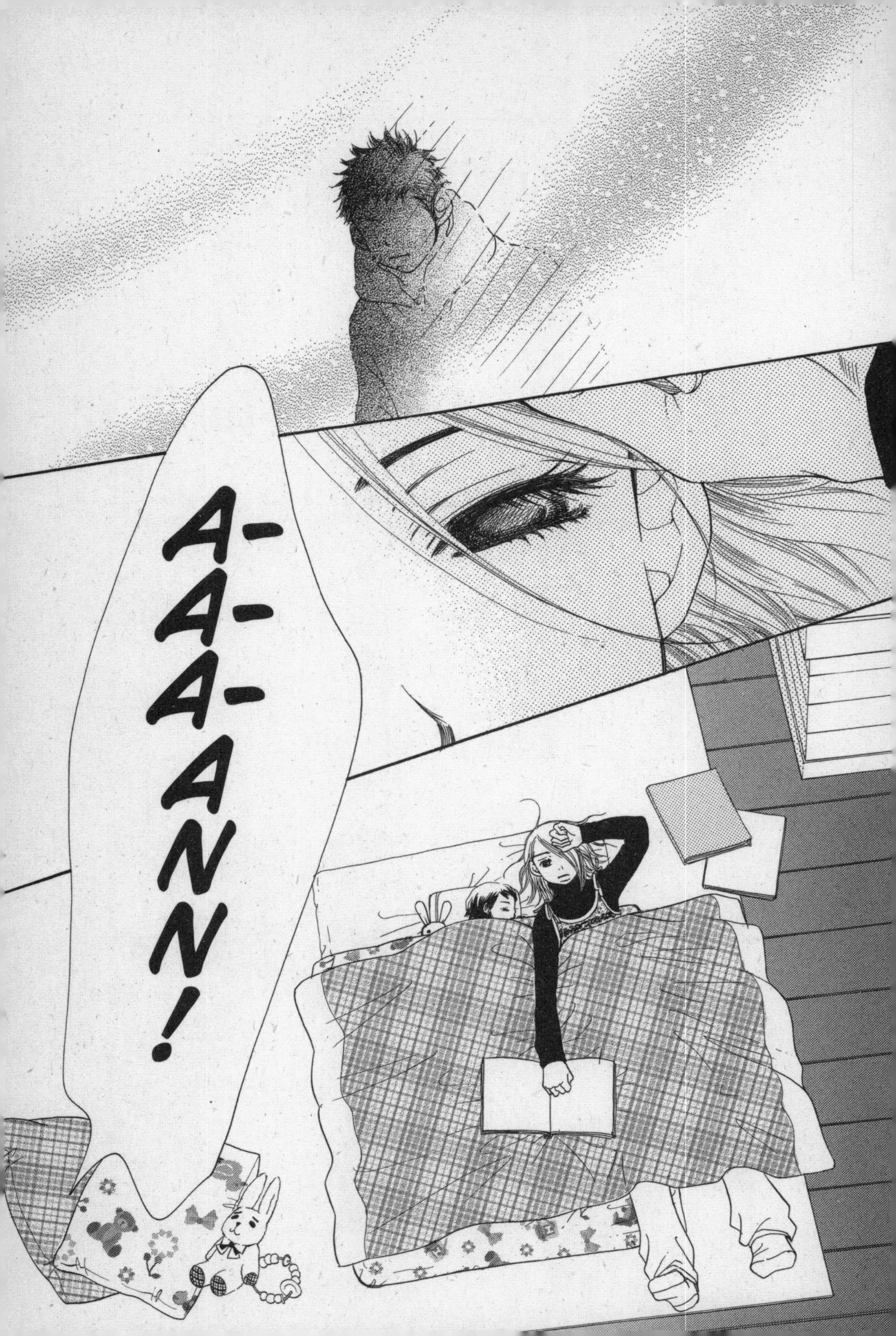
A-A-A-AANN!

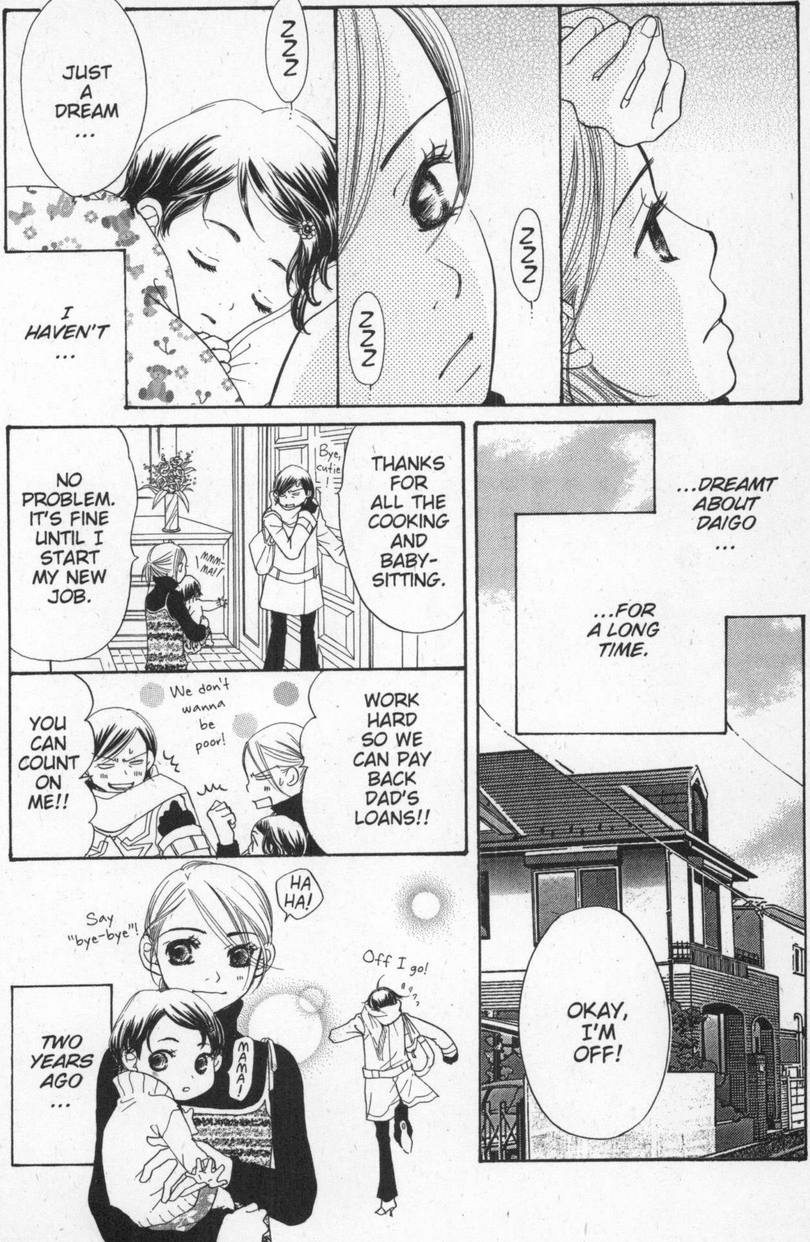
ZZZ
ZZZ
ZZZ
JUST A DREAM...
I HAVEN'T...
...DREAMT ABOUT DAIGO...
...FOR A LONG TIME.
OKAY, I'M OFF!
THANKS FOR ALL THE COOKING AND BABY-SITTING.
Bye, cutie!
mmm-ma!!
NO PROBLEM. IT'S FINE UNTIL I START MY NEW JOB.
WORK HARD SO WE CAN PAY BACK DAD'S LOANS!!
We don't wanna be poor!
YOU CAN COUNT ON ME!!
Off I go!
HA HA!
Say "bye-bye"!
MAMA!
TWO YEARS AGO...

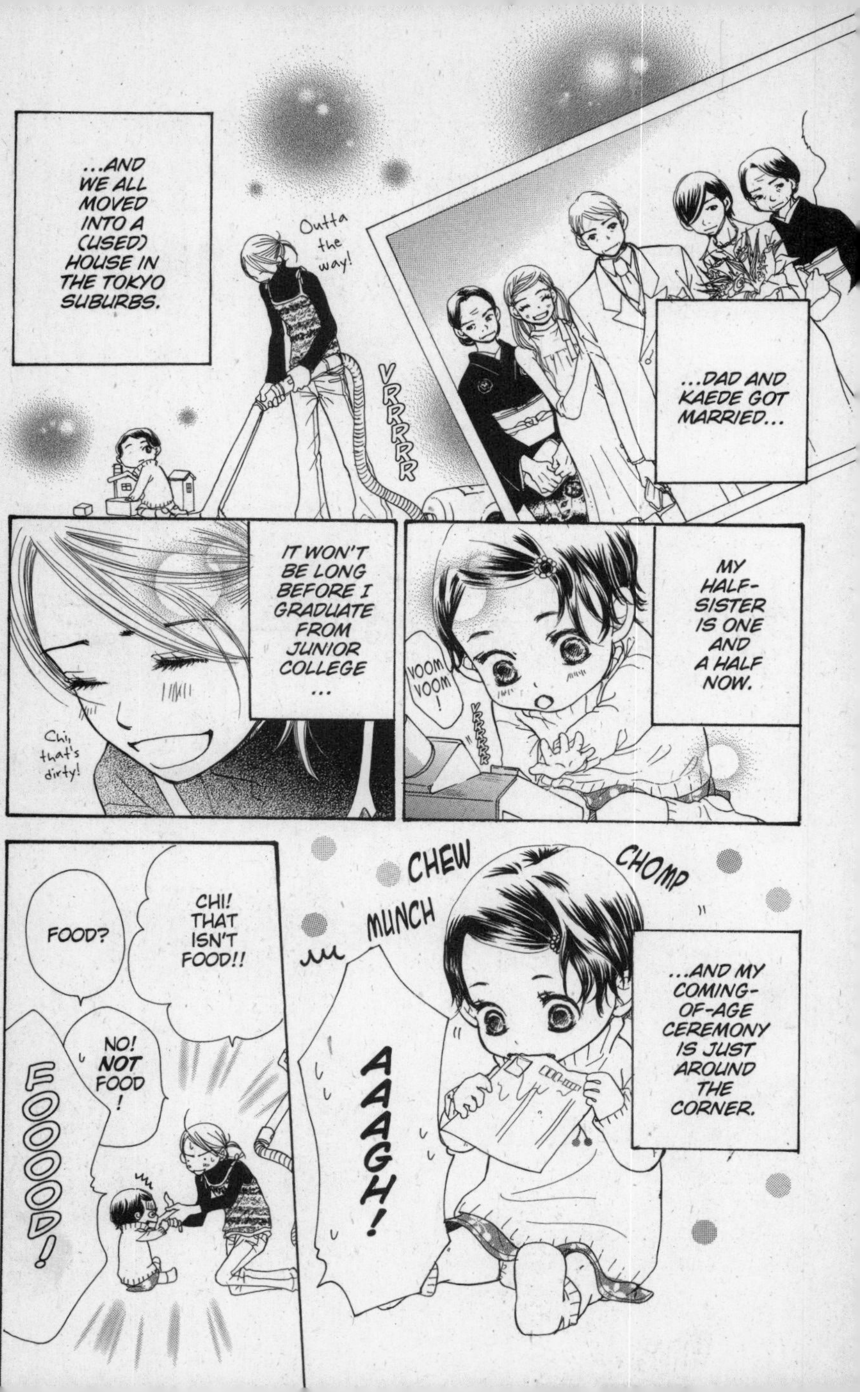
...DAD AND KAEDE GOT MARRIED...
Outta the way!
VRRRRR
...AND WE ALL MOVED INTO A (USED) HOUSE IN THE TOKYO SUBURBS.
MY HALF-SISTER IS ONE AND A HALF NOW.
VRRRRR
VOOM VOOM!
IT WON'T BE LONG BEFORE I GRADUATE FROM JUNIOR COLLEGE ...
Chi, that's dirty!
...AND MY COMING-OF-AGE CEREMONY IS JUST AROUND THE CORNER.
CHOMP
CHEW
MUNCH
AAAGH!
CHI! THAT ISN'T FOOD!!
FOOD?
NO! NOT FOOD!
FOOOOD!

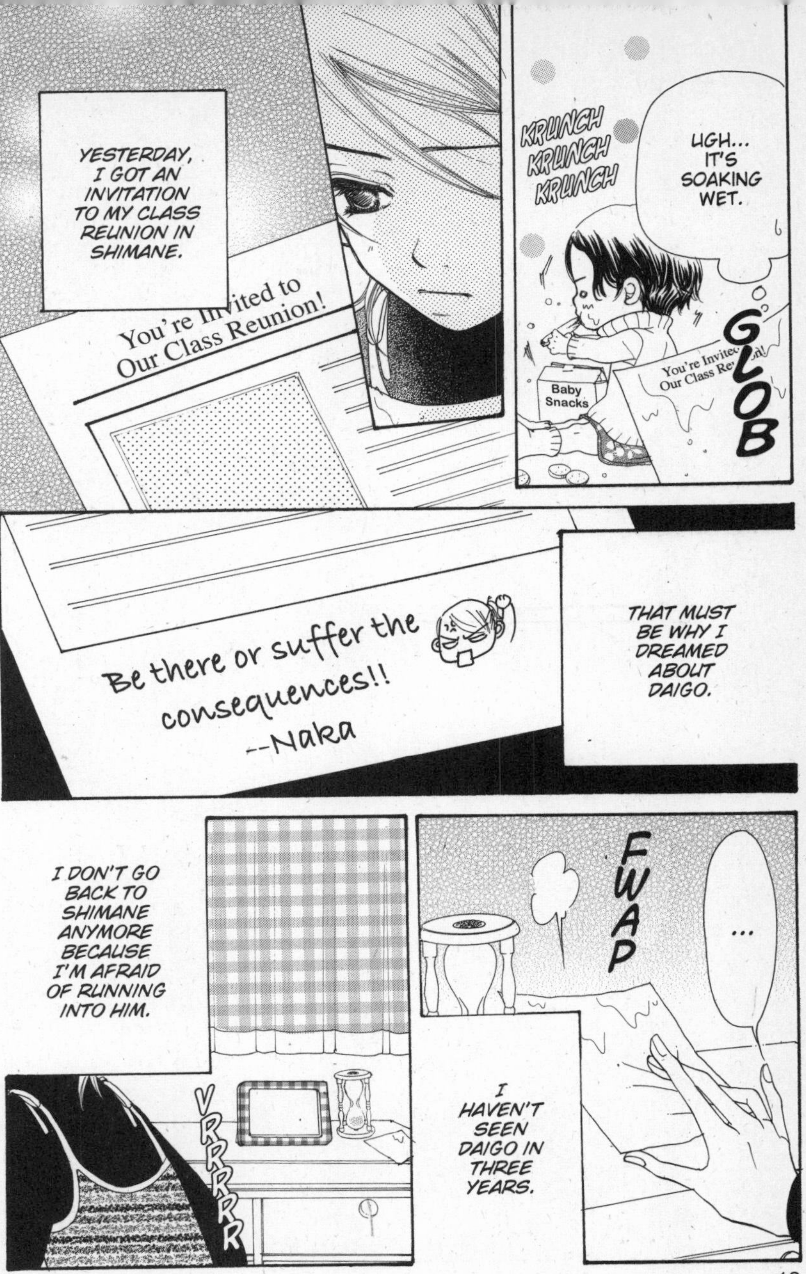
KRUNCH KRUNCH KRUNCH
UGH... IT'S SOAKING WET.
GLOB
You're Invited to Our Class Reunion!
Baby Snacks
YESTERDAY, I GOT AN INVITATION TO MY CLASS REUNION IN SHIMANE.
You're Invited to Our Class Reunion!
THAT MUST BE WHY I DREAMED ABOUT DAIGO.
Be there or suffer the consequences!! --Naka
FWAP
...
I HAVEN'T SEEN DAIGO IN THREE YEARS.
I DON'T GO BACK TO SHIMANE ANYMORE BECAUSE I'M AFRAID OF RUNNING INTO HIM.
VRRRRR

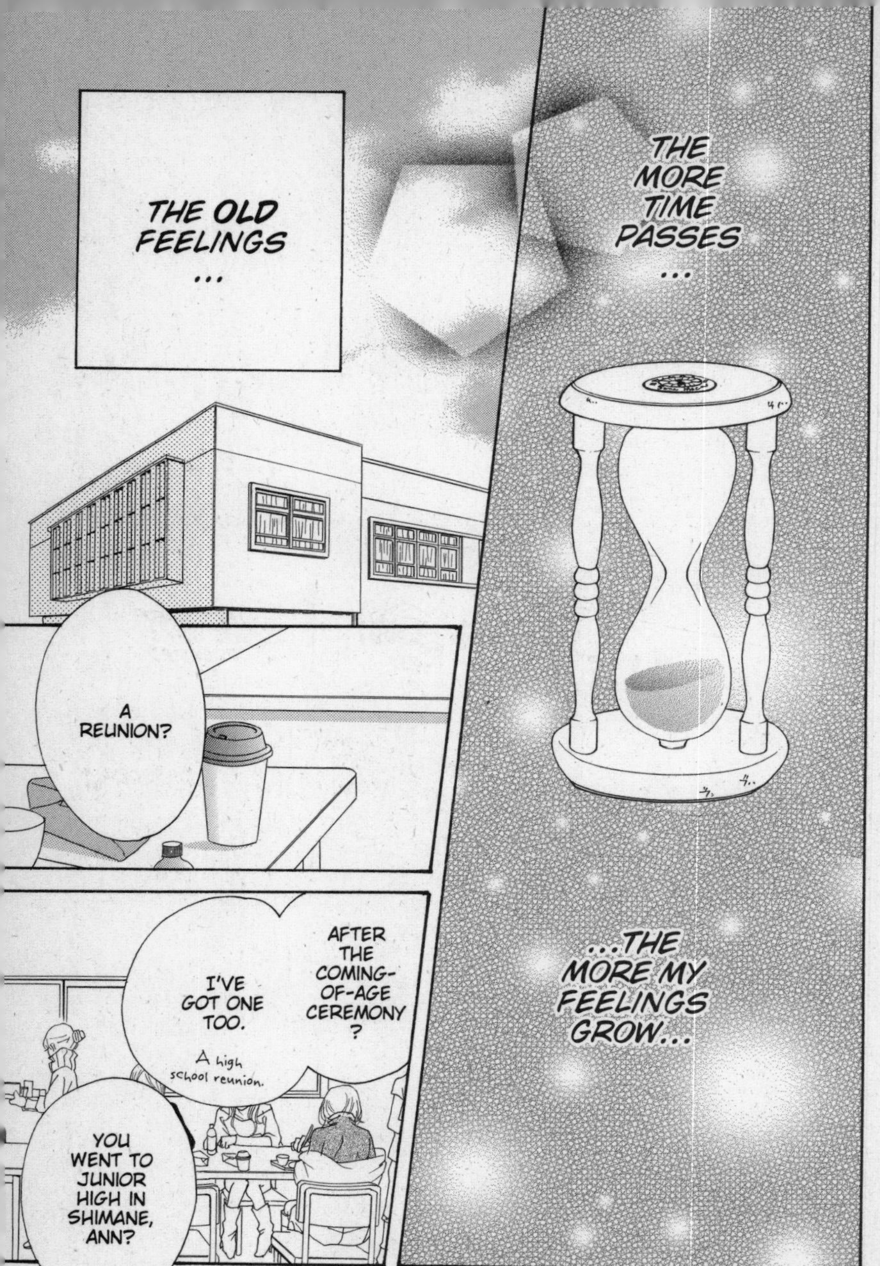
THE MORE TIME PASSES ...
...THE MORE MY FEELINGS GROW...
THE OLD FEELINGS ...
A REUNION?
AFTER THE COMING-OF-AGE CEREMONY?
I'VE GOT ONE TOO.
A high school reunion.
YOU WENT TO JUNIOR HIGH IN SHIMANE, ANN?

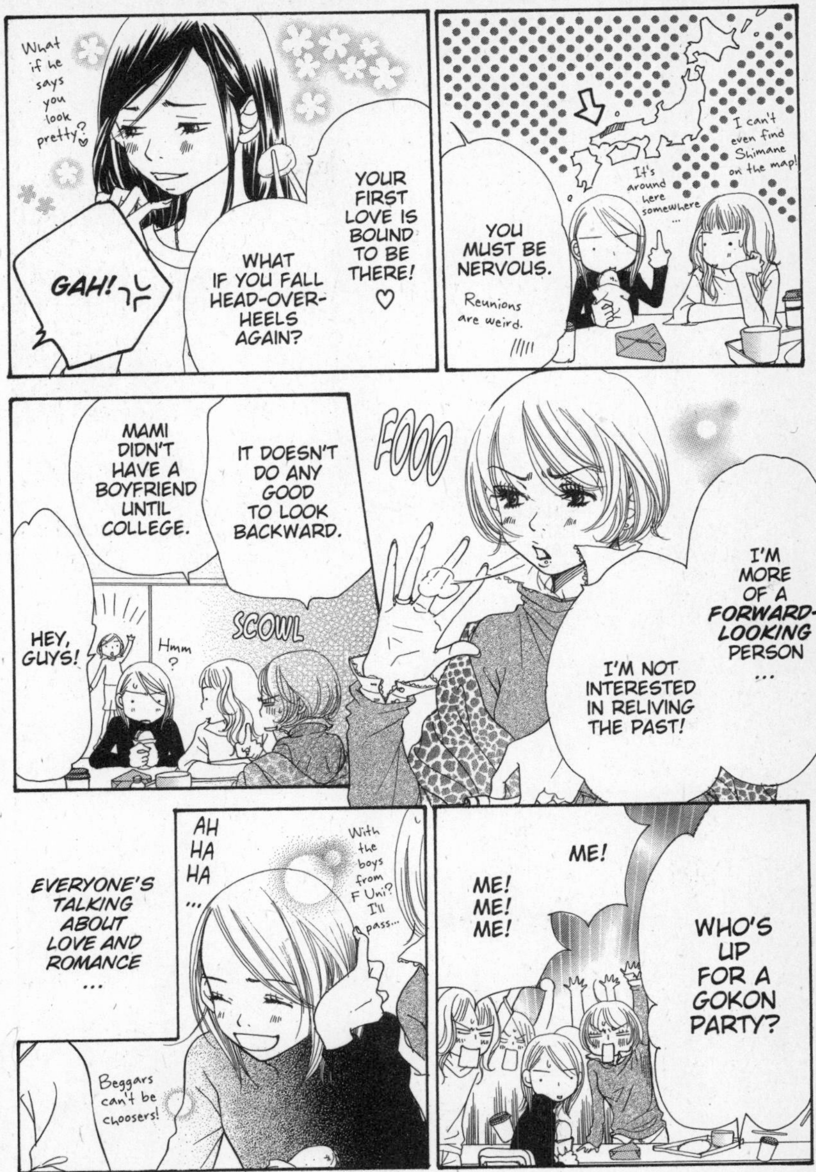
I can't even find Shimane on the map!
It's around here somewhere...
YOU MUST BE NERVOUS.
Reunions are weird.
YOUR FIRST LOVE IS BOUND TO BE THERE! ♡
WHAT IF YOU FALL HEAD-OVER-HEELS AGAIN?
What if he says you look pretty?♡
GAH!
FOOO
I'M MORE OF A FORWARD-LOOKING PERSON...
I'M NOT INTERESTED IN RELIVING THE PAST!
IT DOESN'T DO ANY GOOD TO LOOK BACKWARD.
MAMI DIDN'T HAVE A BOYFRIEND UNTIL COLLEGE.
SCOWL
Hmm?
HEY, GUYS!
WHO'S UP FOR A GOKON PARTY?
ME!
ME! ME! ME!
With the boys from F Uni? I'll pass...
AH HA HA...
EVERYONE'S TALKING ABOUT LOVE AND ROMANCE...
Beggars can't be choosers!

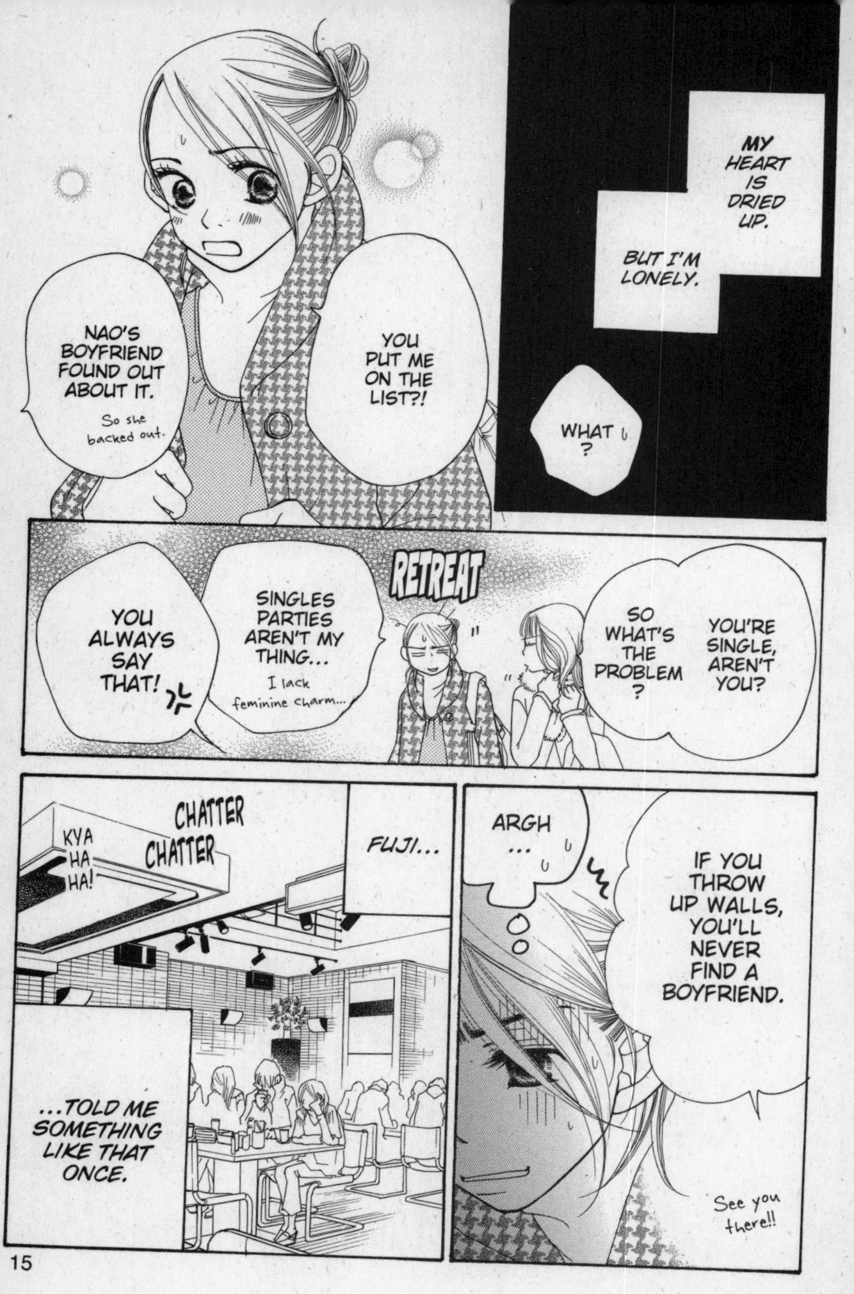
MY HEART IS DRIED UP.
BUT I'M LONELY.
WHAT?
YOU PUT ME ON THE LIST?!
NAO'S BOYFRIEND FOUND OUT ABOUT IT.
So she backed out.
YOU'RE SINGLE, AREN'T YOU?
SO WHAT'S THE PROBLEM?
RETREAT
SINGLES PARTIES AREN'T MY THING...
I lack feminine charm...
YOU ALWAYS SAY THAT!
IF YOU THROW UP WALLS, YOU'LL NEVER FIND A BOYFRIEND.
See you there!!
ARGH...
FUJI...
CHATTER
CHATTER
KYA HA HA!
...TOLD ME SOMETHING LIKE THAT ONCE.

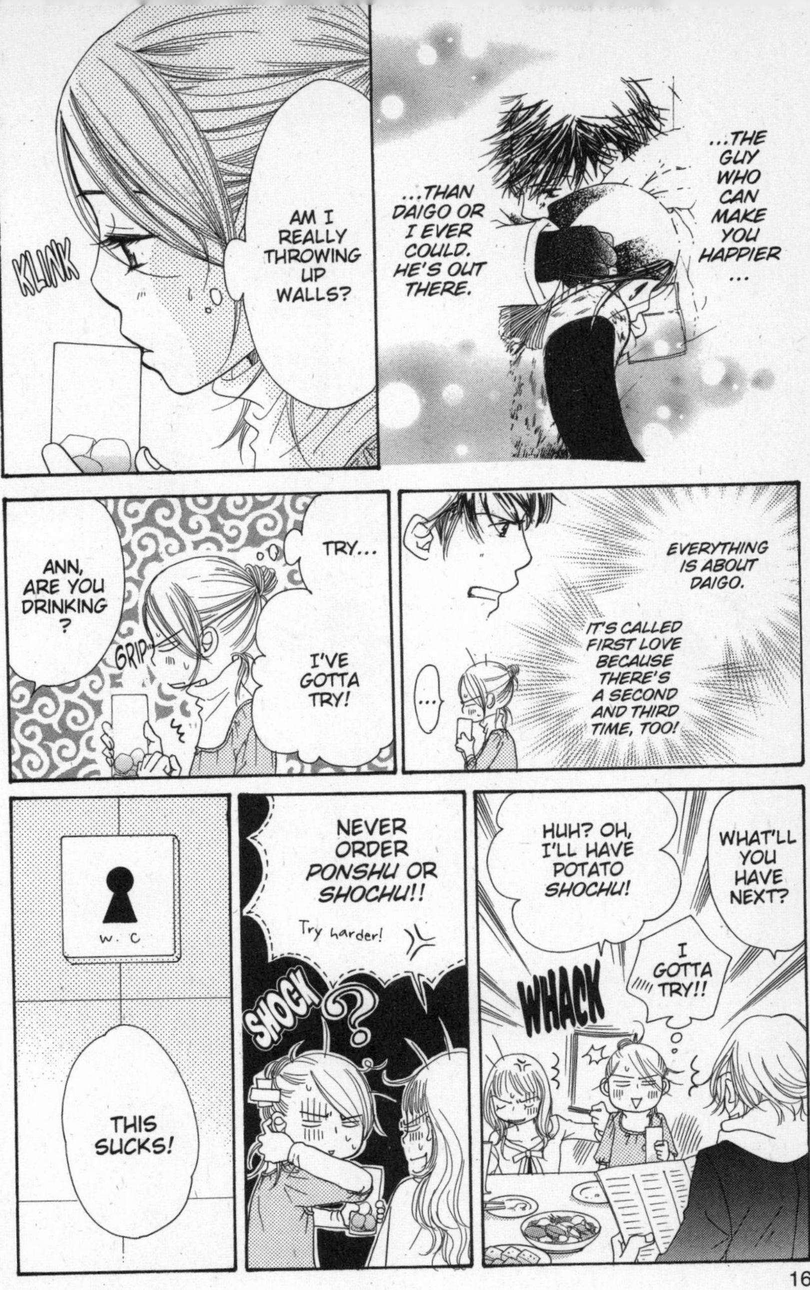
...THE GUY WHO CAN MAKE YOU HAPPIER ...
...THAN DAIGO OR I EVER COULD. HE'S OUT THERE.
AM I REALLY THROWING UP WALLS?
KLINK
EVERYTHING IS ABOUT DAIGO.
IT'S CALLED FIRST LOVE BECAUSE THERE'S A SECOND AND THIRD TIME, TOO!
...
TRY...
I'VE GOTTA TRY!
ANN, ARE YOU DRINKING?
GRIP
WHAT'LL YOU HAVE NEXT?
HUH? OH, I'LL HAVE POTATO SHOCHU!
I GOTTA TRY!!
WHACK
NEVER ORDER *PONSHU* OR *SHOCHU*!!
Try harder!
SHOCK
W. C
THIS SUCKS!

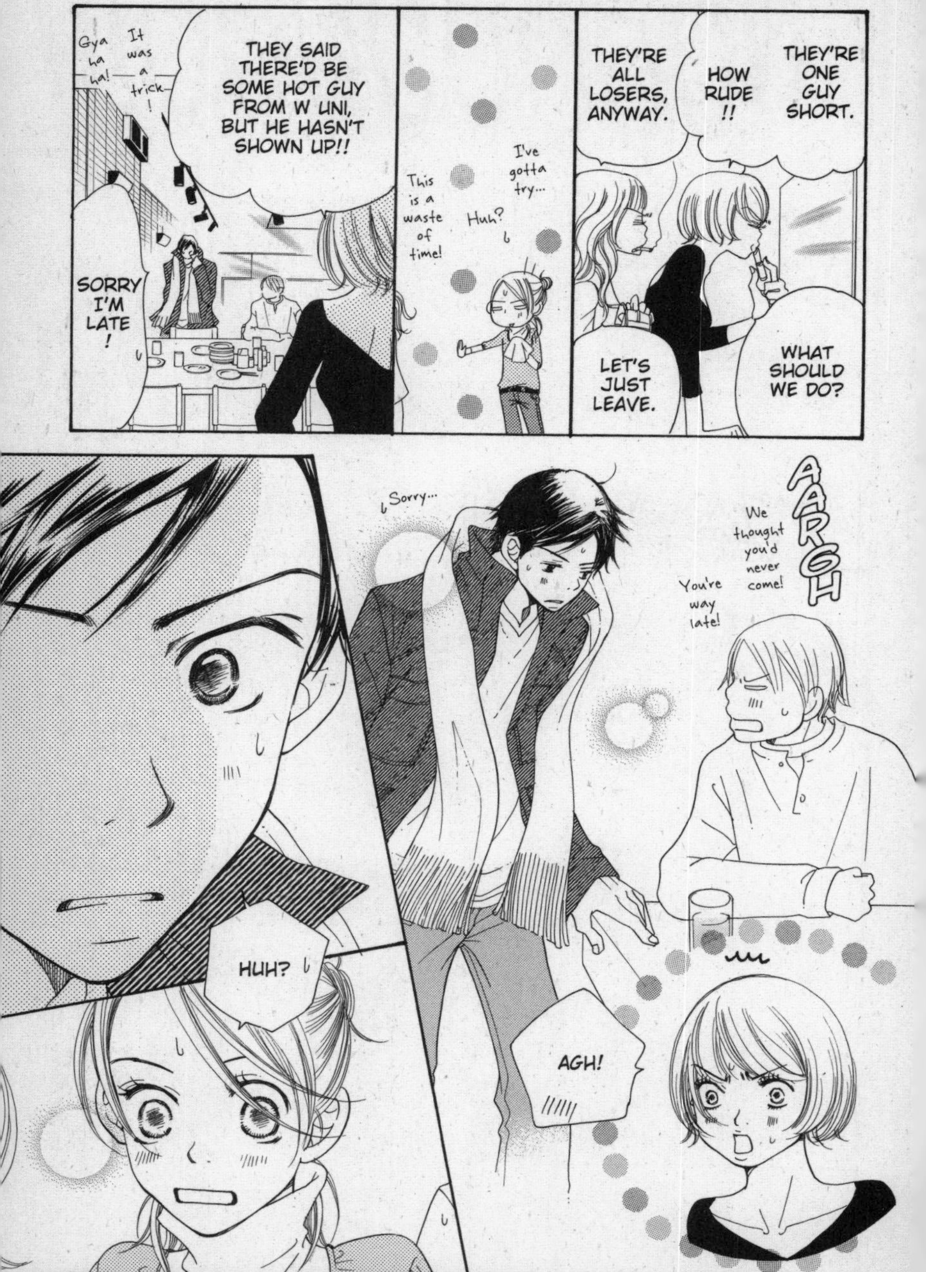
THEY'RE ONE GUY SHORT.
HOW RUDE!!
THEY'RE ALL LOSERS, ANYWAY.
WHAT SHOULD WE DO?
LET'S JUST LEAVE.
I've gotta try...
Huh?
This is a waste of time!
THEY SAID THERE'D BE SOME HOT GUY FROM W UNI, BUT HE HASN'T SHOWN UP!!
It was a trick!
Gya ha ha!
SORRY I'M LATE!
AARGH
We thought you'd never come!
You're way late!
Sorry...
AGH!
HUH?

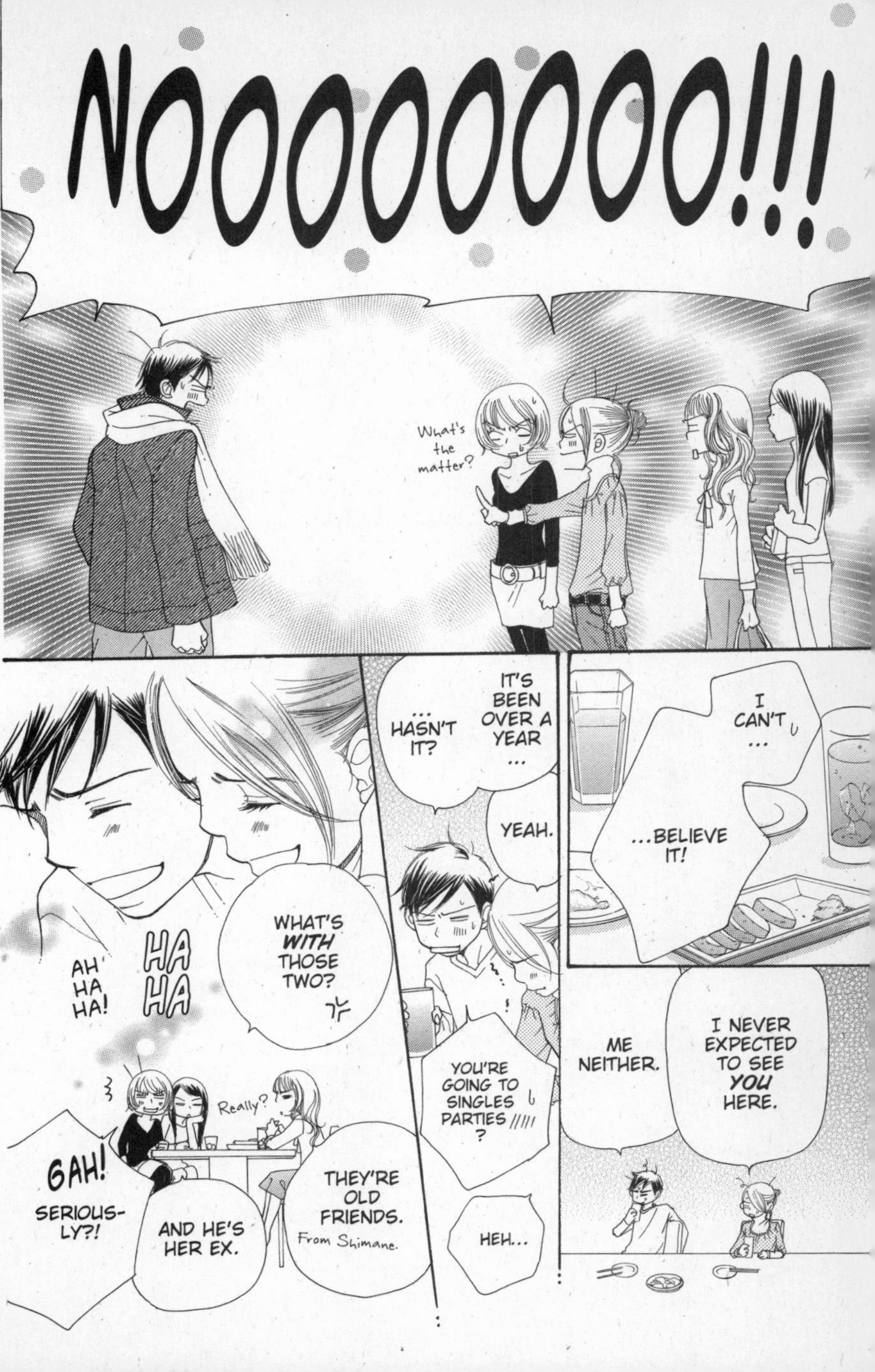
NOOOOOOOO!!!
What's the matter?
I CAN'T ...
...BELIEVE IT!
I NEVER EXPECTED TO SEE YOU HERE.
ME NEITHER.
IT'S BEEN OVER A YEAR ...
... HASN'T IT?
YEAH.
YOU'RE GOING TO SINGLES PARTIES ?
HEH...
WHAT'S WITH THOSE TWO?
HA HA
AH HA HA!
Really?
THEY'RE OLD FRIENDS.
From Shimane.
AND HE'S HER EX.
GAH!
SERIOUSLY?!

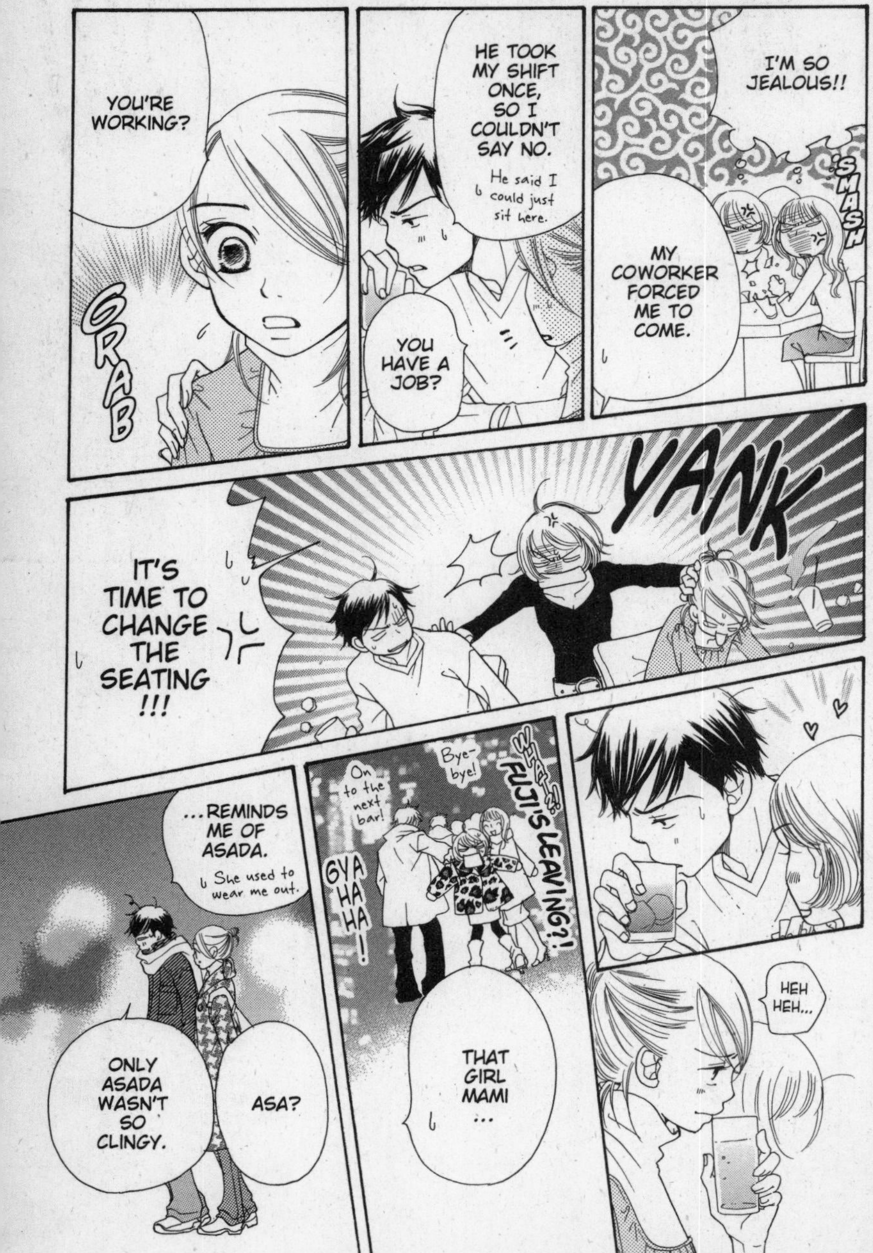
I'M SO JEALOUS!!
SMASH
MY COWORKER FORCED ME TO COME.
HE TOOK MY SHIFT ONCE, SO I COULDN'T SAY NO.
He said I could just sit here.
YOU HAVE A JOB?
YOU'RE WORKING?
GRAB
YANK
IT'S TIME TO CHANGE THE SEATING!!!
HEH HEH...
Bye-bye!
On to the next bar!
WHAT?! FUJI'S LEAVING?!
GYA HA HA!
THAT GIRL MAMI...
...REMINDS ME OF ASADA.
She used to wear me out.
ASA?
ONLY ASADA WASN'T SO CLINGY.

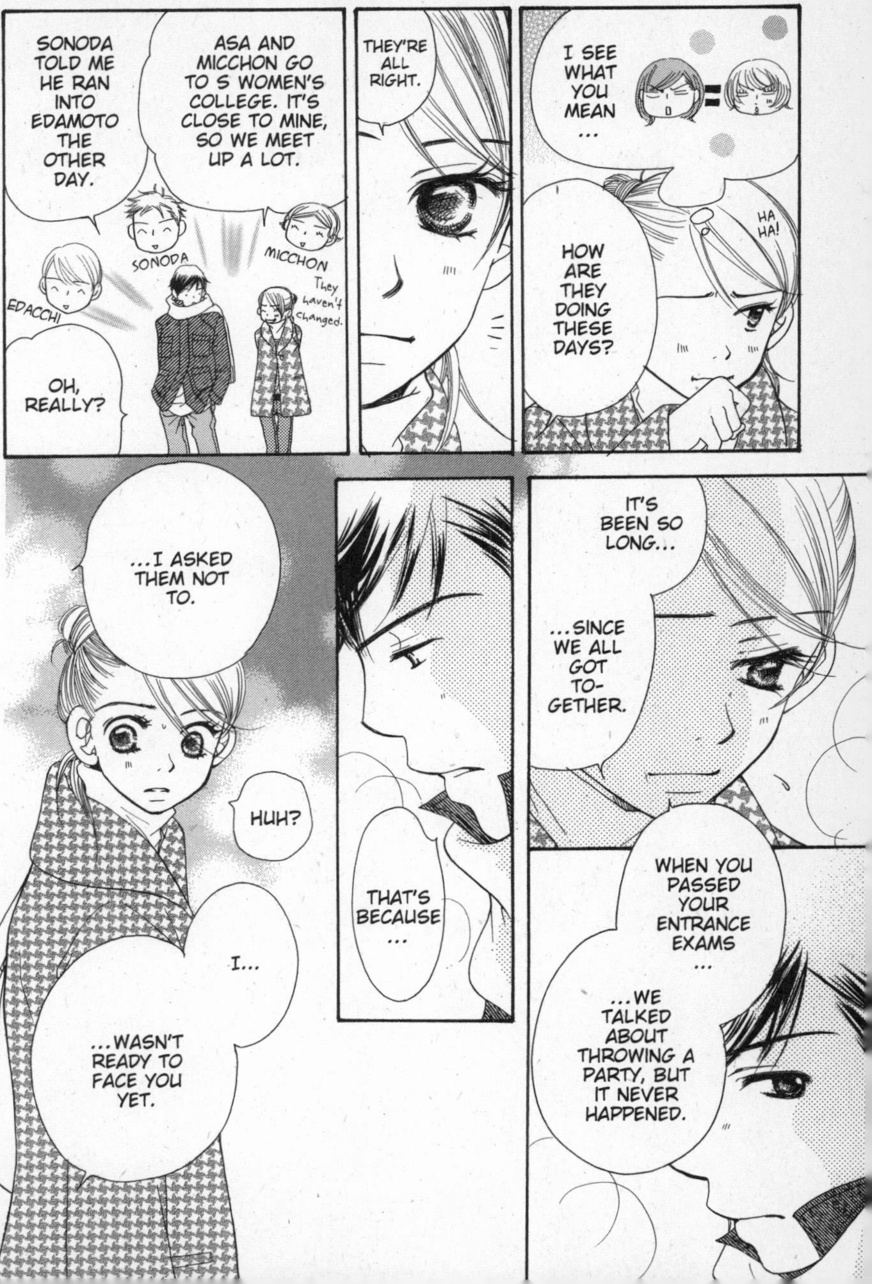
HA HA!
I SEE WHAT YOU MEAN...
HOW ARE THEY DOING THESE DAYS?
THEY'RE ALL RIGHT.
ASA AND MICCHON GO TO S WOMEN'S COLLEGE. IT'S CLOSE TO MINE, SO WE MEET UP A LOT.
SONODA TOLD ME HE RAN INTO EDAMOTO THE OTHER DAY.
MICCHON
SONODA
EDACCHI
They haven't changed.
OH, REALLY?
IT'S BEEN SO LONG...
...SINCE WE ALL GOT TO-GETHER.
WHEN YOU PASSED YOUR ENTRANCE EXAMS...
...WE TALKED ABOUT THROWING A PARTY, BUT IT NEVER HAPPENED.
THAT'S BECAUSE...
...I ASKED THEM NOT TO.
HUH?
I...
...WASN'T READY TO FACE YOU YET.

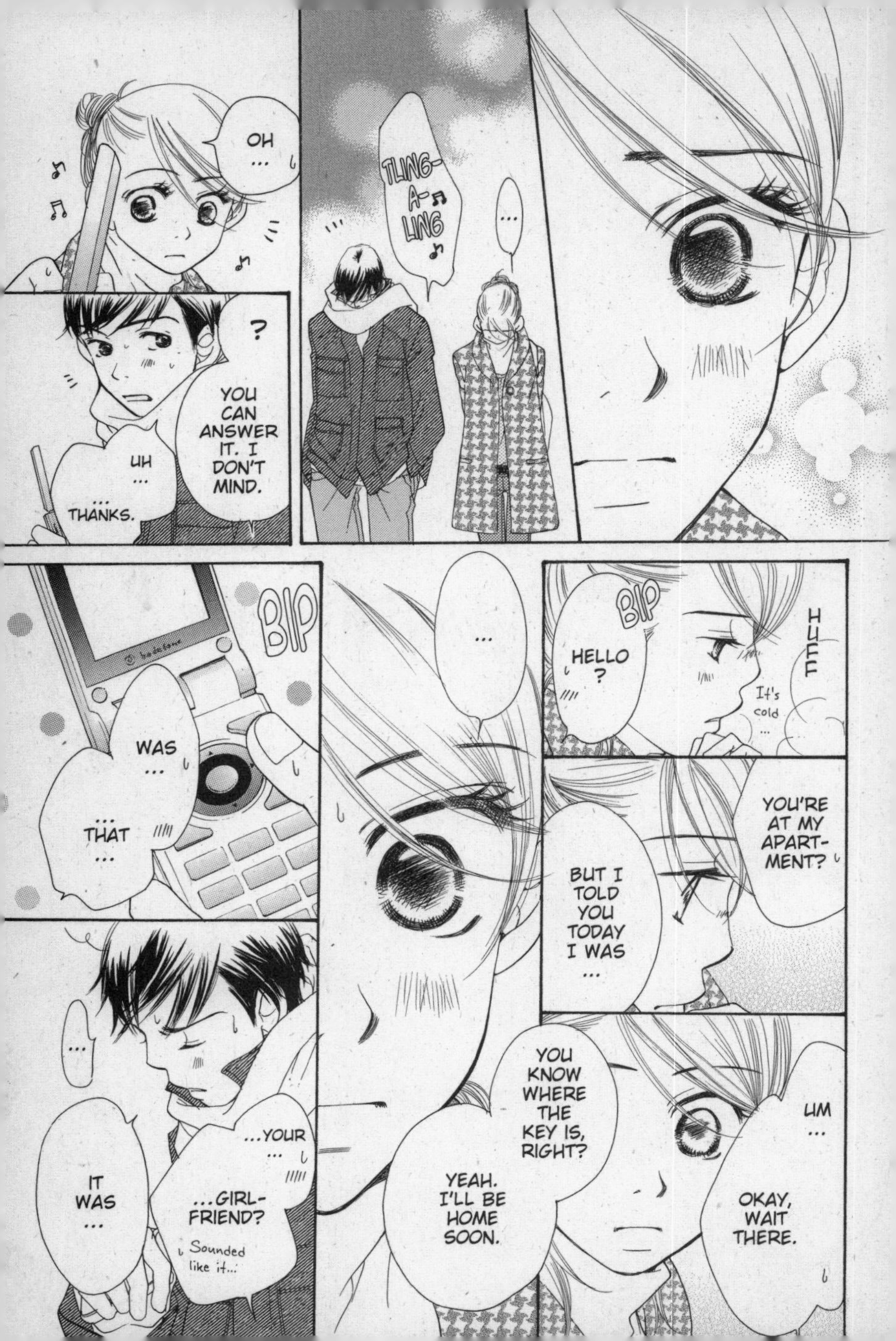
TLING-A-LING
...
OH ...
?
YOU CAN ANSWER IT. I DON'T MIND.
UH ... ... THANKS.
BIP
HUFF
HELLO ?
It's cold ...
YOU'RE AT MY APARTMENT?
BUT I TOLD YOU TODAY I WAS ...
UM ...
YOU KNOW WHERE THE KEY IS, RIGHT?
OKAY, WAIT THERE.
YEAH. I'LL BE HOME SOON.
...
BIP
WAS ... ... THAT ...
...YOUR ... ...GIRL-FRIEND?
...
IT WAS ...
Sounded like it...

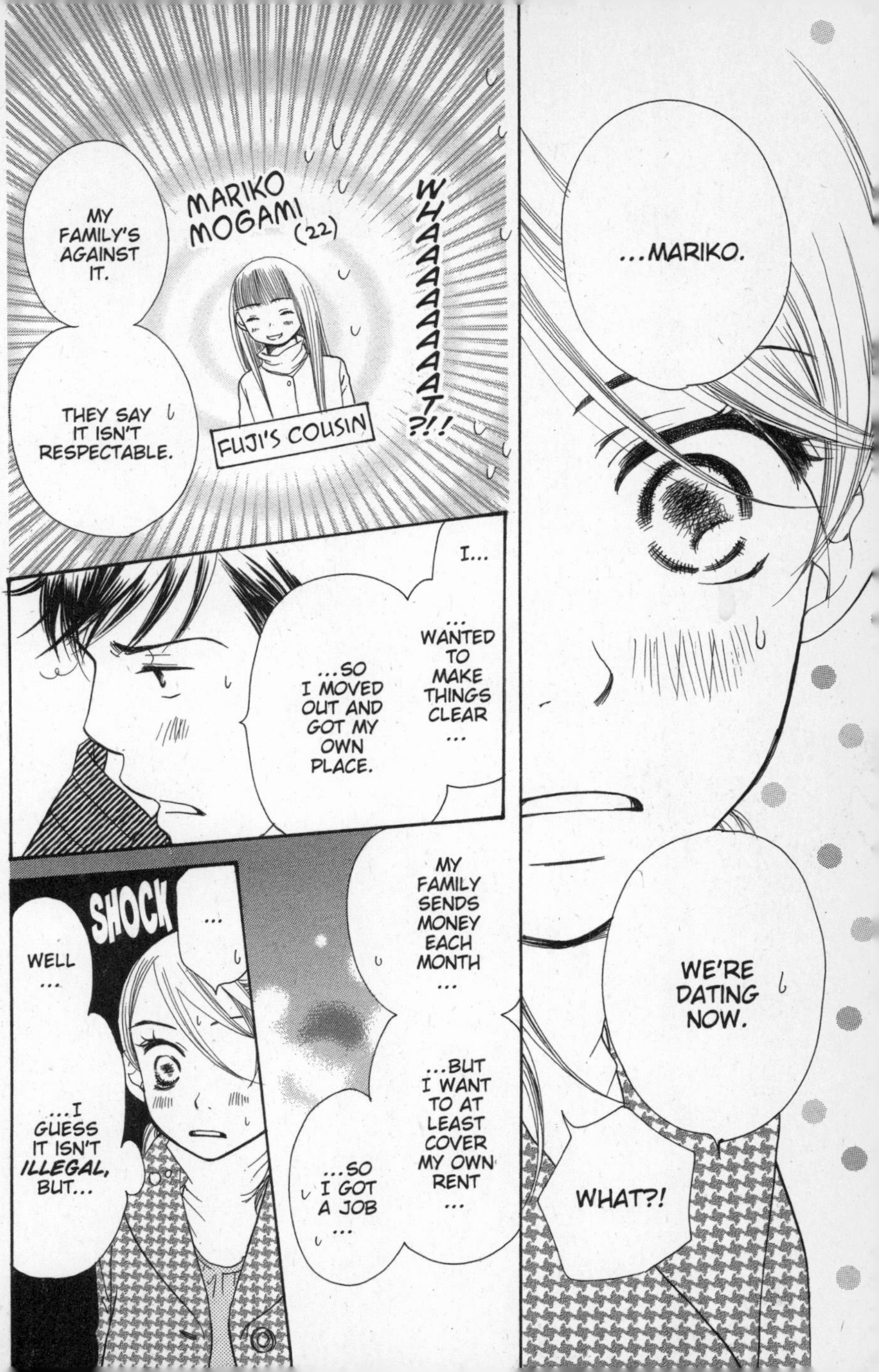
...MARIKO.
WE'RE DATING NOW.
WHAT?!
WHAAAAAAAAAAT?!!
MARIKO MOGAMI (22)
FUJI'S COUSIN
MY FAMILY'S AGAINST IT.
THEY SAY IT ISN'T RESPECTABLE.
I...
...WANTED TO MAKE THINGS CLEAR...
...SO I MOVED OUT AND GOT MY OWN PLACE.
MY FAMILY SENDS MONEY EACH MONTH...
...BUT I WANT TO AT LEAST COVER MY OWN RENT...
...SO I GOT A JOB...
SHOCK
...
WELL...
...I GUESS IT ISN'T ILLEGAL, BUT...

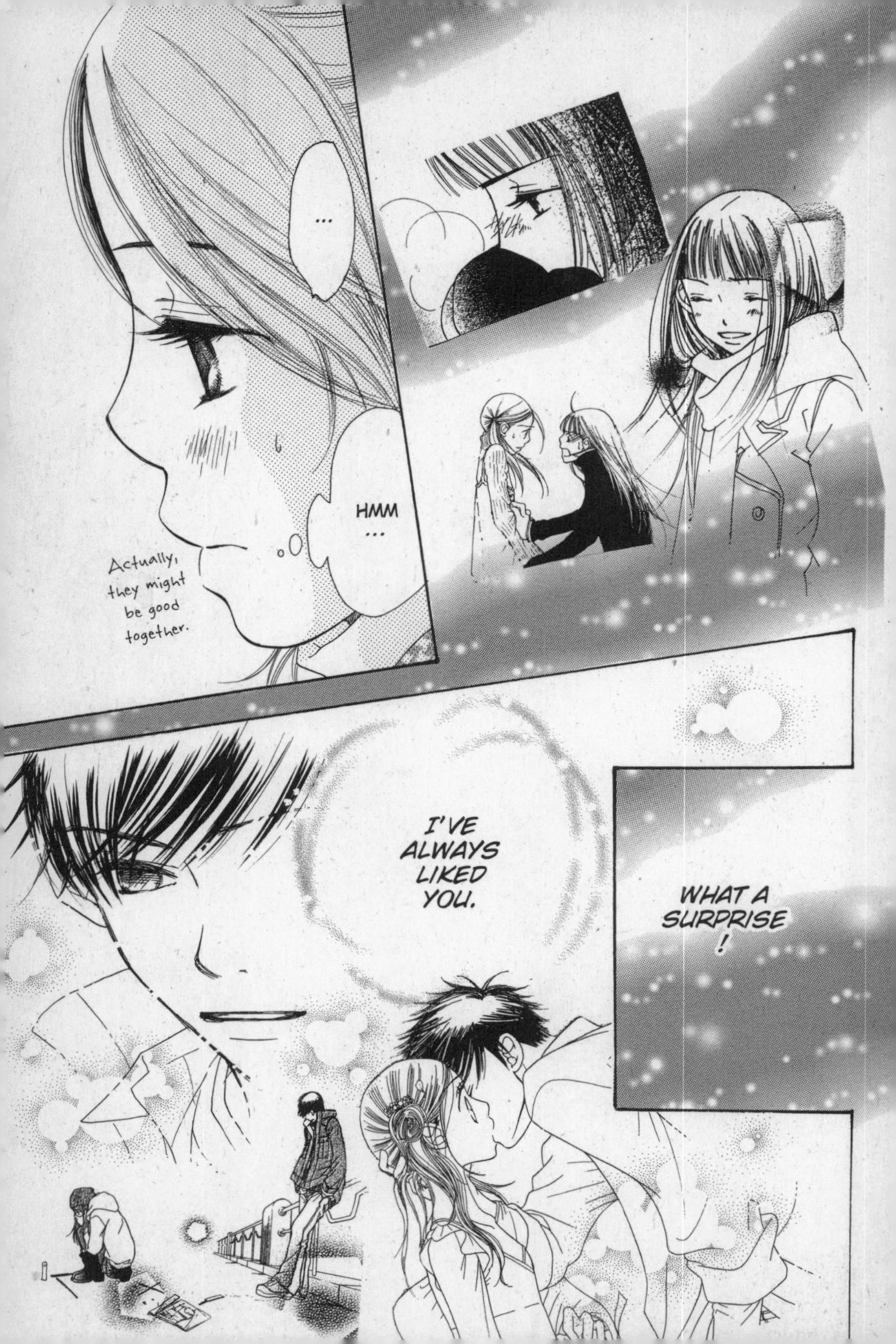
...
HMM ...
Actually, they might be good together.
WHAT A SURPRISE !
I'VE ALWAYS LIKED YOU.

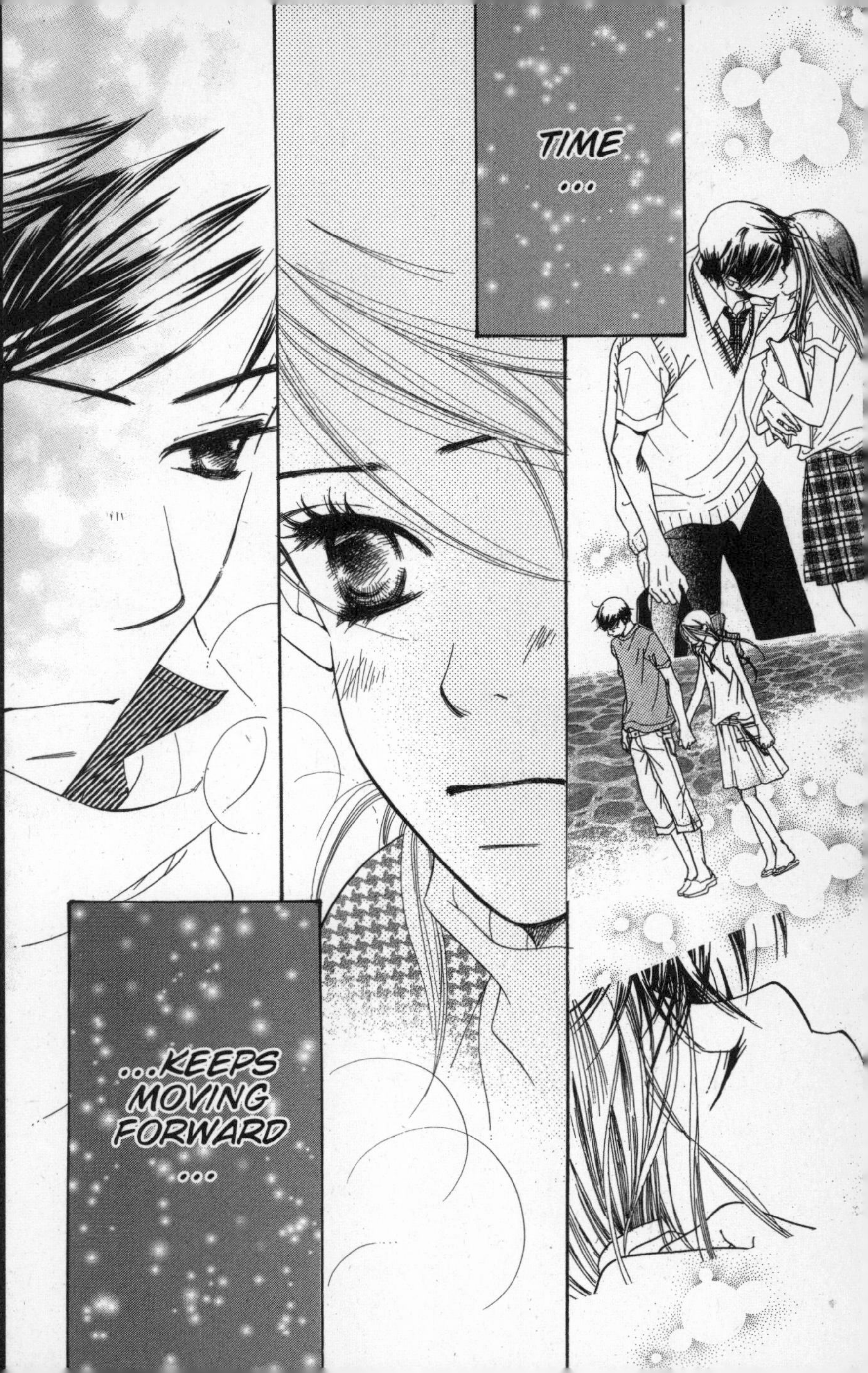
TIME ...
...KEEPS MOVING FORWARD ...

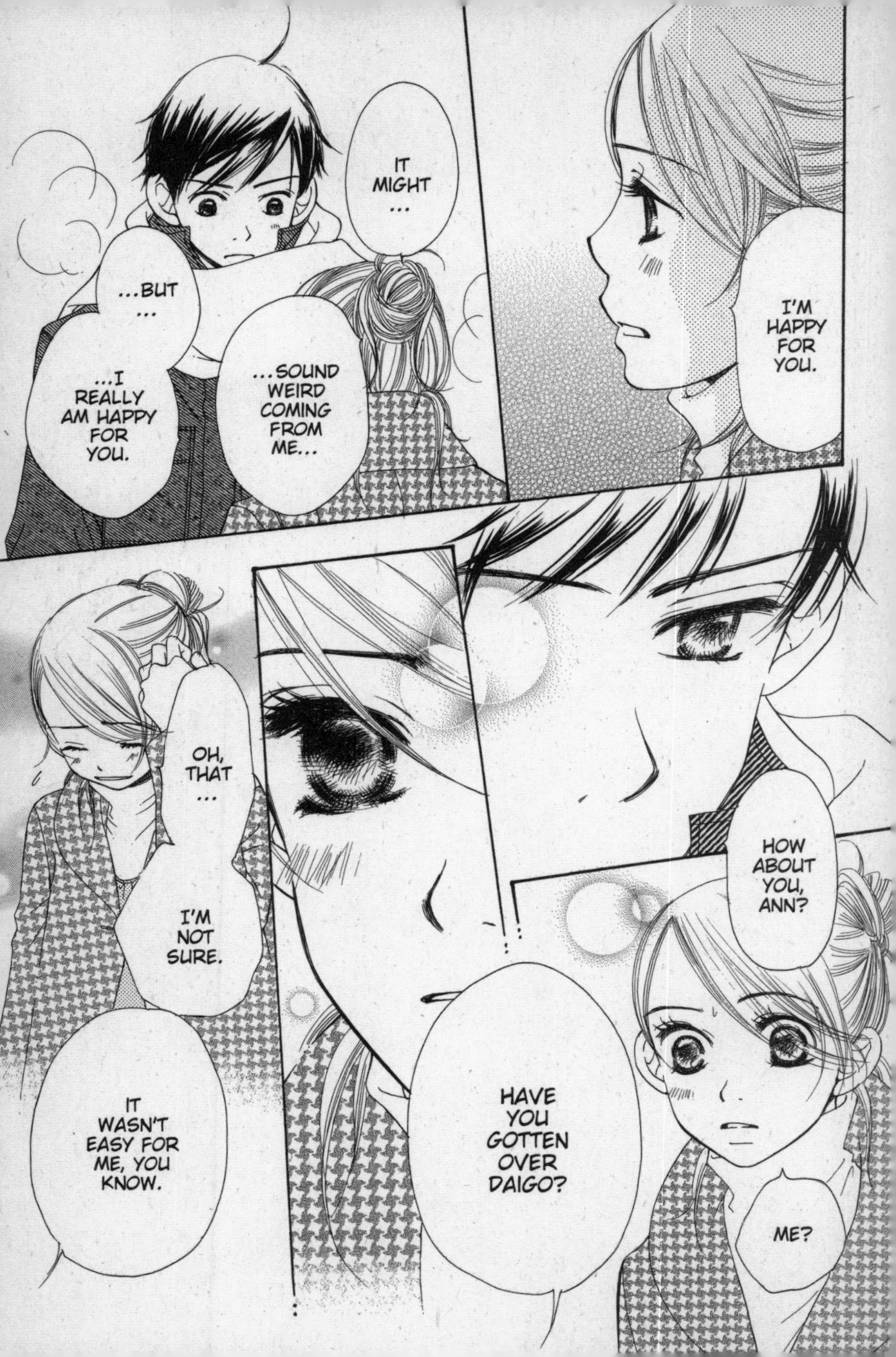
I'M HAPPY FOR YOU.
IT MIGHT ...
...SOUND WEIRD COMING FROM ME...
...BUT ...
...I REALLY AM HAPPY FOR YOU.
HOW ABOUT YOU, ANN?
ME?
HAVE YOU GOTTEN OVER DAIGO?
OH, THAT ...
I'M NOT SURE.
IT WASN'T EASY FOR ME, YOU KNOW.

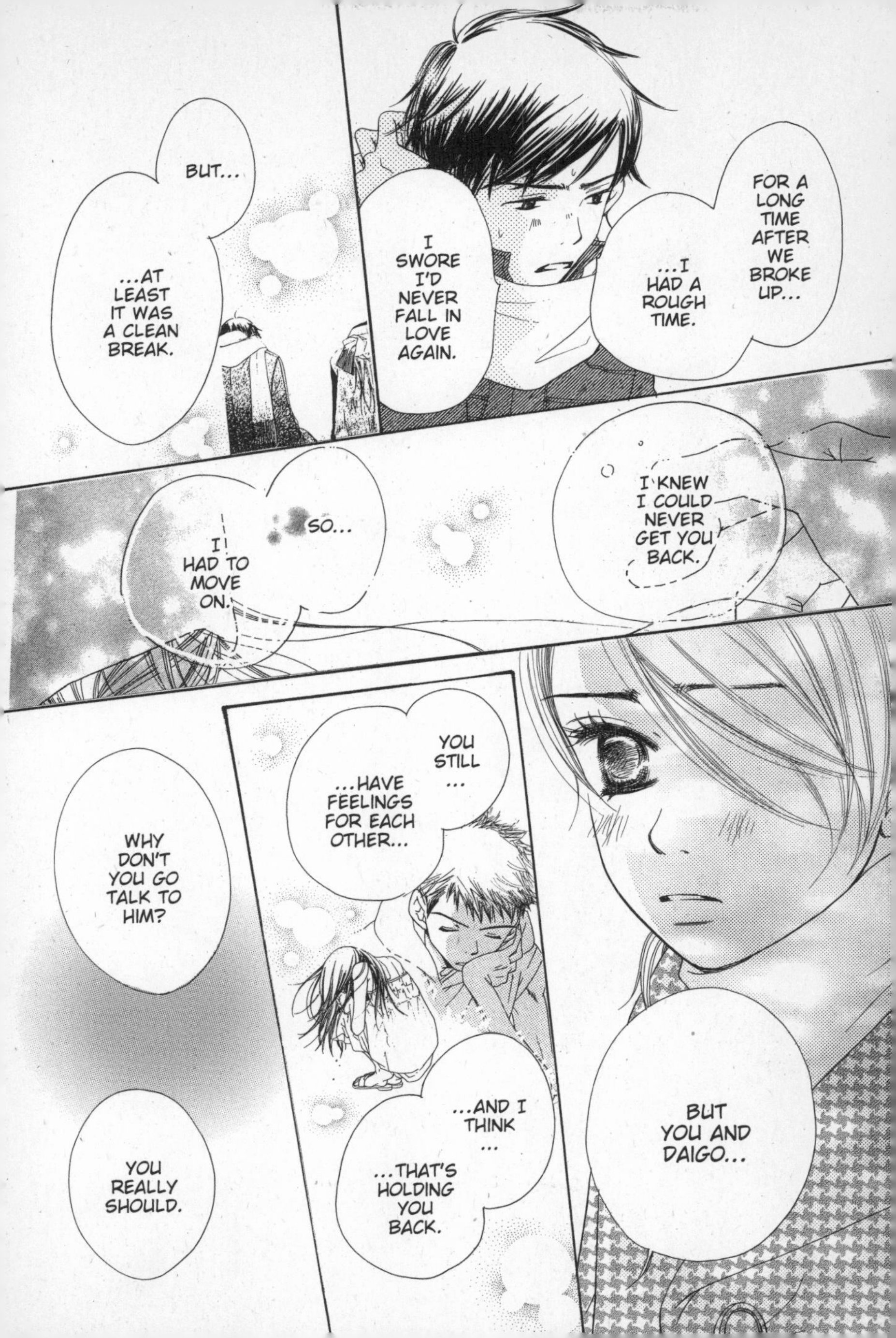
FOR A LONG TIME AFTER WE BROKE UP...
...I HAD A ROUGH TIME.
I SWORE I'D NEVER FALL IN LOVE AGAIN.
BUT...
...AT LEAST IT WAS A CLEAN BREAK.
I KNEW I COULD NEVER GET YOU BACK.
SO...
I HAD TO MOVE ON.
BUT YOU AND DAIGO...
YOU STILL...
...HAVE FEELINGS FOR EACH OTHER...
...AND I THINK...
...THAT'S HOLDING YOU BACK.
WHY DON'T YOU GO TALK TO HIM?
YOU REALLY SHOULD.

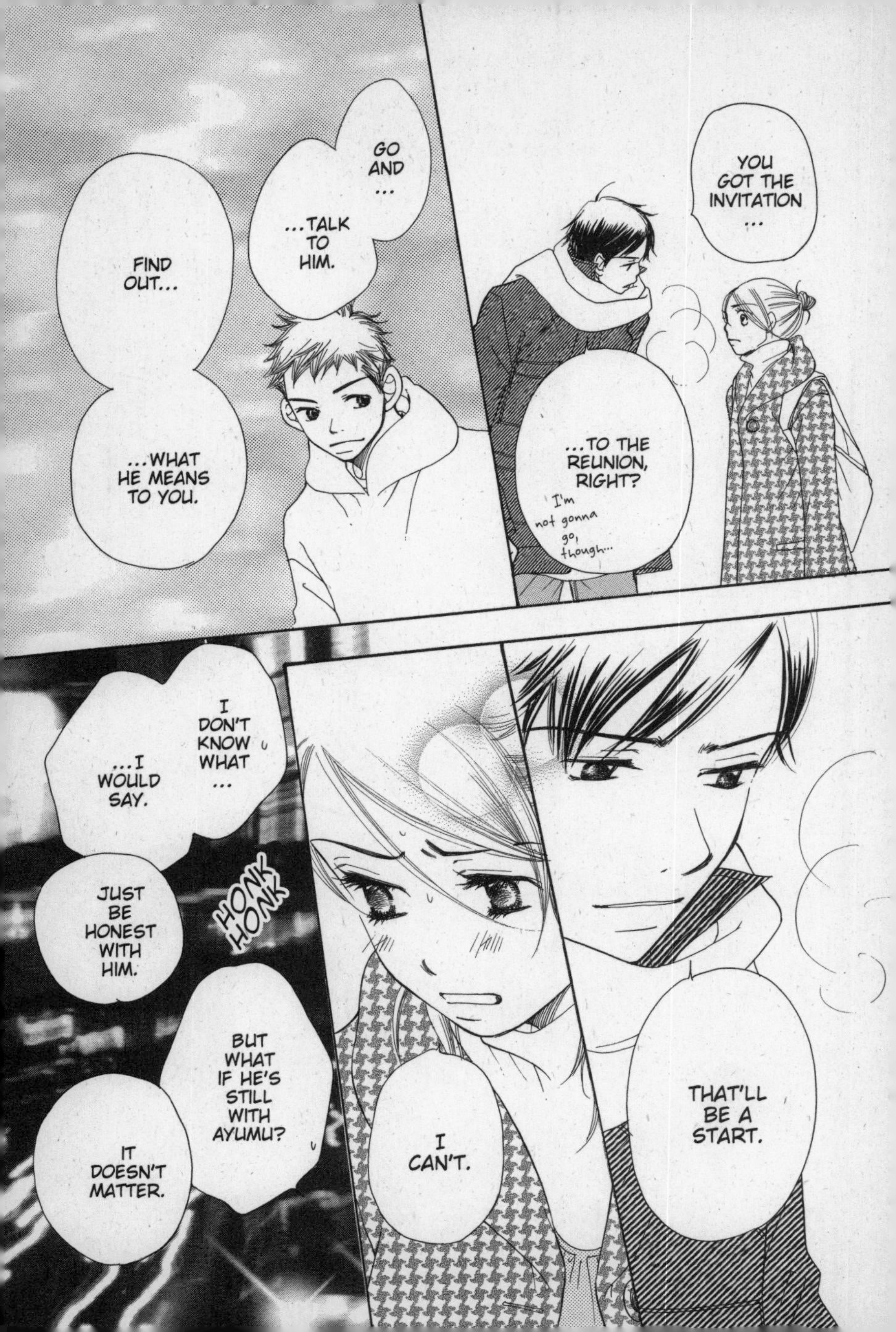
YOU GOT THE INVITATION ...
...TO THE REUNION, RIGHT?
I'm not gonna go, though...
GO AND ...
...TALK TO HIM.
FIND OUT...
...WHAT HE MEANS TO YOU.
THAT'LL BE A START.
I CAN'T.
I DON'T KNOW WHAT ...
...I WOULD SAY.
JUST BE HONEST WITH HIM.
HONK HONK
BUT WHAT IF HE'S STILL WITH AYUMU?
IT DOESN'T MATTER.

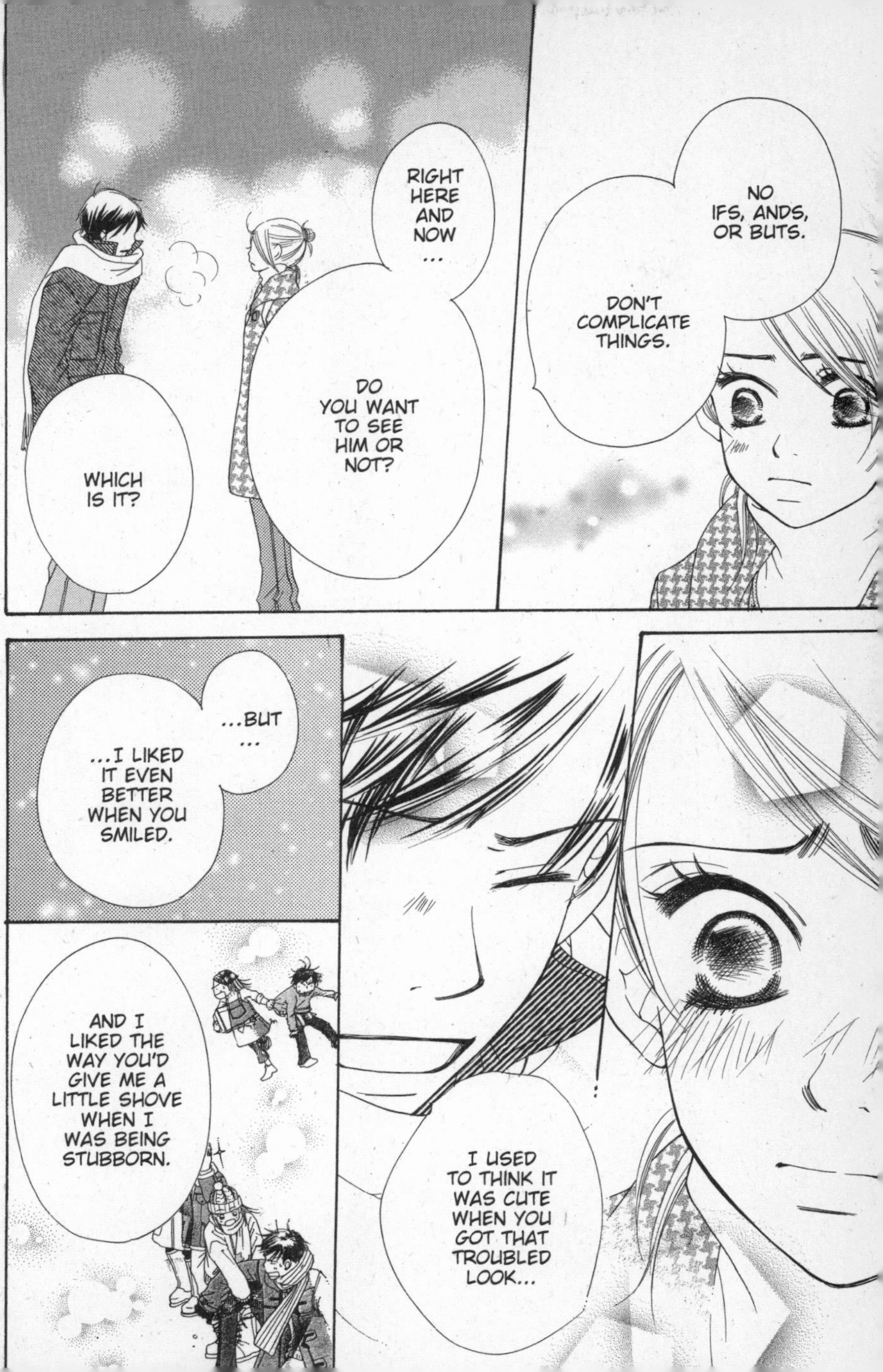
NO IFS, ANDS, OR BUTS.
DON'T COMPLICATE THINGS.
RIGHT HERE AND NOW ...
DO YOU WANT TO SEE HIM OR NOT?
WHICH IS IT?
I USED TO THINK IT WAS CUTE WHEN YOU GOT THAT TROUBLED LOOK...
...BUT ...
...I LIKED IT EVEN BETTER WHEN YOU SMILED.
AND I LIKED THE WAY YOU'D GIVE ME A LITTLE SHOVE WHEN I WAS BEING STUBBORN.

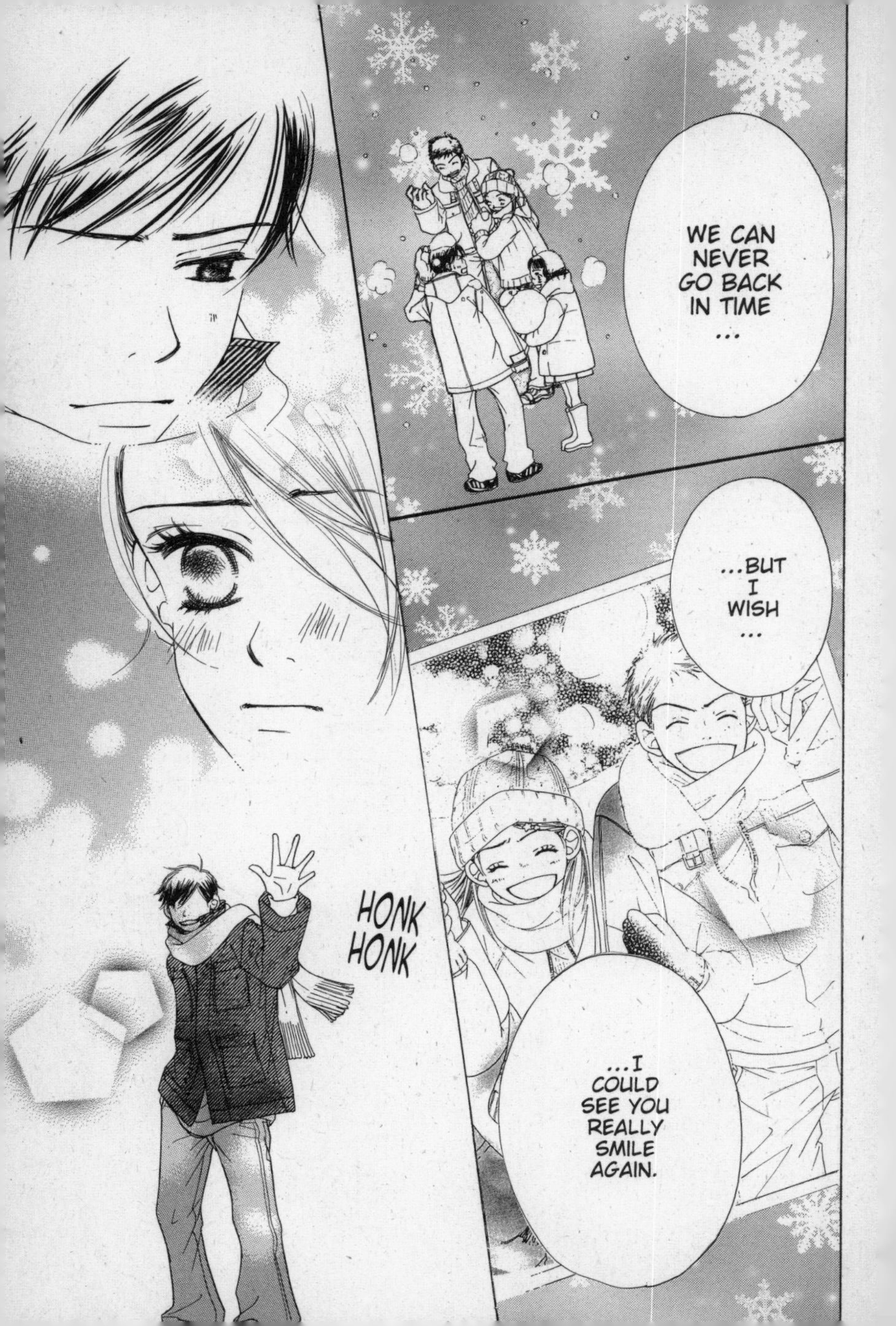
WE CAN NEVER GO BACK IN TIME ...
...BUT I WISH ...
...I COULD SEE YOU REALLY SMILE AGAIN.
HONK HONK

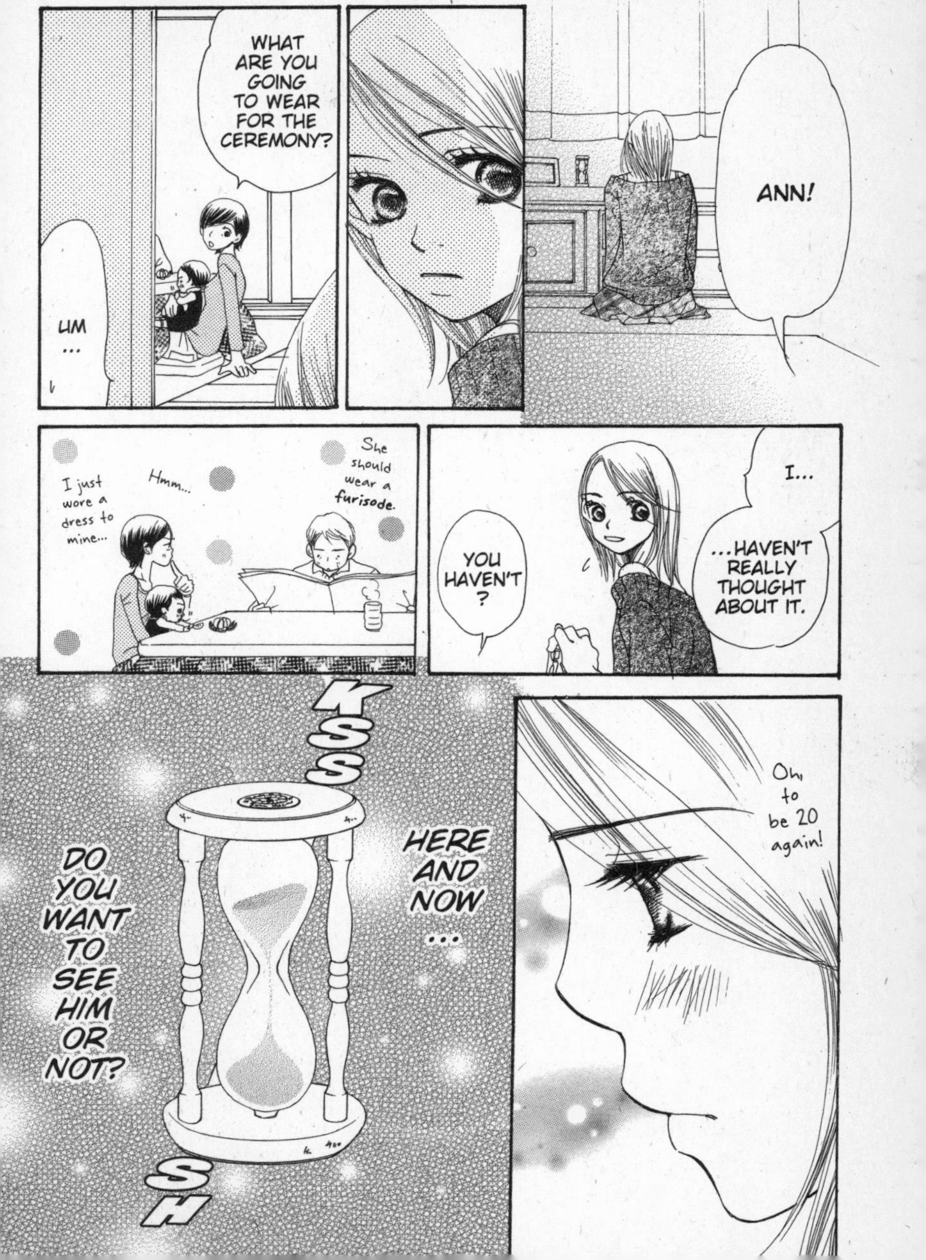
ANN!
WHAT ARE YOU GOING TO WEAR FOR THE CEREMONY?
UM ...
I...
...HAVEN'T REALLY THOUGHT ABOUT IT.
YOU HAVEN'T?
She should wear a furisode.
Hmm...
I just wore a dress to mine...
Oh, to be 20 again!
KSSSH
HERE AND NOW ...
DO YOU WANT TO SEE HIM OR NOT?

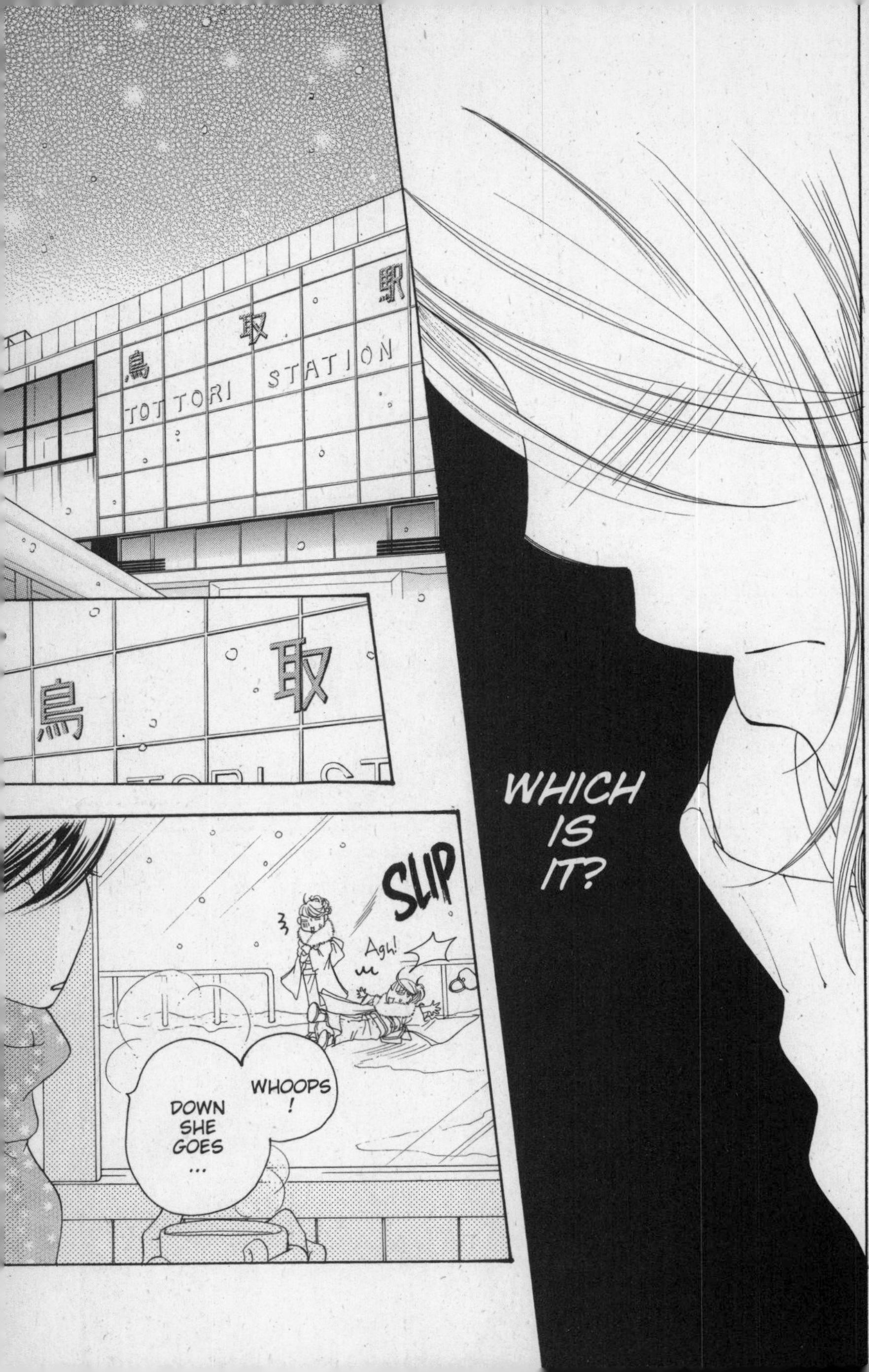
WHICH IS IT?
鳥取駅
TOTTORI STATION
鳥取
SLIP
Agh!
WHOOPS!
DOWN SHE GOES...

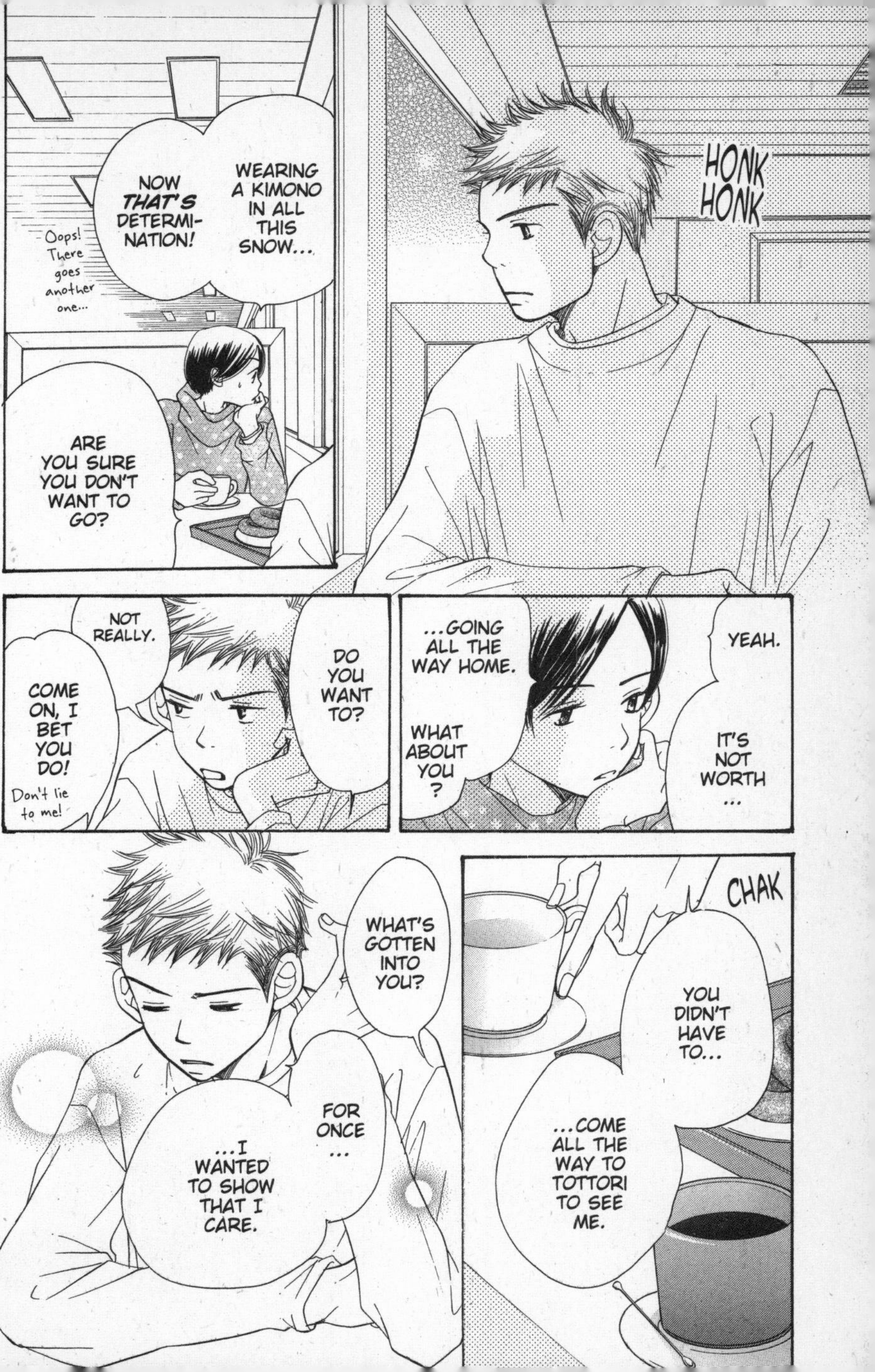
HONK HONK
WEARING A KIMONO IN ALL THIS SNOW...
NOW *THAT'S* DETERMINATION!
Oops! There goes another one...
ARE YOU SURE YOU DON'T WANT TO GO?
YEAH.
IT'S NOT WORTH...
...GOING ALL THE WAY HOME.
WHAT ABOUT YOU?
DO YOU WANT TO?
NOT REALLY.
COME ON, I BET YOU DO!
Don't lie to me!
CHAK
YOU DIDN'T HAVE TO...
...COME ALL THE WAY TO TOTTORI TO SEE ME.
WHAT'S GOTTEN INTO YOU?
FOR ONCE...
...I WANTED TO SHOW THAT I CARE.

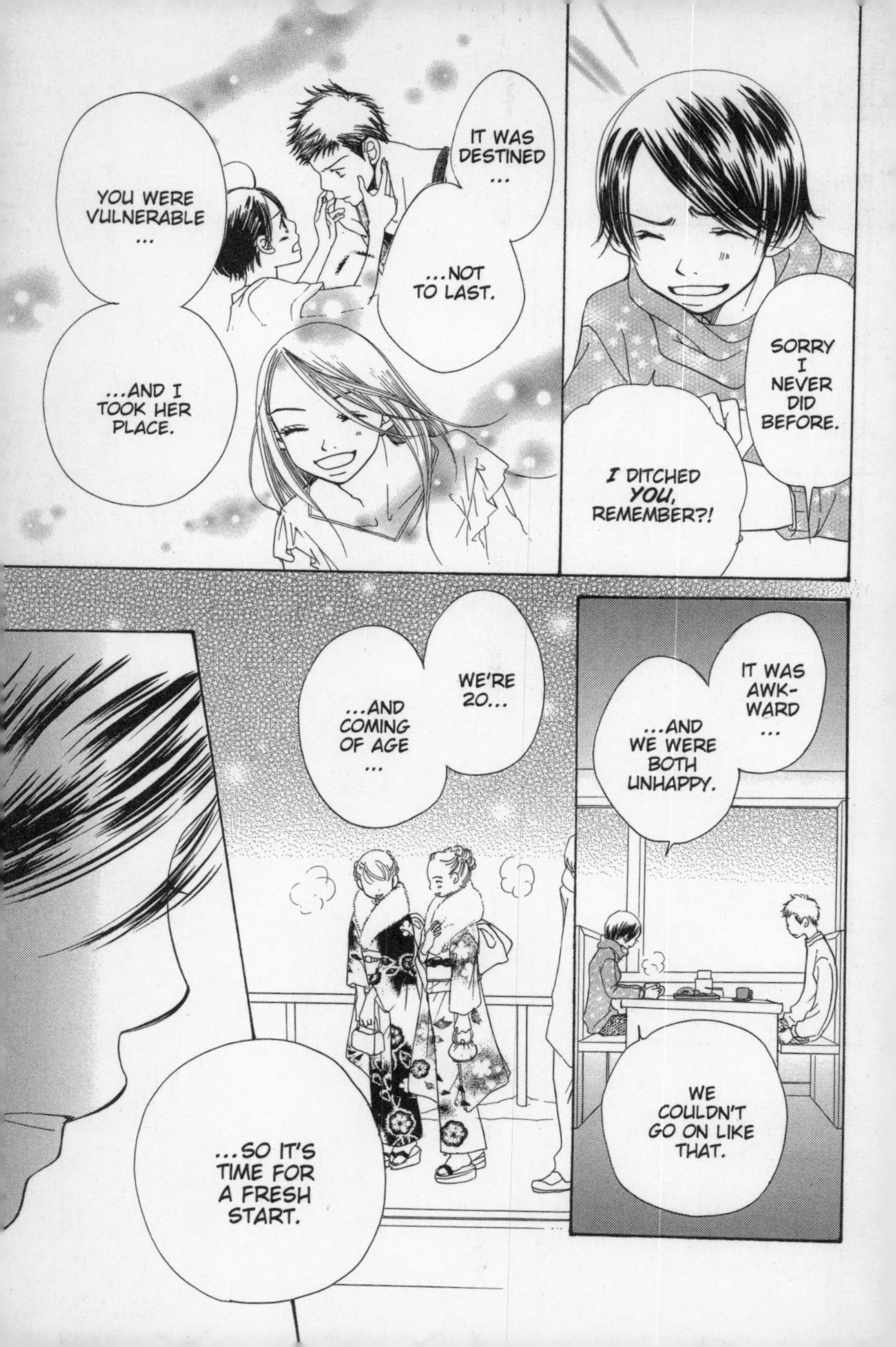
SORRY I NEVER DID BEFORE.
I DITCHED YOU, REMEMBER?!
IT WAS DESTINED ...
...NOT TO LAST.
YOU WERE VULNERABLE ...
...AND I TOOK HER PLACE.
IT WAS AWK-WARD ...
...AND WE WERE BOTH UNHAPPY.
WE COULDN'T GO ON LIKE THAT.
WE'RE 20...
...AND COMING OF AGE ...
...SO IT'S TIME FOR A FRESH START.

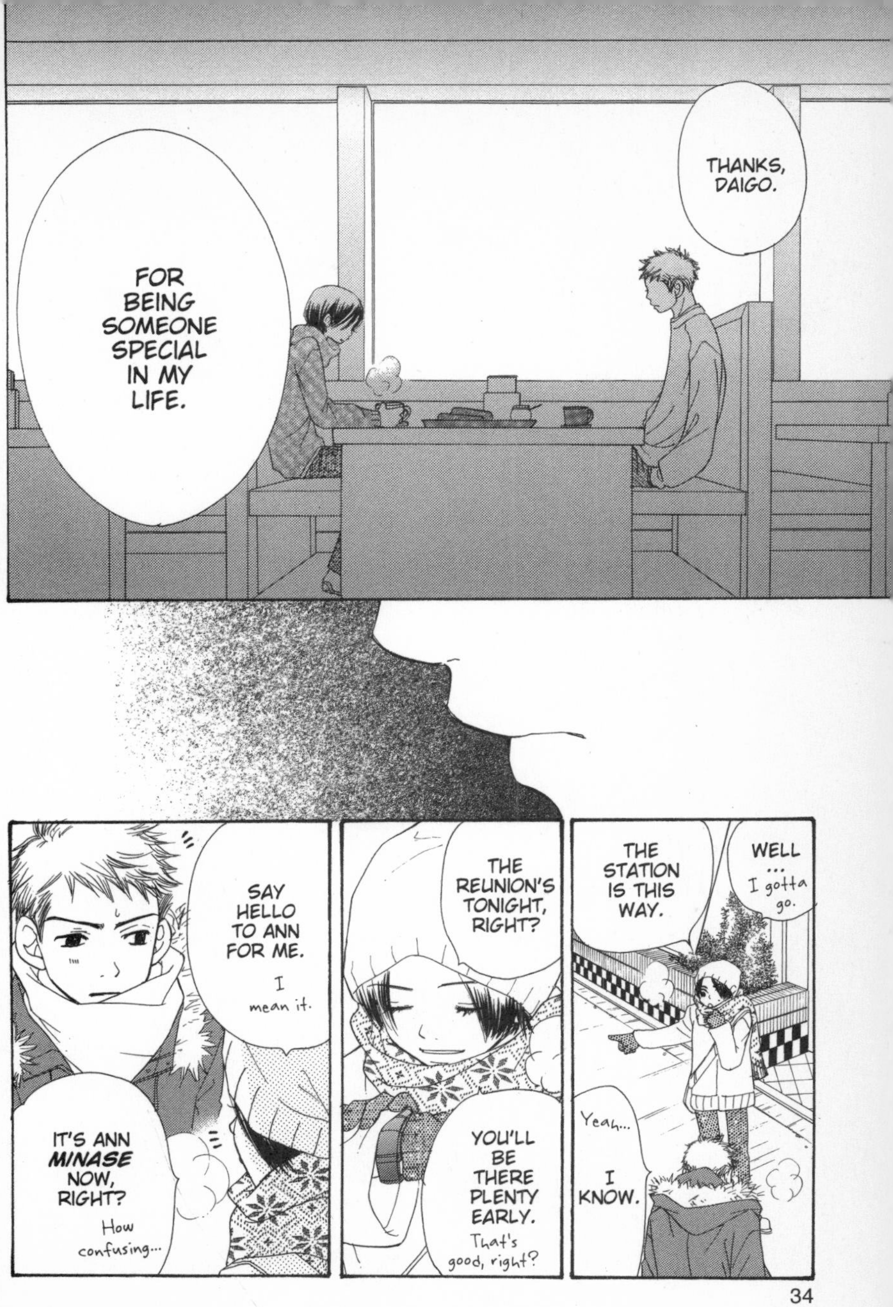
THANKS, DAIGO.
FOR BEING SOMEONE SPECIAL IN MY LIFE.
WELL... I gotta go.
THE STATION IS THIS WAY.
Yeah... I KNOW.
THE REUNION'S TONIGHT, RIGHT?
YOU'LL BE THERE PLENTY EARLY. That's good, right?
SAY HELLO TO ANN FOR ME. I mean it.
IT'S ANN MINASE NOW, RIGHT? How confusing...

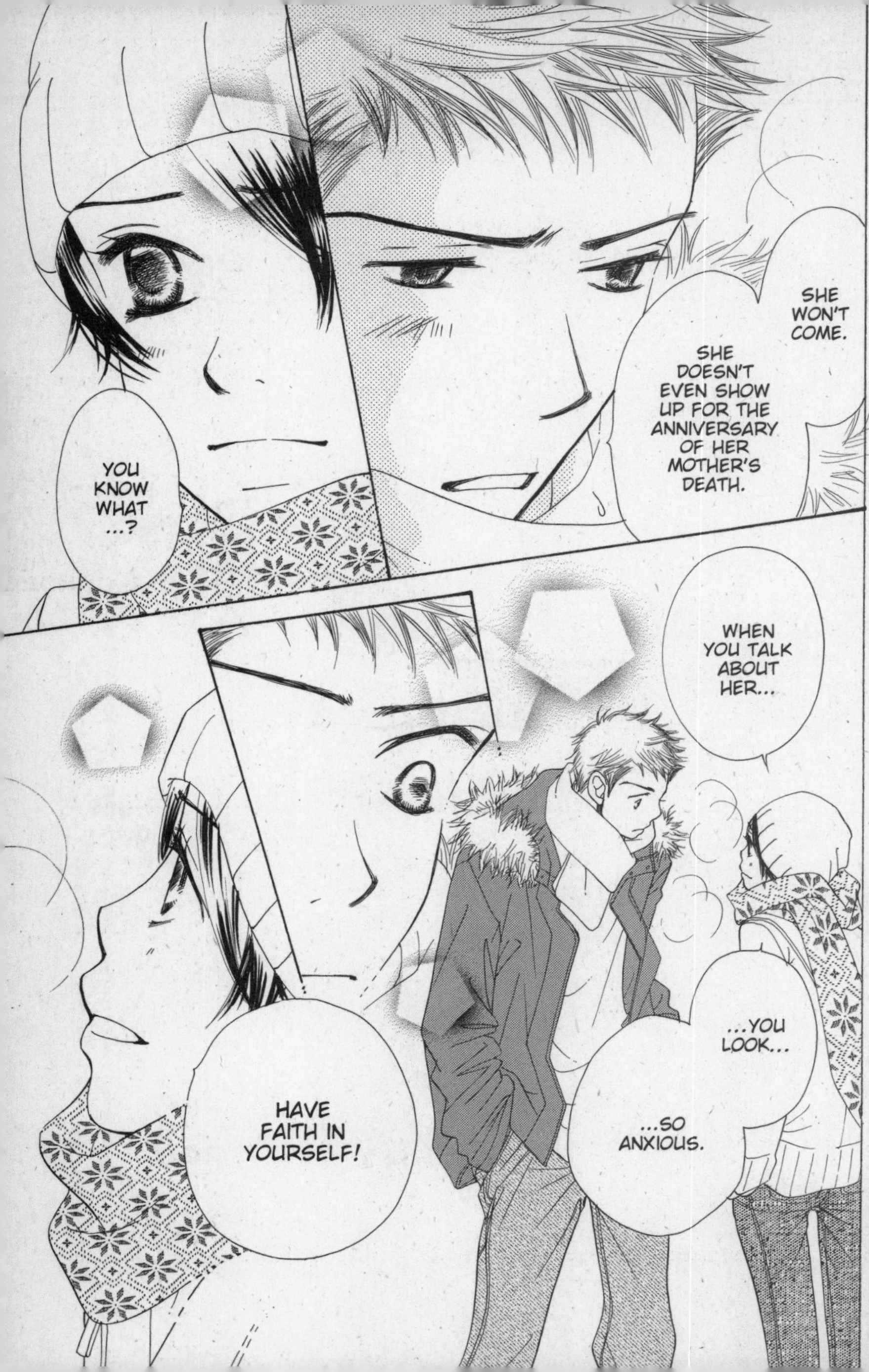
SHE WON'T COME.
SHE DOESN'T EVEN SHOW UP FOR THE ANNIVERSARY OF HER MOTHER'S DEATH.
YOU KNOW WHAT...?
WHEN YOU TALK ABOUT HER...
...YOU LOOK...
...SO ANXIOUS.
HAVE FAITH IN YOURSELF!

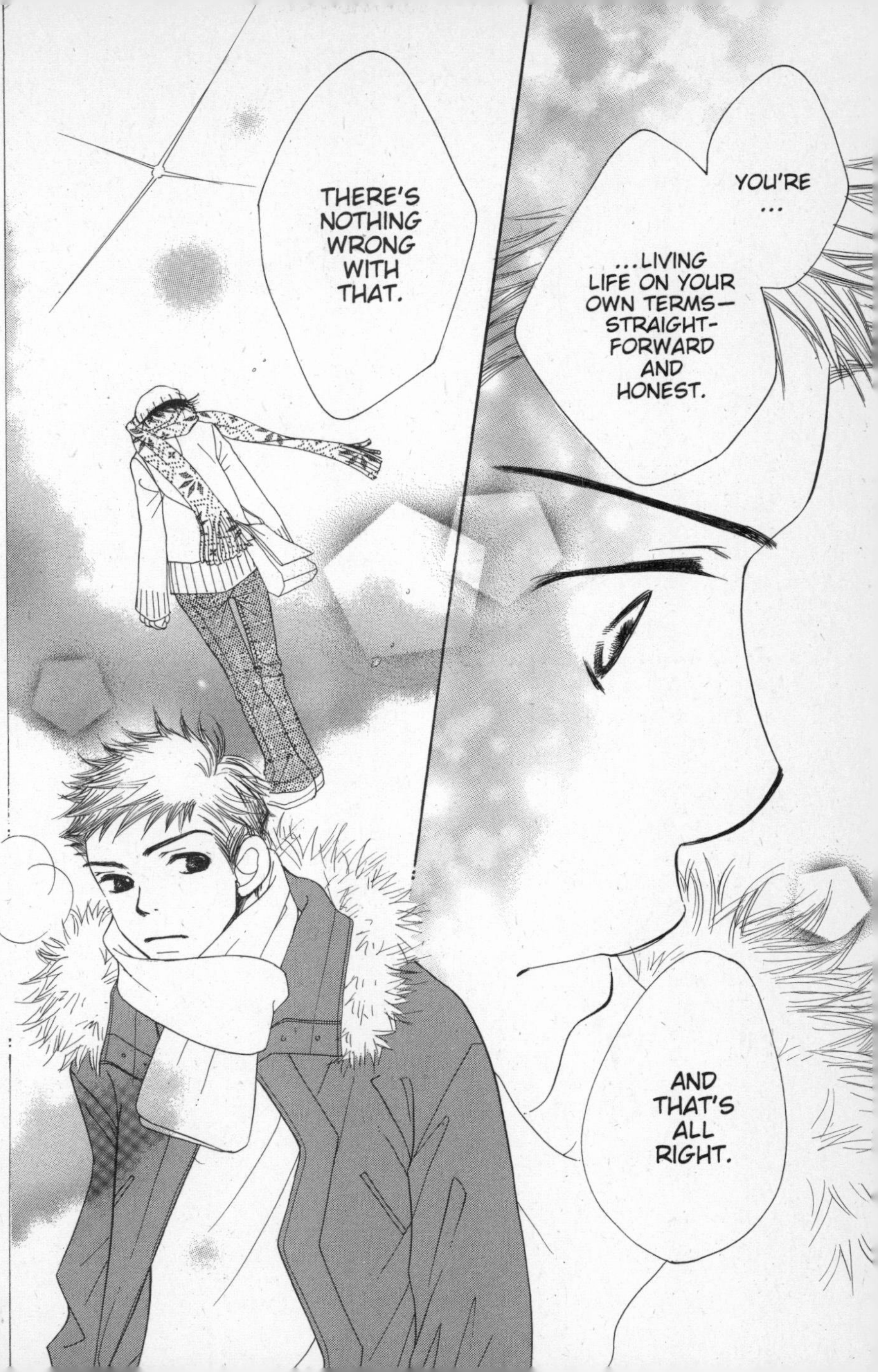
YOU'RE ...
...LIVING LIFE ON YOUR OWN TERMS— STRAIGHT-FORWARD AND HONEST.
AND THAT'S ALL RIGHT.
THERE'S NOTHING WRONG WITH THAT.

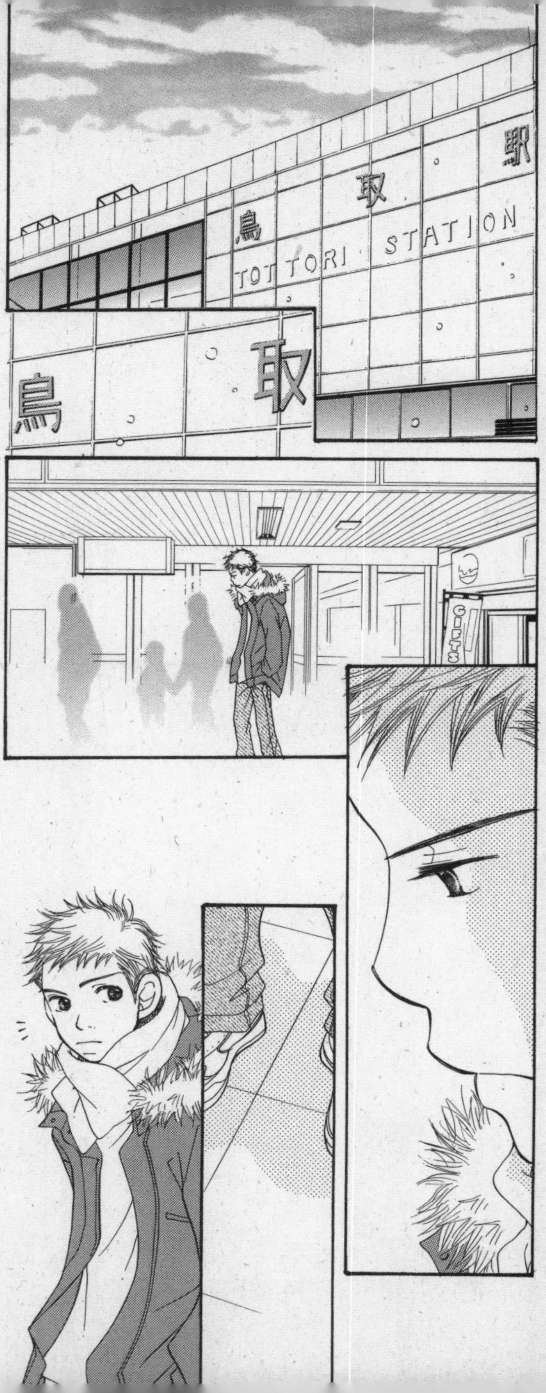
鳥取駅
TOTTORI STATION
鳥取
GIFTS

Winter, Age 20:
Singing Sand

Welcome to Volume 7! And, as always, thanks for reading! Ann and the rest have grown up... Now they're 20 years old. Sometimes I wonder if the younger readers of **Betsucomi** are keeping up.

About the crying sand or... to be more precise, **singing** sand. You can really hear a cute, squeaky sound when you walk on it. When I went to the beach on a research trip, a local man told me that it was squeaking particularly well that day. Lucky me! ♪

As for the Tottori Sand Dunes...there was lots of snow in the Sanin area when I went. The dunes were like ski slopes... I felt so lost out there in the falling snow and dunes. In its own way, that was fun. I like having a research trip as an excuse to travel by train.

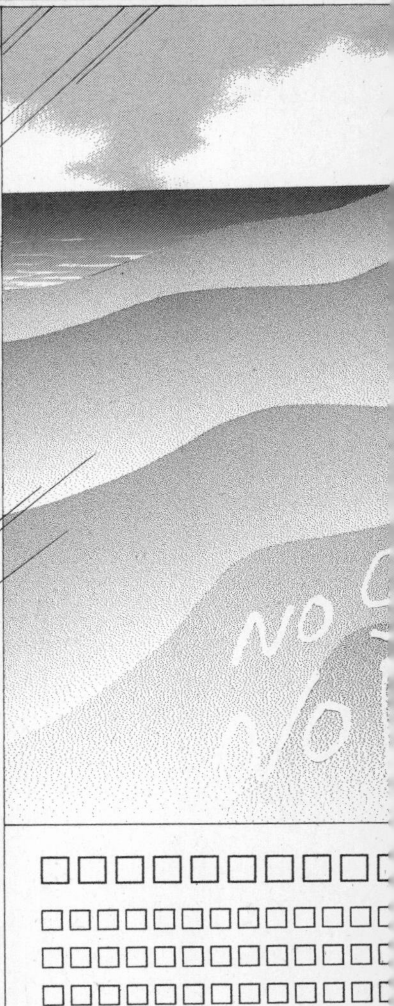

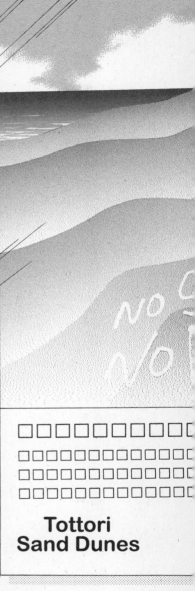

Tottori
Sand Dunes

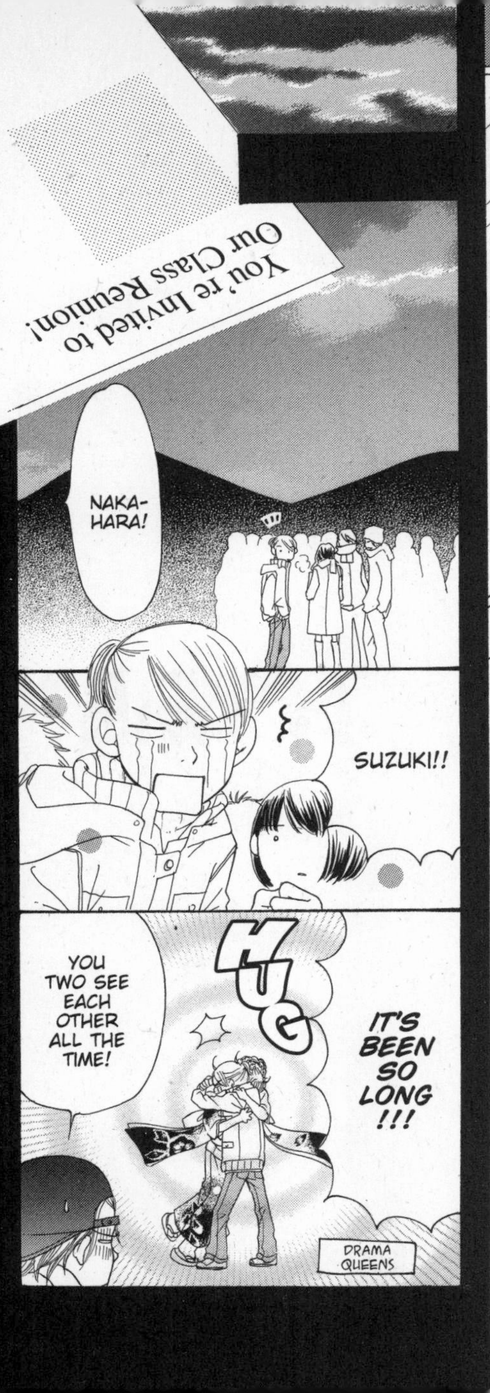
You're Invited to
Our Class Reunion!
NAKA-
HARA!
SUZUKI!!
IT'S BEEN SO LONG!!!
HUG
YOU TWO SEE EACH OTHER ALL THE TIME!
DRAMA QUEENS

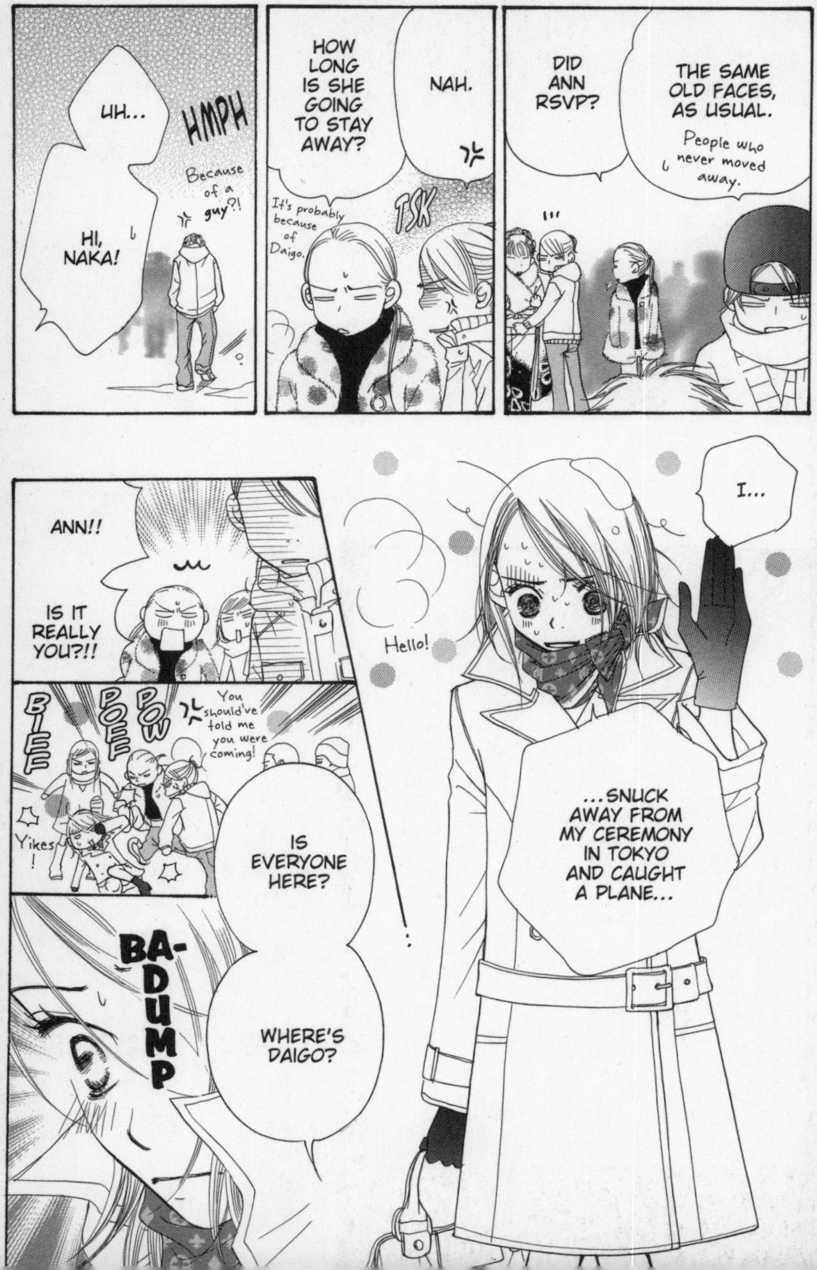
THE SAME OLD FACES, AS USUAL.
People who never moved away.
DID ANN RSVP?
NAH.
HOW LONG IS SHE GOING TO STAY AWAY?
TSK
It's probably because of Daigo.
HMPH
Because of a guy?!
UH...
HI, NAKA!
I...
Hello!
...SNUCK AWAY FROM MY CEREMONY IN TOKYO AND CAUGHT A PLANE...
ANN!!
IS IT REALLY YOU?!!
POW
POFF
BIFF
You should've told me you were coming!
Yikes!
IS EVERYONE HERE?
WHERE'S DAIGO?
BA-DUMP

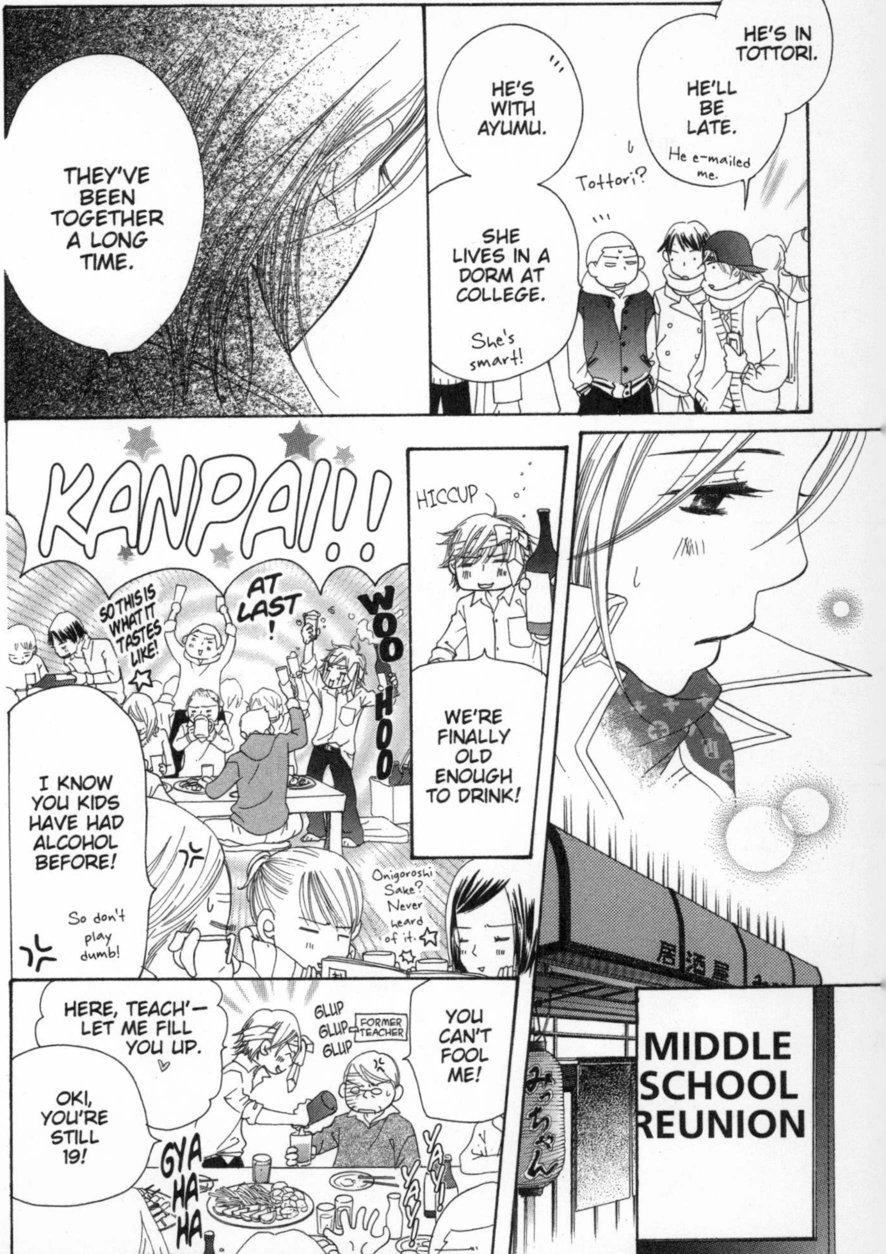
HE'S IN TOTTORI.
HE'LL BE LATE.
He e-mailed me.
Tottori?
...
HE'S WITH AYUMU.
SHE LIVES IN A DORM AT COLLEGE.
She's smart!
THEY'VE BEEN TOGETHER A LONG TIME.
HICCUP
WE'RE FINALLY OLD ENOUGH TO DRINK!
KANPAI!!
WOO HOO
AT LAST!
SO THIS IS WHAT IT TASTES LIKE!
Onigoroshi Sake? Never heard of it.
I KNOW YOU KIDS HAVE HAD ALCOHOL BEFORE!
So don't play dumb!
MIDDLE SCHOOL REUNION
居酒屋
みっちゃん
YOU CAN'T FOOL ME!
FORMER TEACHER
GLUP GLUP GLUP
HERE, TEACH'— LET ME FILL YOU UP.
OKI, YOU'RE STILL 19!
YAY! YAY!
GYA HA HA

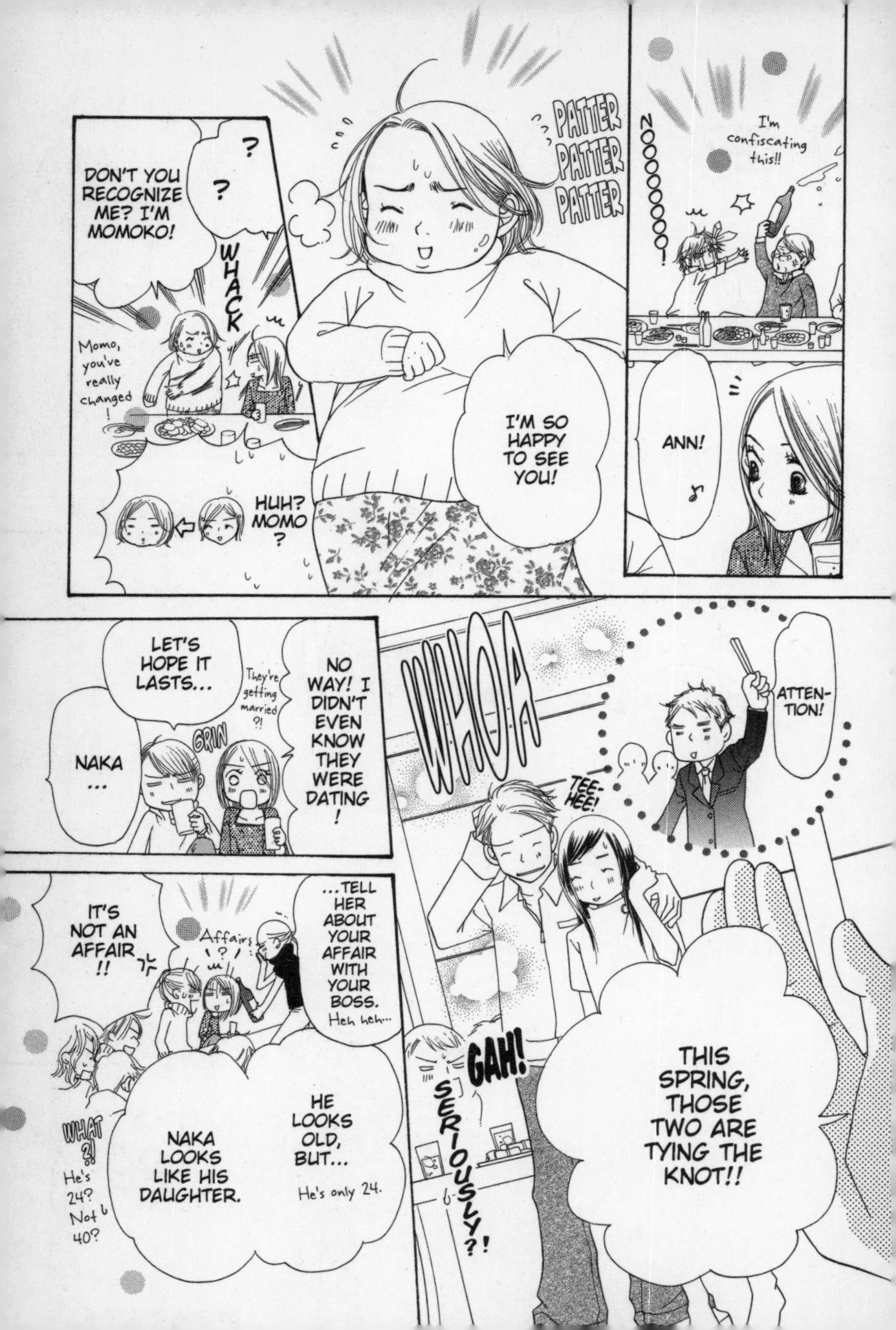

NOOOOOOOO!
I'm confiscating this!!
ANN!
PATTER PATTER PATTER
I'M SO HAPPY TO SEE YOU!
DON'T YOU RECOGNIZE ME? I'M MOMOKO!
?
?
WHACK
Momo, you've really changed!
HUH? MOMO?
ATTENTION!
WHOA
TEE-HEE!
NO WAY! I DIDN'T EVEN KNOW THEY WERE DATING!
They're getting married?!
LET'S HOPE IT LASTS...
GRIN
NAKA...
THIS SPRING, THOSE TWO ARE TYING THE KNOT!!
GAH!
SERIOUSLY?!
...TELL HER ABOUT YOUR AFFAIR WITH YOUR BOSS.
Heh heh...
IT'S NOT AN AFFAIR!!
Affair?!
HE LOOKS OLD, BUT...
He's only 24.
NAKA LOOKS LIKE HIS DAUGHTER.
WHAT?!
He's 24? Not 40?

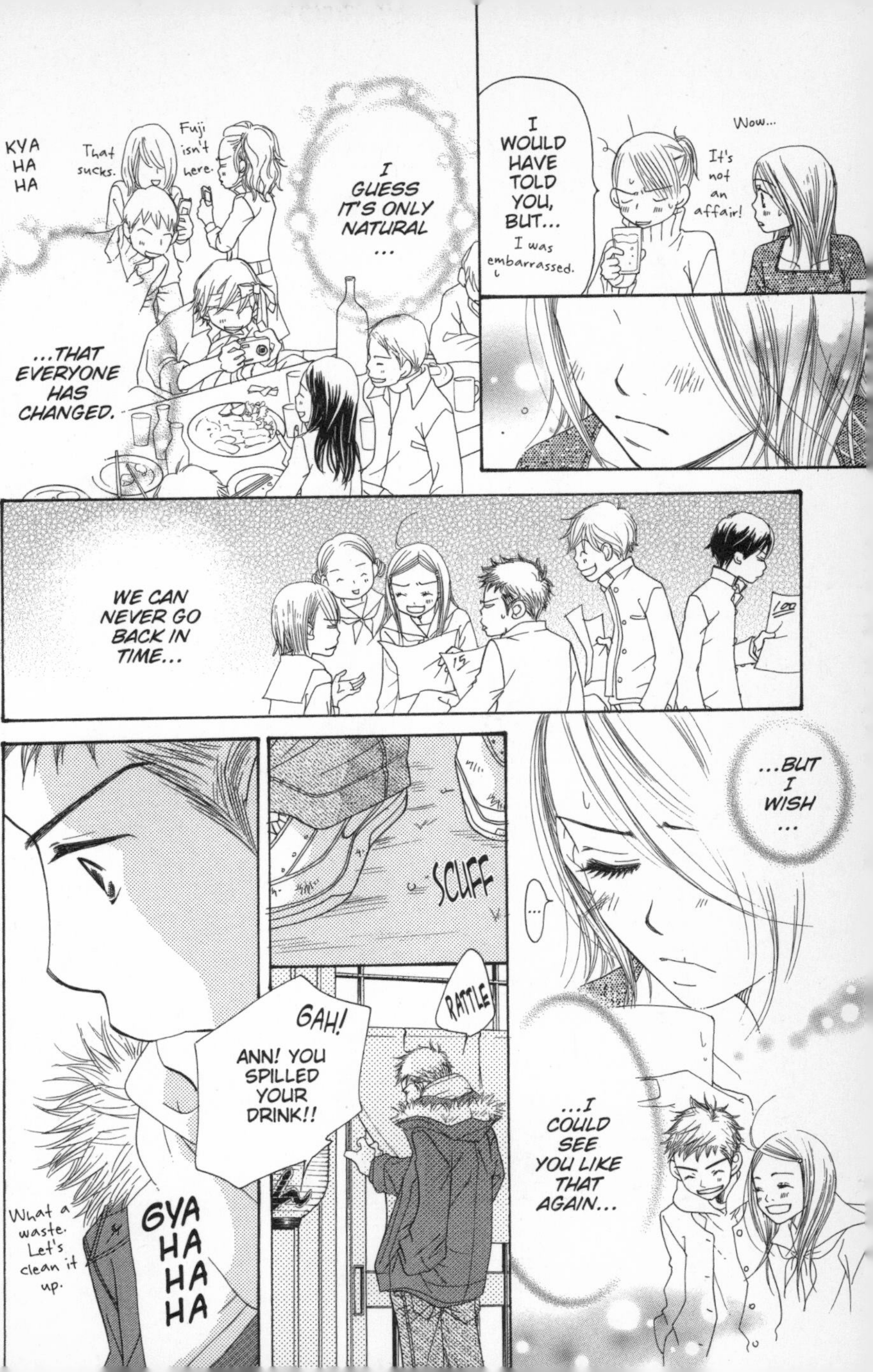
I WOULD HAVE TOLD YOU, BUT...
I was embarrassed.
Wow...
It's not an affair!
I GUESS IT'S ONLY NATURAL...
...THAT EVERYONE HAS CHANGED.
Fuji isn't here.
That sucks.
KYA HA HA
WE CAN NEVER GO BACK IN TIME...
...BUT I WISH...
...
...I COULD SEE YOU LIKE THAT AGAIN...
SCUFF
RATTLE
GAH!
ANN! YOU SPILLED YOUR DRINK!!
GYA HA HA HA
What a waste. Let's clean it up.

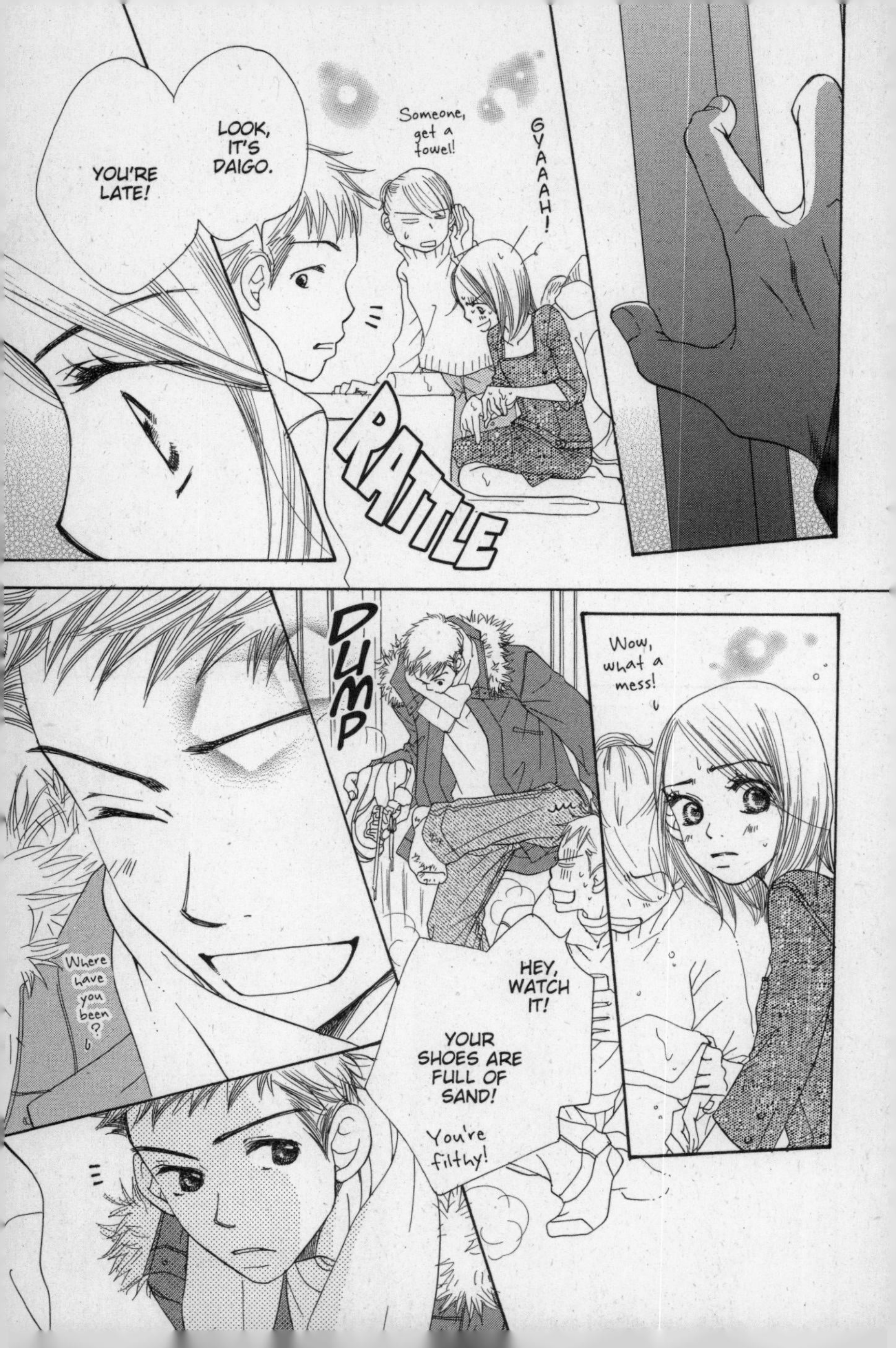

GYAAAAH!
Someone, get a towel!
RATTLE
LOOK, IT'S DAIGO.
YOU'RE LATE!
Wow, what a mess!
DUMP
HEY, WATCH IT!
YOUR SHOES ARE FULL OF SAND!
You're filthy!
Where have you been?

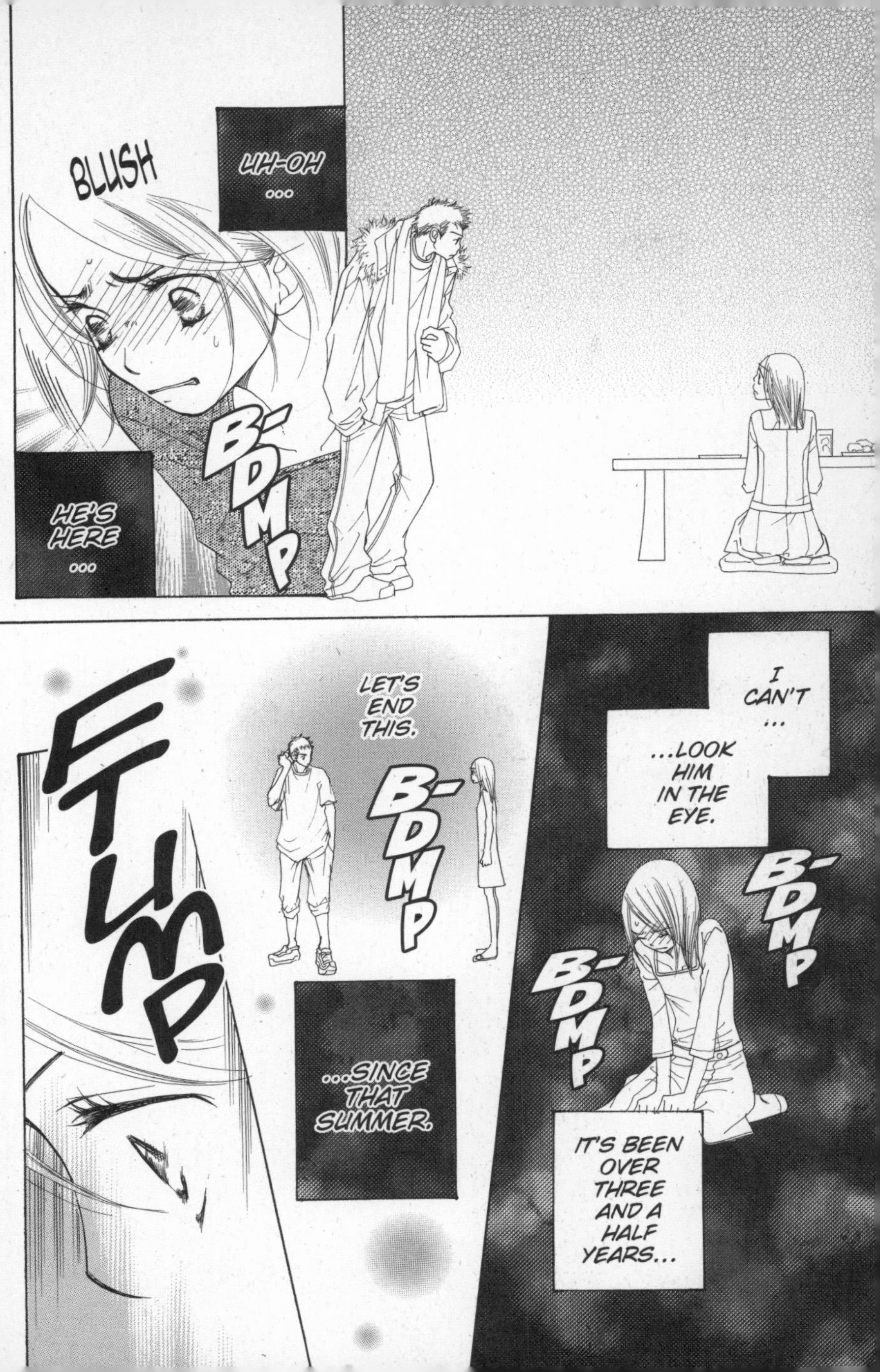
UH-OH ...
BLUSH
B-DMP
HE'S HERE ...
I CAN'T ...
...LOOK HIM IN THE EYE.
B-DMP
B-DMP
IT'S BEEN OVER THREE AND A HALF YEARS...
LET'S END THIS.
B-DMP
...SINCE THAT SUMMER.
FTUMP

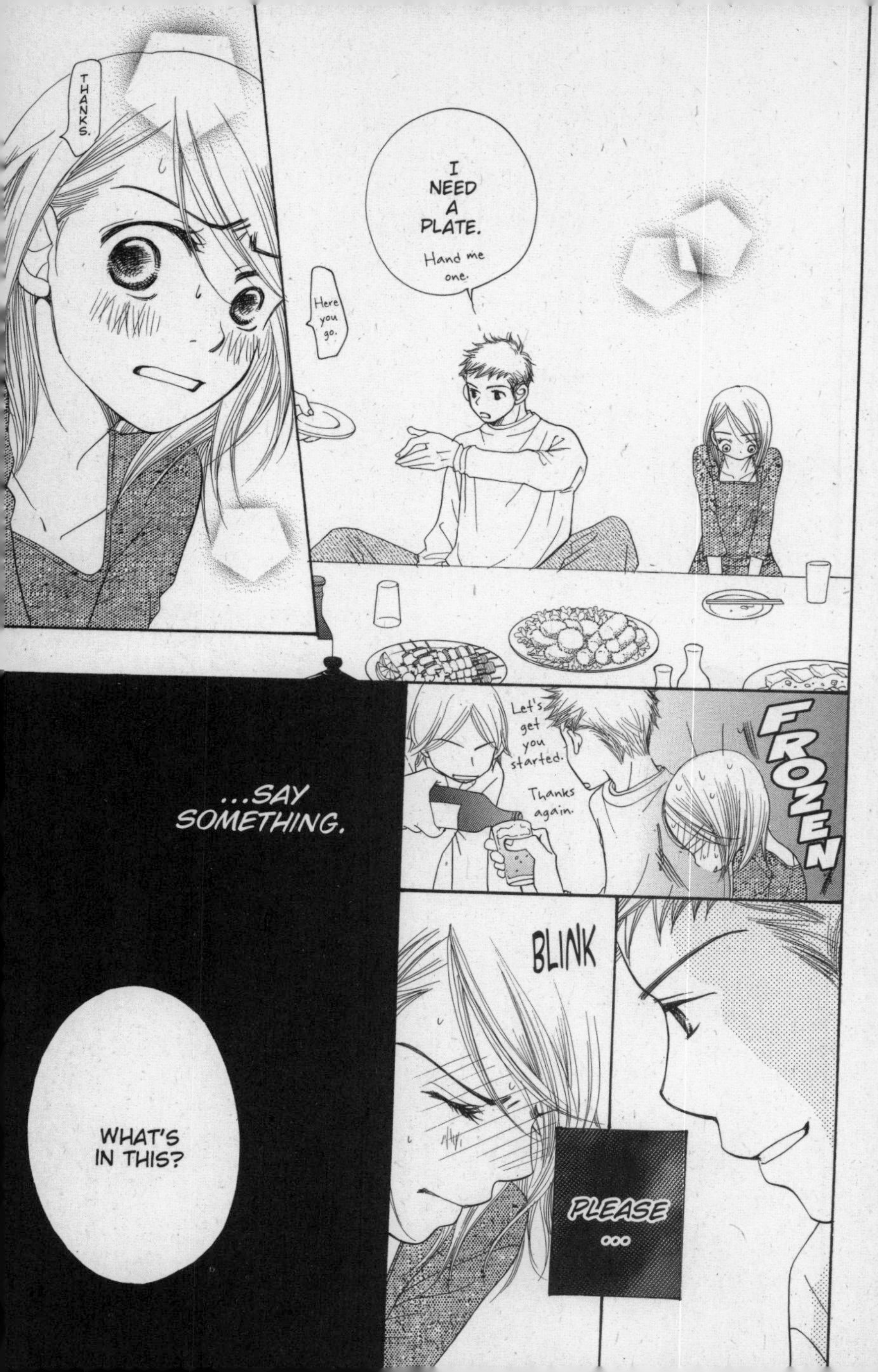
I NEED A PLATE.
Hand me one.
Here you go.
THANKS.
Let's get you started.
Thanks again.
FROZEN
BLINK
PLEASE ...
...SAY SOMETHING.
WHAT'S IN THIS?

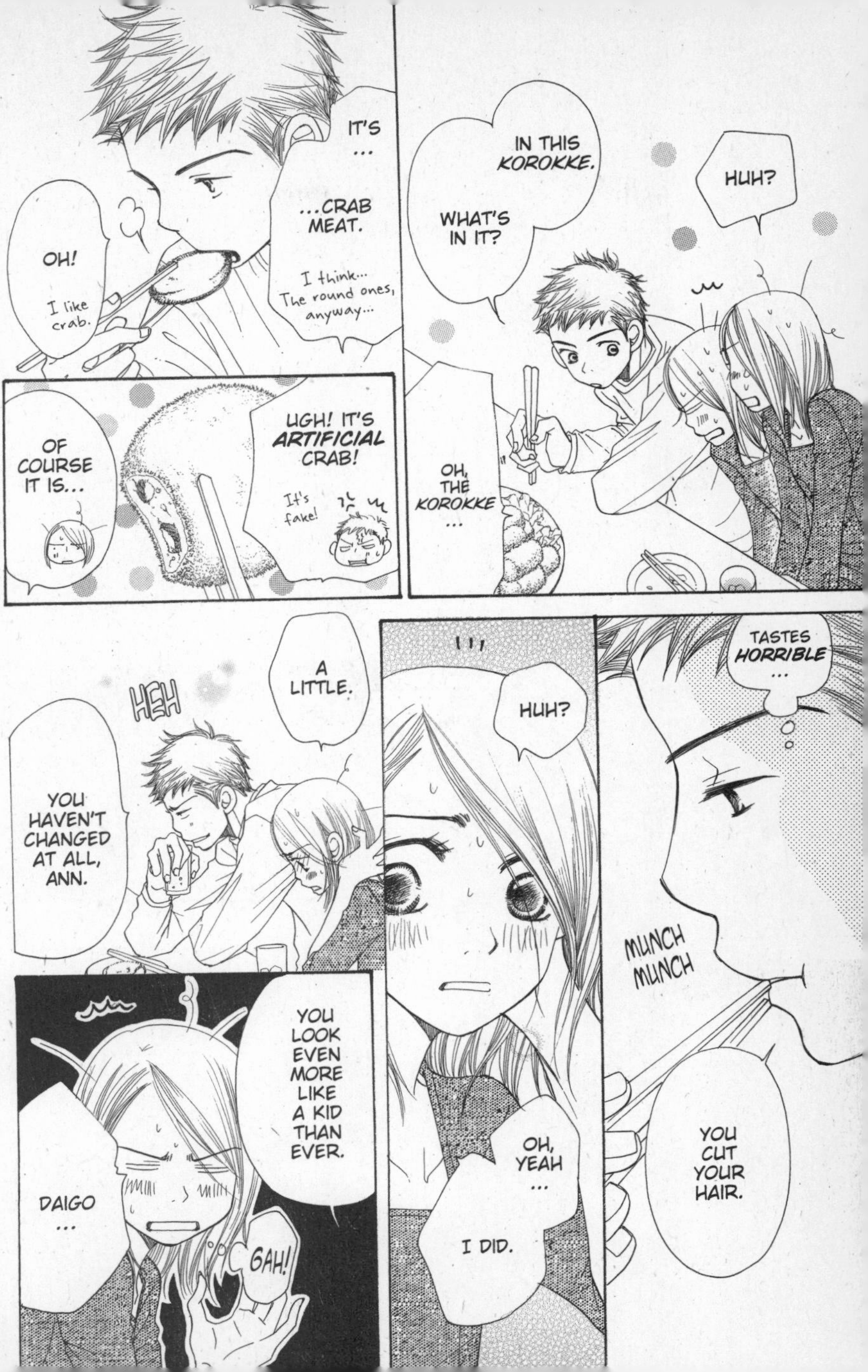
HUH?
IN THIS KOROKKE.
WHAT'S IN IT?
OH, THE KOROKKE...
IT'S...
...CRAB MEAT.
I think... The round ones, anyway...
OH!
I like crab.
UGH! IT'S ARTIFICIAL CRAB!
It's fake!
OF COURSE IT IS...
TASTES HORRIBLE...
MUNCH MUNCH
YOU CUT YOUR HAIR.
HUH?
OH, YEAH...
I DID.
A LITTLE.
HEH
YOU HAVEN'T CHANGED AT ALL, ANN.
YOU LOOK EVEN MORE LIKE A KID THAN EVER.
DAIGO...
GAH!

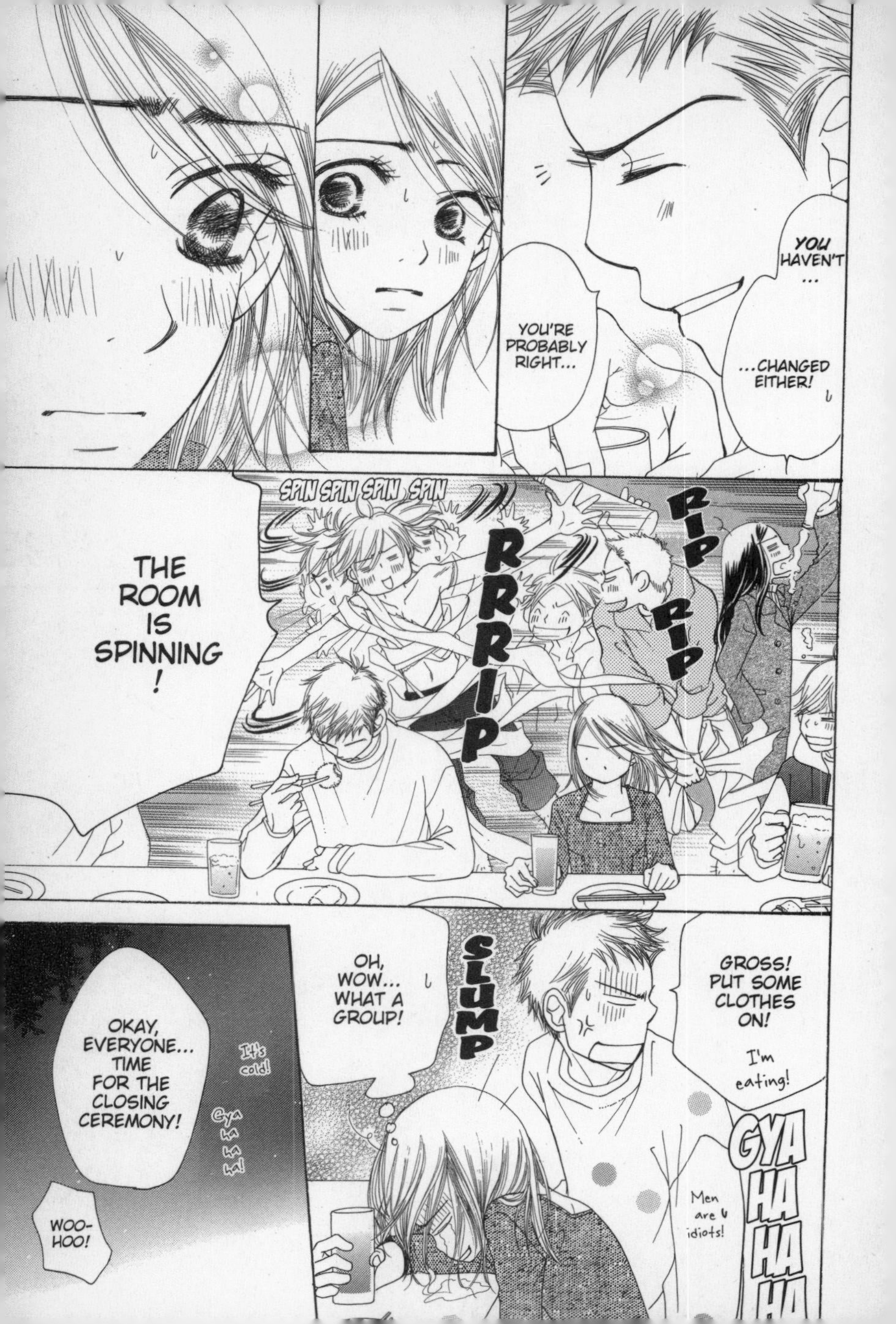
YOU HAVEN'T ...
...CHANGED EITHER!
YOU'RE PROBABLY RIGHT...
RIP RIP
RRRIP
SPIN SPIN SPIN SPIN
THE ROOM IS SPINNING!
GROSS! PUT SOME CLOTHES ON!
I'm eating!
GYA HA HA HA HA
Men are idiots!
SLUMP
OH, WOW... WHAT A GROUP!
OKAY, EVERYONE... TIME FOR THE CLOSING CEREMONY!
It's cold!
Gya ha ha ha!
WOO-HOO!

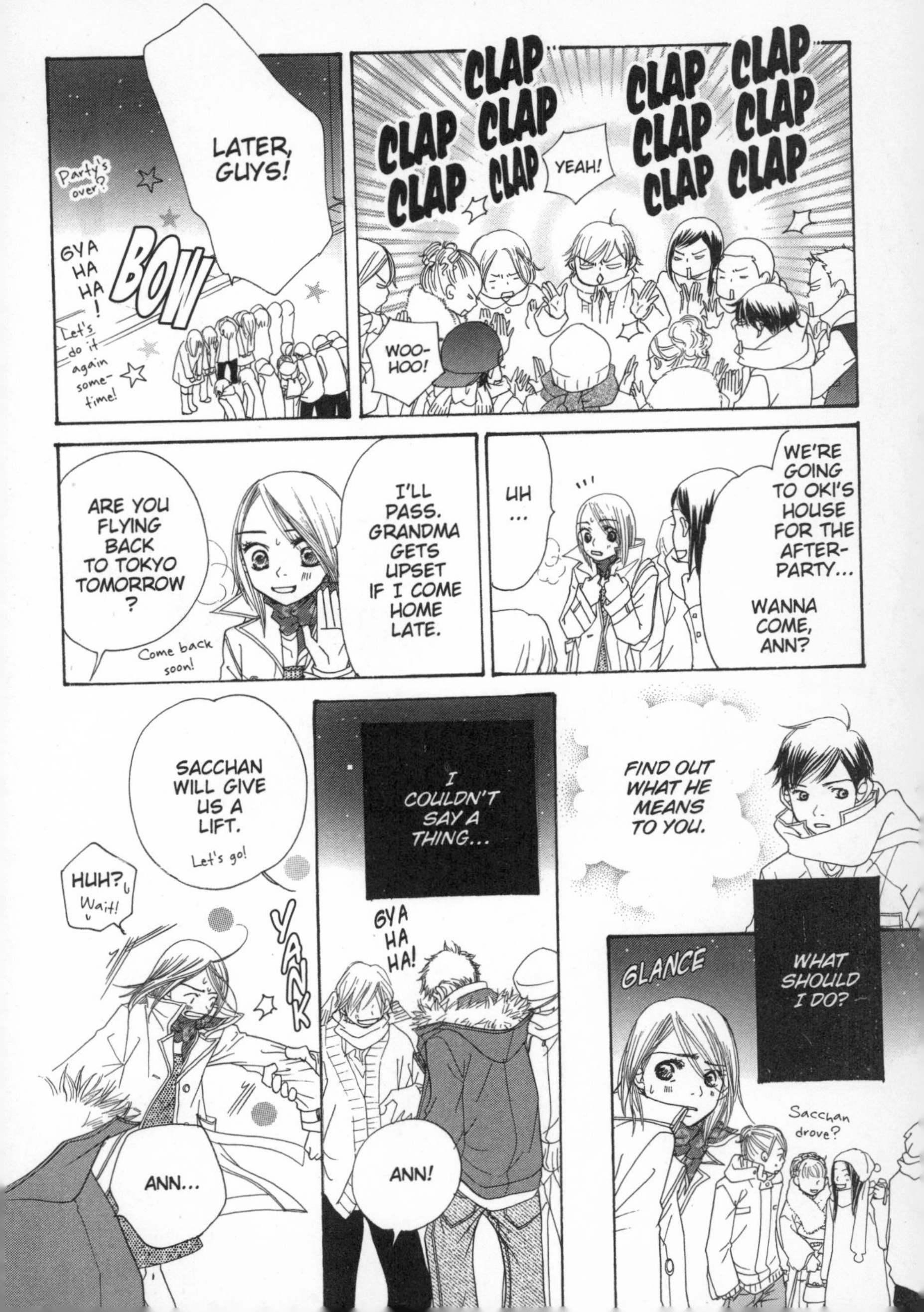
CLAP CLAP CLAP CLAP CLAP CLAP
CLAP CLAP CLAP CLAP CLAP
YEAH!
WOO-HOO!
LATER, GUYS!
Party's over?
GYA HA HA!
BOW
Let's do it again some-time!
WE'RE GOING TO OKI'S HOUSE FOR THE AFTER-PARTY...
WANNA COME, ANN?
UH...
I'LL PASS. GRANDMA GETS UPSET IF I COME HOME LATE.
ARE YOU FLYING BACK TO TOKYO TOMORROW?
Come back soon!
FIND OUT WHAT HE MEANS TO YOU.
GLANCE
WHAT SHOULD I DO?
Sacchan drove?
I COULDN'T SAY A THING...
GYA HA HA!
ANN!
SACCHAN WILL GIVE US A LIFT.
Let's go!
HUH?
Wait!
YANK
ANN...

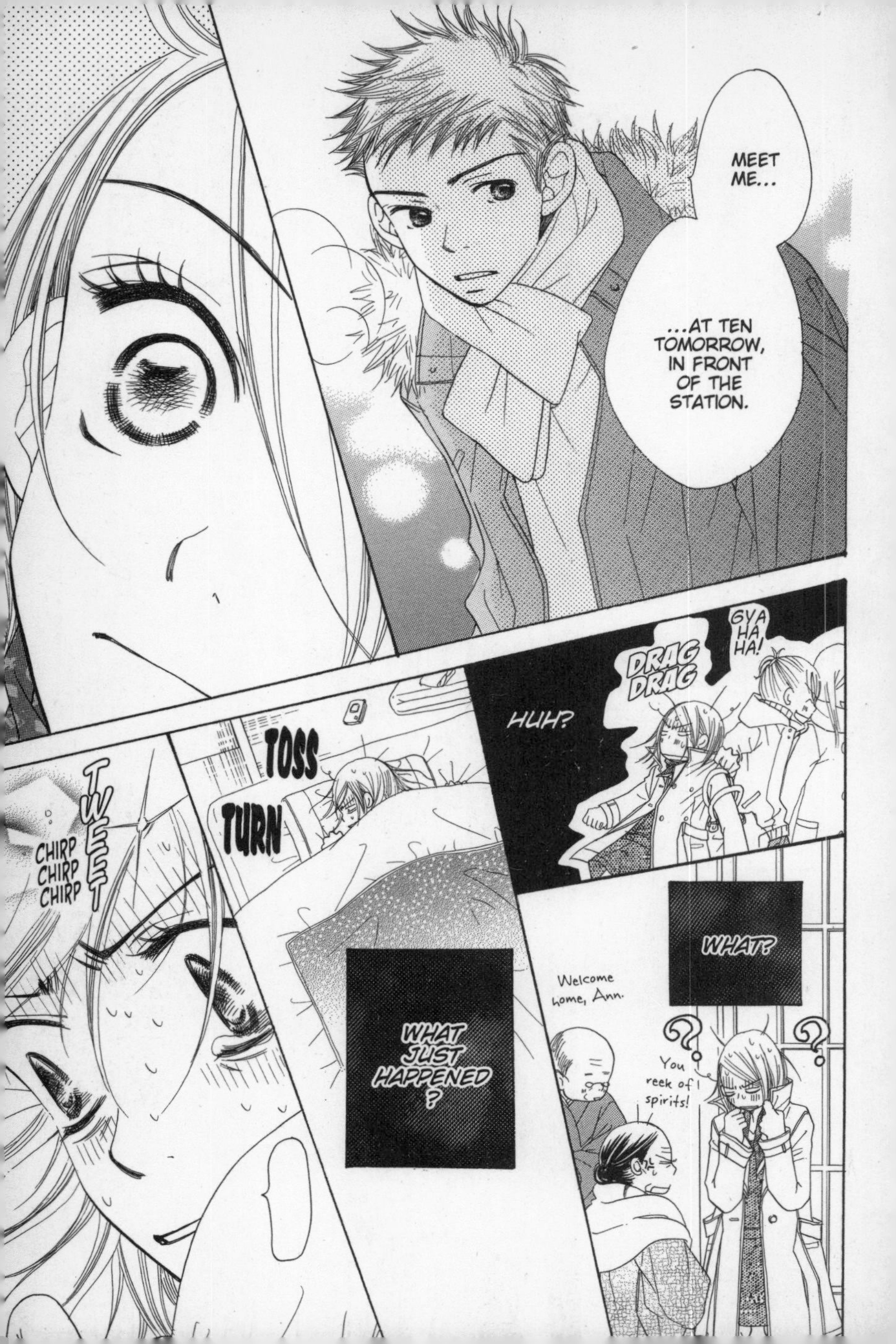
MEET ME...
...AT TEN TOMORROW, IN FRONT OF THE STATION.
GYA HA HA!
DRAG DRAG
HUH?
WHAT?
Welcome home, Ann.
You reek of spirits!
TOSS
TURN
WHAT JUST HAPPENED?
TWEET
CHIRP CHIRP CHIRP

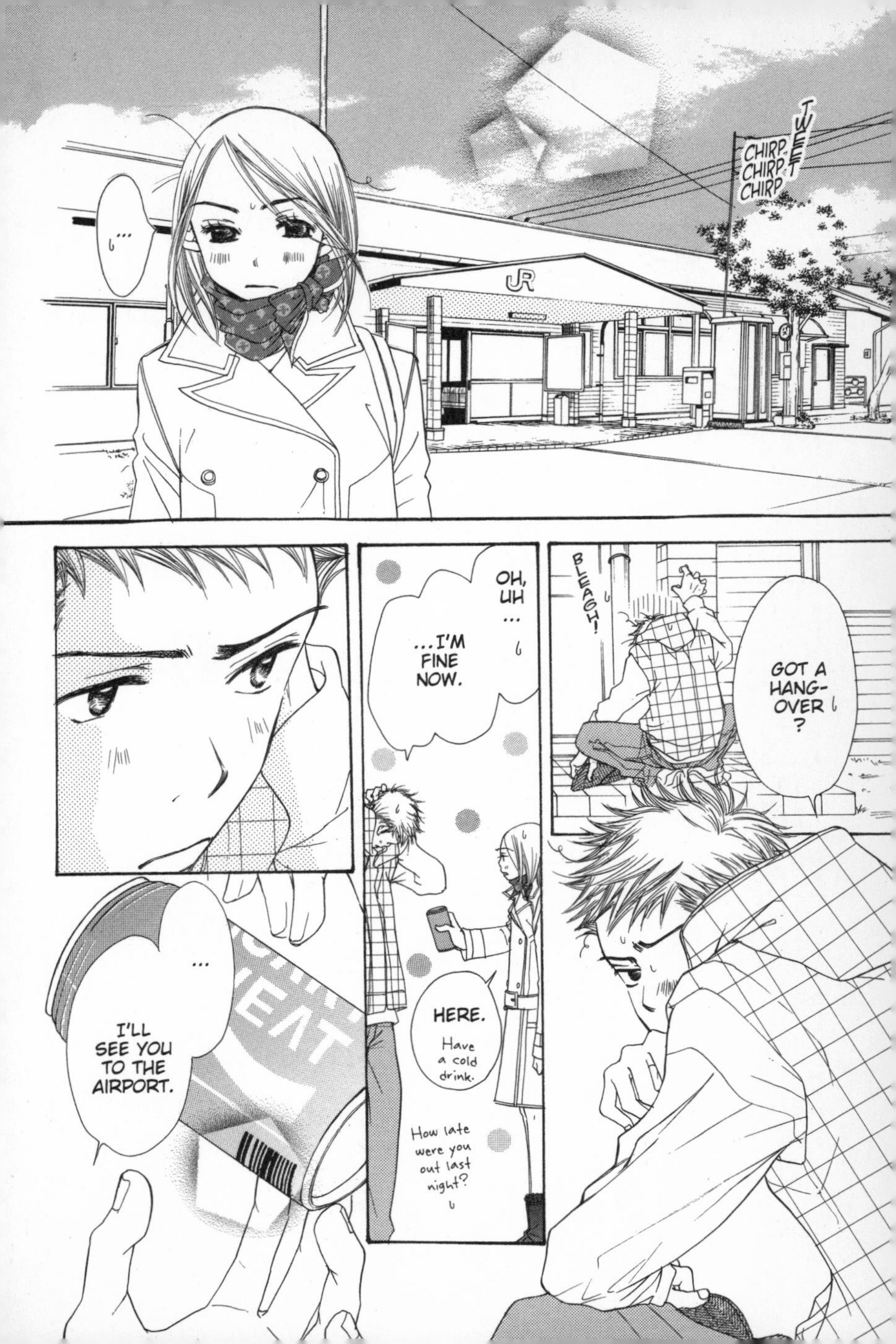
TWEET
CHIRP CHIRP CHIRP
...
BLEACH!
GOT A HANG-OVER?
OH, UH...
...I'M FINE NOW.
HERE.
Have a cold drink.
How late were you out last night?
...
I'LL SEE YOU TO THE AIRPORT.

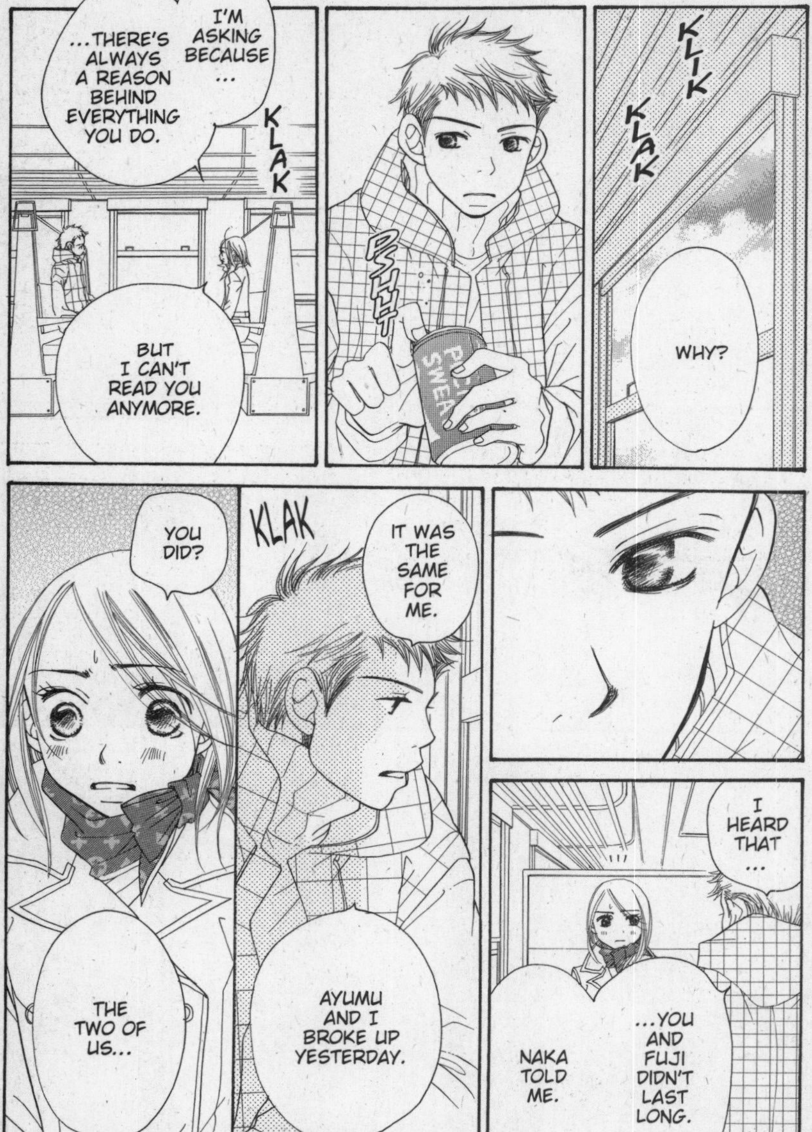
KLIK
KLAK
WHY?
PSHHT
I'M ASKING BECAUSE ...
...THERE'S ALWAYS A REASON BEHIND EVERYTHING YOU DO.
KLAK
BUT I CAN'T READ YOU ANYMORE.
I HEARD THAT ...
...YOU AND FUJI DIDN'T LAST LONG.
NAKA TOLD ME.
KLAK
IT WAS THE SAME FOR ME.
AYUMU AND I BROKE UP YESTERDAY.
YOU DID?
THE TWO OF US...

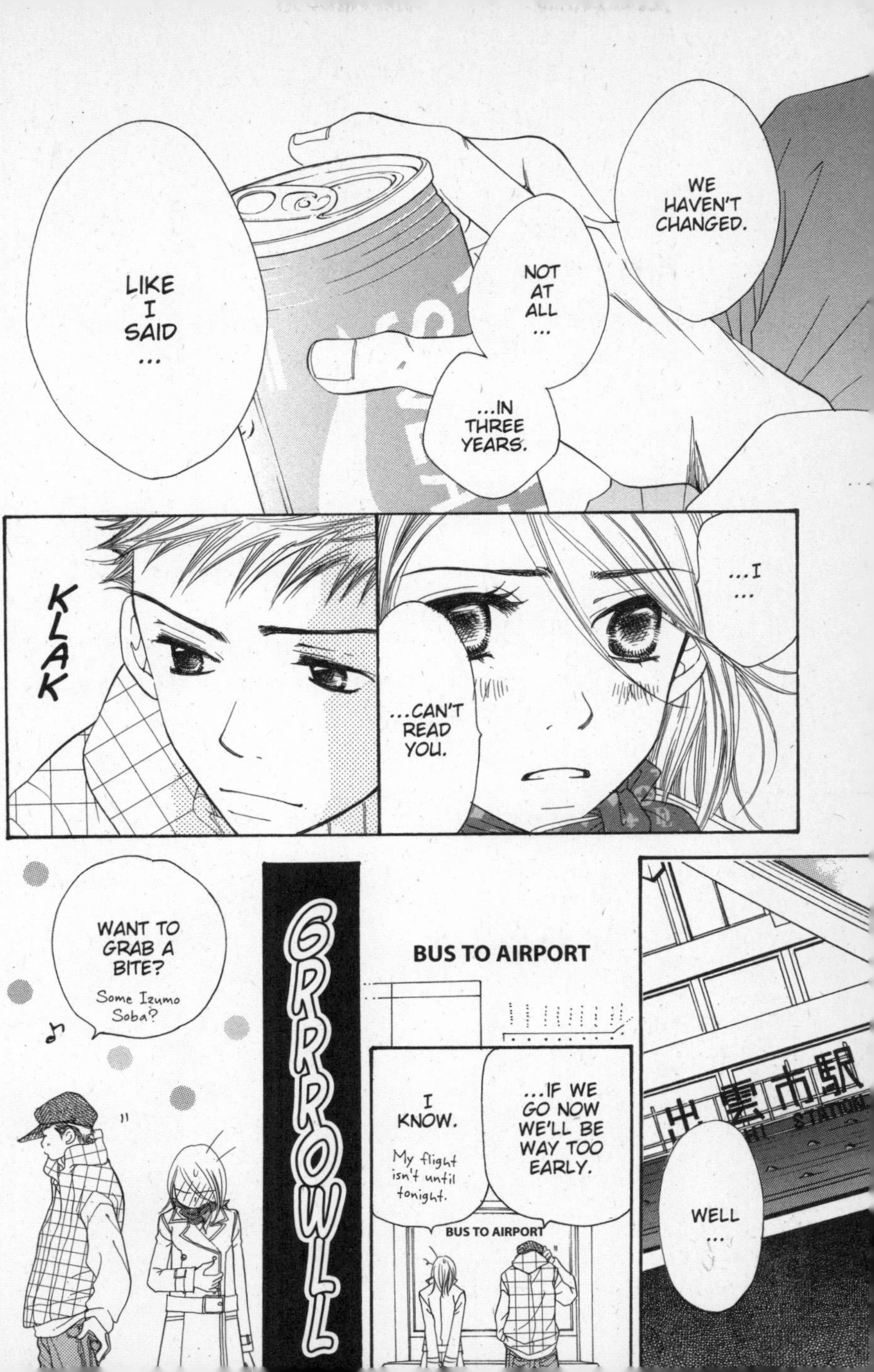
WE HAVEN'T CHANGED.
NOT AT ALL ...
...IN THREE YEARS.
LIKE I SAID ...
...I ...
...CAN'T READ YOU.
KLAK
出雲市駅
WELL ...
BUS TO AIRPORT
...IF WE GO NOW WE'LL BE WAY TOO EARLY.
I KNOW.
My flight isn't until tonight.
BUS TO AIRPORT
GRRROWLL
WANT TO GRAB A BITE?
Some Izumo Soba?

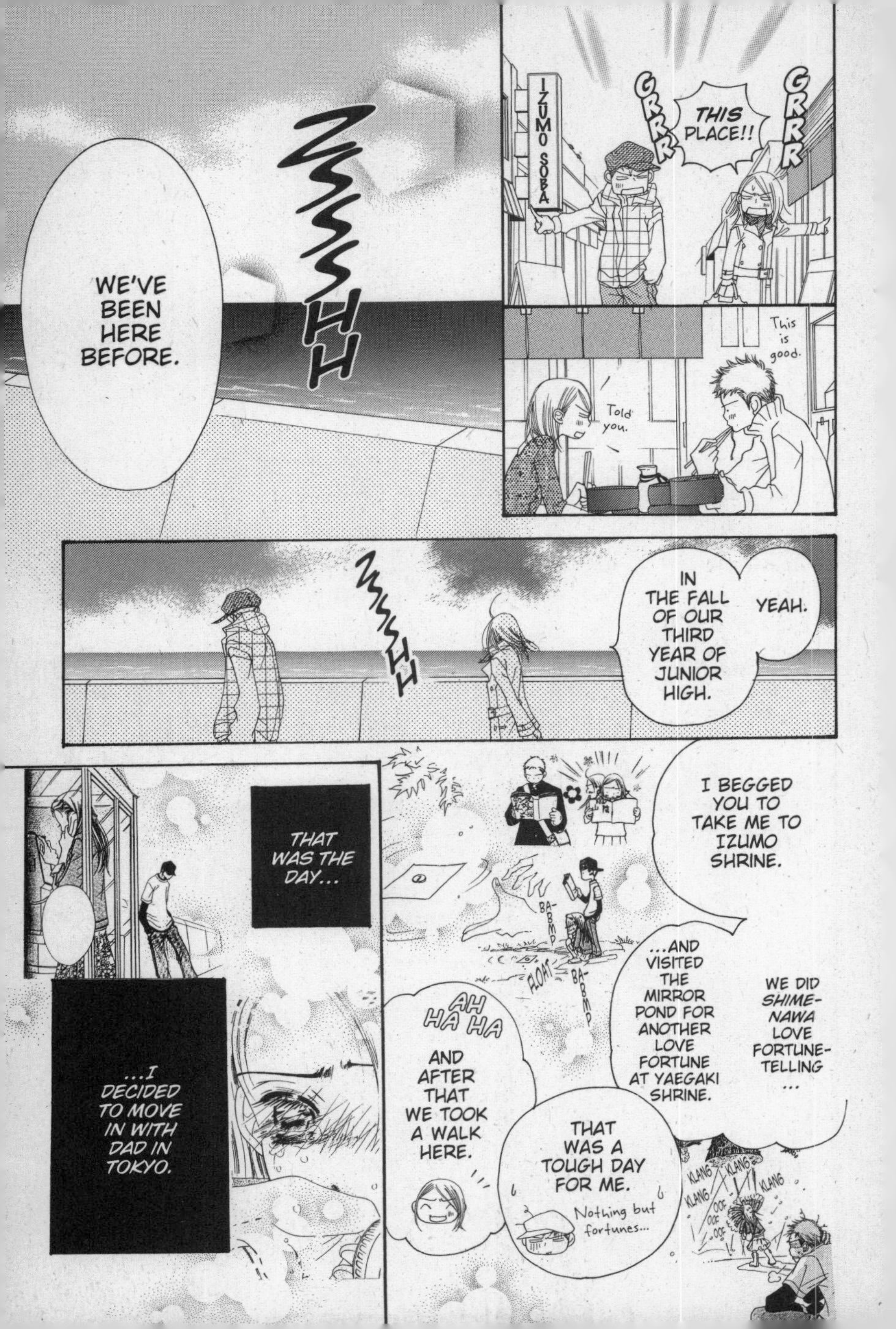
IZUMO SOBA
GRRR
THIS PLACE!!
GRRR
This is good.
Told you.
ZSSHH
WE'VE BEEN HERE BEFORE.
YEAH.
IN THE FALL OF OUR THIRD YEAR OF JUNIOR HIGH.
ZSSHH
I BEGGED YOU TO TAKE ME TO IZUMO SHRINE.
WE DID SHIME-NAWA LOVE FORTUNE-TELLING...
...AND VISITED THE MIRROR POND FOR ANOTHER LOVE FORTUNE AT YAEGAKI SHRINE.
BA-BMP
BA-BMP
FLOAT
KLANG KLANG KLANG KLANG
OOF OOF OOF
AH HA HA
AND AFTER THAT WE TOOK A WALK HERE.
THAT WAS A TOUGH DAY FOR ME.
Nothing but fortunes...
THAT WAS THE DAY...
...I DECIDED TO MOVE IN WITH DAD IN TOKYO.

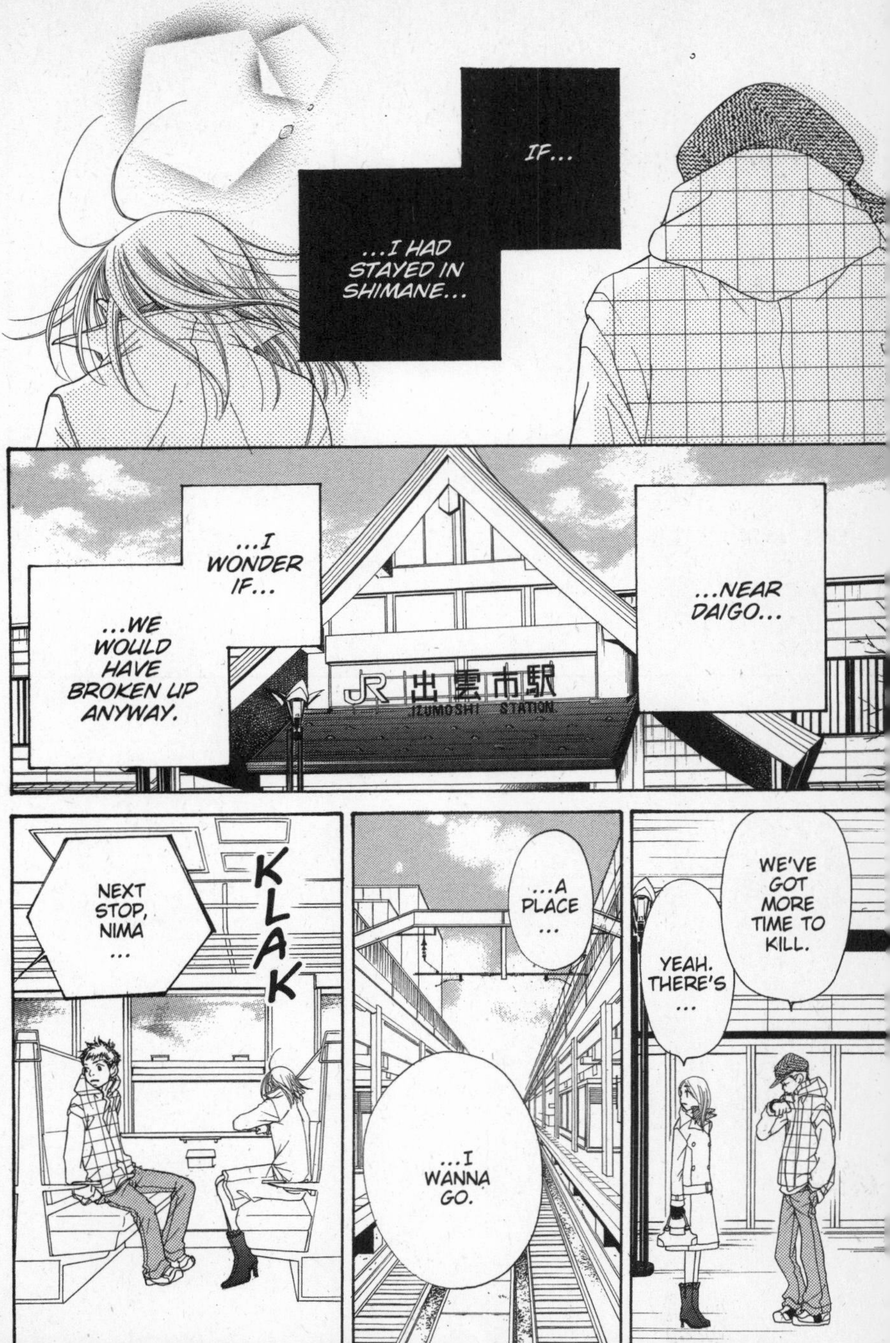
IF...
...I HAD STAYED IN SHIMANE...
...NEAR DAIGO...
...I WONDER IF...
...WE WOULD HAVE BROKEN UP ANYWAY.
JR 出雲市駅
IZUMOSHI STATION
WE'VE GOT MORE TIME TO KILL.
YEAH. THERE'S ...
...A PLACE ...
...I WANNA GO.
KLAK
NEXT STOP, NIMA ...

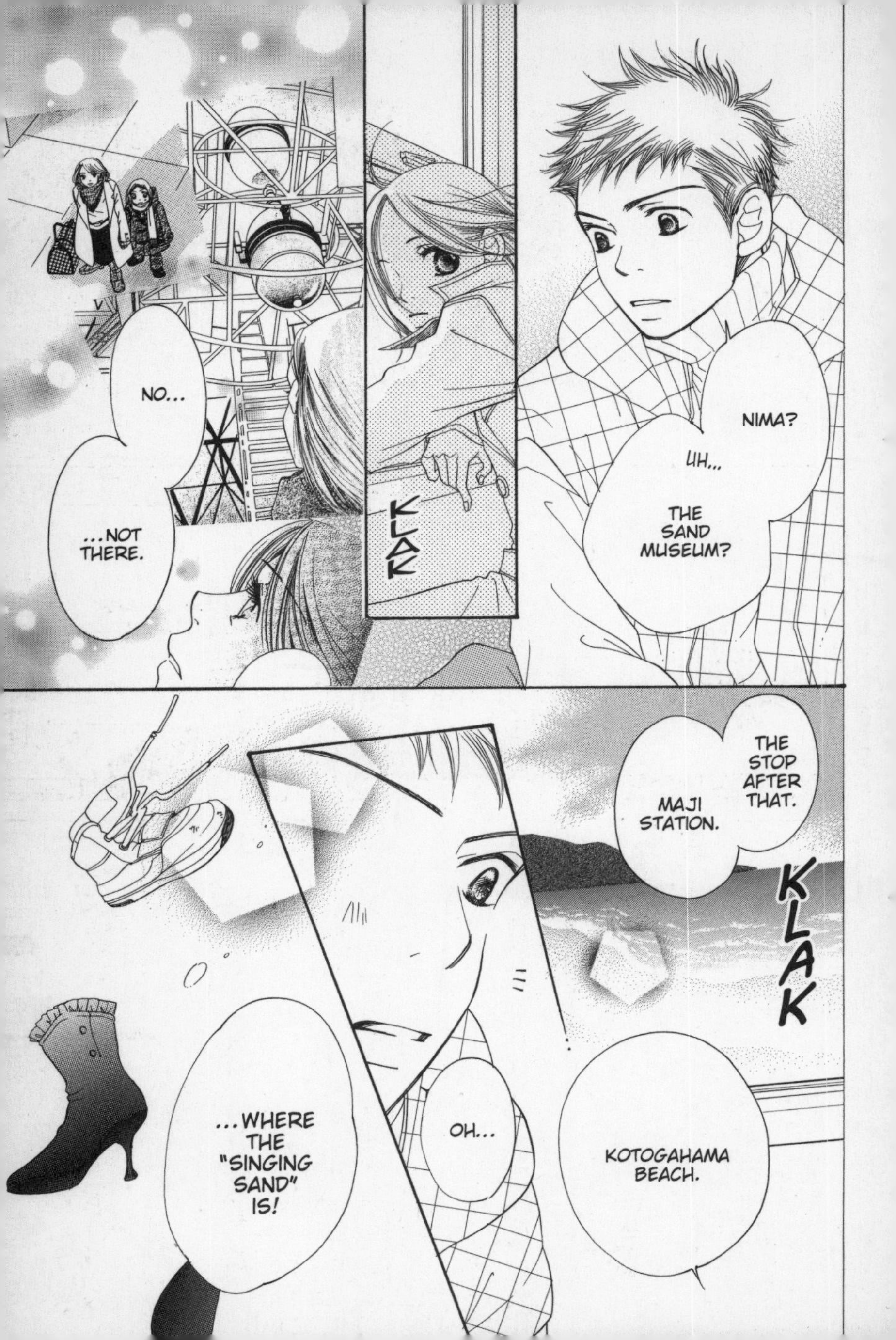
NIMA?
UH... THE SAND MUSEUM?
KLAK
NO...
...NOT THERE.
THE STOP AFTER THAT.
MAJI STATION.
KLAK
KOTOGAHAMA BEACH.
OH...
...WHERE THE "SINGING SAND" IS!

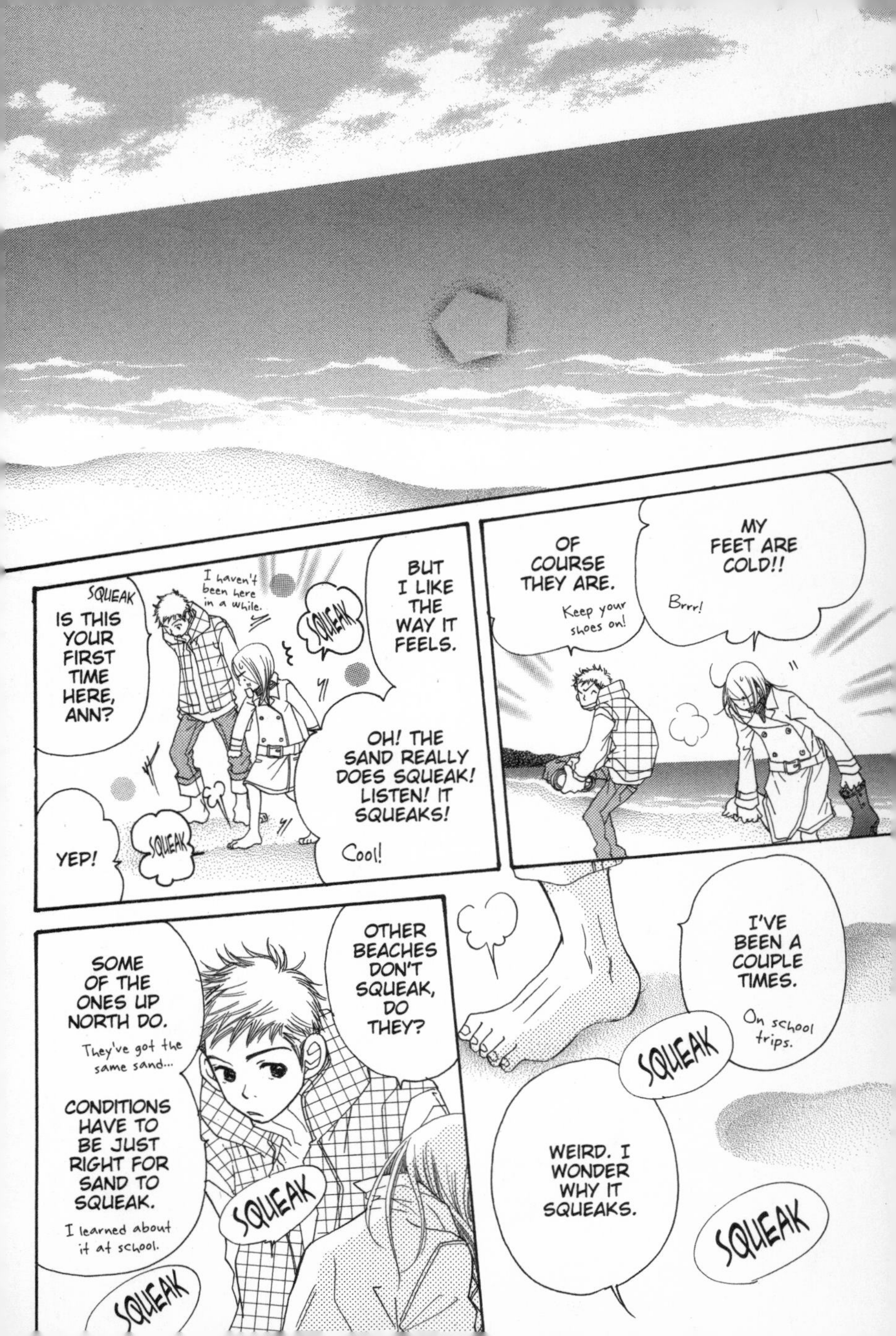
MY FEET ARE COLD!!
Brrr!
OF COURSE THEY ARE.
Keep your shoes on!
BUT I LIKE THE WAY IT FEELS.
I haven't been here in a while.
SQUEAK
SQUEAK
IS THIS YOUR FIRST TIME HERE, ANN?
OH! THE SAND REALLY DOES SQUEAK! LISTEN! IT SQUEAKS!
Cool!
SQUEAK
YEP!
I'VE BEEN A COUPLE TIMES.
On school trips.
SQUEAK
WEIRD. I WONDER WHY IT SQUEAKS.
SQUEAK
OTHER BEACHES DON'T SQUEAK, DO THEY?
SOME OF THE ONES UP NORTH DO.
They've got the same sand...
CONDITIONS HAVE TO BE JUST RIGHT FOR SAND TO SQUEAK.
I learned about it at school.
SQUEAK
SQUEAK

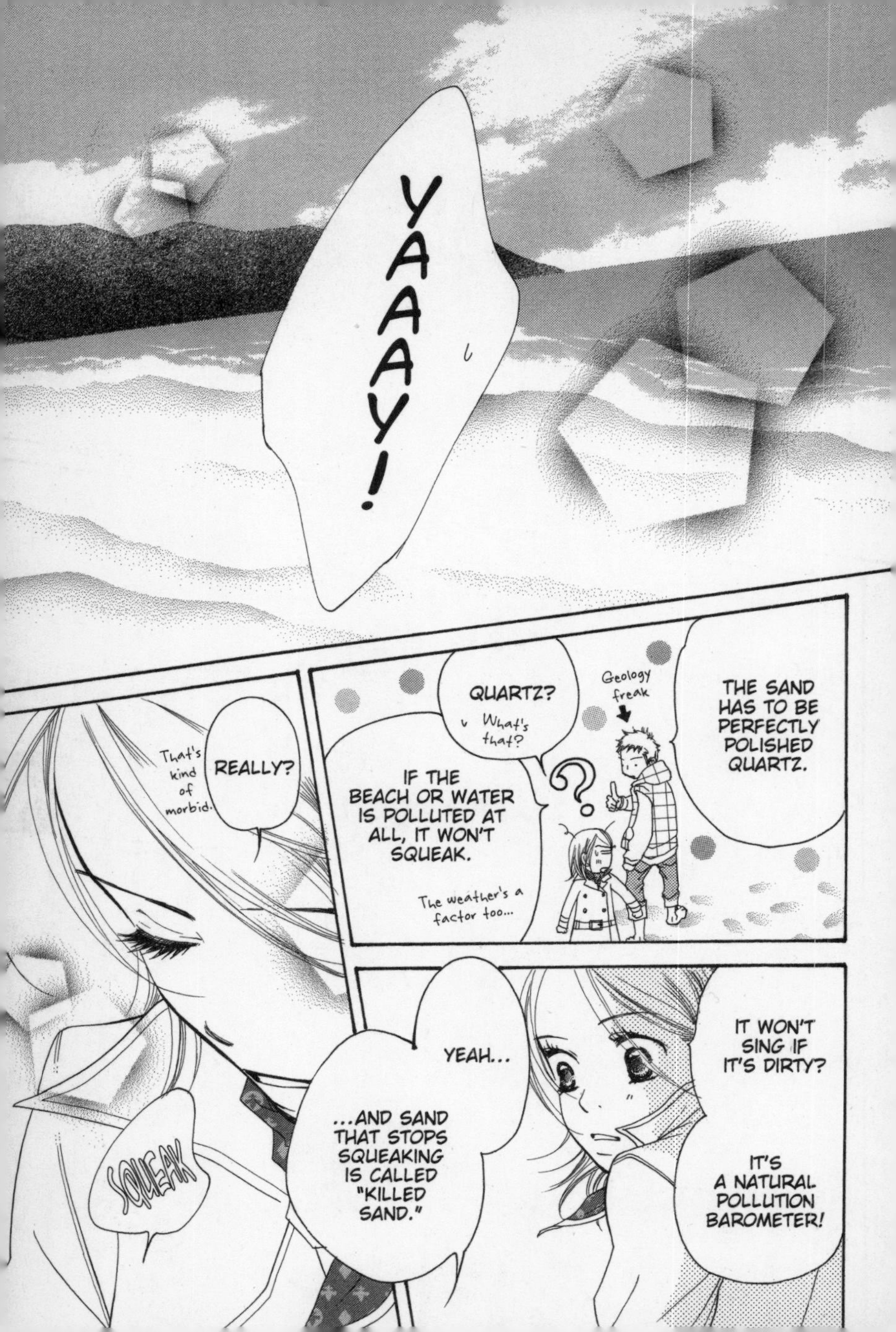
YAAAAY!
THE SAND HAS TO BE PERFECTLY POLISHED QUARTZ.
Geology freak
QUARTZ?
What's that?
IF THE BEACH OR WATER IS POLLUTED AT ALL, IT WON'T SQUEAK.
The weather's a factor too...
IT WON'T SING IF IT'S DIRTY?
IT'S A NATURAL POLLUTION BAROMETER!
REALLY?
That's kind of morbid.
YEAH...
...AND SAND THAT STOPS SQUEAKING IS CALLED "KILLED SAND."
SQUEAK

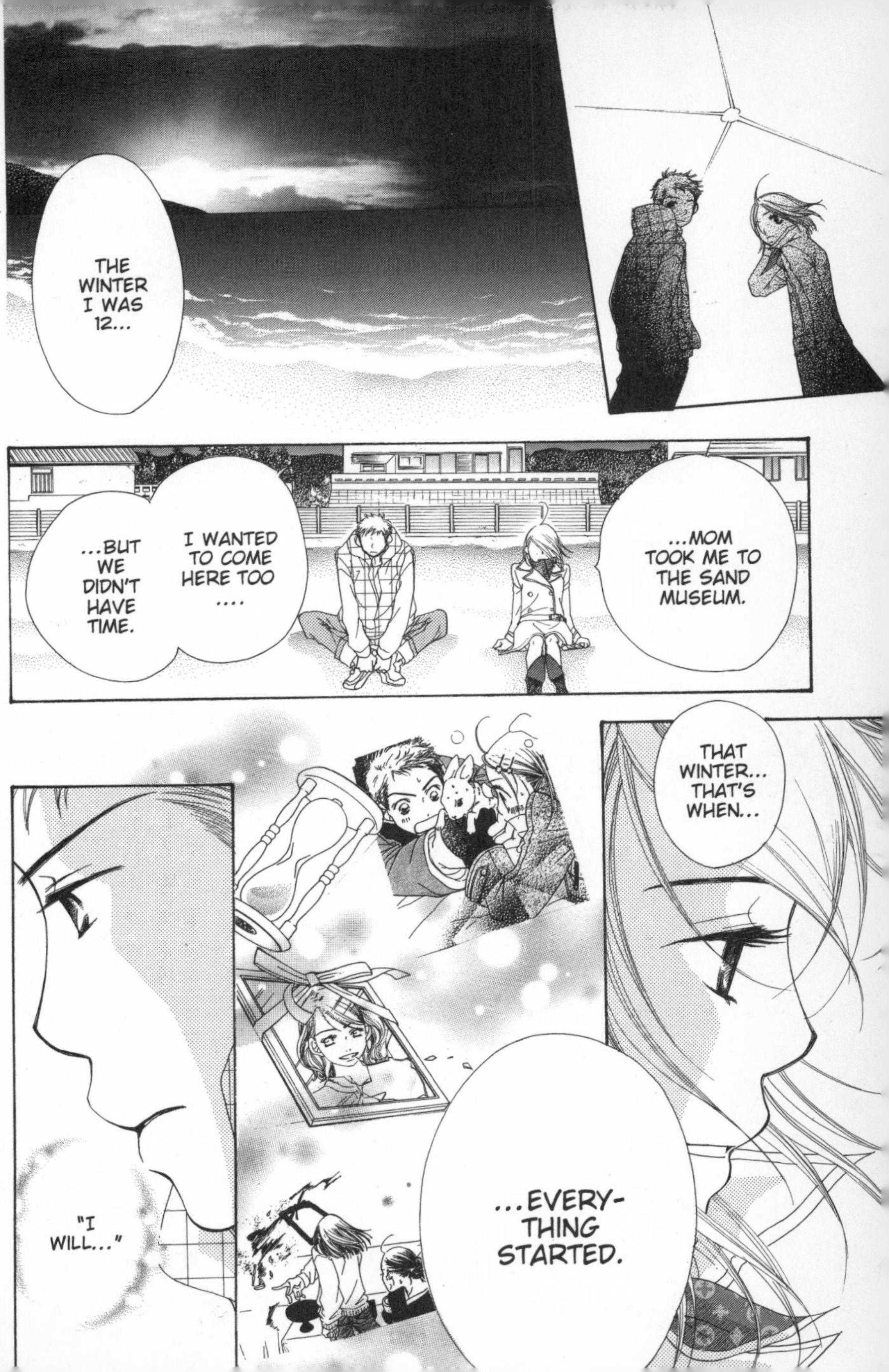
THE WINTER I WAS 12...
...MOM TOOK ME TO THE SAND MUSEUM.
I WANTED TO COME HERE TOO ....
...BUT WE DIDN'T HAVE TIME.
THAT WINTER... THAT'S WHEN...
...EVERY-THING STARTED.
"I WILL..."

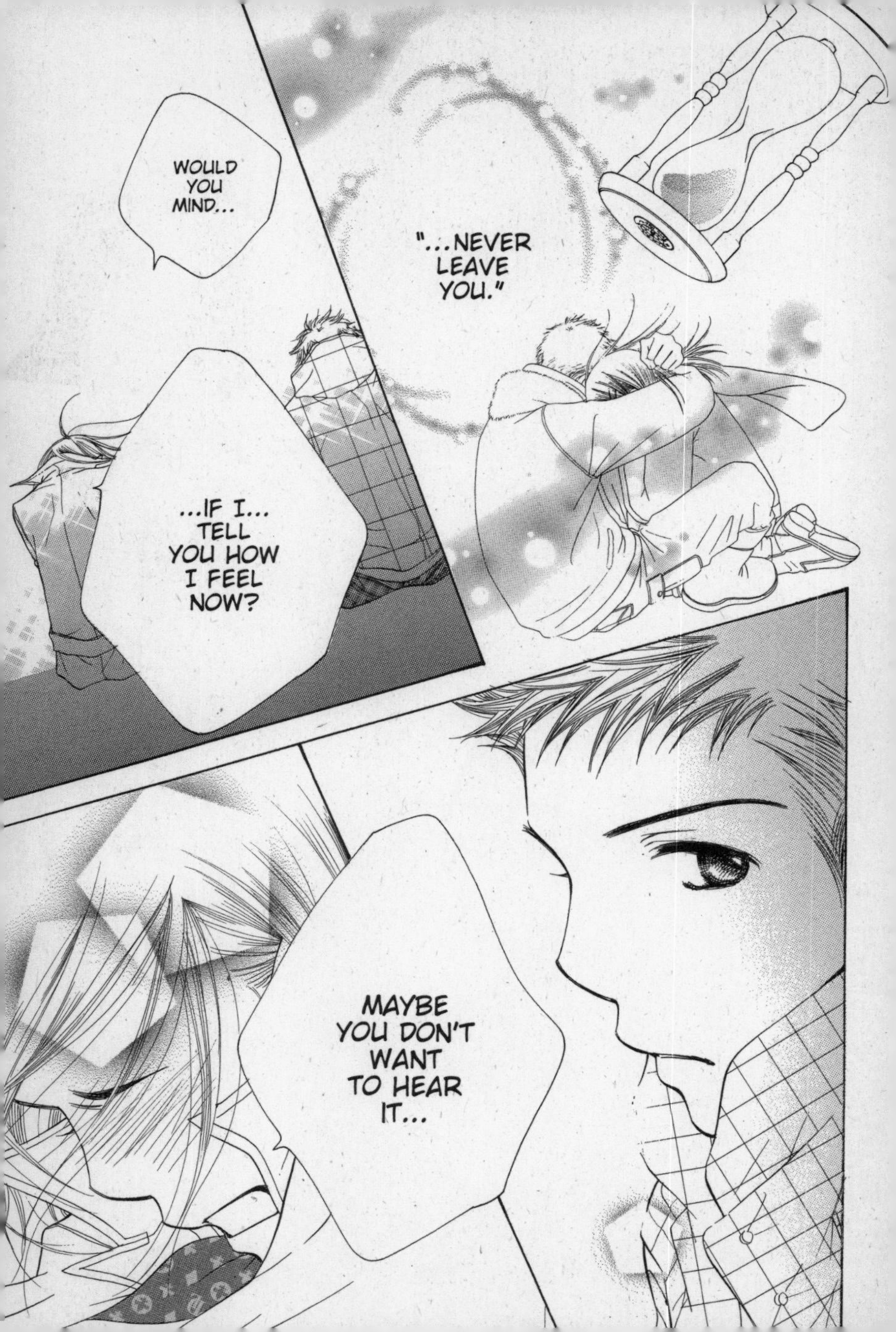
"...NEVER LEAVE YOU."
WOULD YOU MIND...
...IF I... TELL YOU HOW I FEEL NOW?
MAYBE YOU DON'T WANT TO HEAR IT...

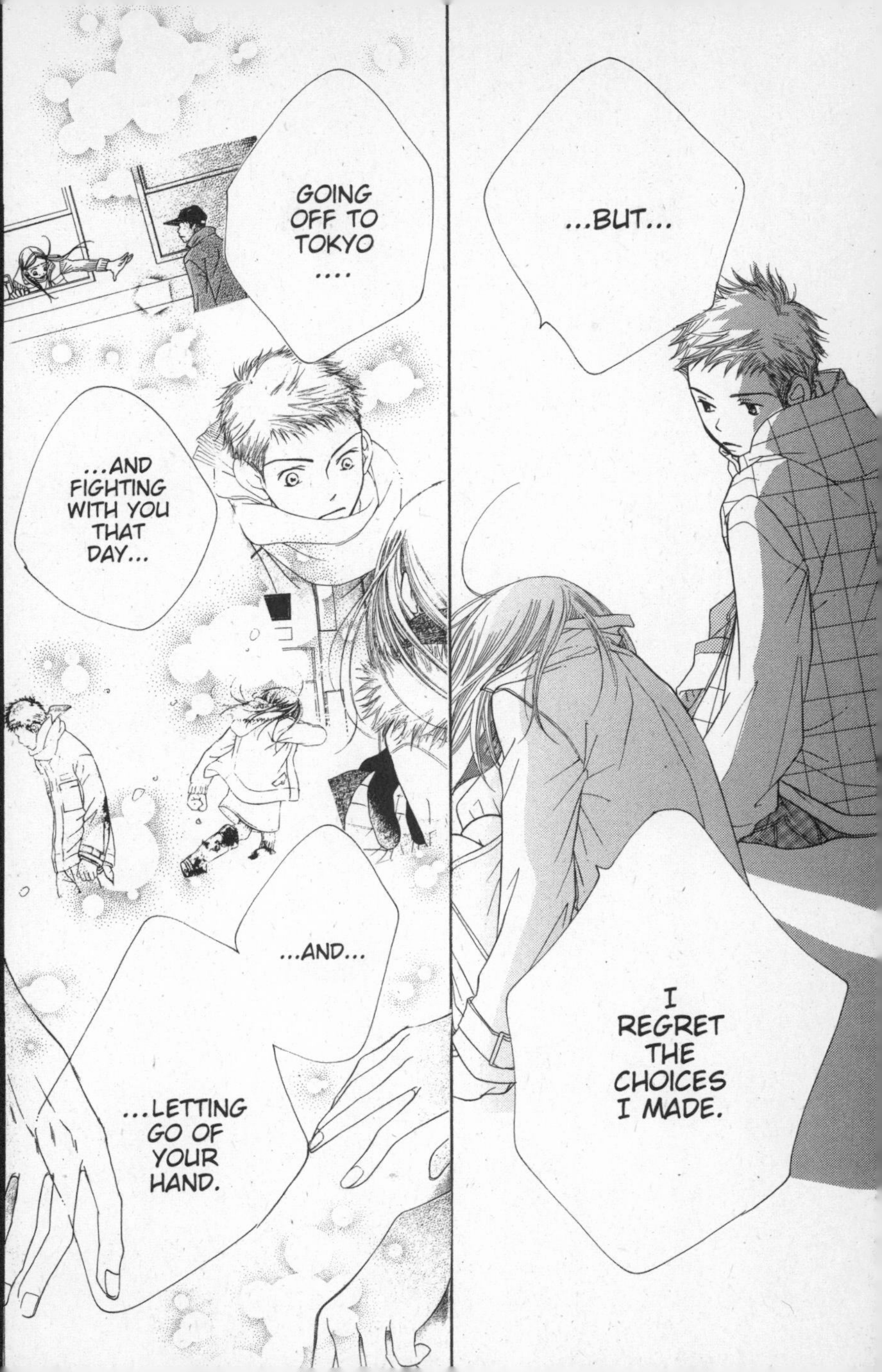
...BUT...
I REGRET THE CHOICES I MADE.
GOING OFF TO TOKYO ....
...AND FIGHTING WITH YOU THAT DAY...
...AND...
...LETTING GO OF YOUR HAND.

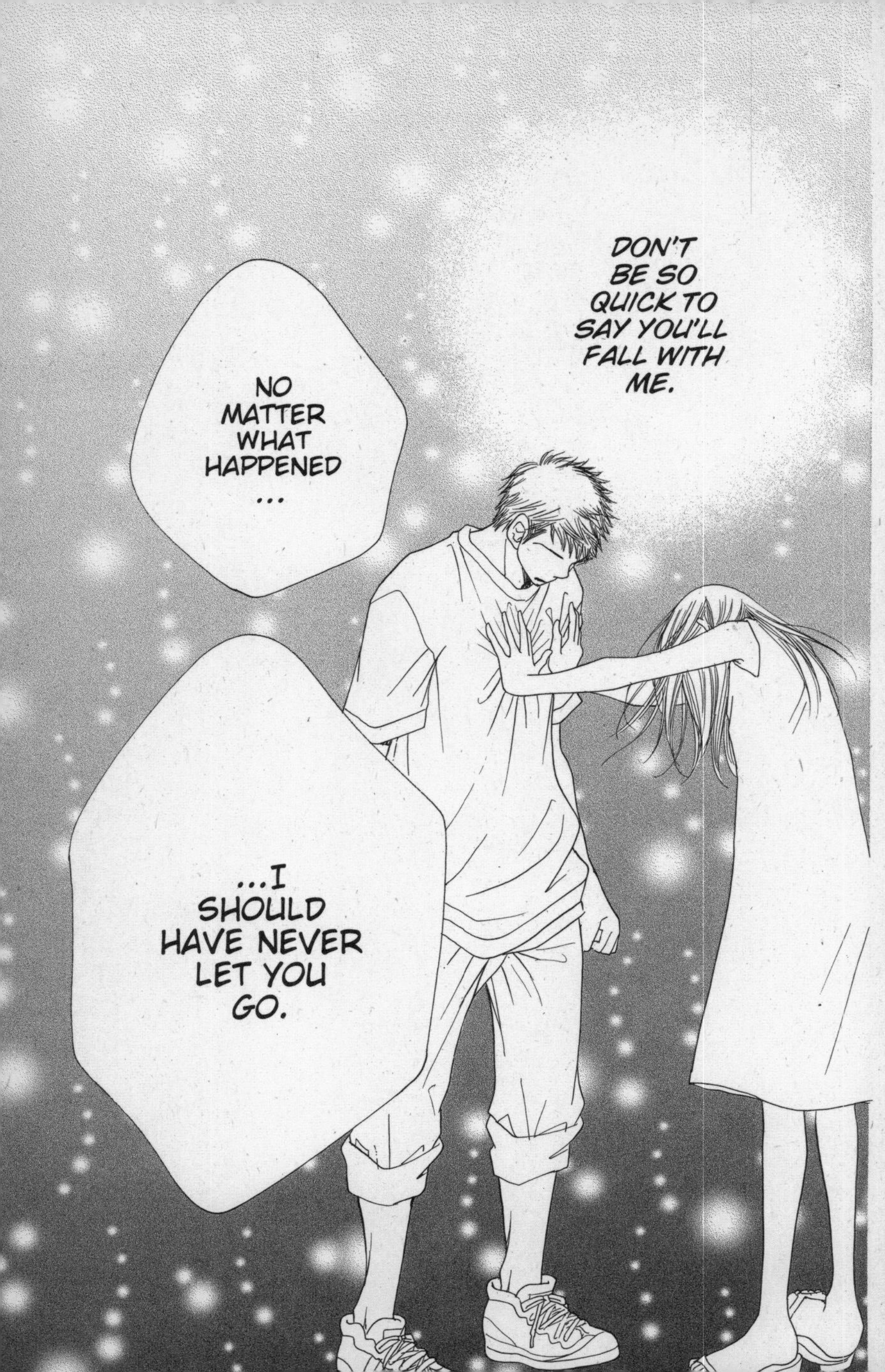
DON'T BE SO QUICK TO SAY YOU'LL FALL WITH ME.
NO MATTER WHAT HAPPENED ...
...I SHOULD HAVE NEVER LET YOU GO.

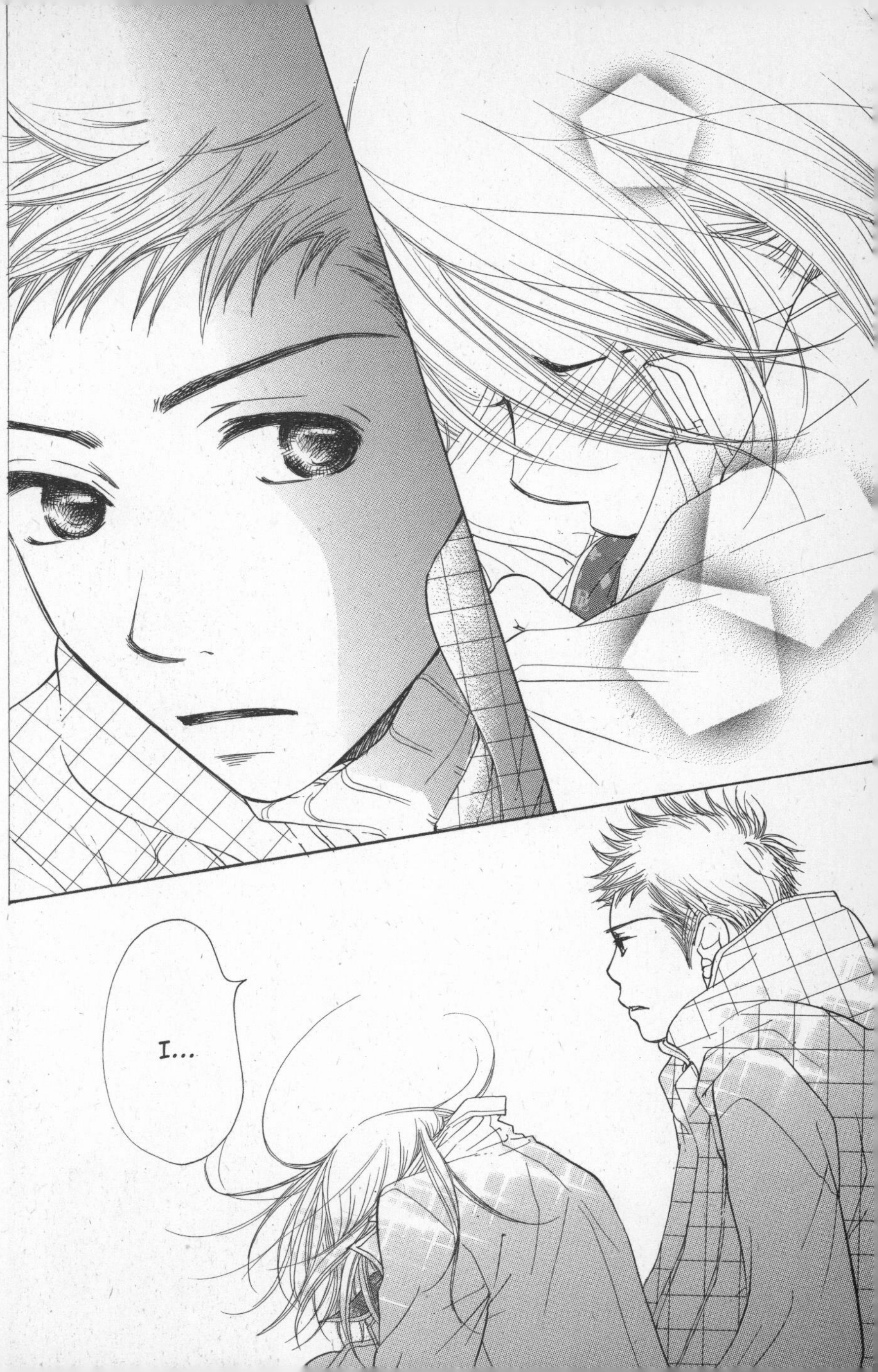
I...

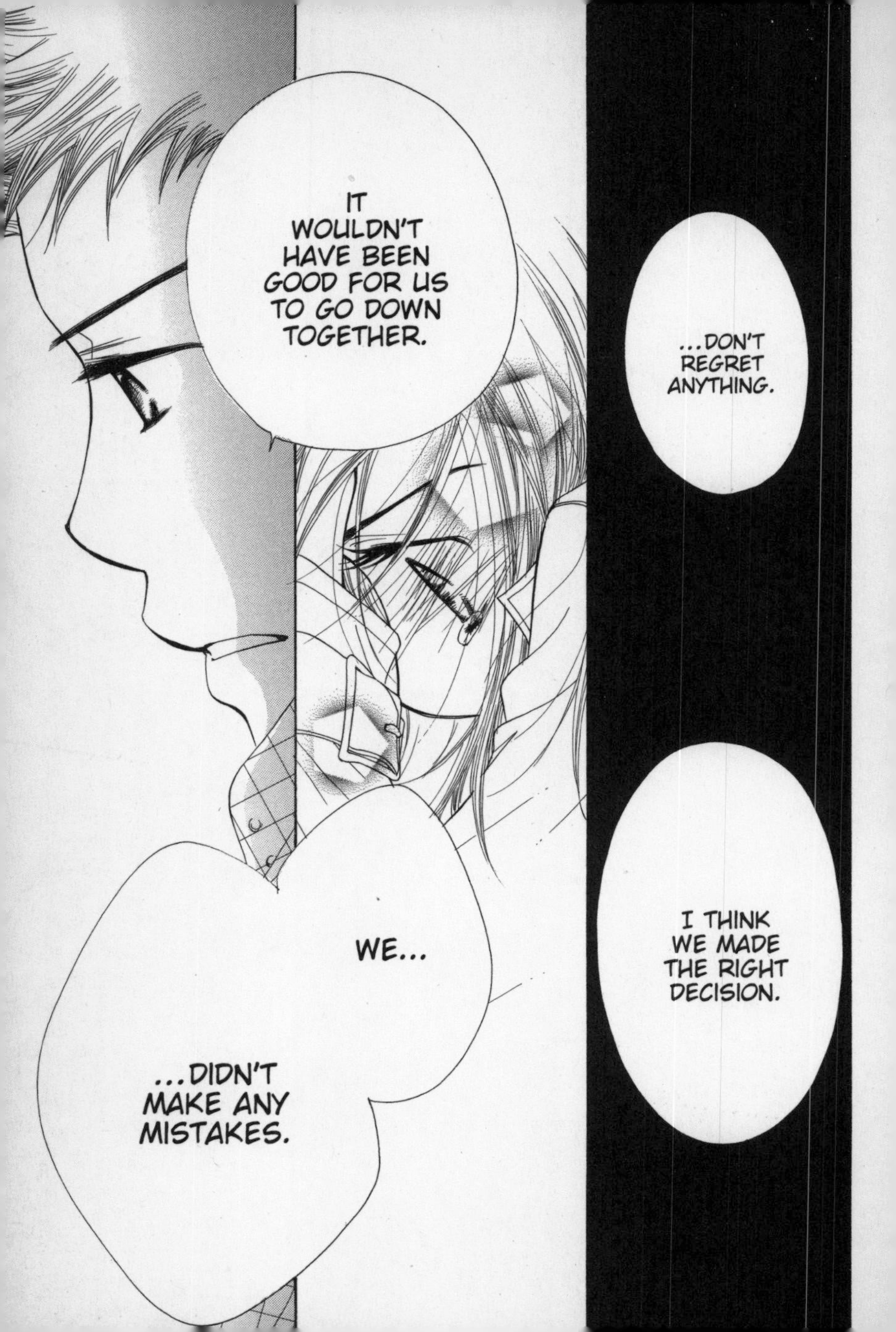
...DON'T REGRET ANYTHING.
I THINK WE MADE THE RIGHT DECISION.
IT WOULDN'T HAVE BEEN GOOD FOR US TO GO DOWN TOGETHER.
WE...
...DIDN'T MAKE ANY MISTAKES.

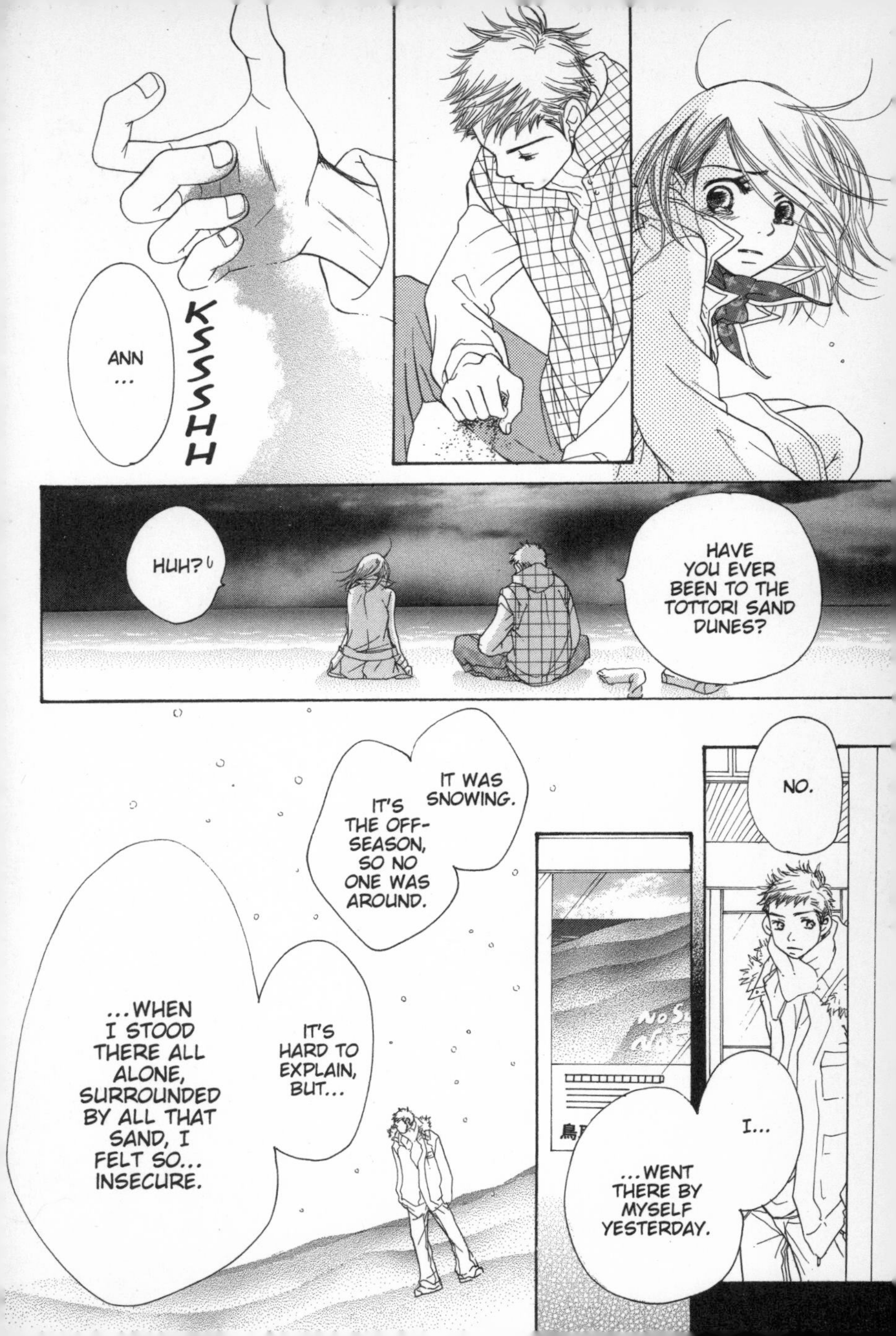
KSSSHH
ANN ...
HAVE YOU EVER BEEN TO THE TOTTORI SAND DUNES?
HUH?
NO.
I...
...WENT THERE BY MYSELF YESTERDAY.
IT WAS SNOWING.
IT'S THE OFF-SEASON, SO NO ONE WAS AROUND.
IT'S HARD TO EXPLAIN, BUT...
...WHEN I STOOD THERE ALL ALONE, SURROUNDED BY ALL THAT SAND, I FELT SO... INSECURE.

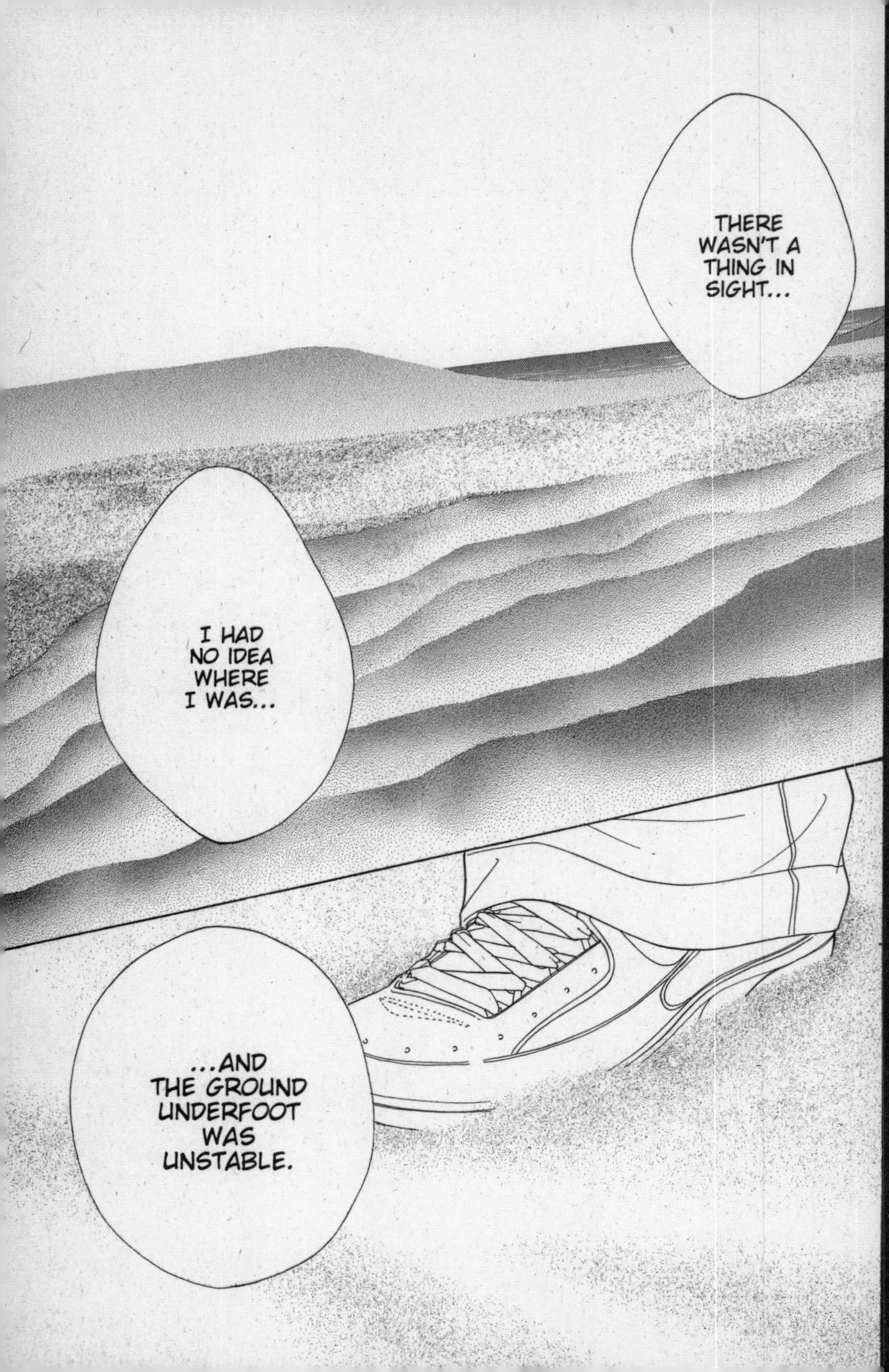
THERE WASN'T A THING IN SIGHT...
I HAD NO IDEA WHERE I WAS...
...AND THE GROUND UNDERFOOT WAS UNSTABLE.

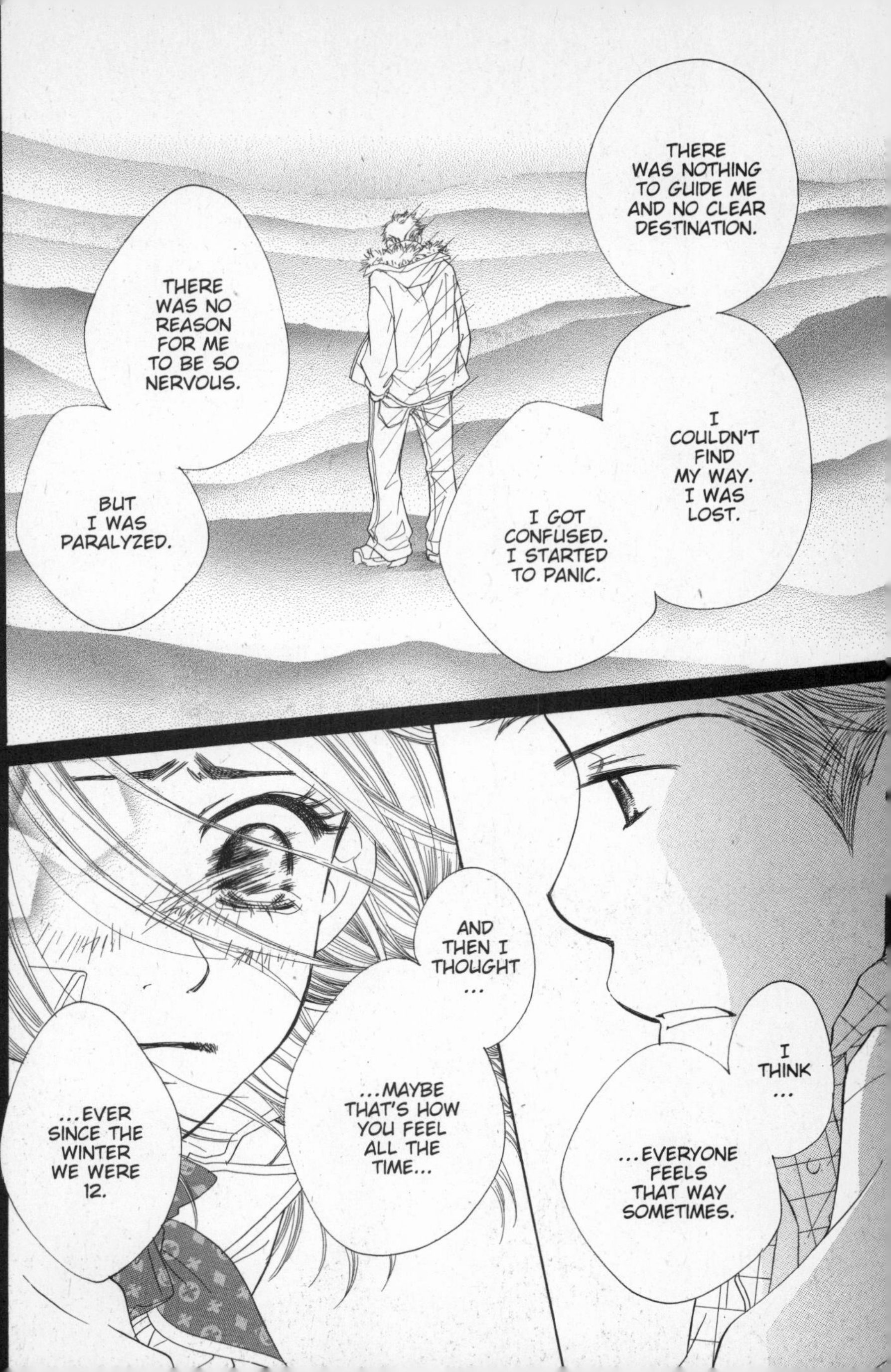
THERE WAS NOTHING TO GUIDE ME AND NO CLEAR DESTINATION.
I COULDN'T FIND MY WAY. I WAS LOST.
I GOT CONFUSED. I STARTED TO PANIC.
THERE WAS NO REASON FOR ME TO BE SO NERVOUS.
BUT I WAS PARALYZED.
AND THEN I THOUGHT...
...MAYBE THAT'S HOW YOU FEEL ALL THE TIME...
...EVER SINCE THE WINTER WE WERE 12.
I THINK...
...EVERYONE FEELS THAT WAY SOMETIMES.

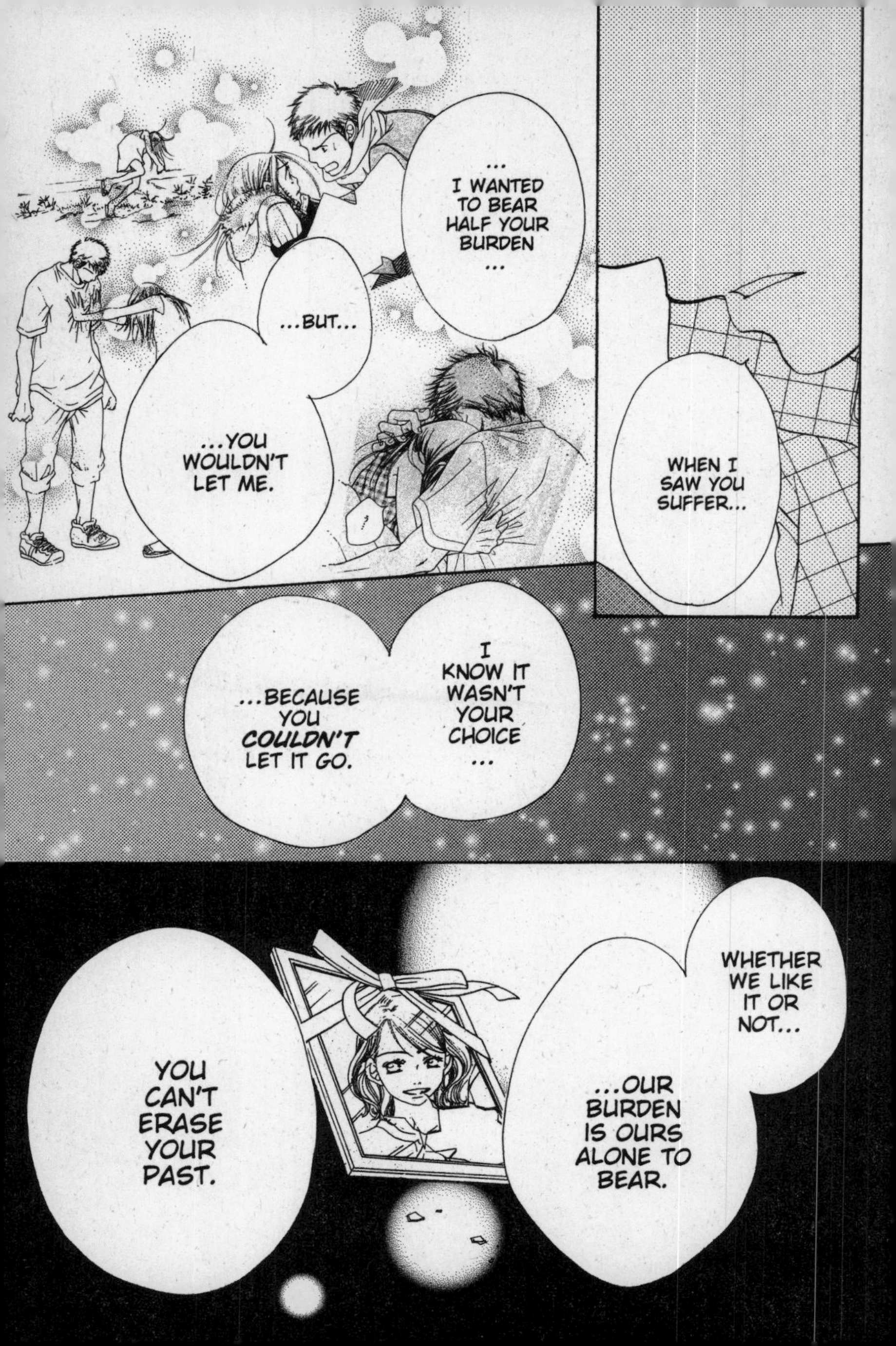
WHEN I SAW YOU SUFFER...
... I WANTED TO BEAR HALF YOUR BURDEN ...
...BUT...
...YOU WOULDN'T LET ME.
I KNOW IT WASN'T YOUR CHOICE ...
...BECAUSE YOU *COULDN'T* LET IT GO.
WHETHER WE LIKE IT OR NOT...
...OUR BURDEN IS OURS ALONE TO BEAR.
YOU CAN'T ERASE YOUR PAST.

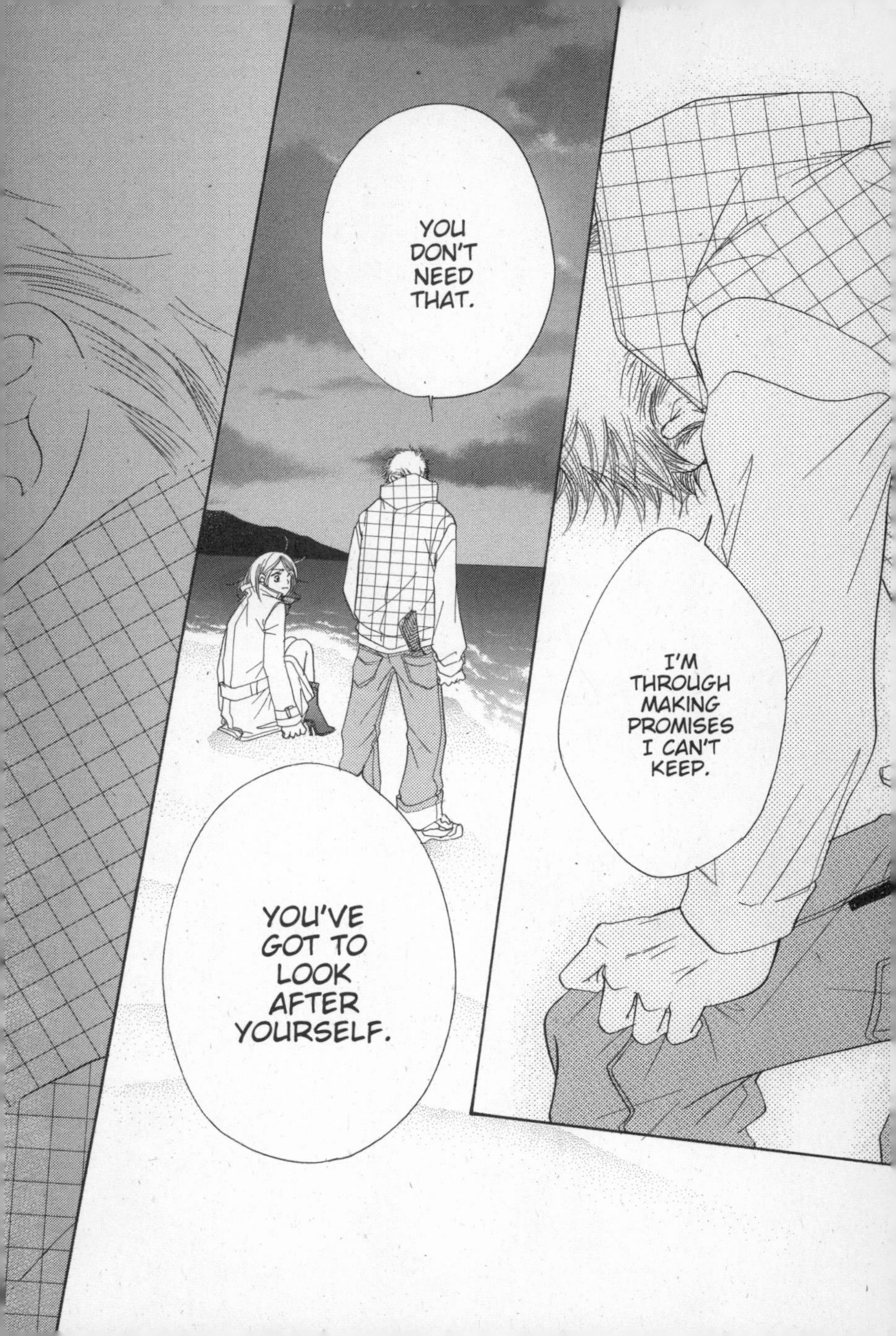
I'M THROUGH MAKING PROMISES I CAN'T KEEP.
YOU DON'T NEED THAT.
YOU'VE GOT TO LOOK AFTER YOURSELF.

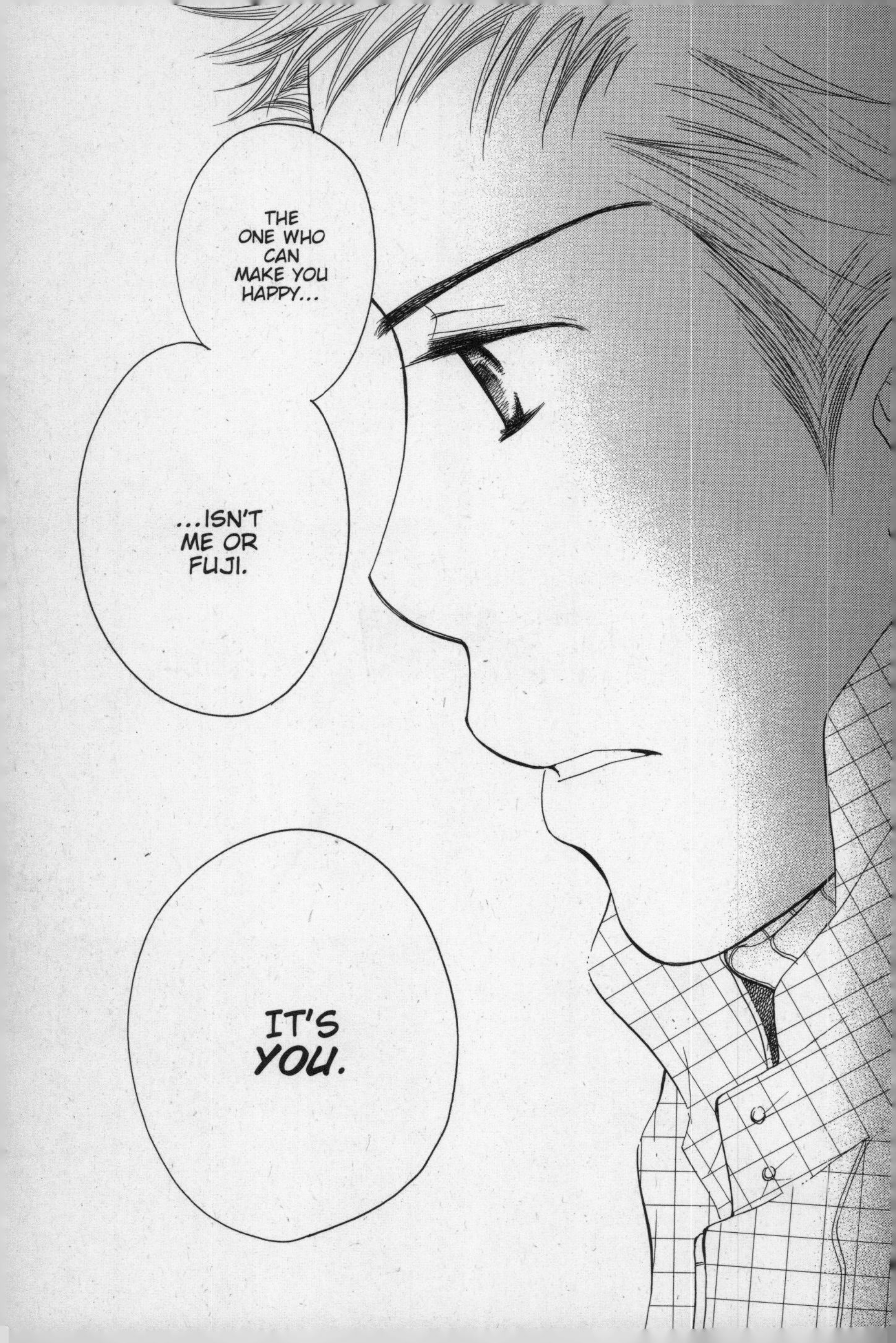
THE ONE WHO CAN MAKE YOU HAPPY...
...ISN'T ME OR FUJI.
IT'S YOU.

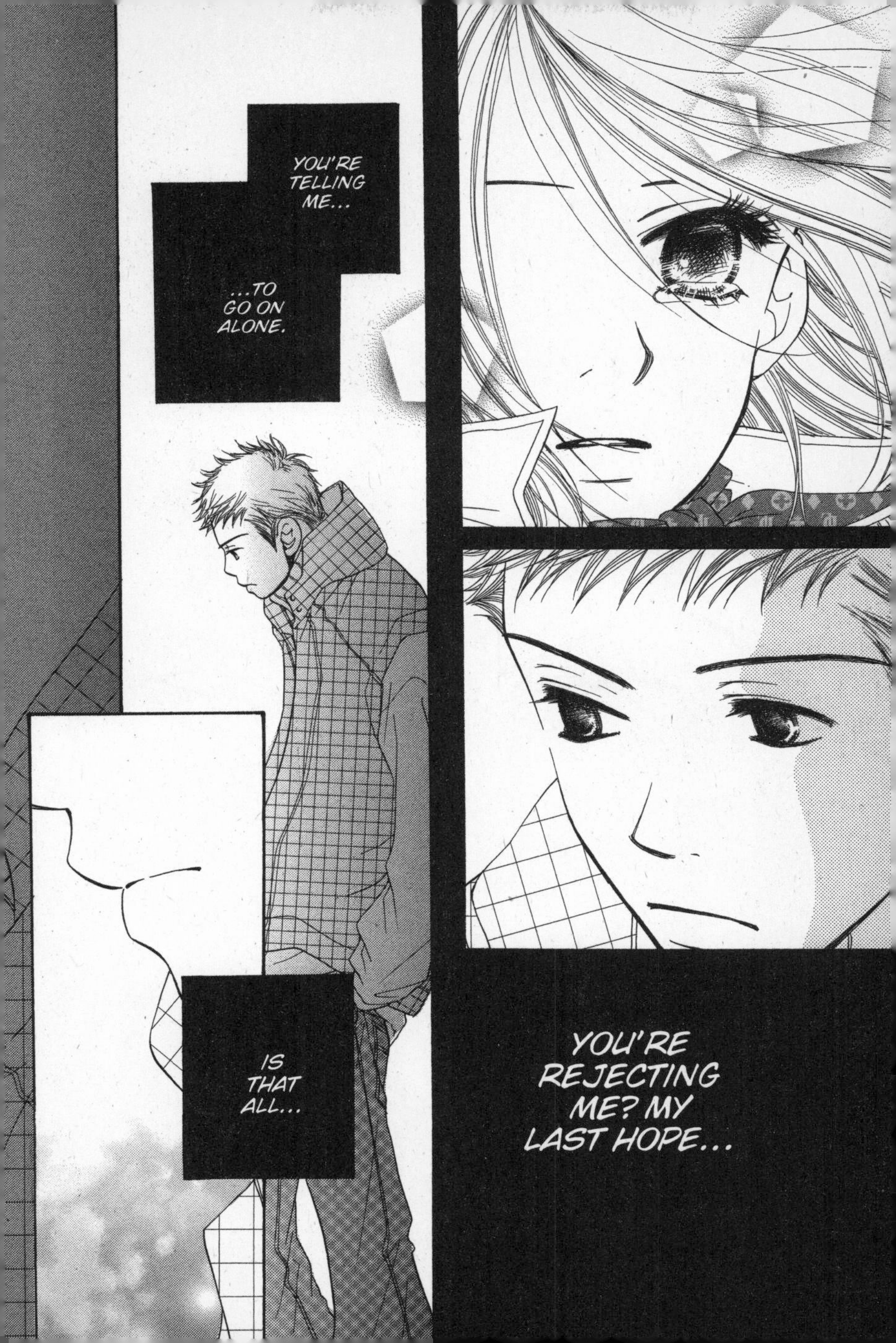
YOU'RE REJECTING ME? MY LAST HOPE...
YOU'RE TELLING ME...
...TO GO ON ALONE.
IS THAT ALL...

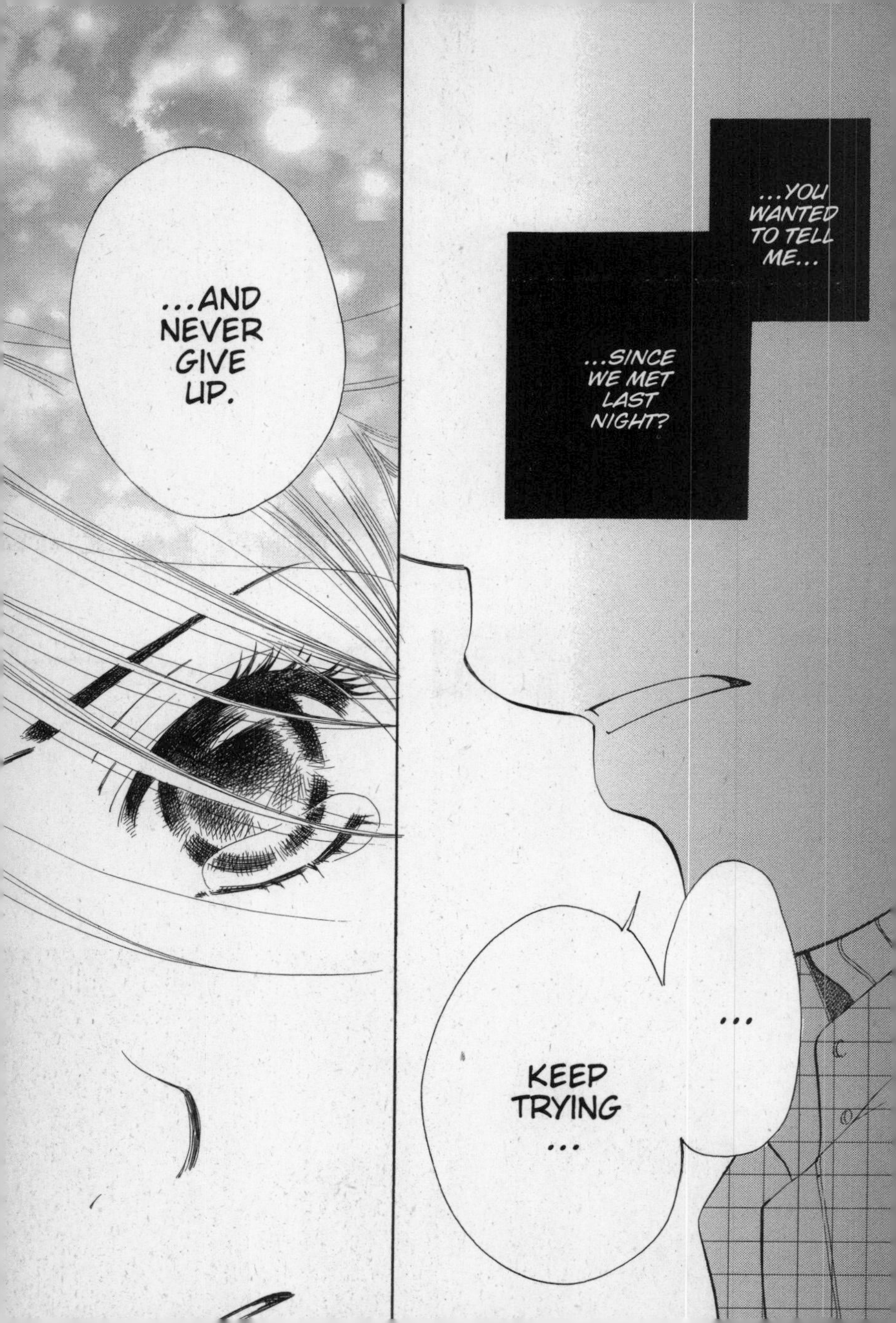
...YOU WANTED TO TELL ME...
...SINCE WE MET LAST NIGHT?
... KEEP TRYING ...
...AND NEVER GIVE UP.

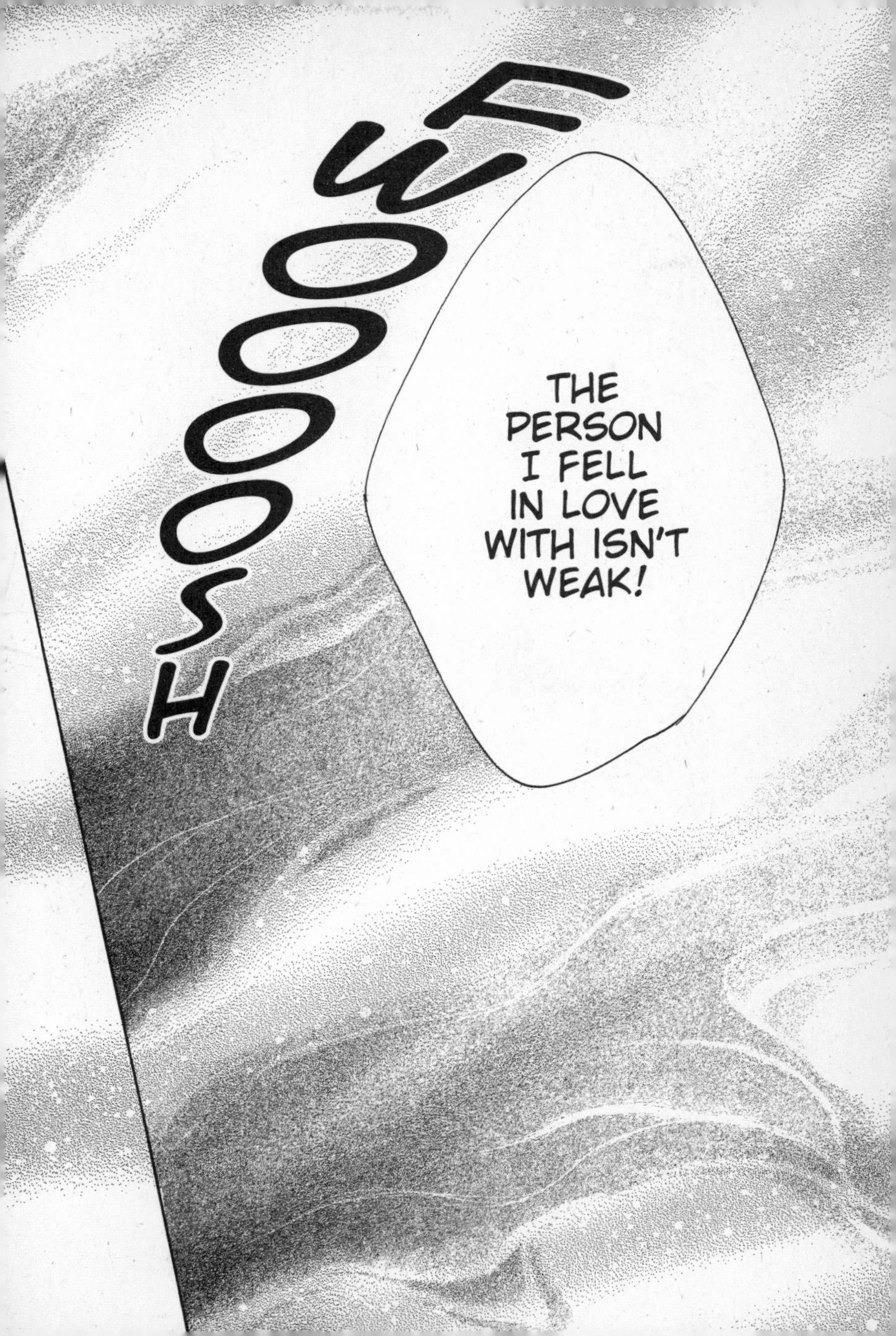
FWOOOOSH
THE PERSON I FELL IN LOVE WITH ISN'T WEAK!

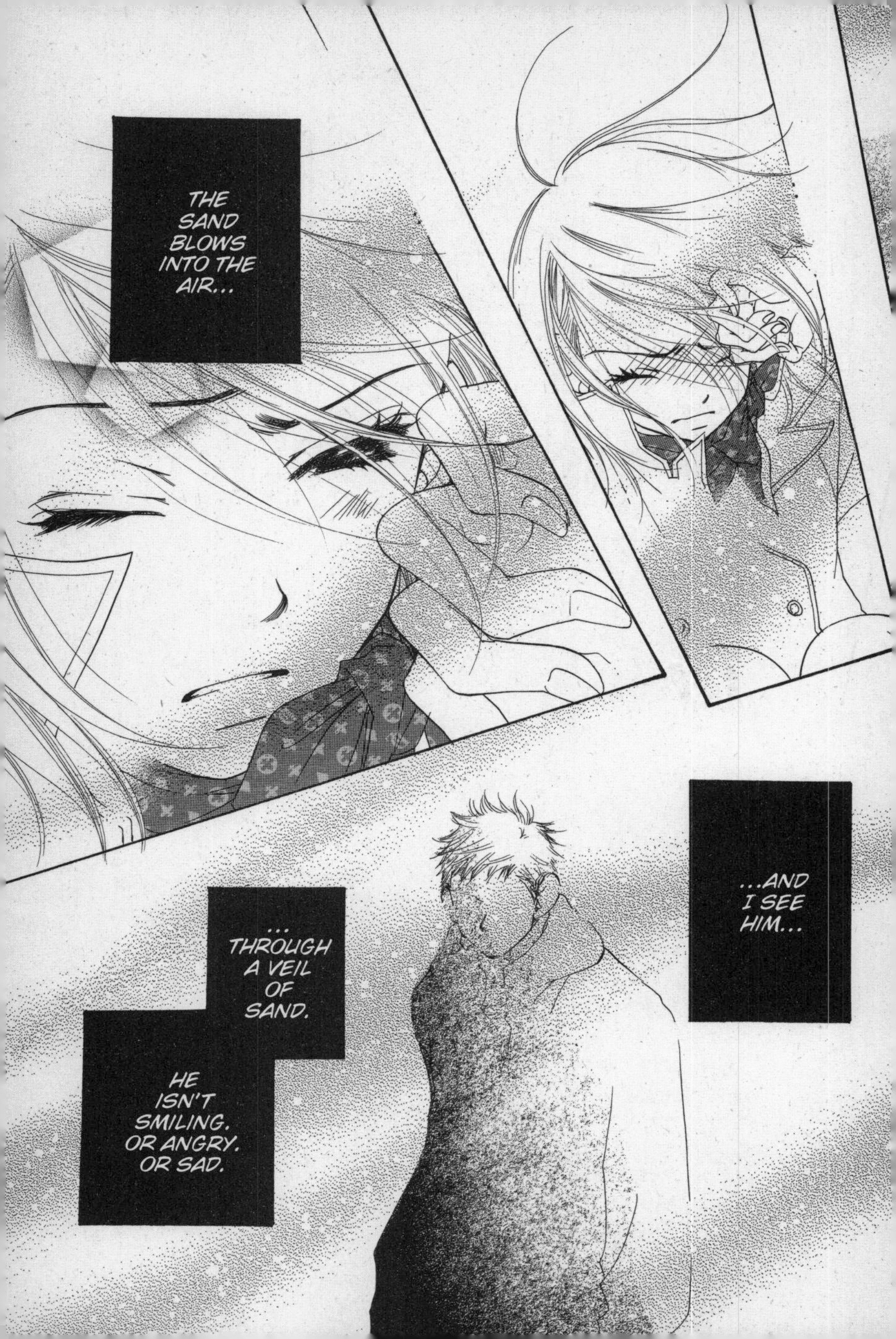
THE SAND BLOWS INTO THE AIR...
...AND I SEE HIM...
...THROUGH A VEIL OF SAND.
HE ISN'T SMILING. OR ANGRY. OR SAD.

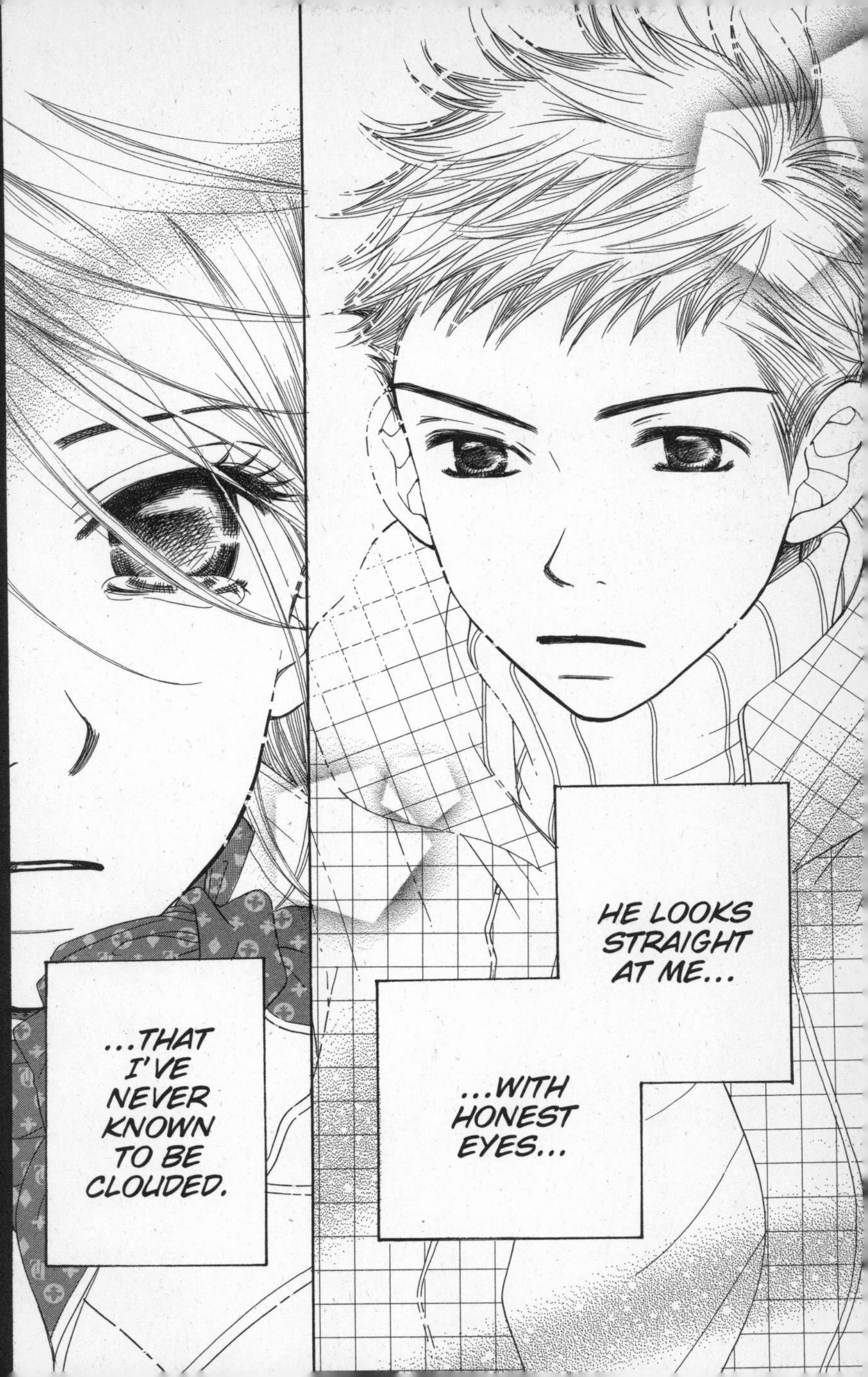
HE LOOKS STRAIGHT AT ME...
...WITH HONEST EYES...
...THAT I'VE NEVER KNOWN TO BE CLOUDED.

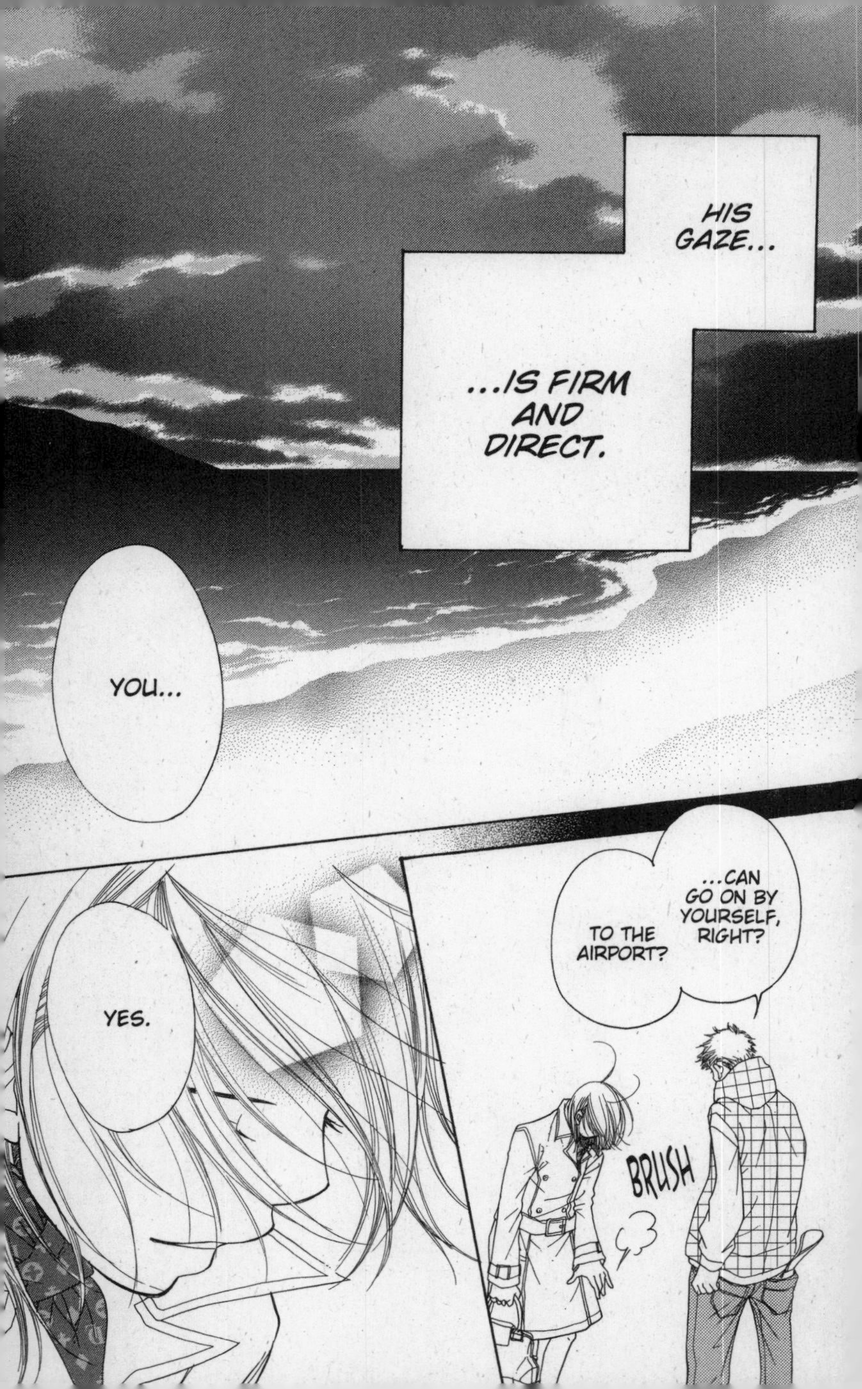
HIS GAZE...
...IS FIRM AND DIRECT.
YOU...
...CAN GO ON BY YOURSELF, RIGHT?
TO THE AIRPORT?
BRUSH
YES.

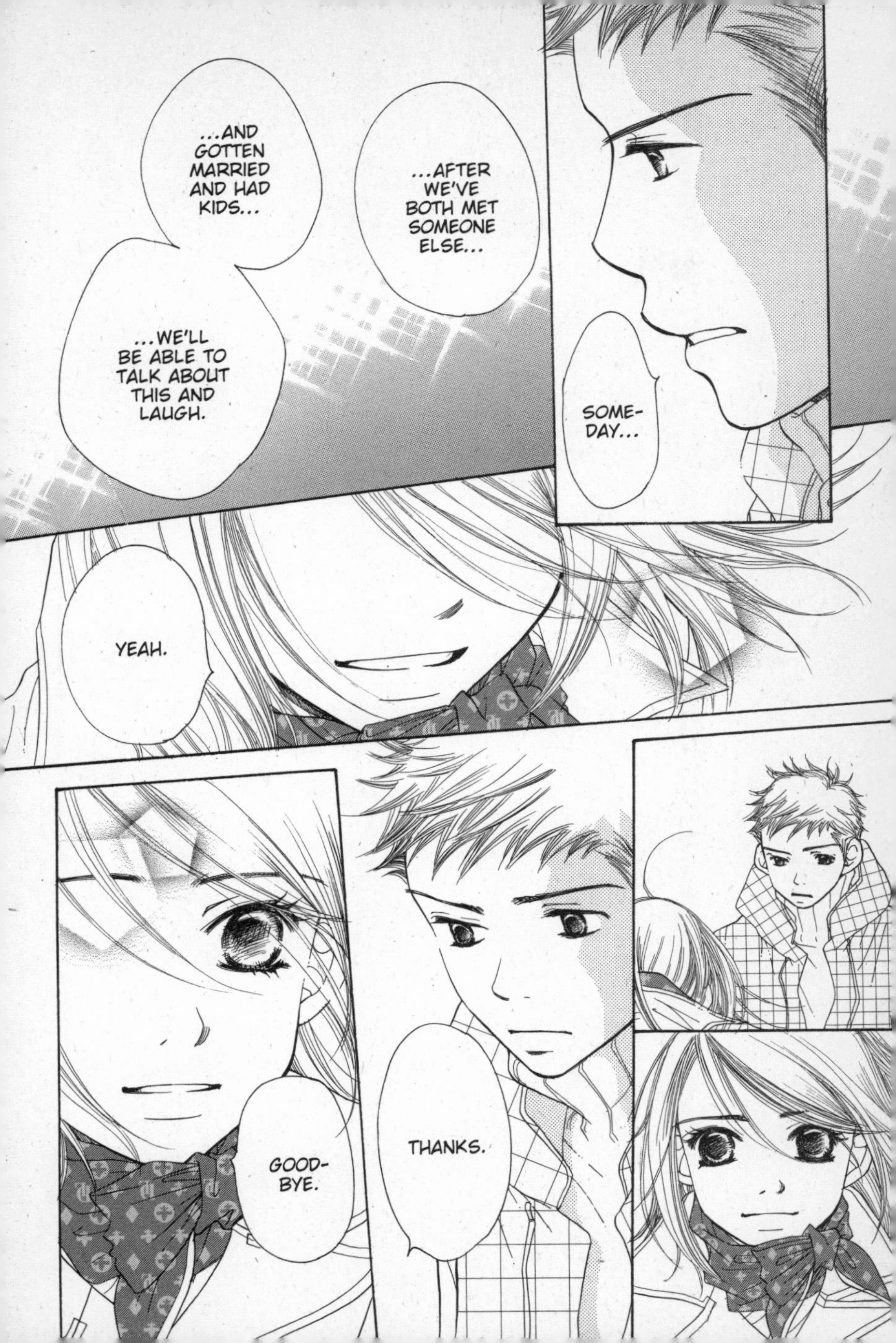
SOME-DAY...
...AFTER WE'VE BOTH MET SOMEONE ELSE...
...AND GOTTEN MARRIED AND HAD KIDS...
...WE'LL BE ABLE TO TALK ABOUT THIS AND LAUGH.
YEAH.
THANKS.
GOOD-BYE.

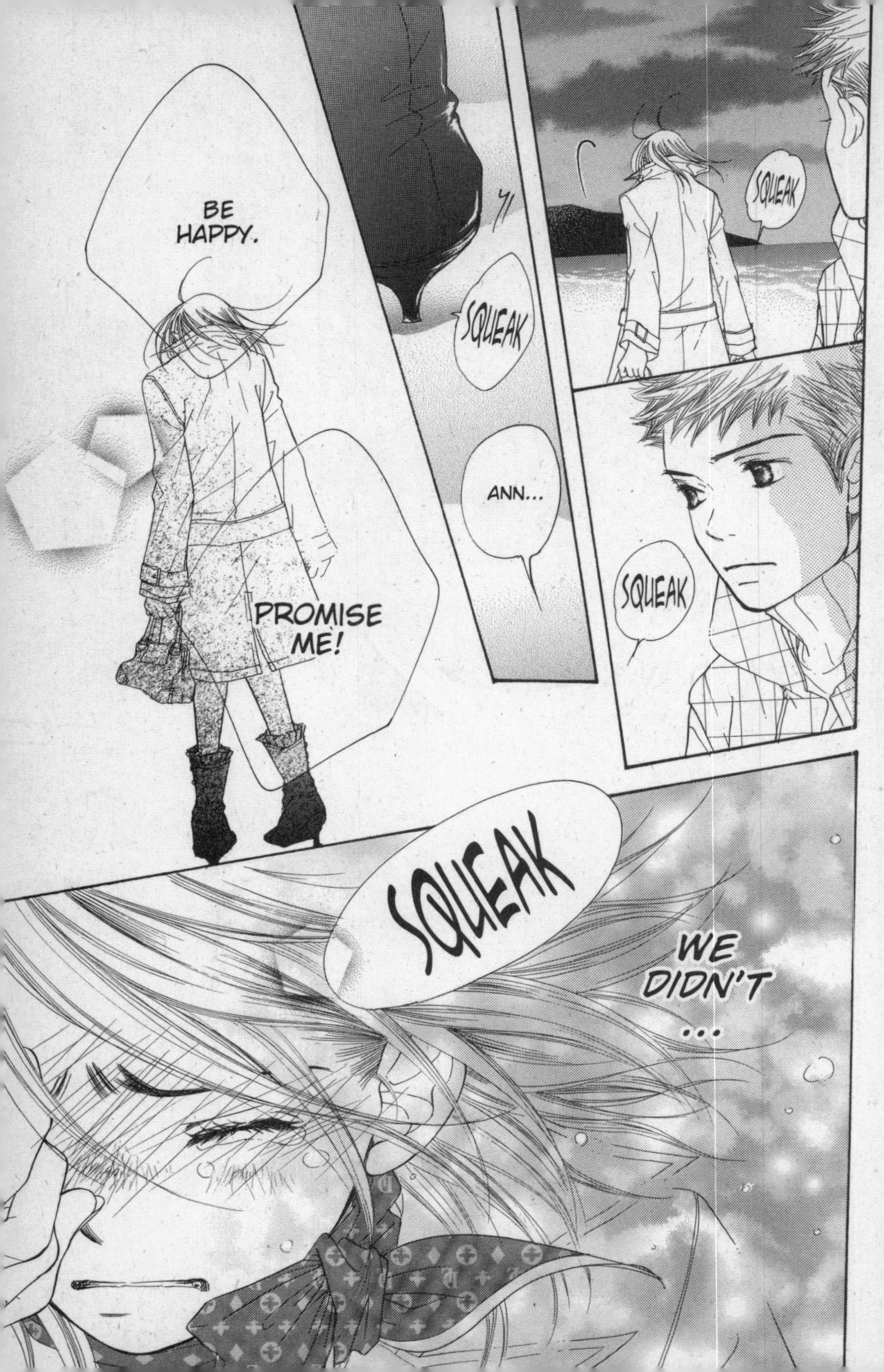
SQUEAK
SQUEAK
SQUEAK
ANN...
BE HAPPY.
PROMISE ME!
SQUEAK
WE DIDN'T ...

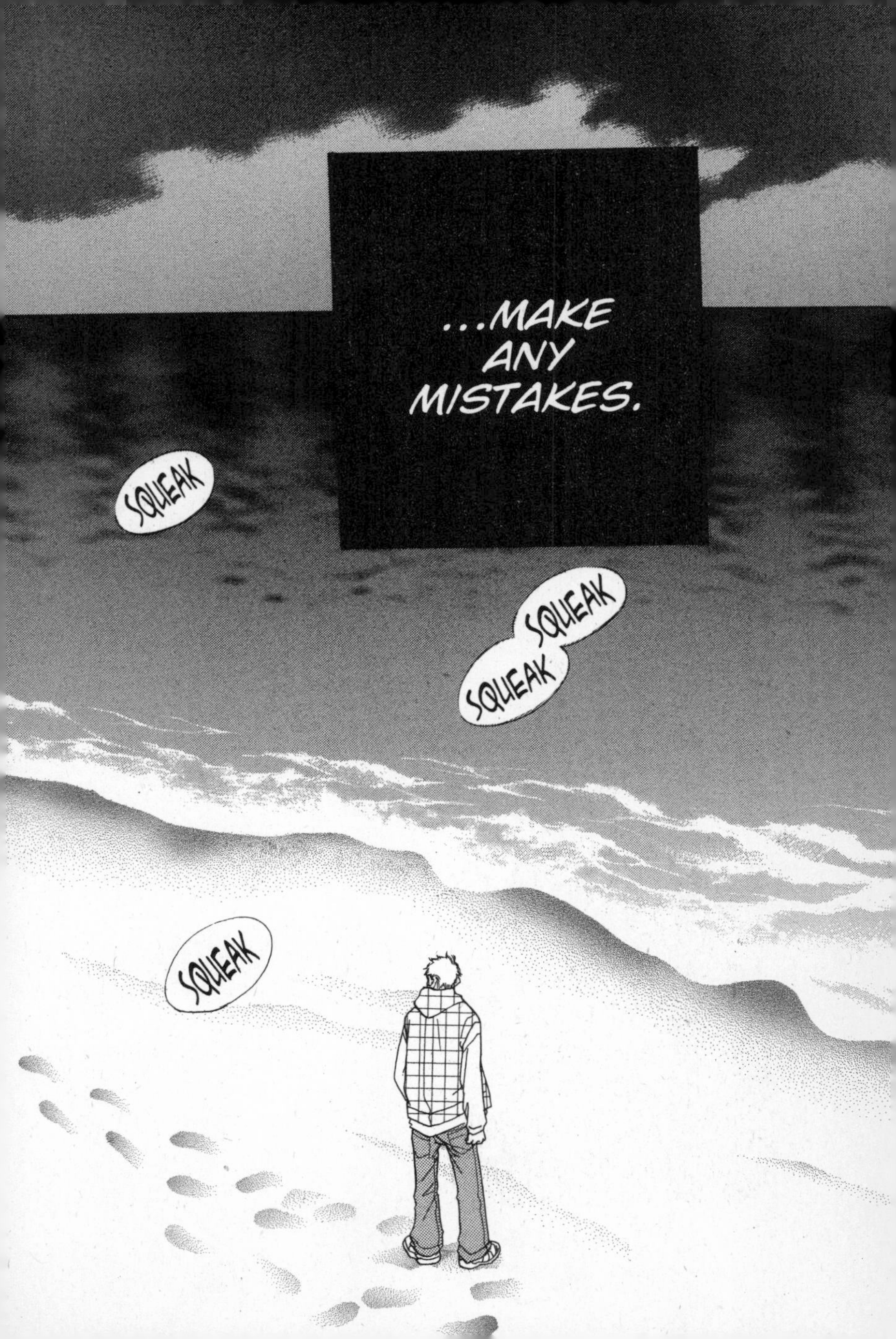
...MAKE ANY MISTAKES.
SQUEAK
SQUEAK
SQUEAK
SQUEAK

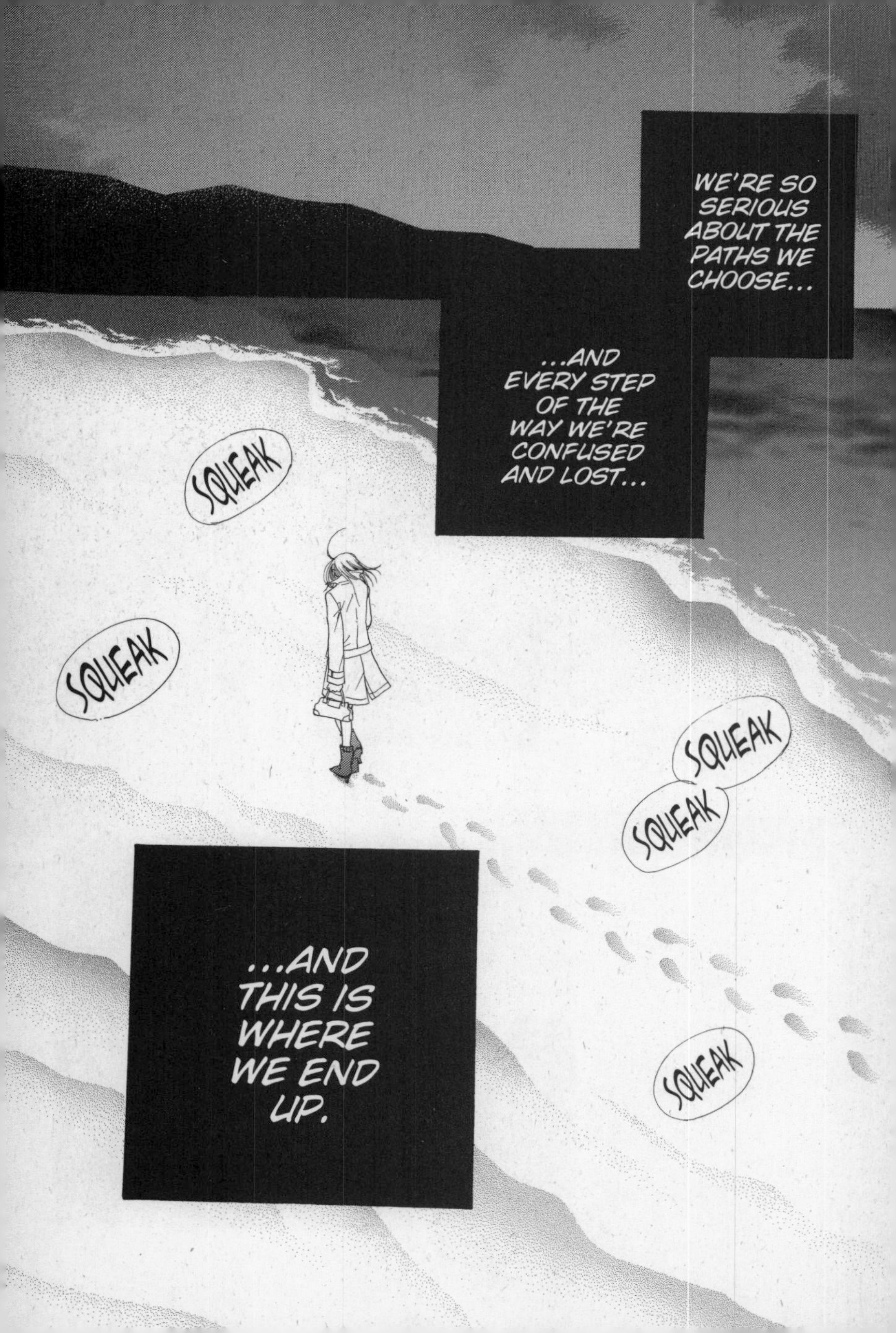
WE'RE SO SERIOUS ABOUT THE PATHS WE CHOOSE...
...AND EVERY STEP OF THE WAY WE'RE CONFUSED AND LOST...
SQUEAK
SQUEAK
SQUEAK
SQUEAK
SQUEAK
...AND THIS IS WHERE WE END UP.

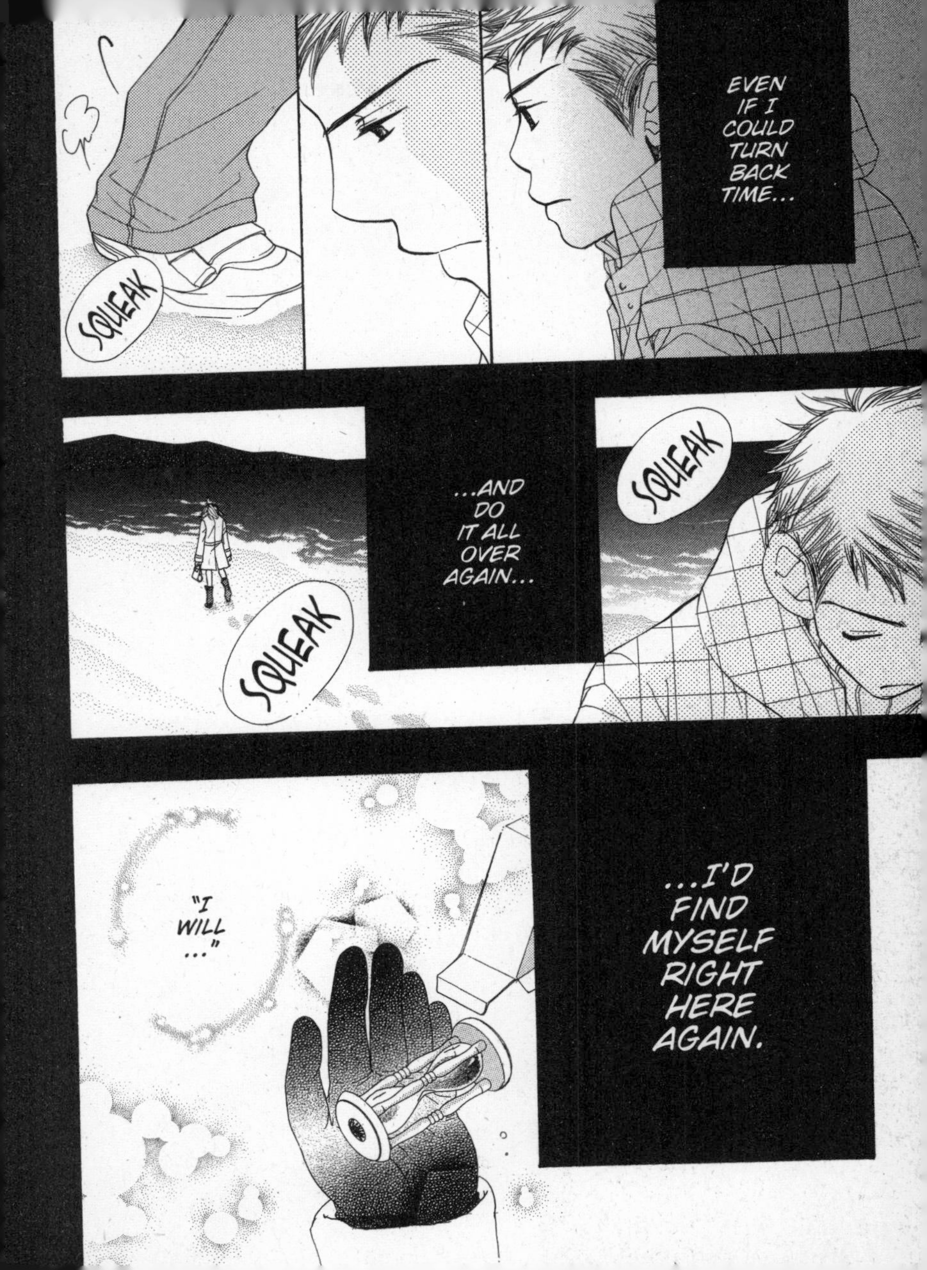
EVEN IF I COULD TURN BACK TIME...
SQUEAK
SQUEAK
...AND DO IT ALL OVER AGAIN...
SQUEAK
...I'D FIND MYSELF RIGHT HERE AGAIN.
"I WILL ..."

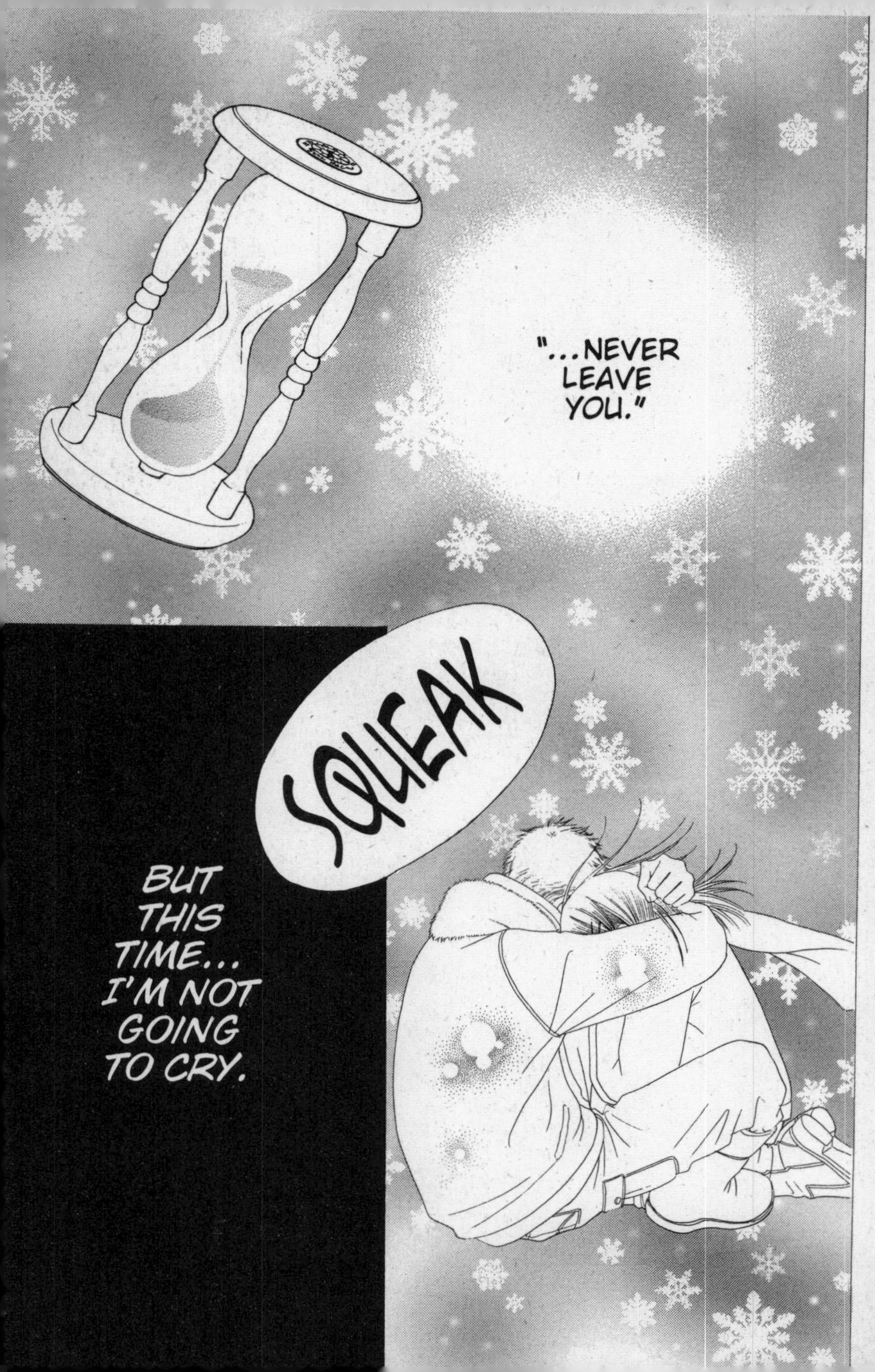
"...NEVER LEAVE YOU."
SQUEAK
BUT THIS TIME... I'M NOT GOING TO CRY.

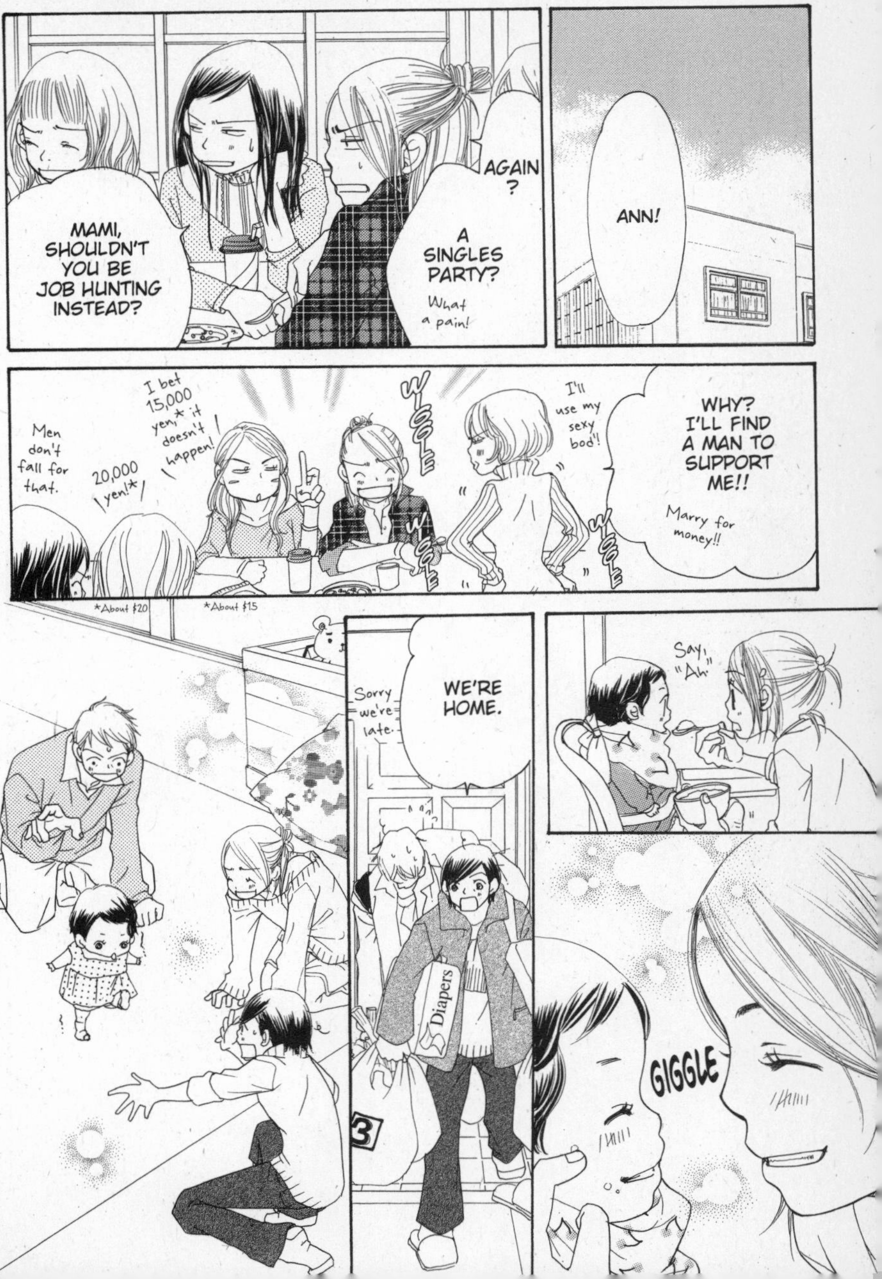
ANN!
AGAIN?
A SINGLES PARTY?
What a pain!
MAMI, SHOULDN'T YOU BE JOB HUNTING INSTEAD?
WHY? I'LL FIND A MAN TO SUPPORT ME!!
Marry for money!!
I'll use my sexy bod!
WIGGLE
WIGGLE
WIGGLE
I bet 15,000 yen,* it doesn't happen!
20,000 yen!*
Men don't fall for that.
*About $20
*About $15
Say, "Ah"
WE'RE HOME.
Sorry we're late.
Diapers
GIGGLE

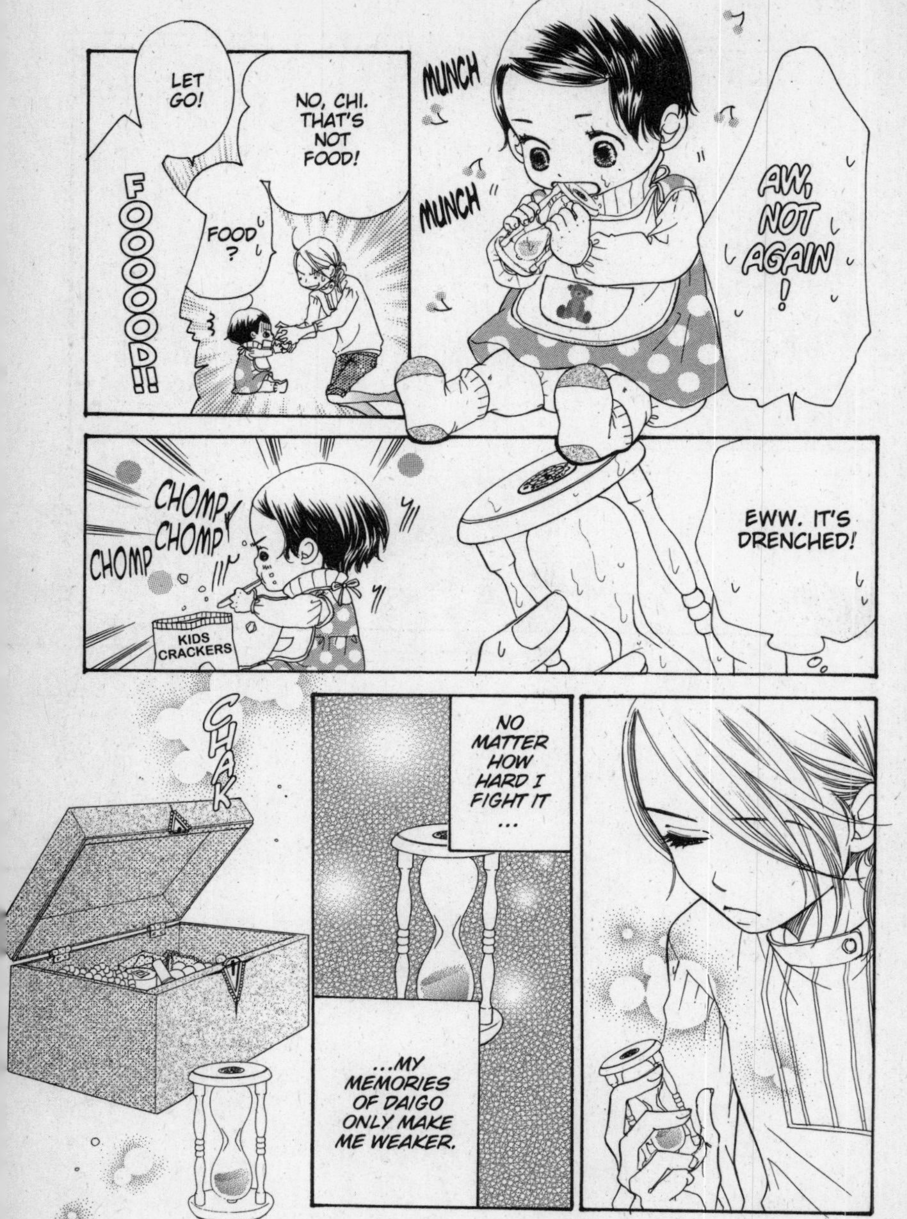
MUNCH
MUNCH
AW, NOT AGAIN!
NO, CHI. THAT'S NOT FOOD!
LET GO!
FOOD?
FOOOOOD!!
EWW. IT'S DRENCHED!
CHOMP CHOMP CHOMP
KIDS CRACKERS
NO MATTER HOW HARD I FIGHT IT...
...MY MEMORIES OF DAIGO ONLY MAKE ME WEAKER.
CHAK

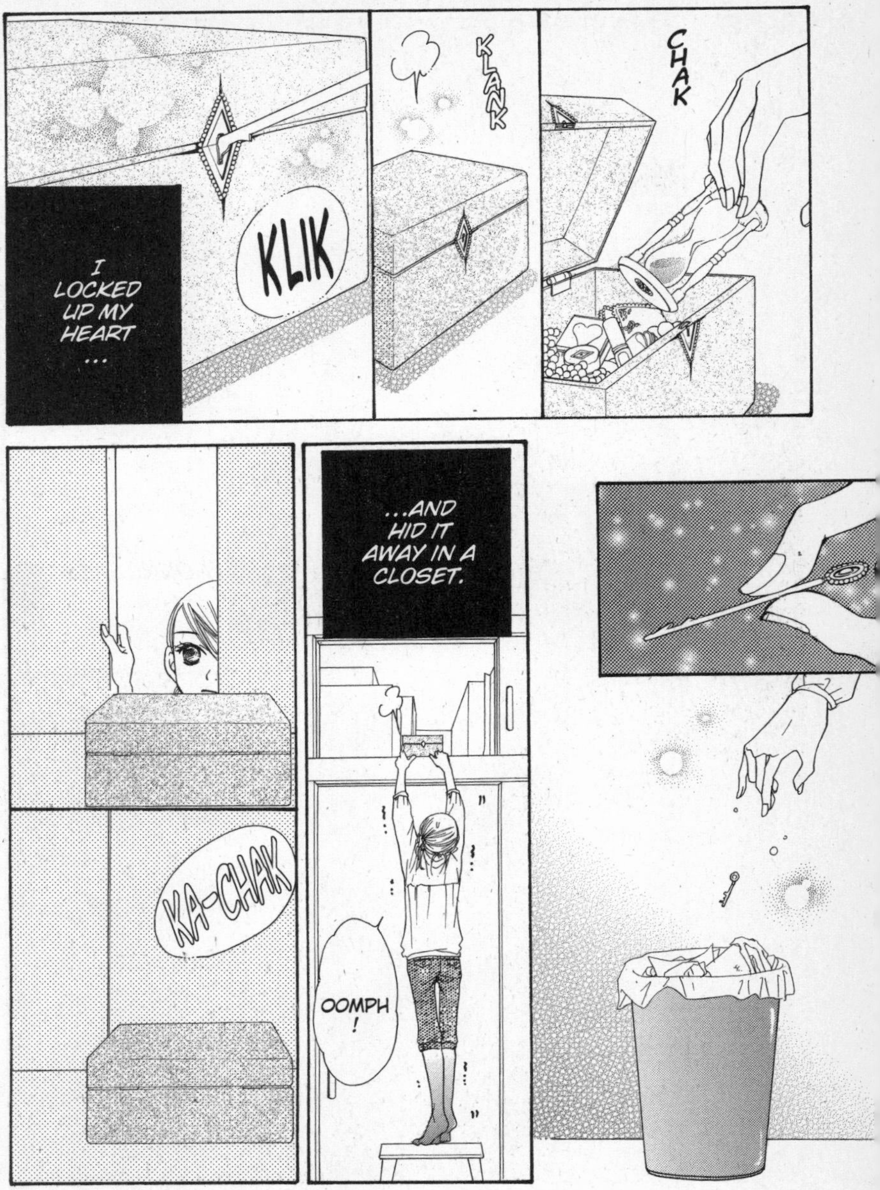
CHAK
KLANK
I LOCKED UP MY HEART ...
KLIK
...AND HID IT AWAY IN A CLOSET.
OOMPH!
KA-CHAK

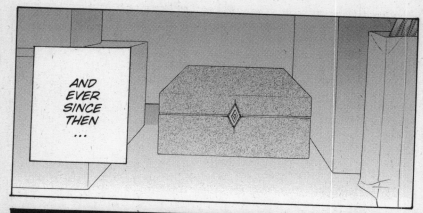

AND EVER SINCE THEN...

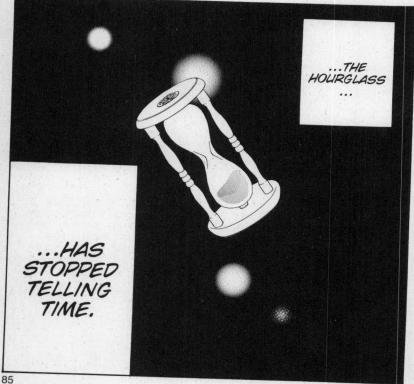

...THE HOURGLASS...

...HAS STOPPED TELLING TIME.

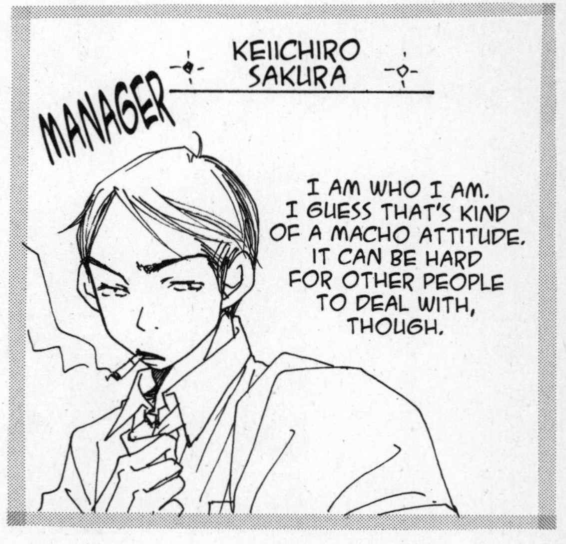
KEIICHIRO SAKURA
MANAGER
I AM WHO I AM. I GUESS THAT'S KIND OF A MACHO ATTITUDE. IT CAN BE HARD FOR OTHER PEOPLE TO DEAL WITH, THOUGH.

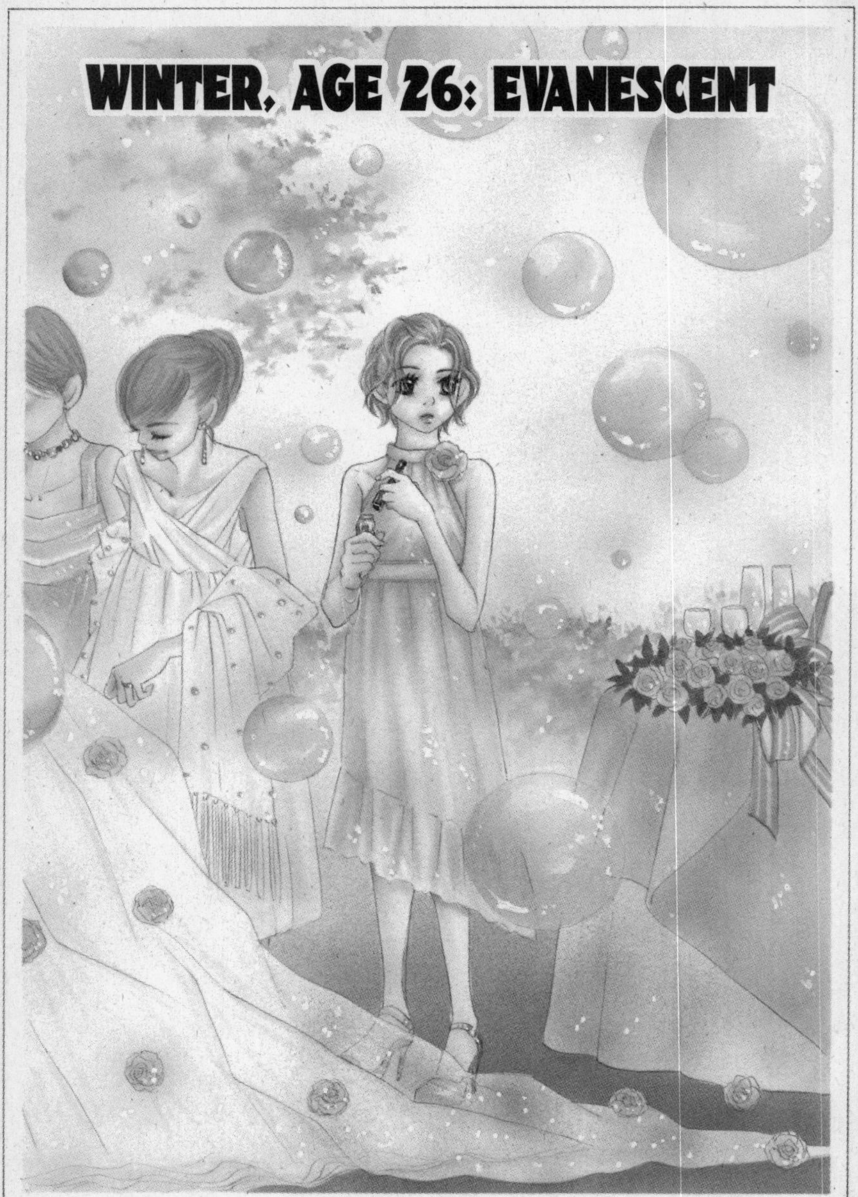
WINTER, AGE 26: EVANESCENT

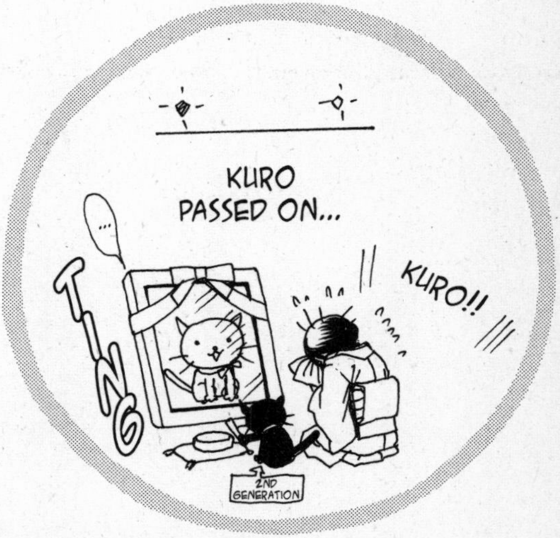
KURO
PASSED ON...
KURO!!
...
TING
2ND
GENERATION

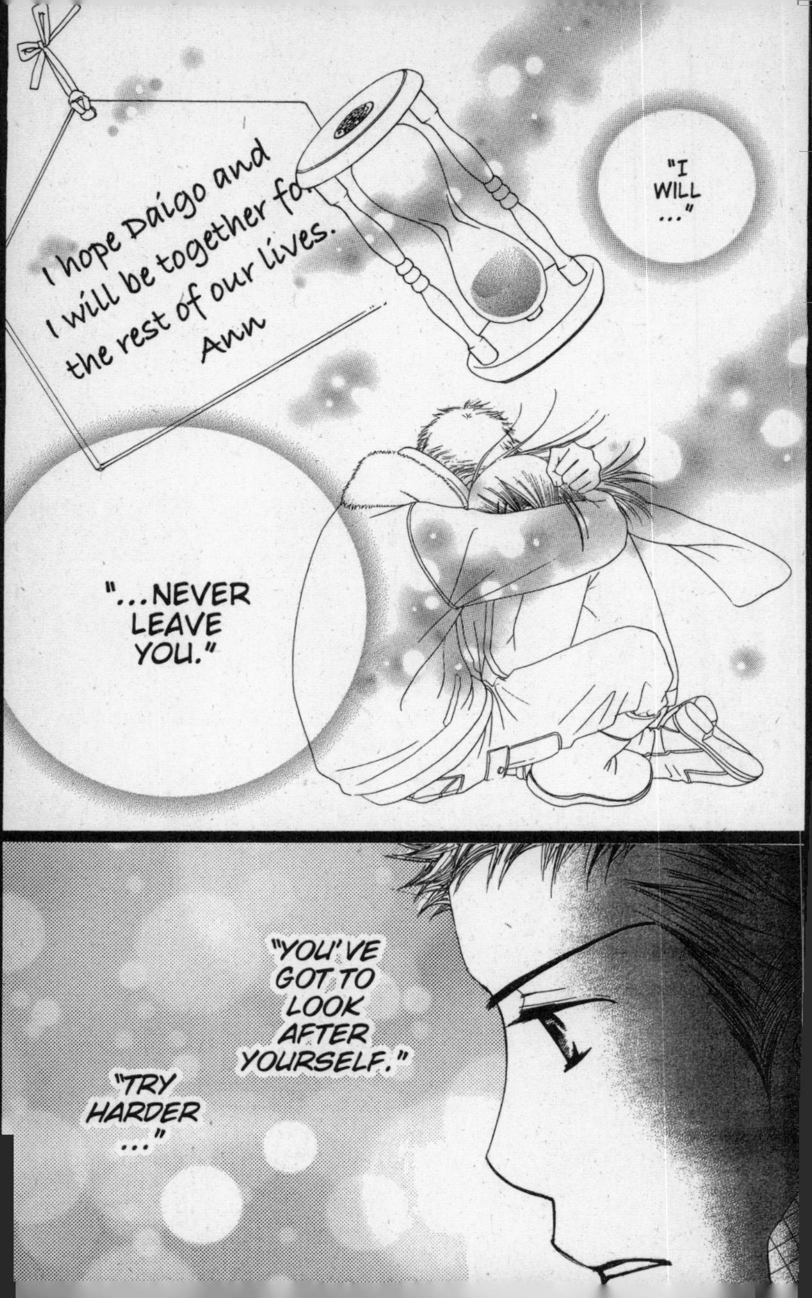
"I WILL ..."
I hope Daigo and I will be together for the rest of our lives. Ann
"...NEVER LEAVE YOU."
"YOU'VE GOT TO LOOK AFTER YOURSELF."
"TRY HARDER ..."

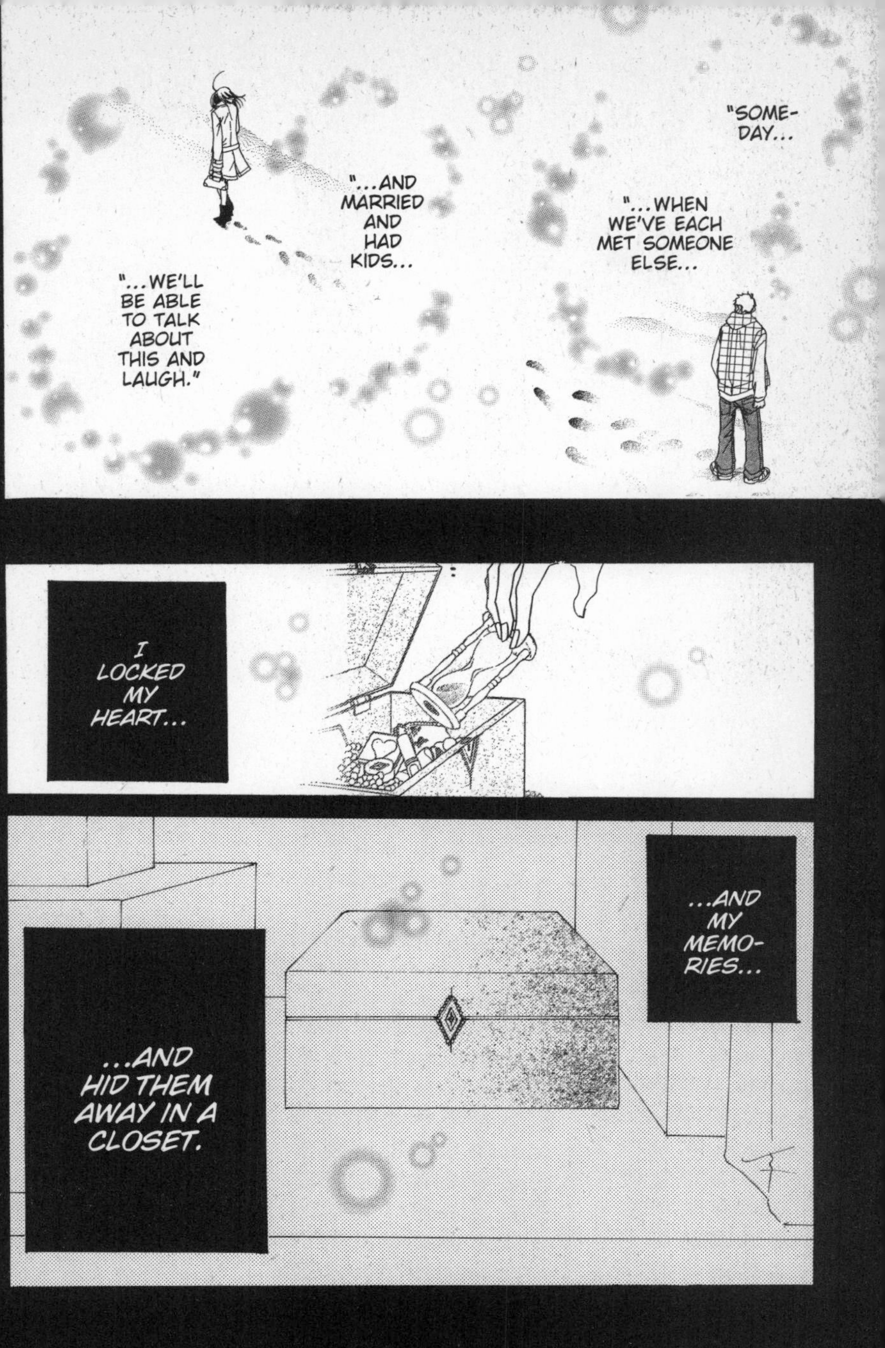
"SOME-DAY...
"...WHEN WE'VE EACH MET SOMEONE ELSE...
"...AND MARRIED AND HAD KIDS...
"...WE'LL BE ABLE TO TALK ABOUT THIS AND LAUGH."
I LOCKED MY HEART...
...AND MY MEMO-RIES...
...AND HID THEM AWAY IN A CLOSET.

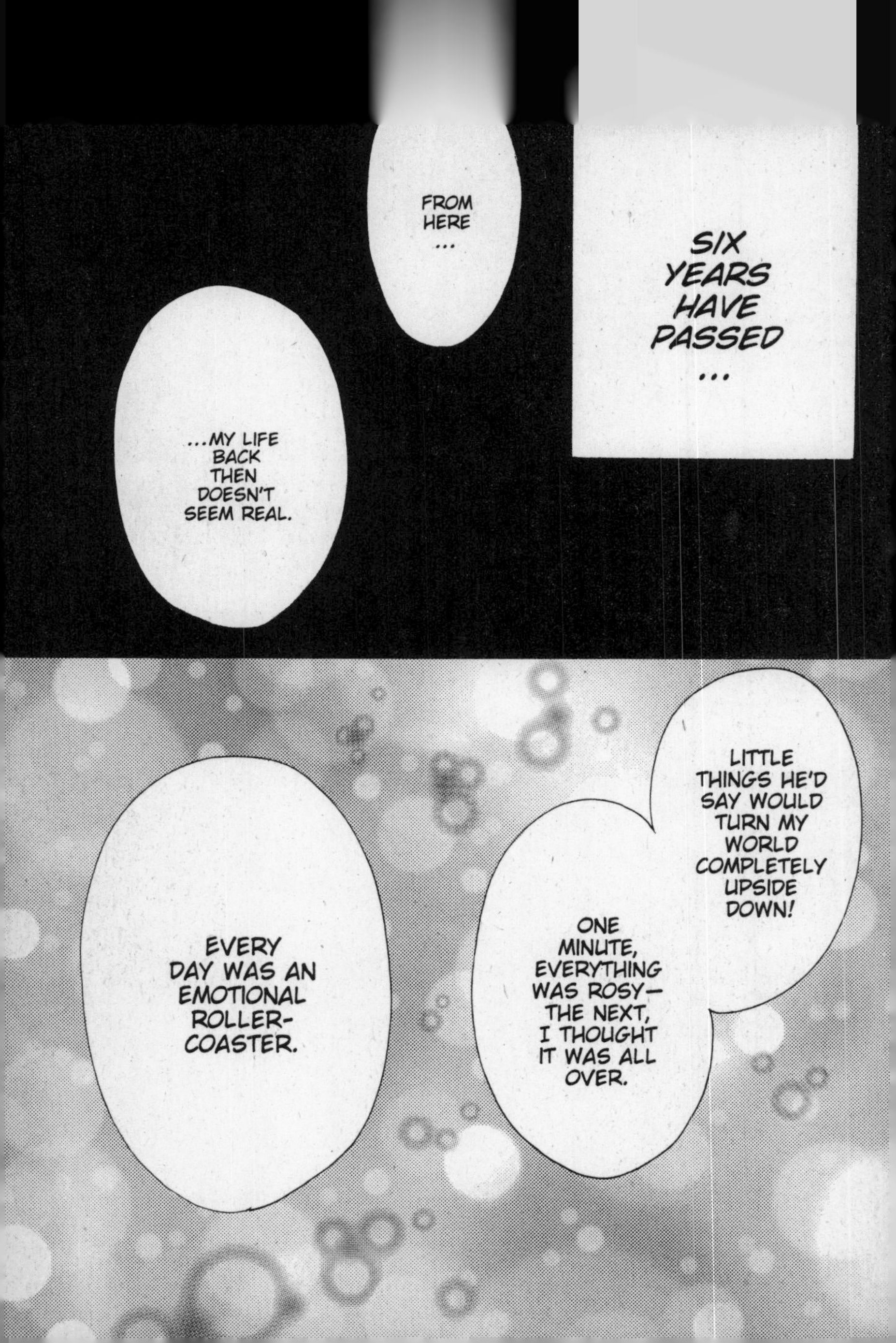
SIX YEARS HAVE PASSED...
FROM HERE...
...MY LIFE BACK THEN DOESN'T SEEM REAL.
LITTLE THINGS HE'D SAY WOULD TURN MY WORLD COMPLETELY UPSIDE DOWN!
ONE MINUTE, EVERYTHING WAS ROSY— THE NEXT, I THOUGHT IT WAS ALL OVER.
EVERY DAY WAS AN EMOTIONAL ROLLER-COASTER.

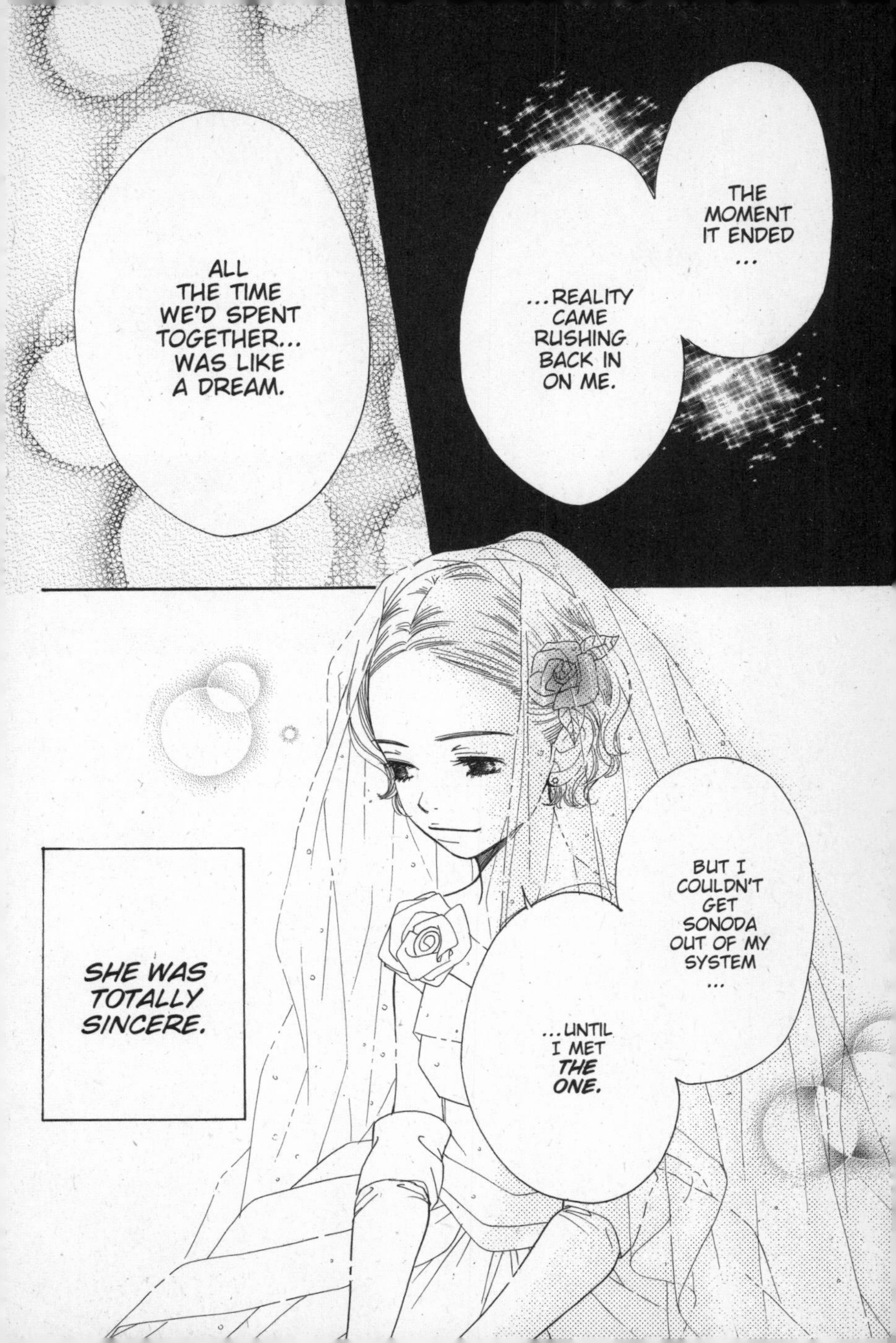

THE MOMENT IT ENDED ...
...REALITY CAME RUSHING BACK IN ON ME.
ALL THE TIME WE'D SPENT TOGETHER... WAS LIKE A DREAM.
BUT I COULDN'T GET SONODA OUT OF MY SYSTEM ...
...UNTIL I MET *THE ONE.*
SHE WAS TOTALLY SINCERE.

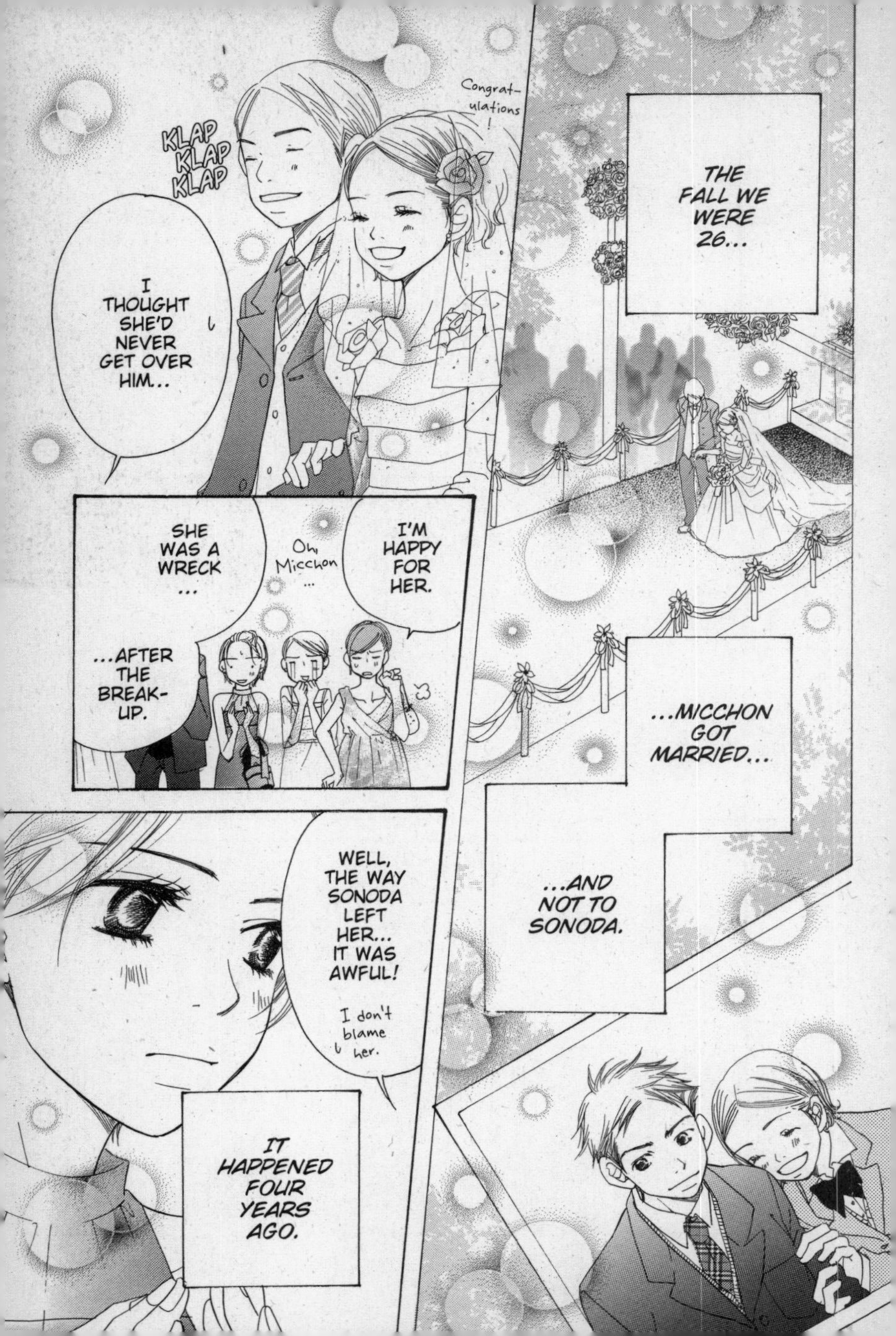
THE FALL WE WERE 26...
...MICCHON GOT MARRIED...
...AND NOT TO SONODA.
Congrat-ulations!
KLAP KLAP KLAP
I THOUGHT SHE'D NEVER GET OVER HIM...
I'M HAPPY FOR HER.
Oh, Micchon...
SHE WAS A WRECK...
...AFTER THE BREAK-UP.
WELL, THE WAY SONODA LEFT HER... IT WAS AWFUL!
I don't blame her.
IT HAPPENED FOUR YEARS AGO.

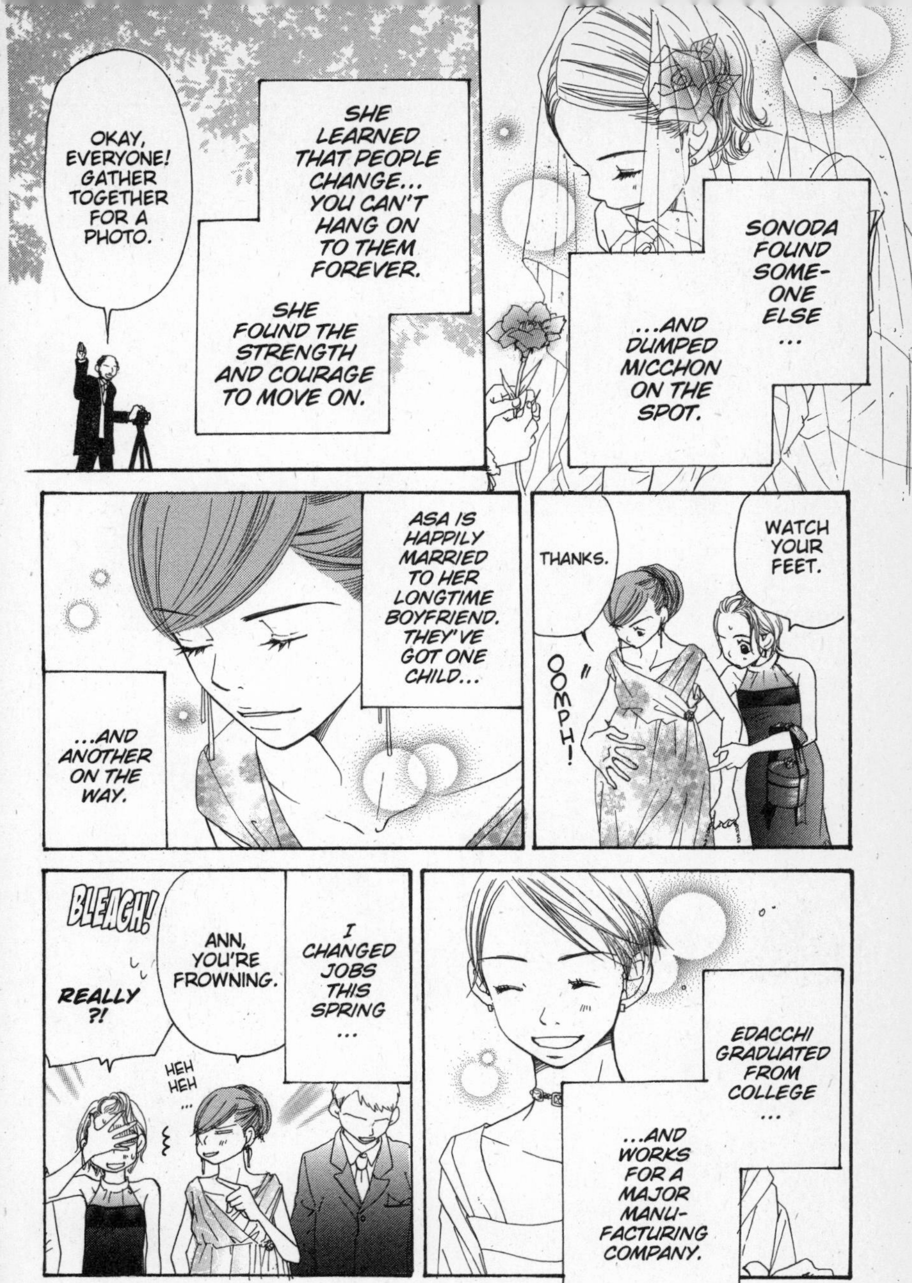
SONODA FOUND SOME-ONE ELSE ...
...AND DUMPED MICCHON ON THE SPOT.
SHE LEARNED THAT PEOPLE CHANGE... YOU CAN'T HANG ON TO THEM FOREVER.
SHE FOUND THE STRENGTH AND COURAGE TO MOVE ON.
OKAY, EVERYONE! GATHER TOGETHER FOR A PHOTO.
WATCH YOUR FEET.
THANKS.
OOMPH!
ASA IS HAPPILY MARRIED TO HER LONGTIME BOYFRIEND. THEY'VE GOT ONE CHILD...
...AND ANOTHER ON THE WAY.
EDACCHI GRADUATED FROM COLLEGE ...
...AND WORKS FOR A MAJOR MANU-FACTURING COMPANY.
I CHANGED JOBS THIS SPRING ...
ANN, YOU'RE FROWNING.
BLEAGH!
REALLY ?!
HEH HEH ...

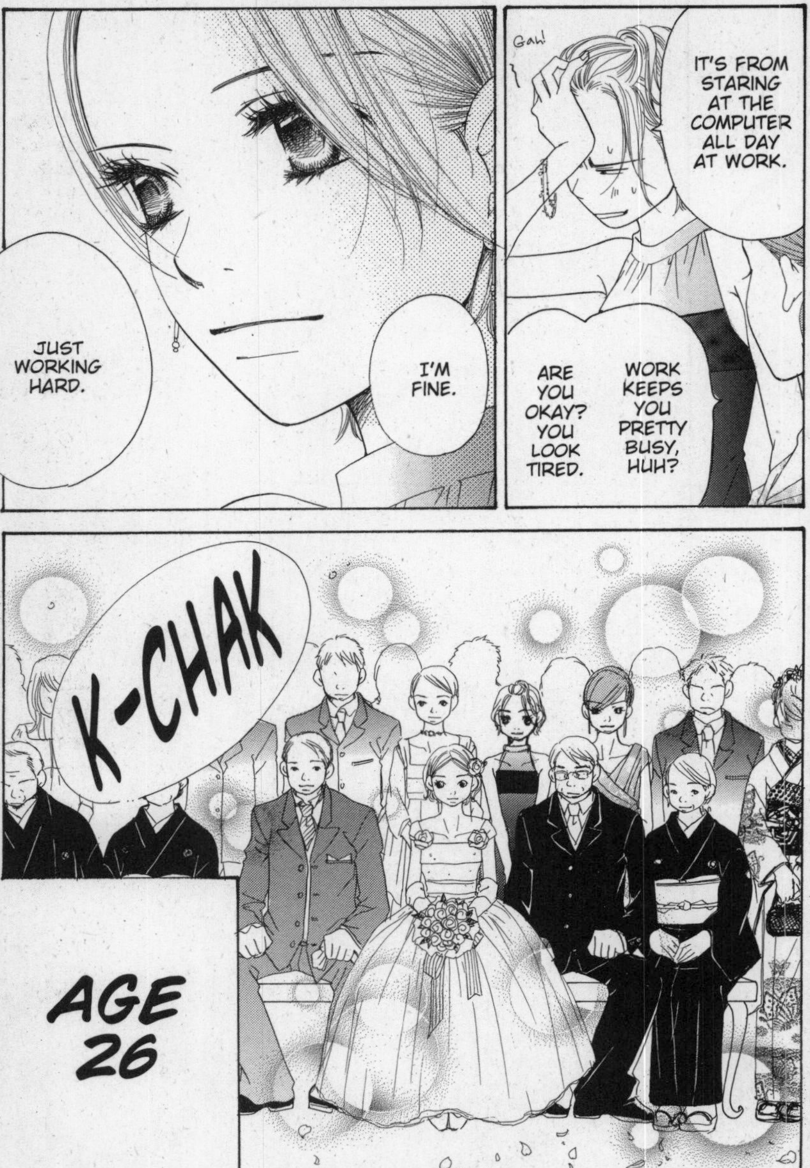
IT'S FROM STARING AT THE COMPUTER ALL DAY AT WORK.
Gah!
WORK KEEPS YOU PRETTY BUSY, HUH?
ARE YOU OKAY? YOU LOOK TIRED.
I'M FINE.
JUST WORKING HARD.
K-CHAK
AGE 26

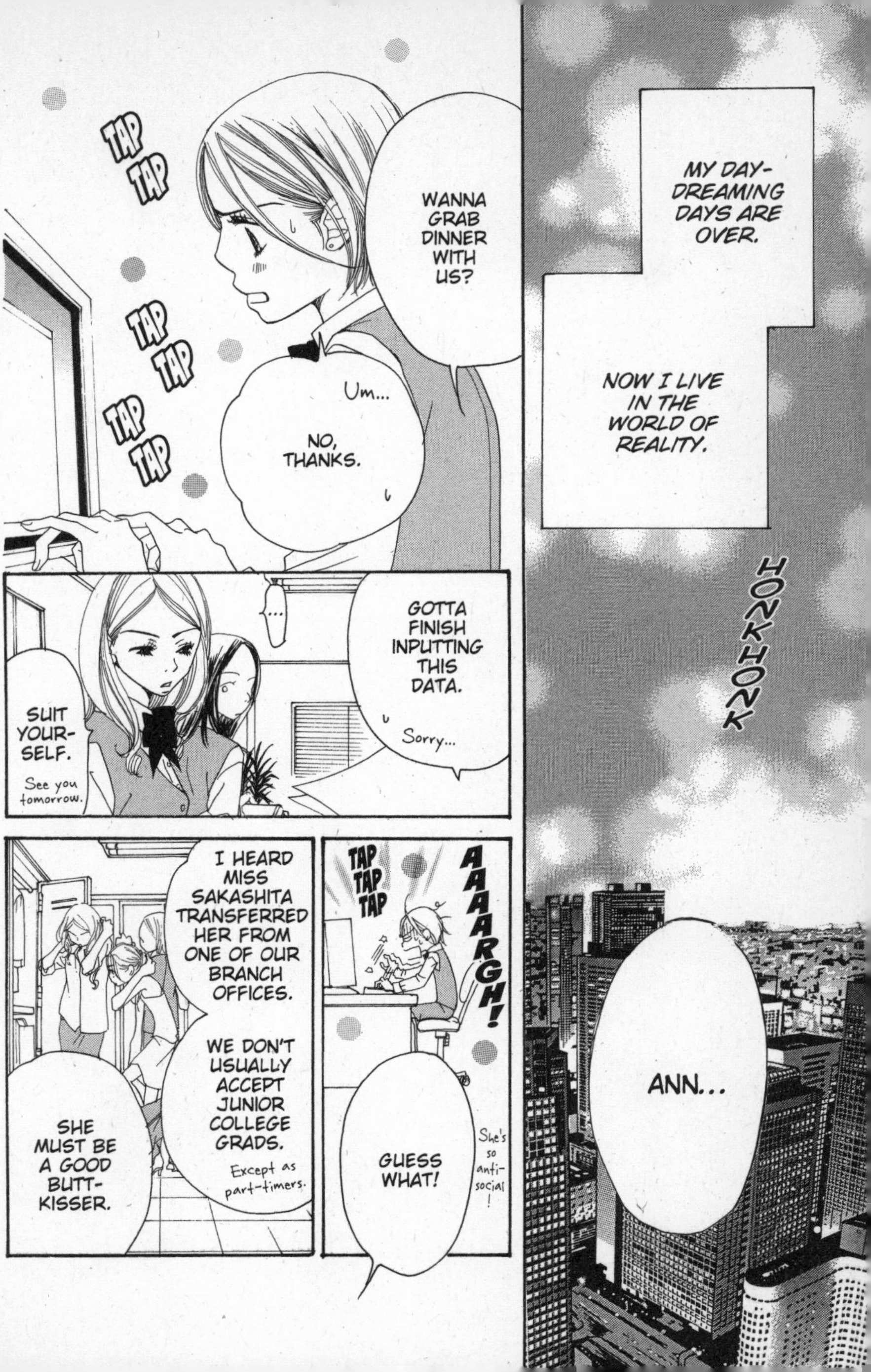
MY DAY-DREAMING DAYS ARE OVER.
NOW I LIVE IN THE WORLD OF REALITY.
HONKHONK
ANN...
WANNA GRAB DINNER WITH US?
Um...
NO, THANKS.
TAP TAP
TAP TAP
TAP TAP
GOTTA FINISH INPUTTING THIS DATA.
Sorry...
...
SUIT YOURSELF.
See you tomorrow.
AAAARGH!
TAP TAP TAP
GUESS WHAT!
She's so anti-social!
I HEARD MISS SAKASHITA TRANSFERRED HER FROM ONE OF OUR BRANCH OFFICES.
WE DON'T USUALLY ACCEPT JUNIOR COLLEGE GRADS.
Except as part-timers.
SHE MUST BE A GOOD BUTT-KISSER.

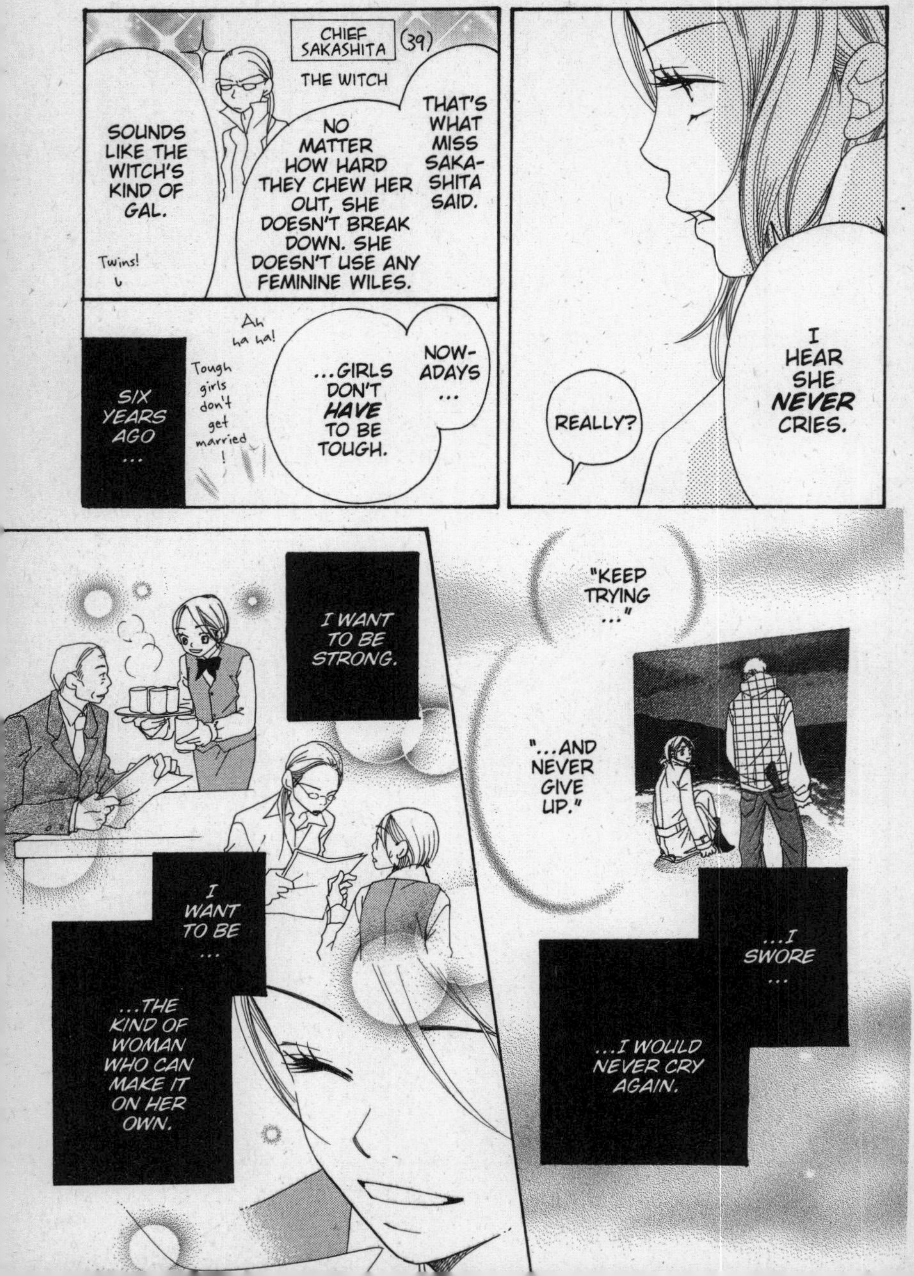
I HEAR SHE **NEVER** CRIES.
REALLY?
THAT'S WHAT MISS SAKASHITA SAID.
CHIEF SAKASHITA (39)
THE WITCH
NO MATTER HOW HARD THEY CHEW HER OUT, SHE DOESN'T BREAK DOWN. SHE DOESN'T USE ANY FEMININE WILES.
SOUNDS LIKE THE WITCH'S KIND OF GAL.
Twins!
NOW-ADAYS...
...GIRLS DON'T **HAVE** TO BE TOUGH.
Ah ha ha!
Tough girls don't get married!
SIX YEARS AGO...
"KEEP TRYING..."
"...AND NEVER GIVE UP."
...I SWORE...
...I WOULD NEVER CRY AGAIN.
I WANT TO BE STRONG.
I WANT TO BE...
...THE KIND OF WOMAN WHO CAN MAKE IT ON HER OWN.

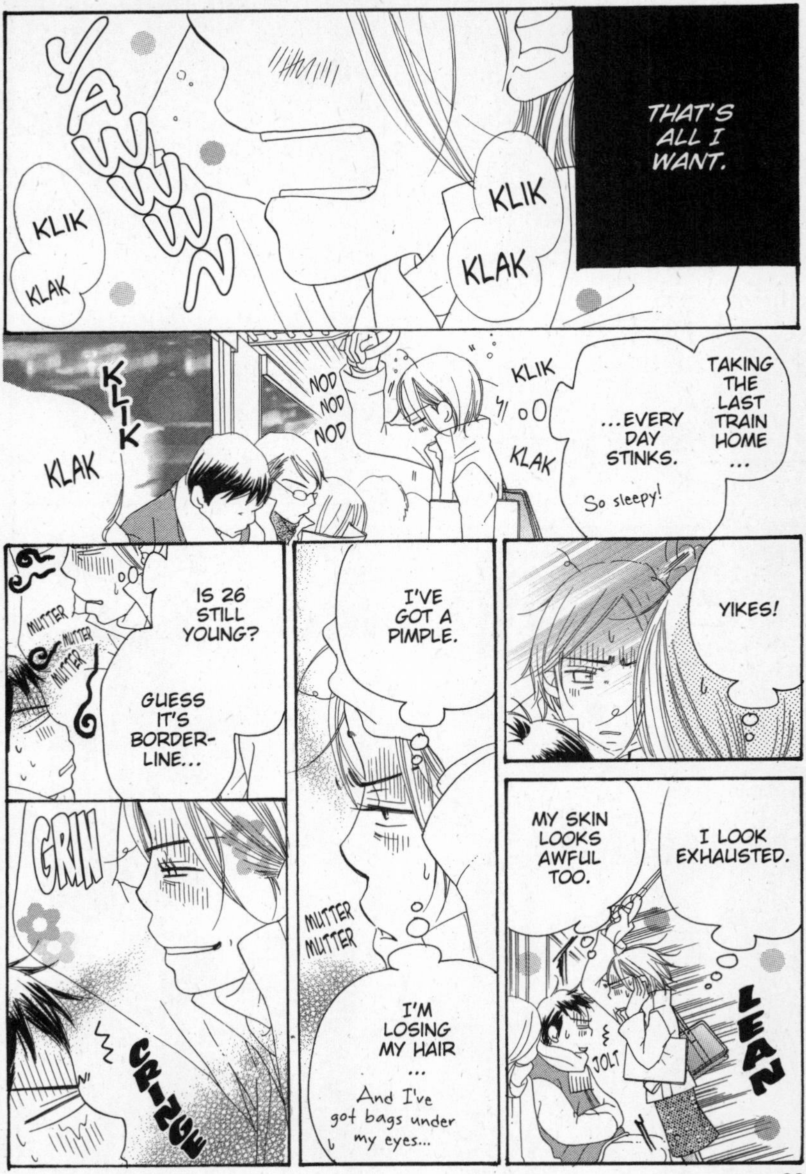
THAT'S ALL I WANT.
KLIK
KLAK
YAWWWN
KLIK
KLAK
TAKING THE LAST TRAIN HOME...
...EVERY DAY STINKS.
So sleepy!
KLIK
KLAK
NOD NOD NOD
KLIK
KLAK
YIKES!
I LOOK EXHAUSTED.
MY SKIN LOOKS AWFUL TOO.
JOLT
LEAN
I'VE GOT A PIMPLE.
MUTTER MUTTER
I'M LOSING MY HAIR...
And I've got bags under my eyes...
IS 26 STILL YOUNG?
GUESS IT'S BORDER-LINE...
MUTTER MUTTER MUTTER
GRIN
CRINGE

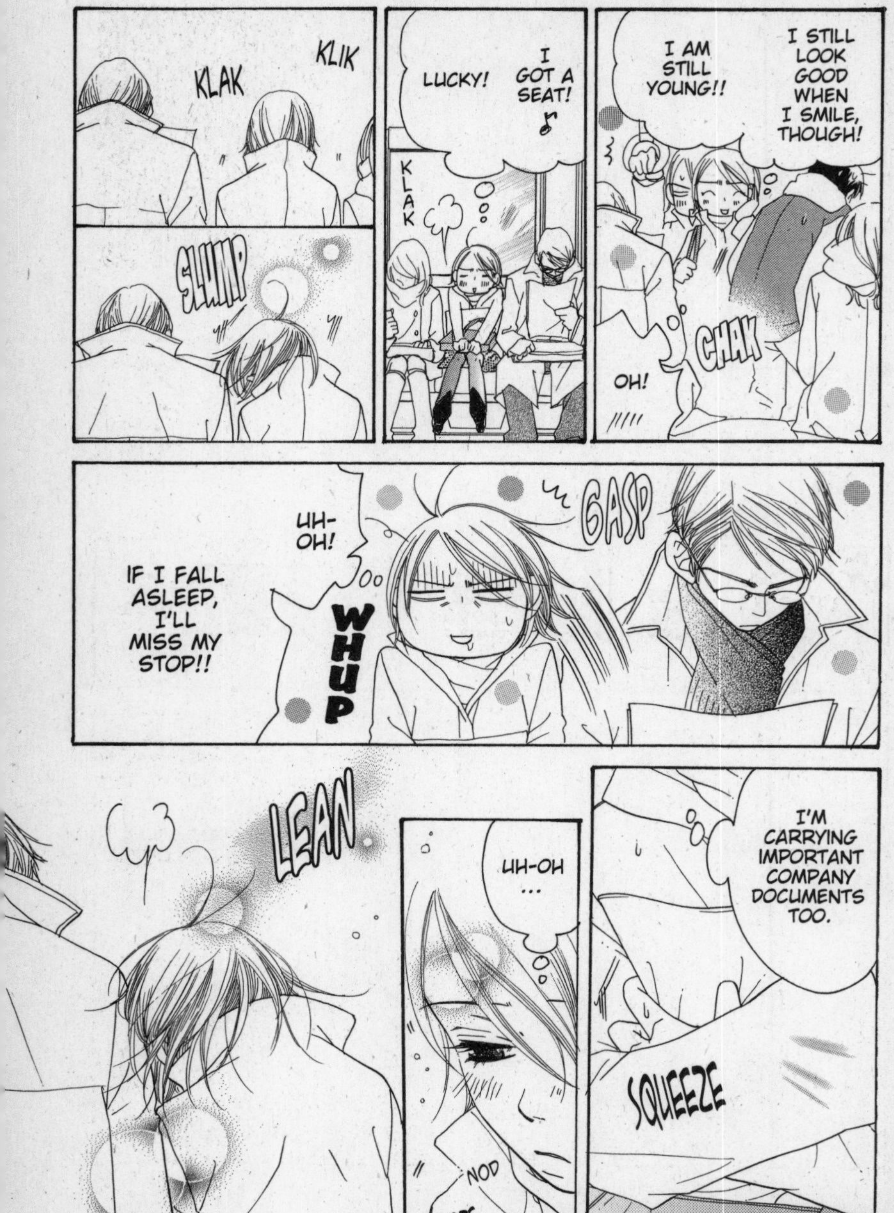
I STILL LOOK GOOD WHEN I SMILE, THOUGH!
I AM STILL YOUNG!!
CHAK
OH!
I GOT A SEAT! ♪
LUCKY!
KLAK
KLIK
KLAK
SLUMP
GASP
WHUP
UH-OH!
IF I FALL ASLEEP, I'LL MISS MY STOP!!
I'M CARRYING IMPORTANT COMPANY DOCUMENTS TOO.
SQUEEZE
UH-OH ...
NOD
DOZE
LEAN

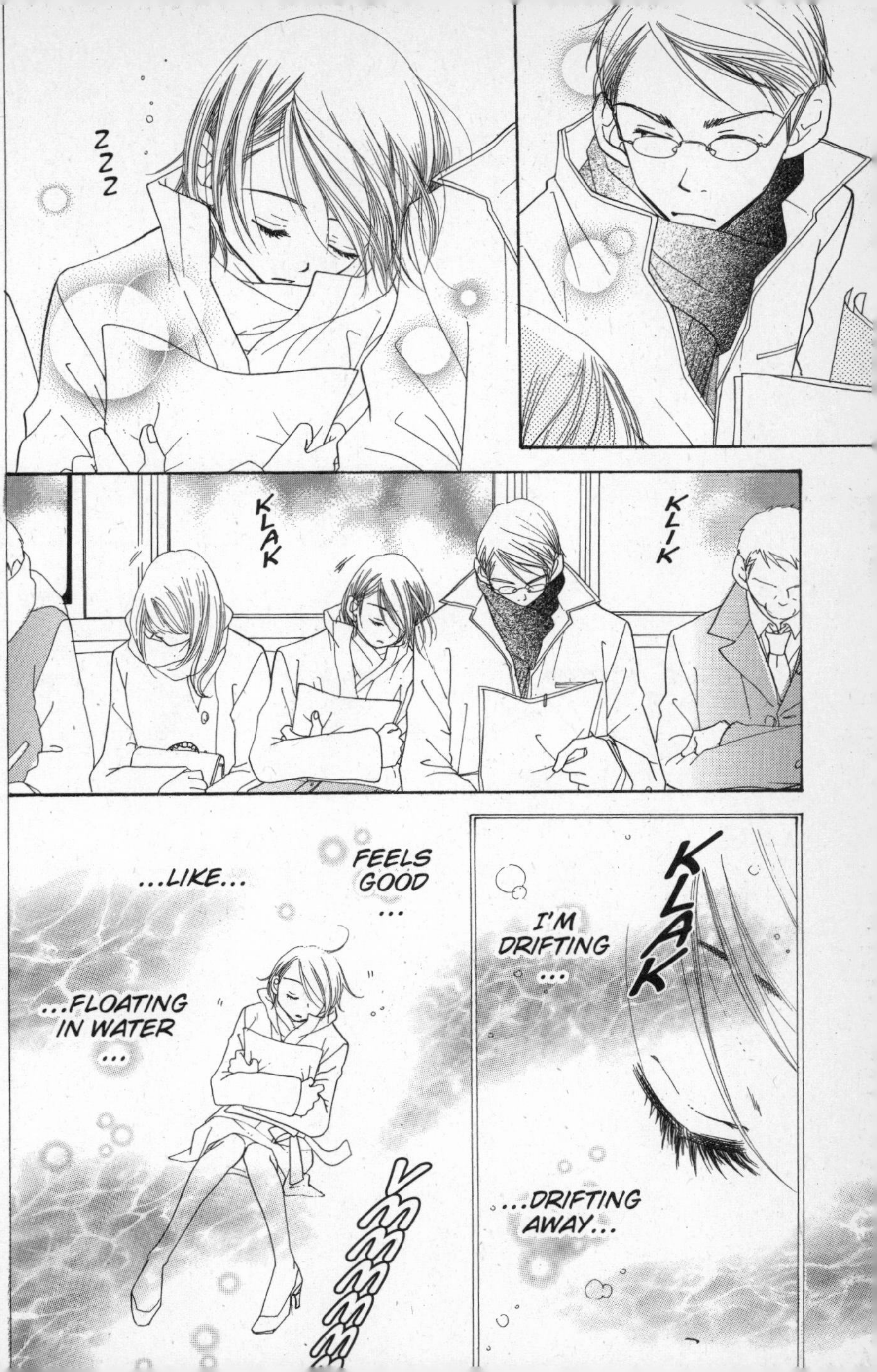
ZZZ
KLIK
KLAK
KLAK
I'M DRIFTING ...
...DRIFTING AWAY...
FEELS GOOD ...
...LIKE...
...FLOATING IN WATER ...
VMMMMMMMMM

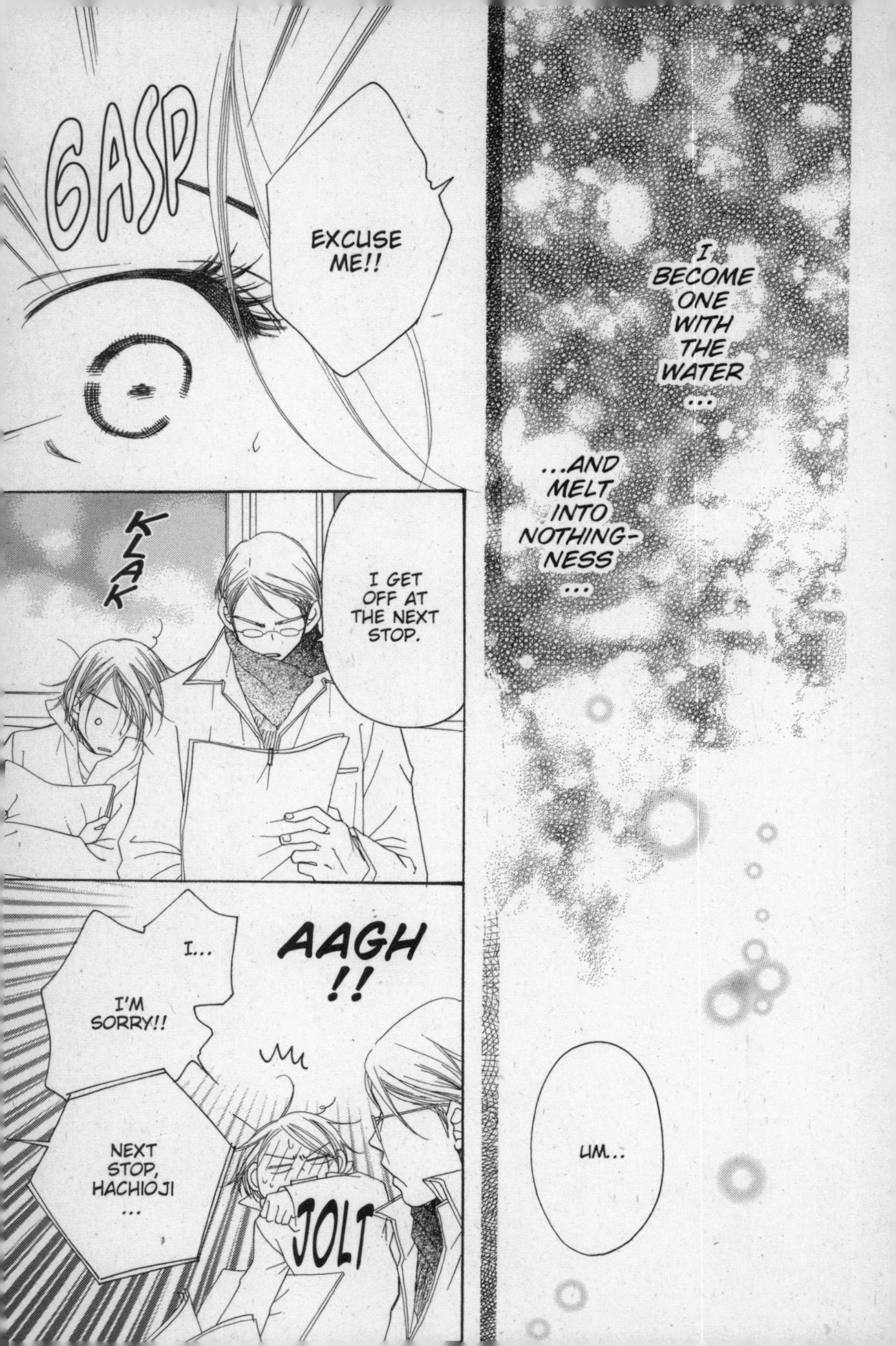
I BECOME ONE WITH THE WATER ...
...AND MELT INTO NOTHINGNESS ...
UM...
EXCUSE ME!!
GASP
I GET OFF AT THE NEXT STOP.
KLAK
AAGH!!
I... I'M SORRY!!
NEXT STOP, HACHIOJI ...
JOLT

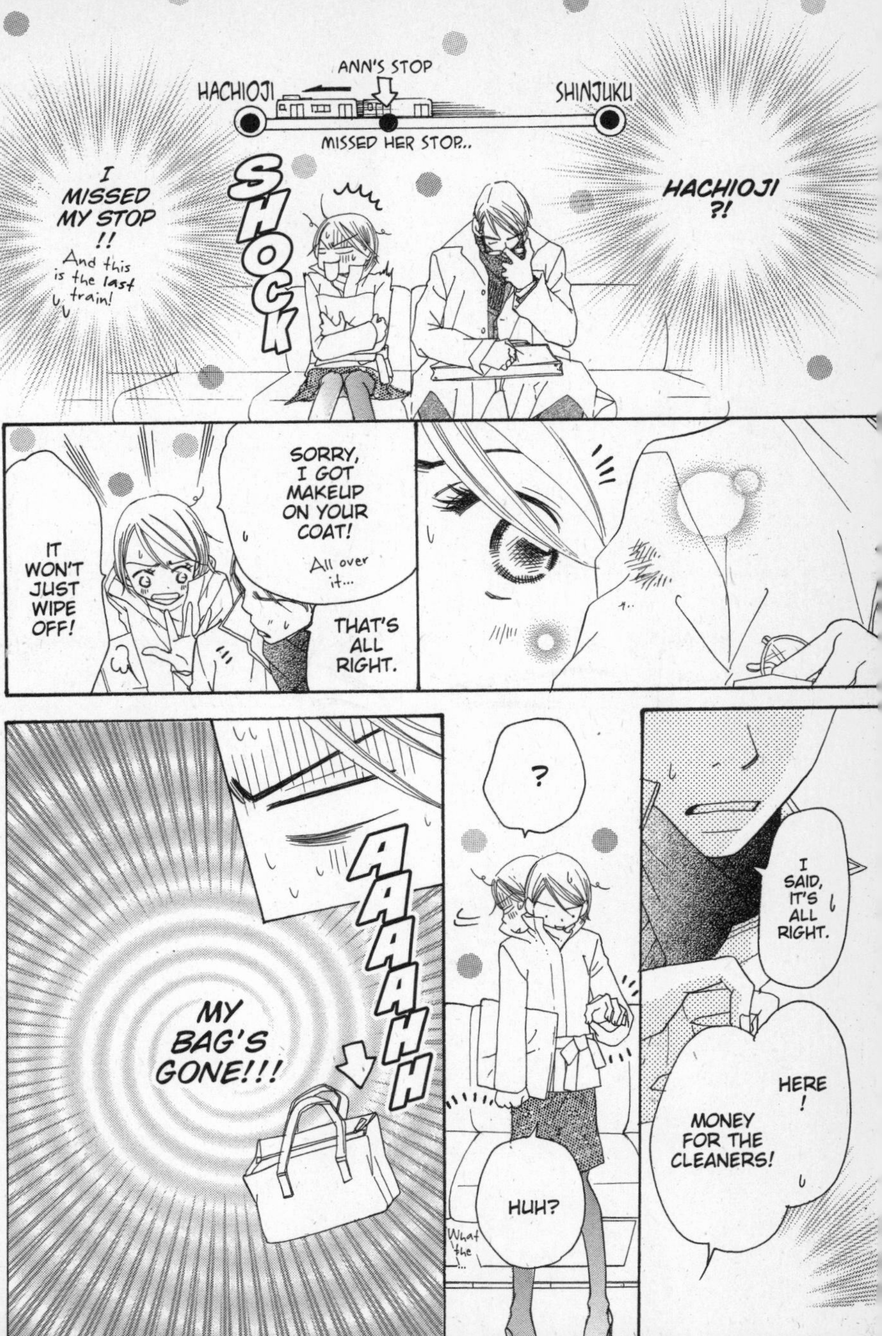
ANN'S STOP
HACHIOJI
SHINJUKU
MISSED HER STOP...
HACHIOJI ?!
SHOCK
I MISSED MY STOP !!
And this is the last train!
SORRY, I GOT MAKEUP ON YOUR COAT!
All over it...
THAT'S ALL RIGHT.
IT WON'T JUST WIPE OFF!
I SAID, IT'S ALL RIGHT.
HERE!
MONEY FOR THE CLEANERS!
?
HUH?
What the...!
AAAAAHH
MY BAG'S GONE!!!

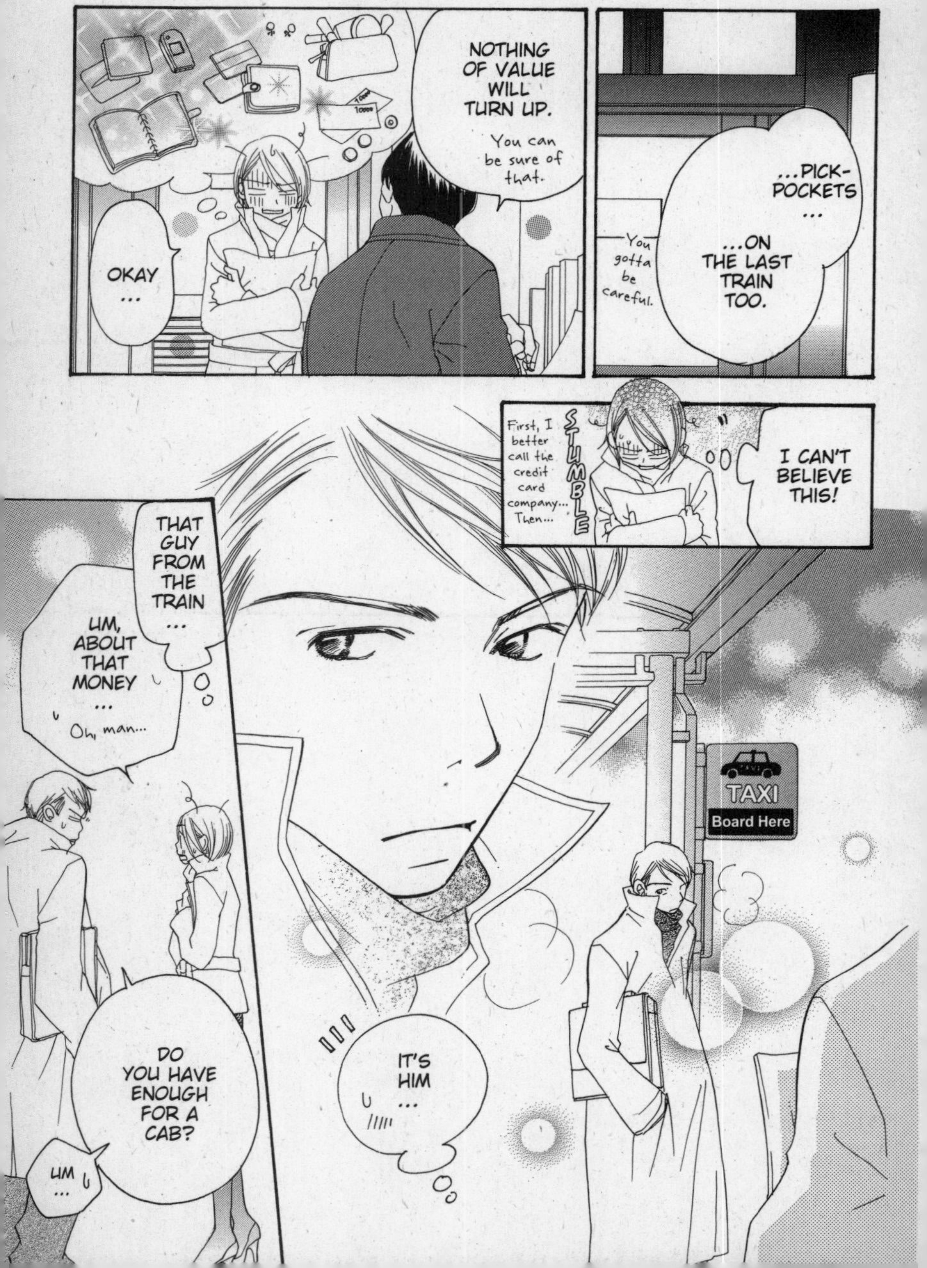
...PICK-POCKETS ...
...ON THE LAST TRAIN TOO.
You gotta be careful.
NOTHING OF VALUE WILL TURN UP.
You can be sure of that.
OKAY ...
I CAN'T BELIEVE THIS!
STUMBLE
First, I better call the credit card company... Then...
IT'S HIM ...
TAXI
Board Here
THAT GUY FROM THE TRAIN ...
UM, ABOUT THAT MONEY ...
Oh, man...
DO YOU HAVE ENOUGH FOR A CAB?
UM ...

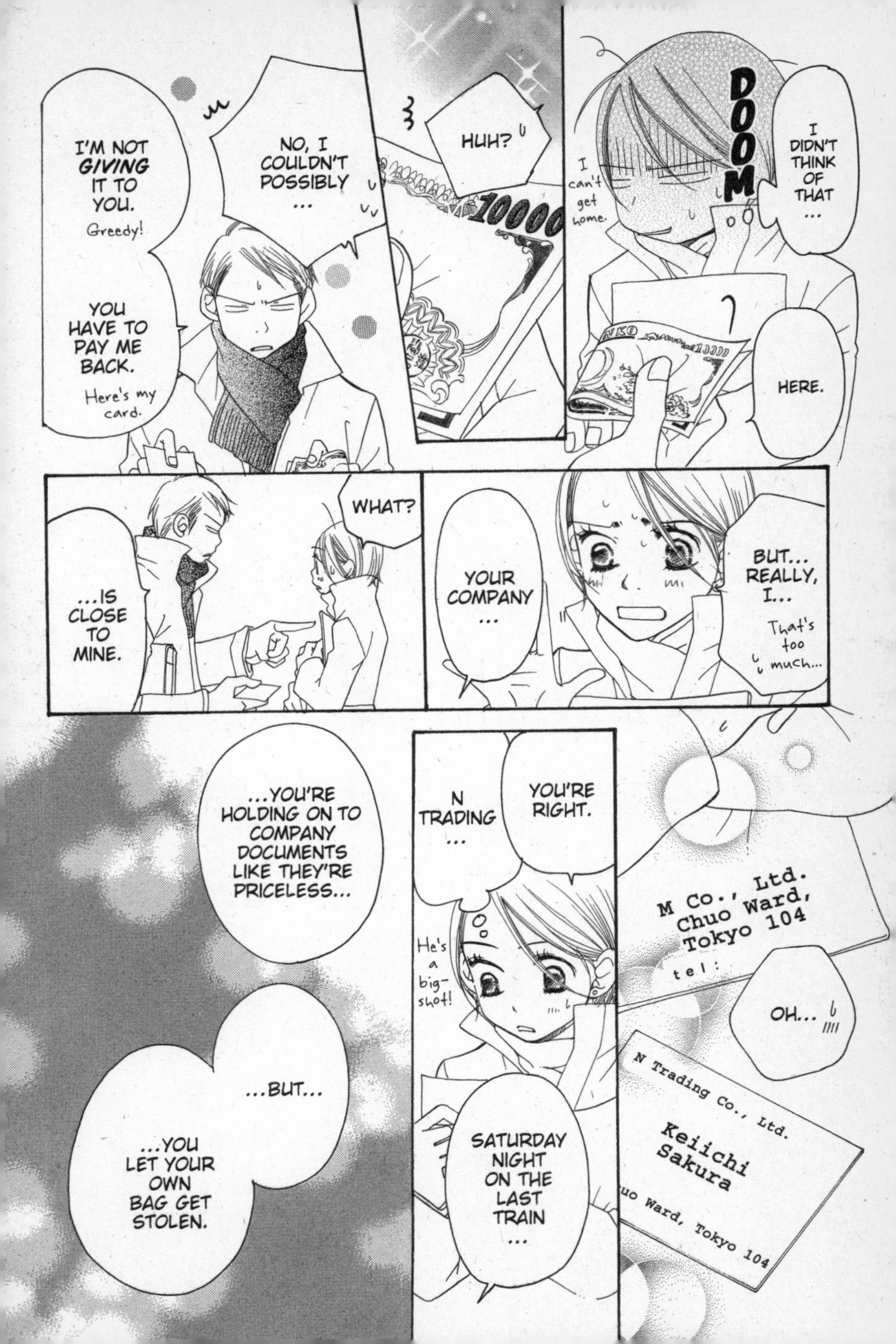
DOOM
I DIDN'T THINK OF THAT ...
I can't get home.
HERE.
HUH?
NO, I COULDN'T POSSIBLY ...
I'M NOT GIVING IT TO YOU.
Greedy!
YOU HAVE TO PAY ME BACK.
Here's my card.
BUT... REALLY, I...
That's too much...
YOUR COMPANY ...
WHAT?
...IS CLOSE TO MINE.
M Co., Ltd.
Chuo Ward, Tokyo 104
tel:
OH...
N Trading Co., Ltd.
Keiichi Sakura
uo Ward, Tokyo 104
YOU'RE RIGHT.
N TRADING ...
He's a big-shot!
SATURDAY NIGHT ON THE LAST TRAIN ...
...YOU'RE HOLDING ON TO COMPANY DOCUMENTS LIKE THEY'RE PRICELESS...
...BUT...
...YOU LET YOUR OWN BAG GET STOLEN.

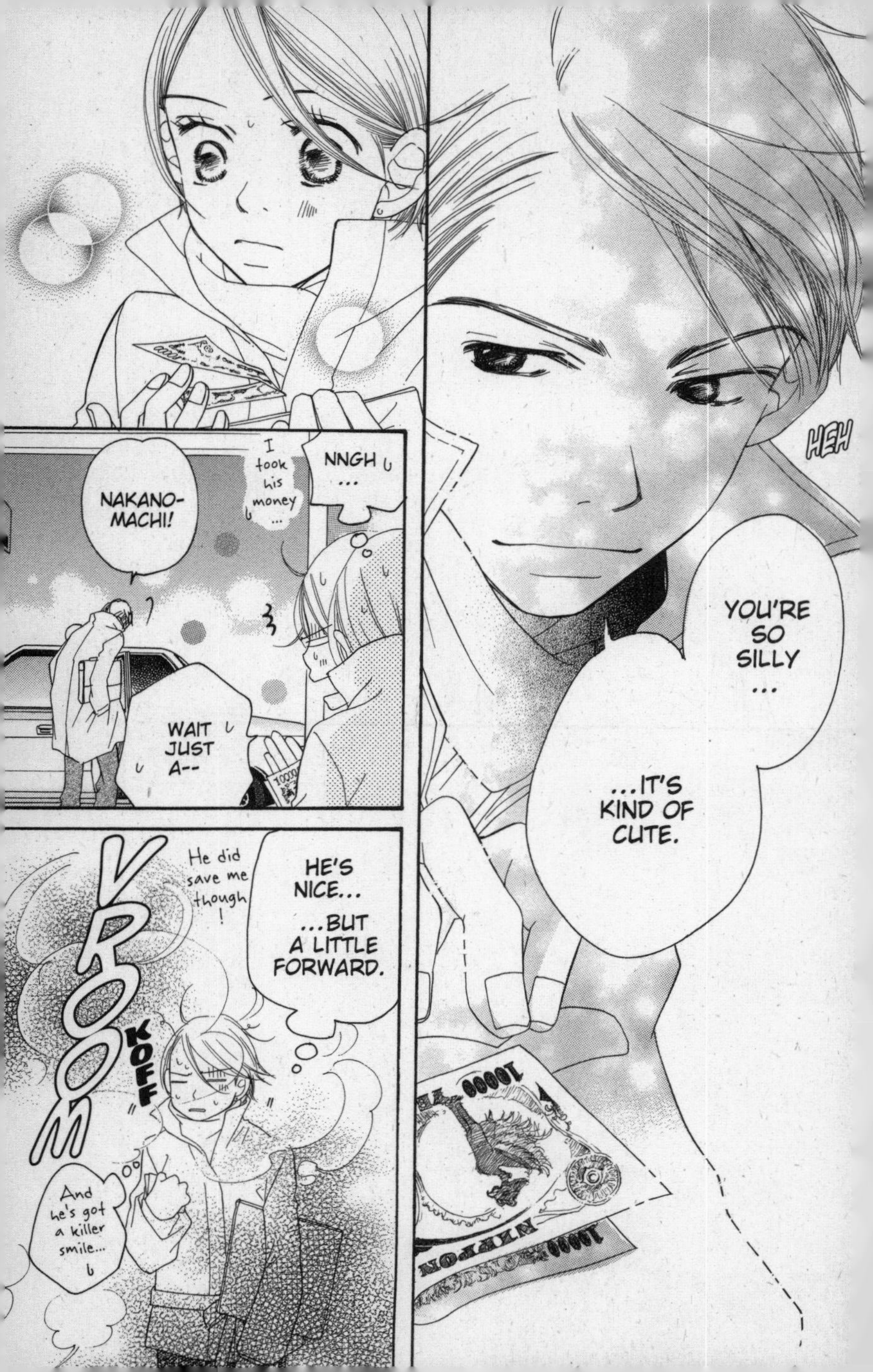
HEH
YOU'RE SO SILLY...
...IT'S KIND OF CUTE.
NNGH...
I took his money...
NAKANO-MACHI!
WAIT JUST A--
HE'S NICE...
...BUT A LITTLE FORWARD.
He did save me though!
VROOM
KOFF
And he's got a killer smile...

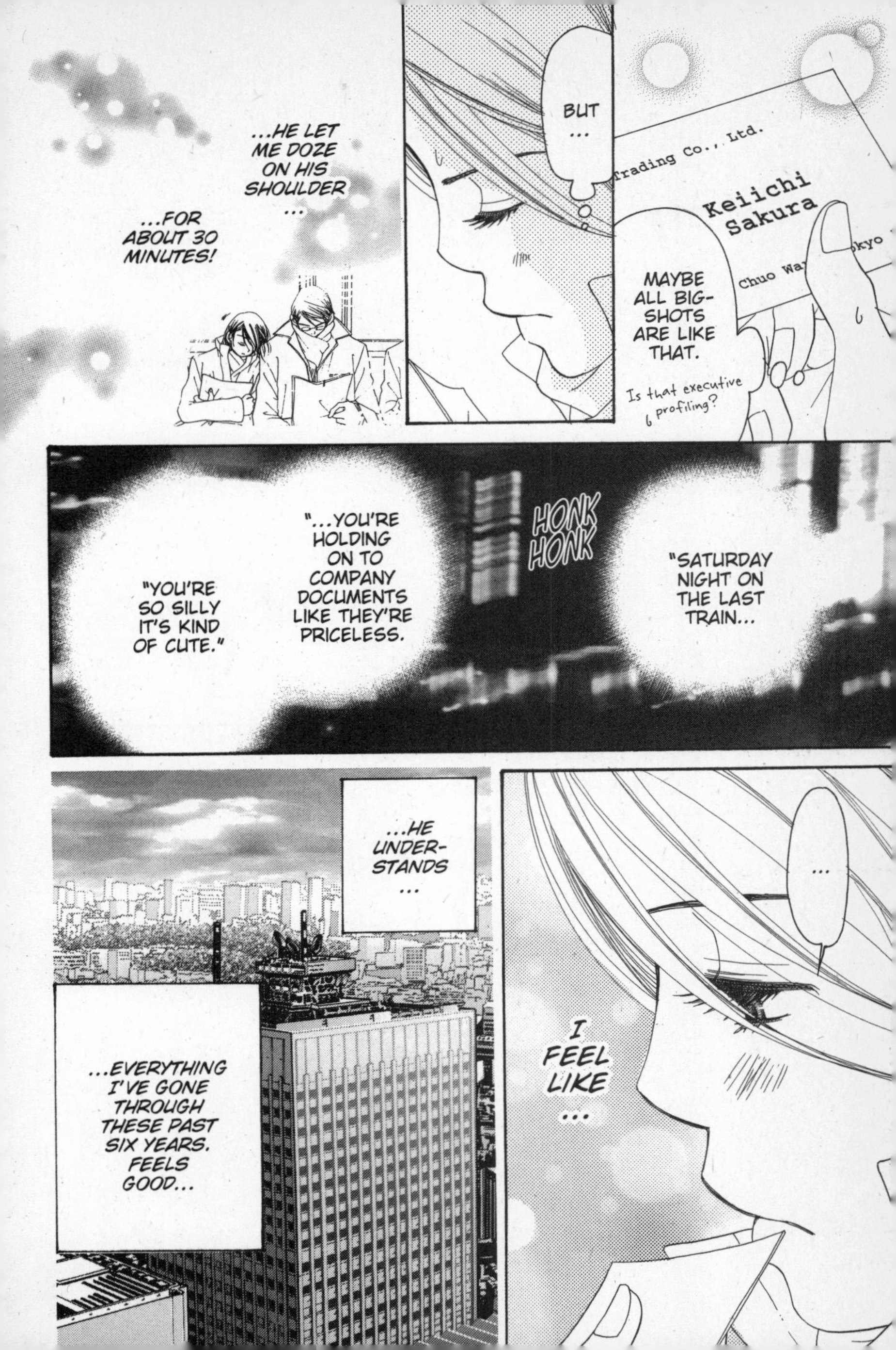

BUT ...
rading Co., Ltd.
Keiichi Sakura
MAYBE ALL BIG-SHOTS ARE LIKE THAT.
Is that executive profiling?
...HE LET ME DOZE ON HIS SHOULDER ...
...FOR ABOUT 30 MINUTES!
"SATURDAY NIGHT ON THE LAST TRAIN...
HONK HONK
"...YOU'RE HOLDING ON TO COMPANY DOCUMENTS LIKE THEY'RE PRICELESS.
"YOU'RE SO SILLY IT'S KIND OF CUTE."
...
I FEEL LIKE ...
...HE UNDER-STANDS ...
...EVERYTHING I'VE GONE THROUGH THESE PAST SIX YEARS. FEELS GOOD...

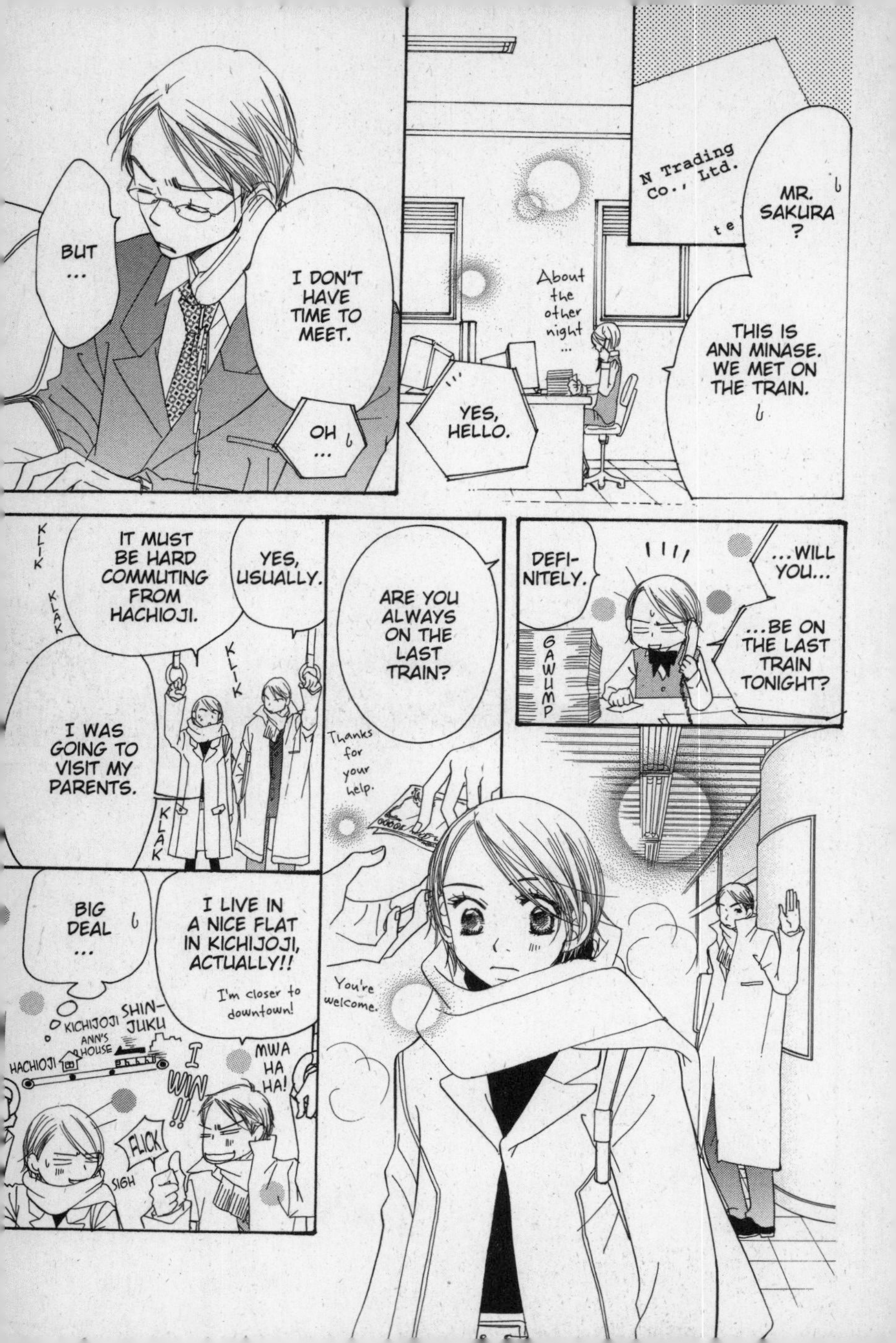

N Trading Co., Ltd.
MR. SAKURA?
te
THIS IS ANN MINASE. WE MET ON THE TRAIN.
About the other night ...
YES, HELLO.
I DON'T HAVE TIME TO MEET.
OH ...
BUT ...
...WILL YOU...
...BE ON THE LAST TRAIN TONIGHT?
DEFI-NITELY.
GAWUMP
ARE YOU ALWAYS ON THE LAST TRAIN?
Thanks for your help.
You're welcome.
YES, USUALLY.
IT MUST BE HARD COMMUTING FROM HACHIOJI.
KLIK KLAK
KLIK KLAK
I WAS GOING TO VISIT MY PARENTS.
I LIVE IN A NICE FLAT IN KICHIJOJI, ACTUALLY!!
I'm closer to downtown!
BIG DEAL ...
KICHIJOJI
ANN'S HOUSE
SHIN-JUKU
HACHIOJI
MWA HA HA!
I WIN!!
FLICK
SIGH

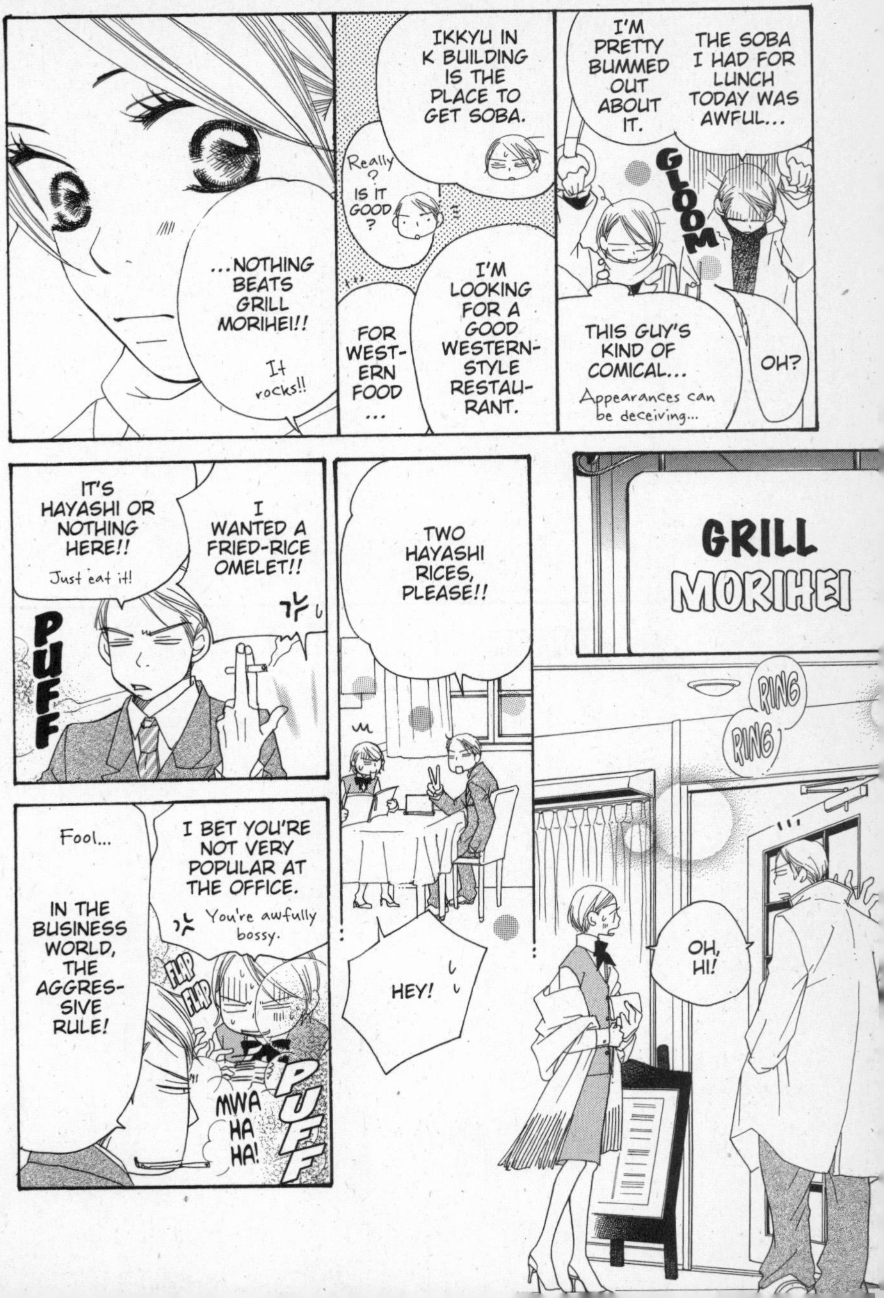
THE SOBA I HAD FOR LUNCH TODAY WAS AWFUL...
I'M PRETTY BUMMED OUT ABOUT IT.
GLOOM
OH?
THIS GUY'S KIND OF COMICAL...
Appearances can be deceiving...
IKKYU IN K BUILDING IS THE PLACE TO GET SOBA.
Really? IS IT GOOD?
I'M LOOKING FOR A GOOD WESTERN-STYLE RESTAURANT.
FOR WESTERN FOOD...
...NOTHING BEATS GRILL MORIHEI!!
It rocks!!
GRILL MORIHEI
RING
RING
OH, HI!
TWO HAYASHI RICES, PLEASE!!
HEY!
IT'S HAYASHI OR NOTHING HERE!!
Just eat it!
I WANTED A FRIED-RICE OMELET!!
PUFF
I BET YOU'RE NOT VERY POPULAR AT THE OFFICE.
You're awfully bossy.
Fool...
IN THE BUSINESS WORLD, THE AGGRESSIVE RULE!
FLAP
FLAP
MWA HA HA!
PUFF

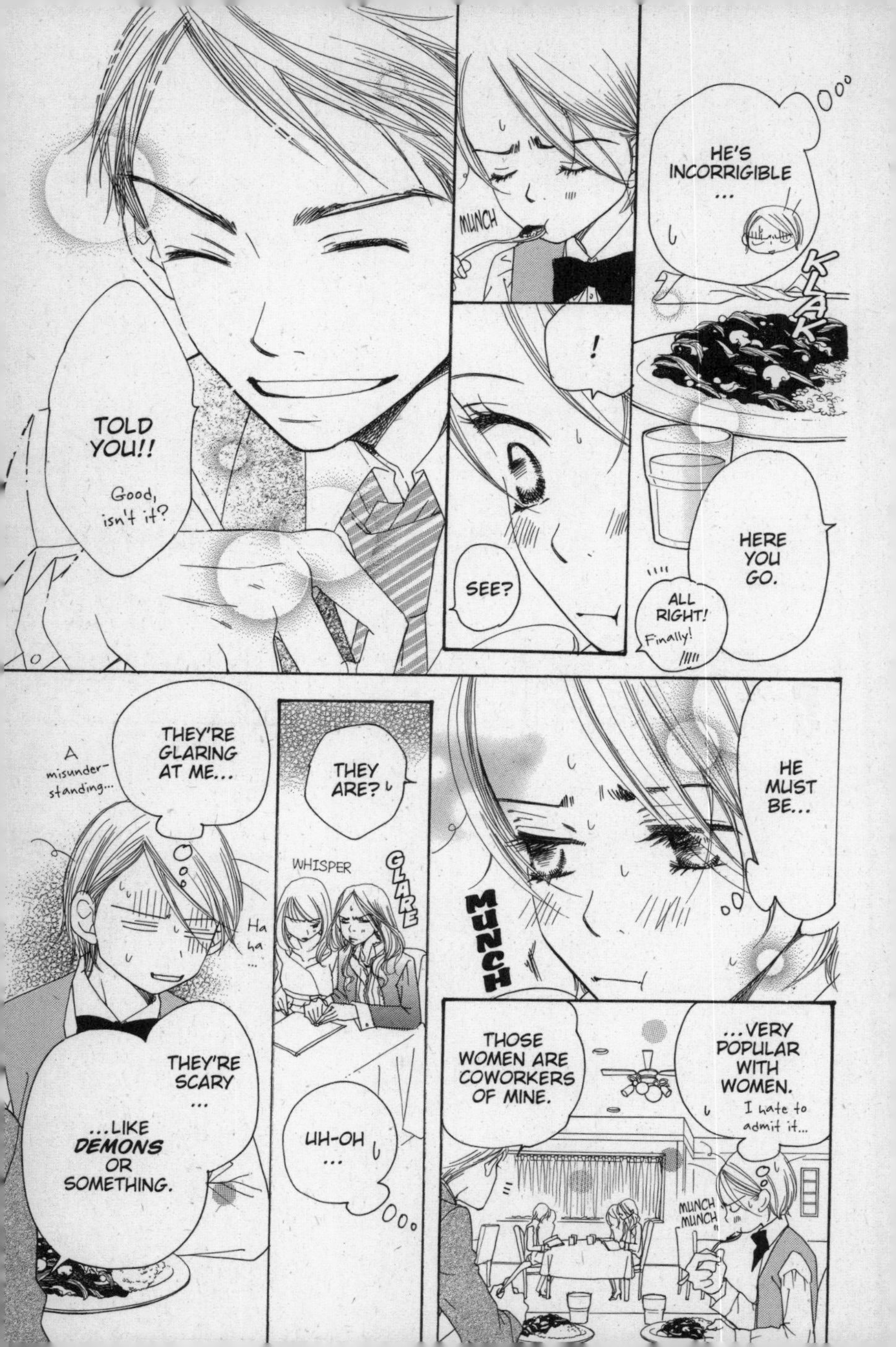
HE'S INCORRIGIBLE ...
KLAK
HERE YOU GO.
ALL RIGHT!
Finally!
MUNCH
!
SEE?
TOLD YOU!!
Good, isn't it?
HE MUST BE...
MUNCH
...VERY POPULAR WITH WOMEN.
I hate to admit it...
THOSE WOMEN ARE COWORKERS OF MINE.
MUNCH MUNCH
THEY ARE?
WHISPER
GLARE
UH-OH ...
THEY'RE GLARING AT ME...
A misunder-standing...
Ha ha ...
THEY'RE SCARY ...
...LIKE DEMONS OR SOMETHING.

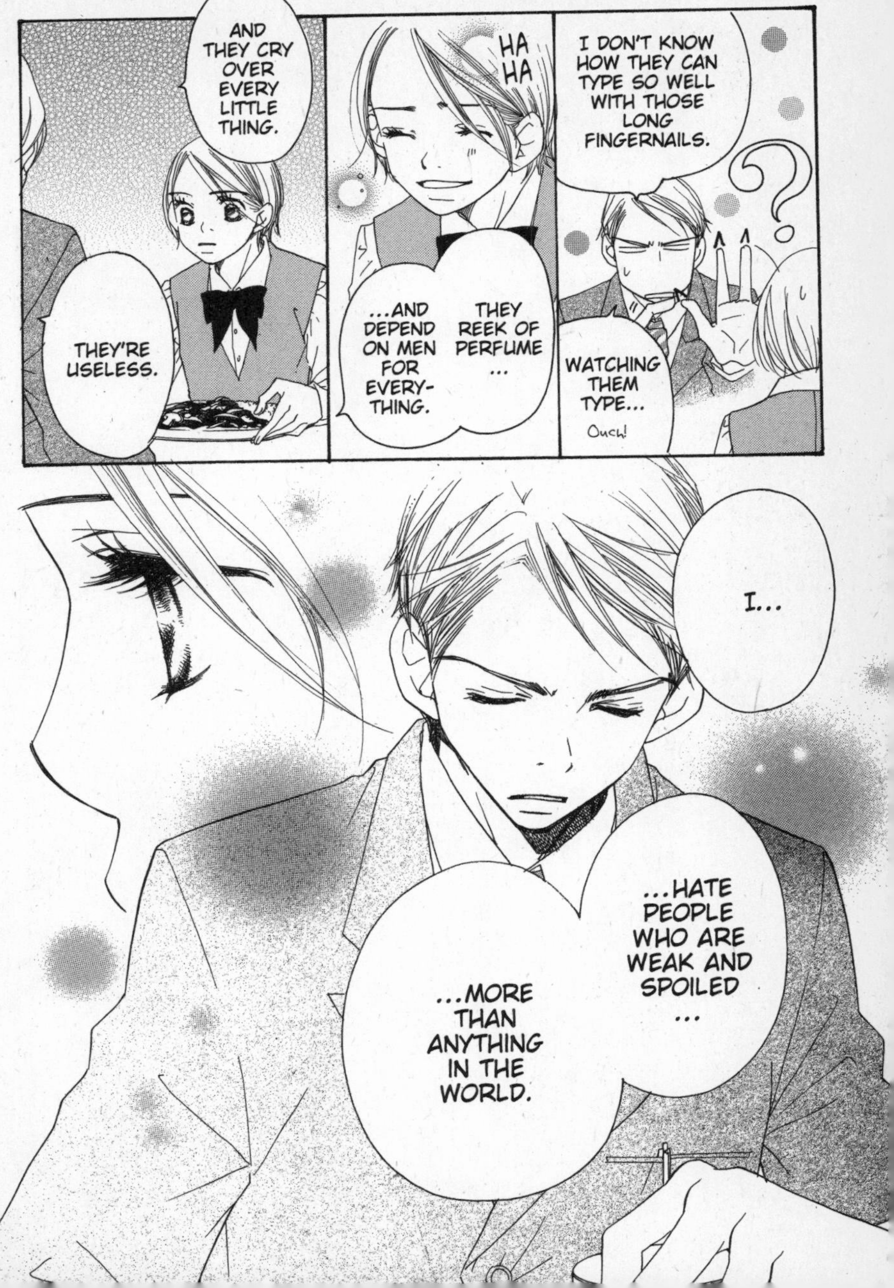
I DON'T KNOW HOW THEY CAN TYPE SO WELL WITH THOSE LONG FINGERNAILS.
WATCHING THEM TYPE...
Ouch!
HA HA
THEY REEK OF PERFUME...
...AND DEPEND ON MEN FOR EVERY-THING.
AND THEY CRY OVER EVERY LITTLE THING.
THEY'RE USELESS.
I...
...HATE PEOPLE WHO ARE WEAK AND SPOILED...
...MORE THAN ANYTHING IN THE WORLD.

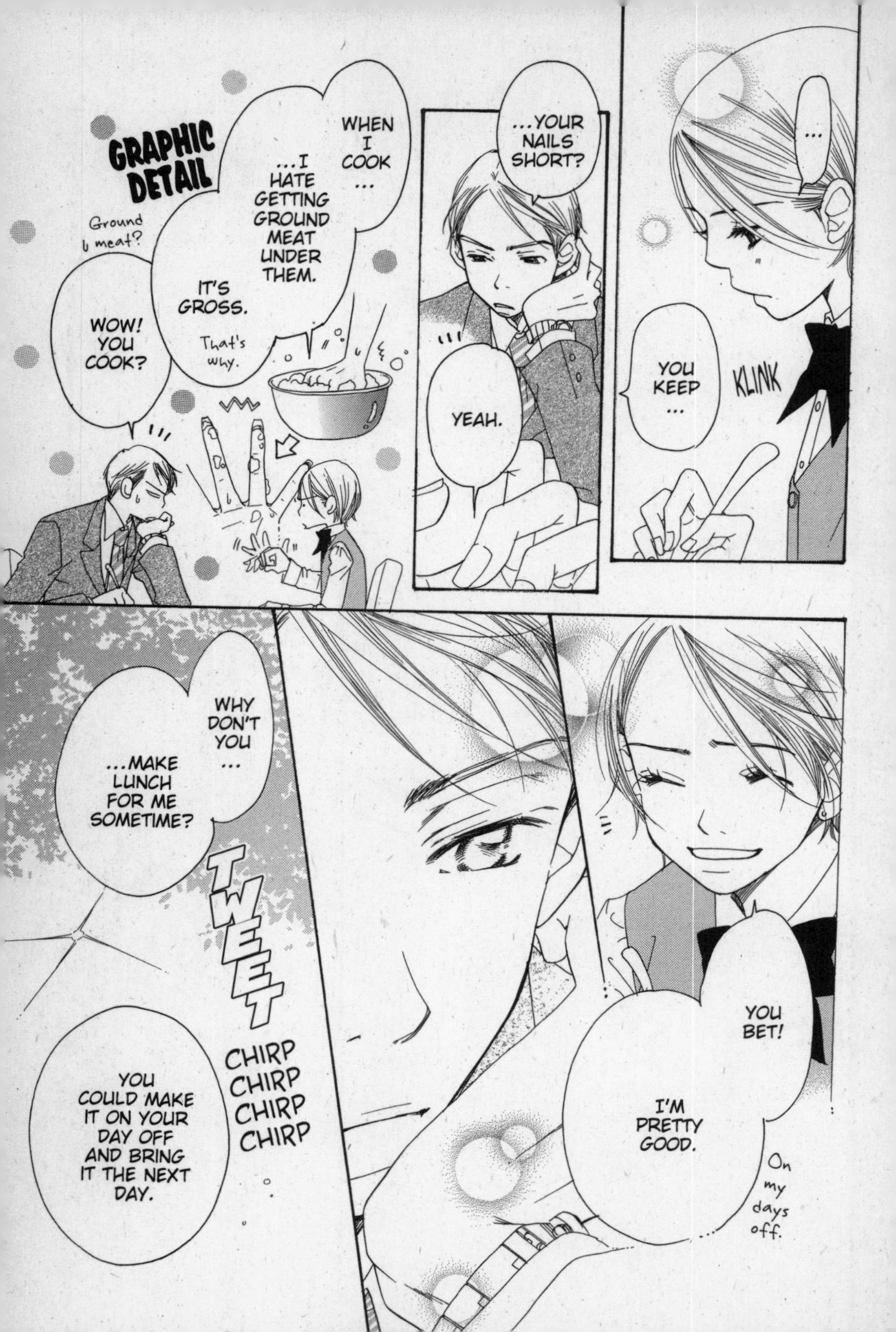
...
YOU KEEP ...
KLINK
...YOUR NAILS SHORT?
YEAH.
WHEN I COOK ...
...I HATE GETTING GROUND MEAT UNDER THEM.
IT'S GROSS.
That's why.
GRAPHIC DETAIL
Ground meat?
WOW! YOU COOK?
YOU BET!
I'M PRETTY GOOD.
On my days off.
WHY DON'T YOU ...
...MAKE LUNCH FOR ME SOMETIME?
TWEET
CHIRP CHIRP CHIRP CHIRP
YOU COULD MAKE IT ON YOUR DAY OFF AND BRING IT THE NEXT DAY.

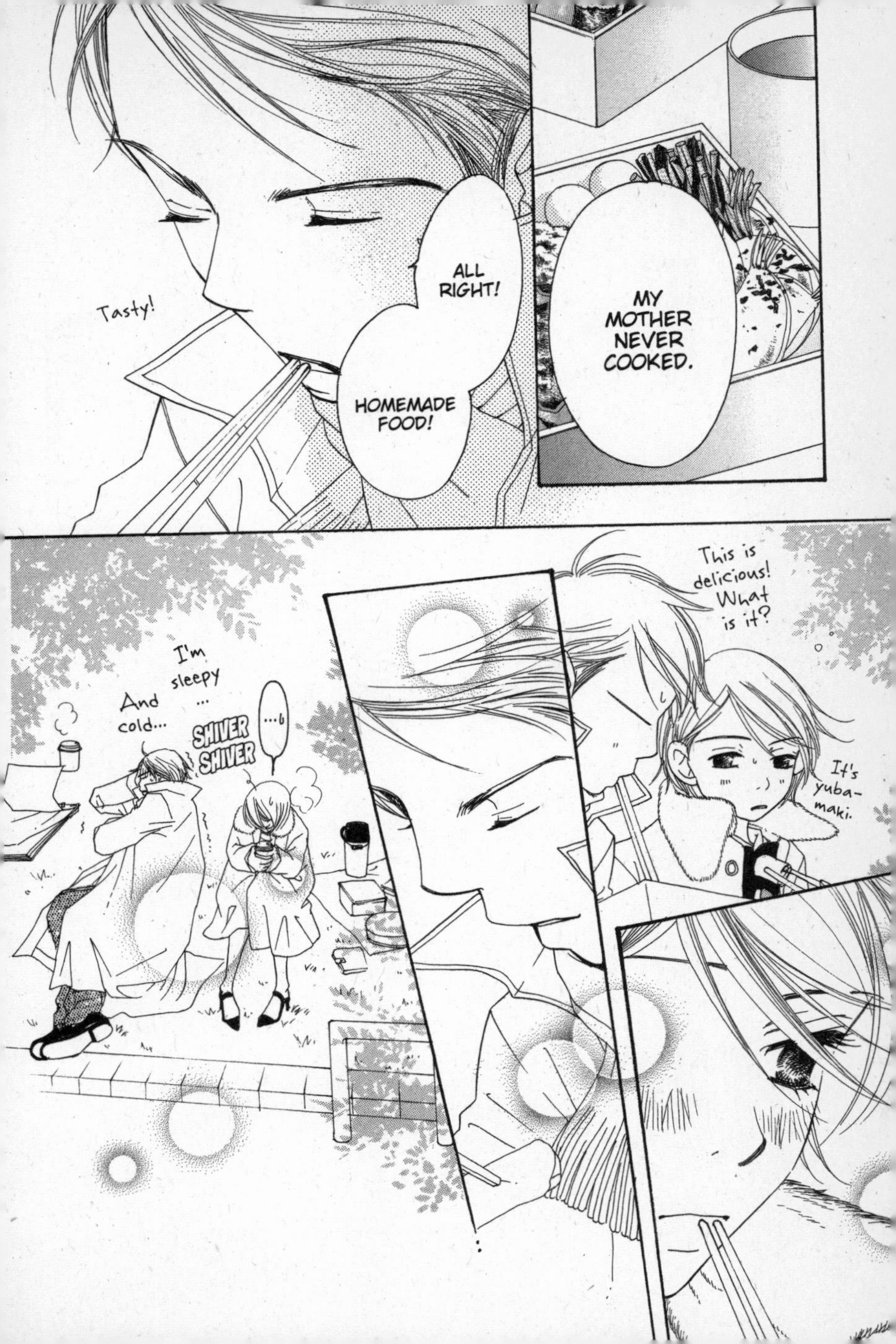
MY MOTHER NEVER COOKED.
ALL RIGHT!
HOMEMADE FOOD!
Tasty!
This is delicious! What is it?
It's yuba-maki.
I'm sleepy ...
And cold...
SHIVER SHIVER
...

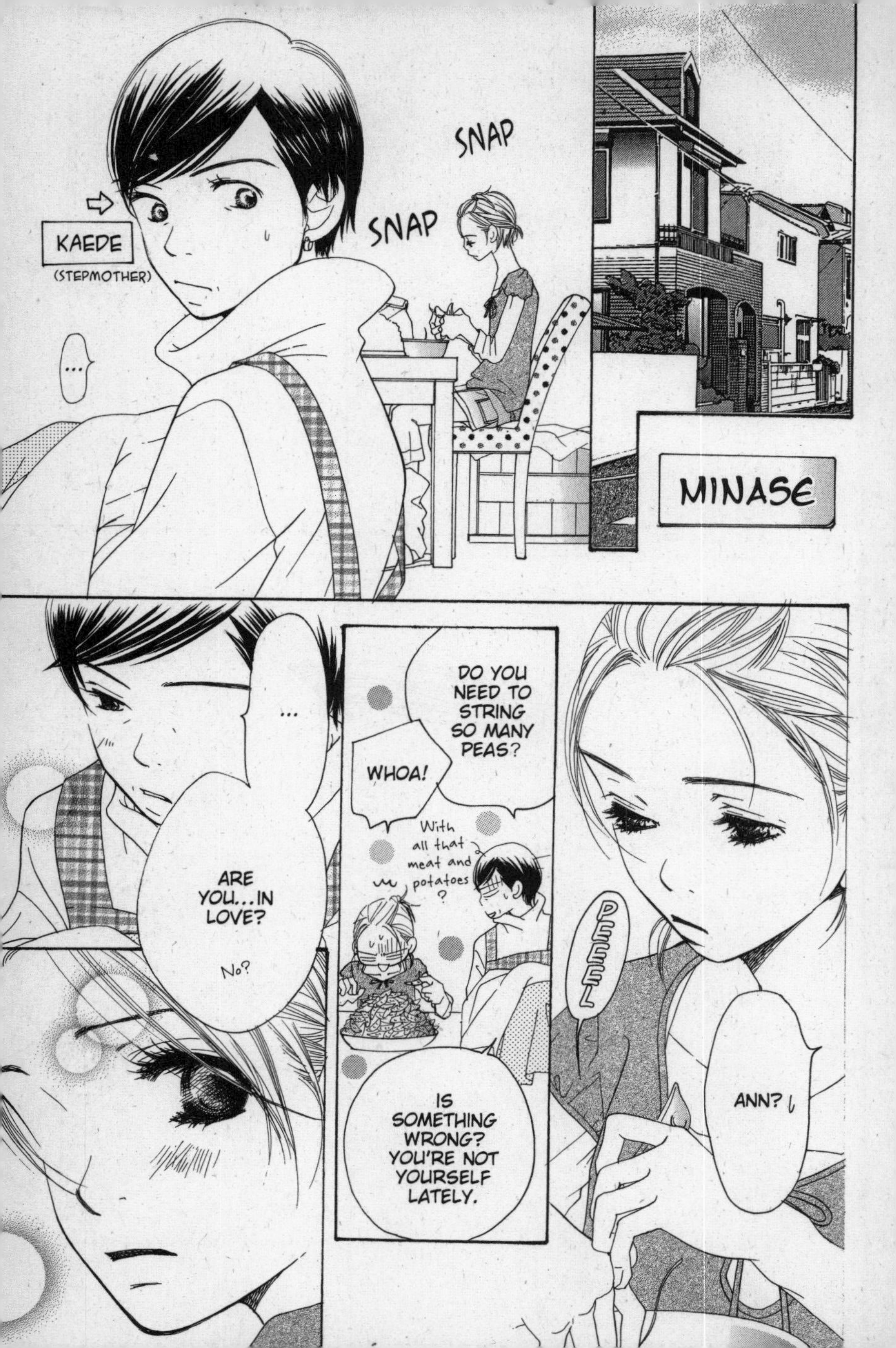
MINASE
SNAP
SNAP
KAEDE
(STEPMOTHER)
...
PEEEL
ANN?
DO YOU NEED TO STRING SO MANY PEAS?
WHOA!
With all that meat and potatoes?
IS SOMETHING WRONG? YOU'RE NOT YOURSELF LATELY.
...
ARE YOU...IN LOVE?
No?

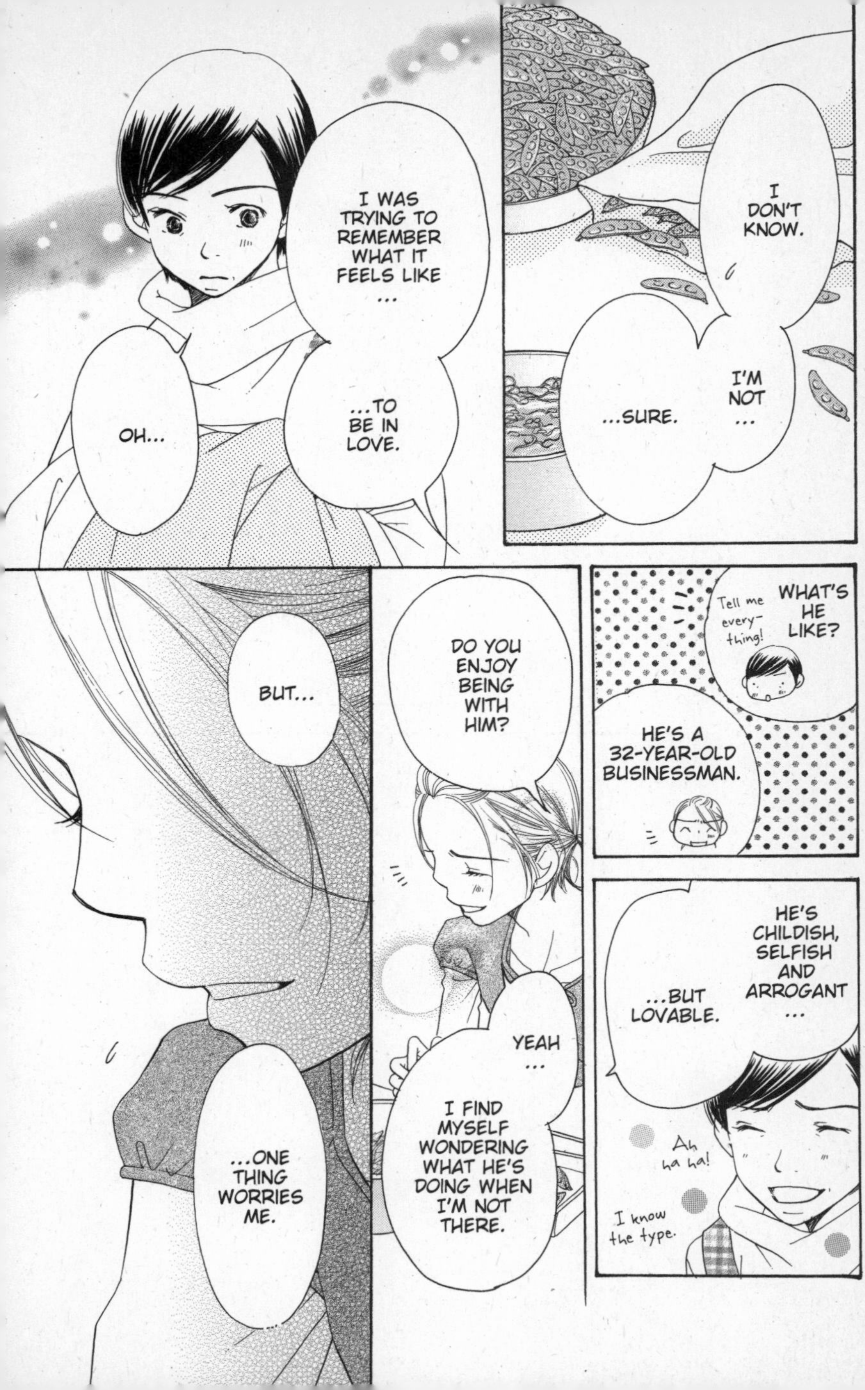
I DON'T KNOW.
I'M NOT...
...SURE.
I WAS TRYING TO REMEMBER WHAT IT FEELS LIKE...
...TO BE IN LOVE.
OH...
WHAT'S HE LIKE?
Tell me every-thing!
HE'S A 32-YEAR-OLD BUSINESSMAN.
HE'S CHILDISH, SELFISH AND ARROGANT...
...BUT LOVABLE.
Ah ha ha!
I know the type.
DO YOU ENJOY BEING WITH HIM?
YEAH...
I FIND MYSELF WONDERING WHAT HE'S DOING WHEN I'M NOT THERE.
BUT...
...ONE THING WORRIES ME.

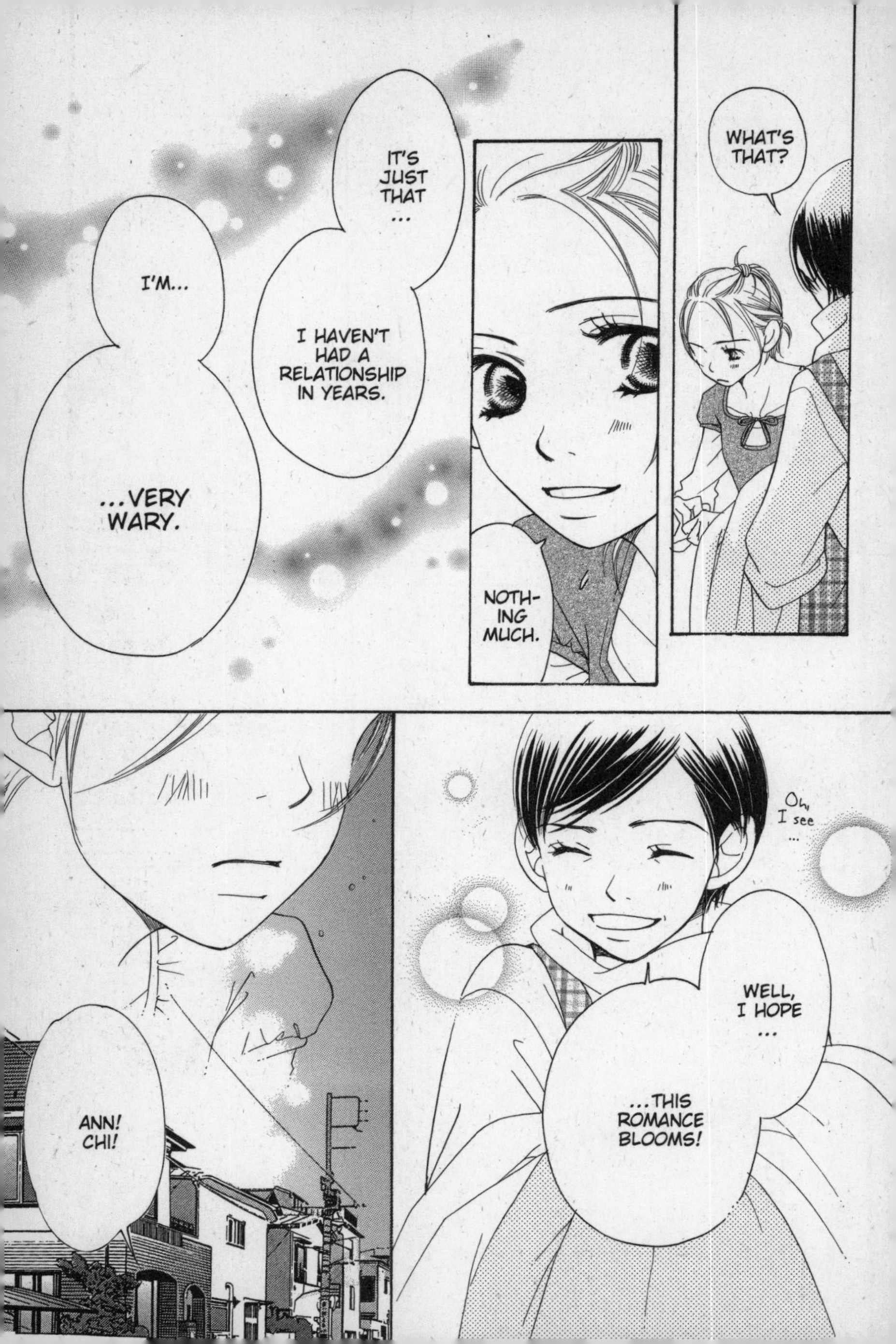
WHAT'S THAT?
NOTH-ING MUCH.
IT'S JUST THAT ...
I HAVEN'T HAD A RELATIONSHIP IN YEARS.
I'M...
...VERY WARY.
Oh, I see ...
WELL, I HOPE ...
...THIS ROMANCE BLOOMS!
ANN! CHI!

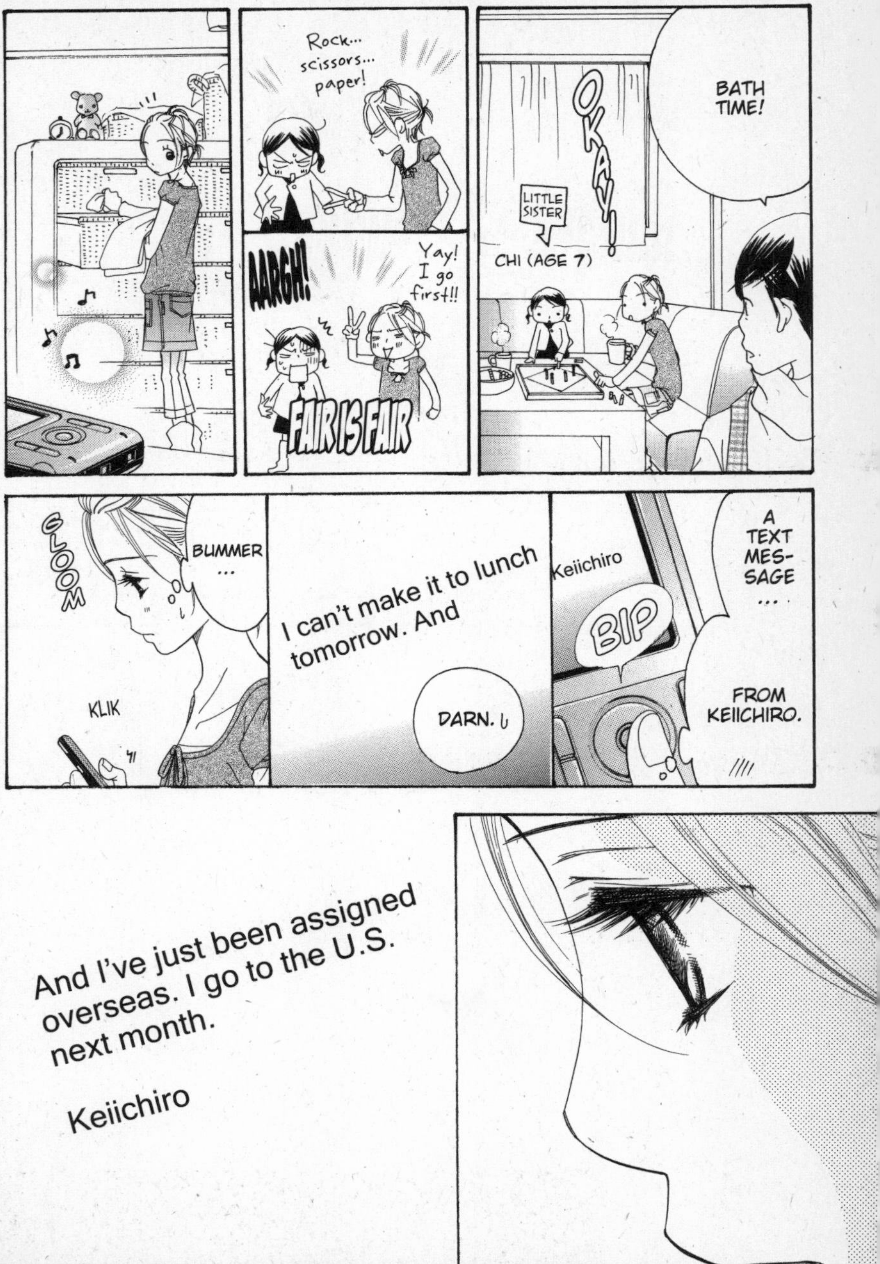
BATH TIME!
OKAY!
LITTLE SISTER
CHI (AGE 7)
Rock... scissors... paper!
Yay! I go first!!
AARGH!
FAIR IS FAIR
A TEXT MES-SAGE ...
FROM KEIICHIRO.
Keiichiro
BIP
I can't make it to lunch tomorrow. And
DARN.
BUMMER ...
GLOOM
KLIK
And I've just been assigned overseas. I go to the U.S. next month.
Keiichiro

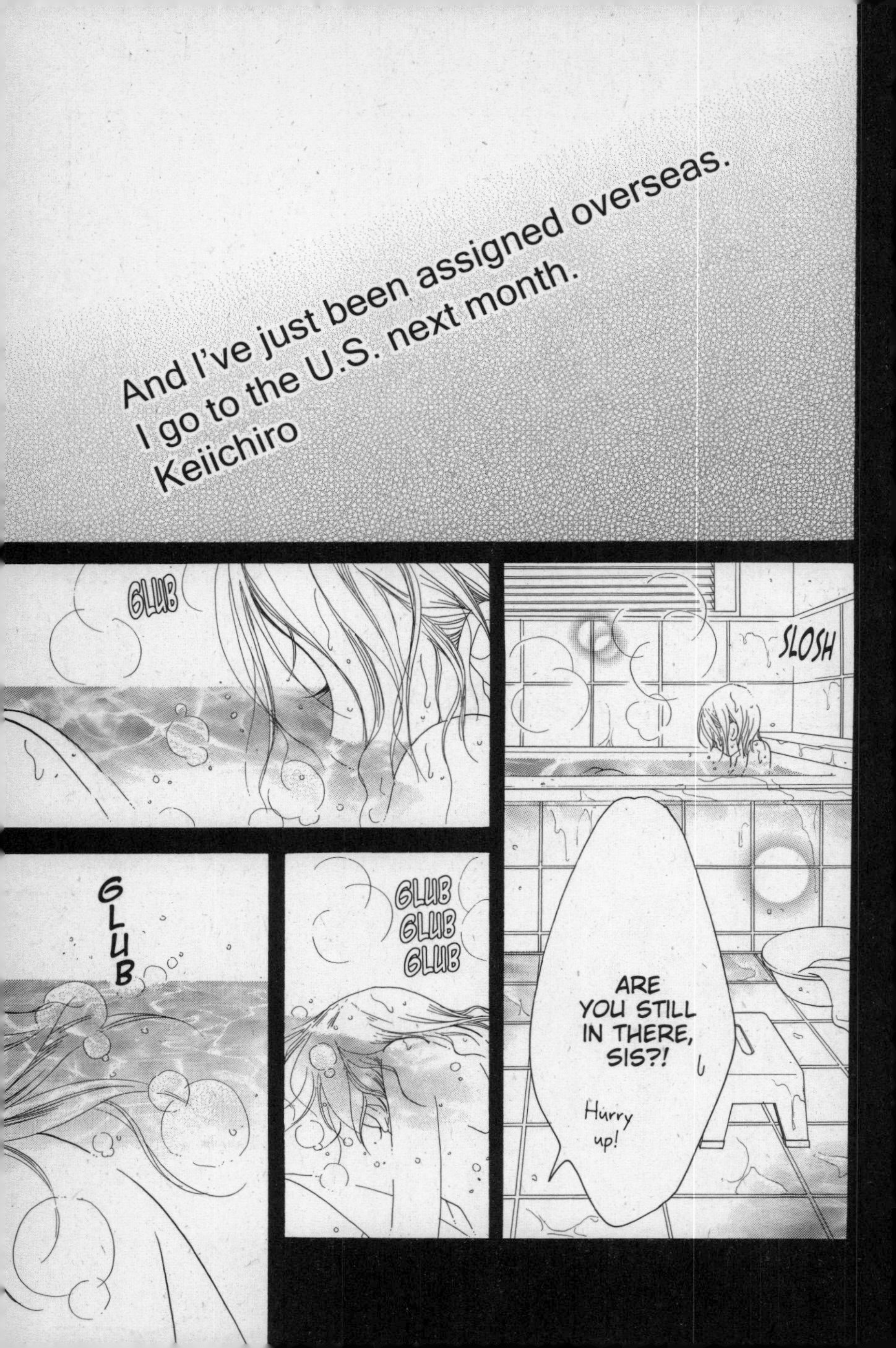
And I've just been assigned overseas.
I go to the U.S. next month.
Keiichiro
SLOSH
ARE YOU STILL IN THERE, SIS?!
Hurry up!
GLUB
GLUB GLUB GLUB
GLUB

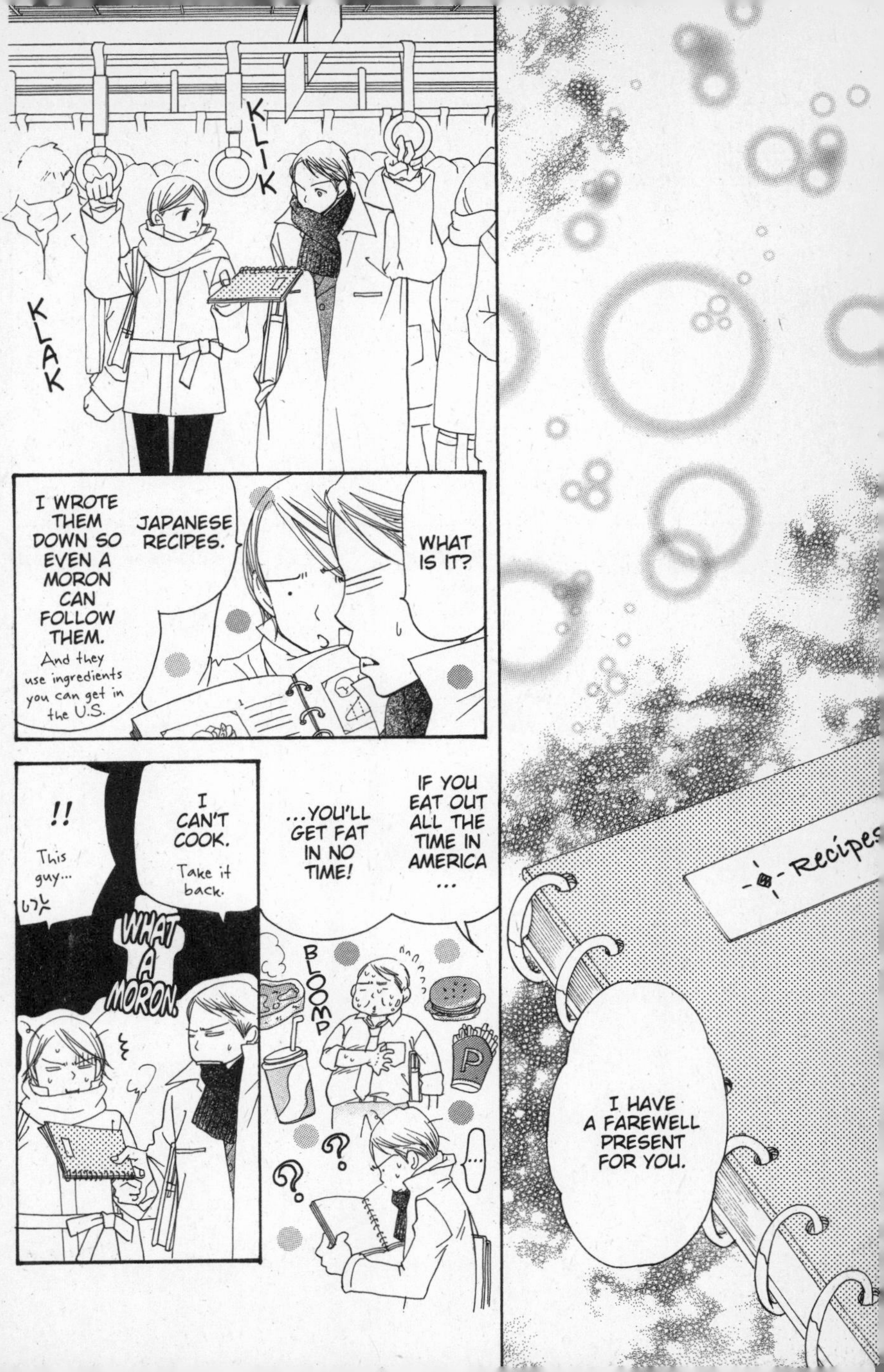
Recipes
I HAVE A FAREWELL PRESENT FOR YOU.
KLIK
KLAK
WHAT IS IT?
JAPANESE RECIPES.
I WROTE THEM DOWN SO EVEN A MORON CAN FOLLOW THEM.
And they use ingredients you can get in the U.S.
IF YOU EAT OUT ALL THE TIME IN AMERICA...
...YOU'LL GET FAT IN NO TIME!
BLOOMP
P
??
...
I CAN'T COOK.
Take it back.
!!
This guy...
WHAT A MORON.

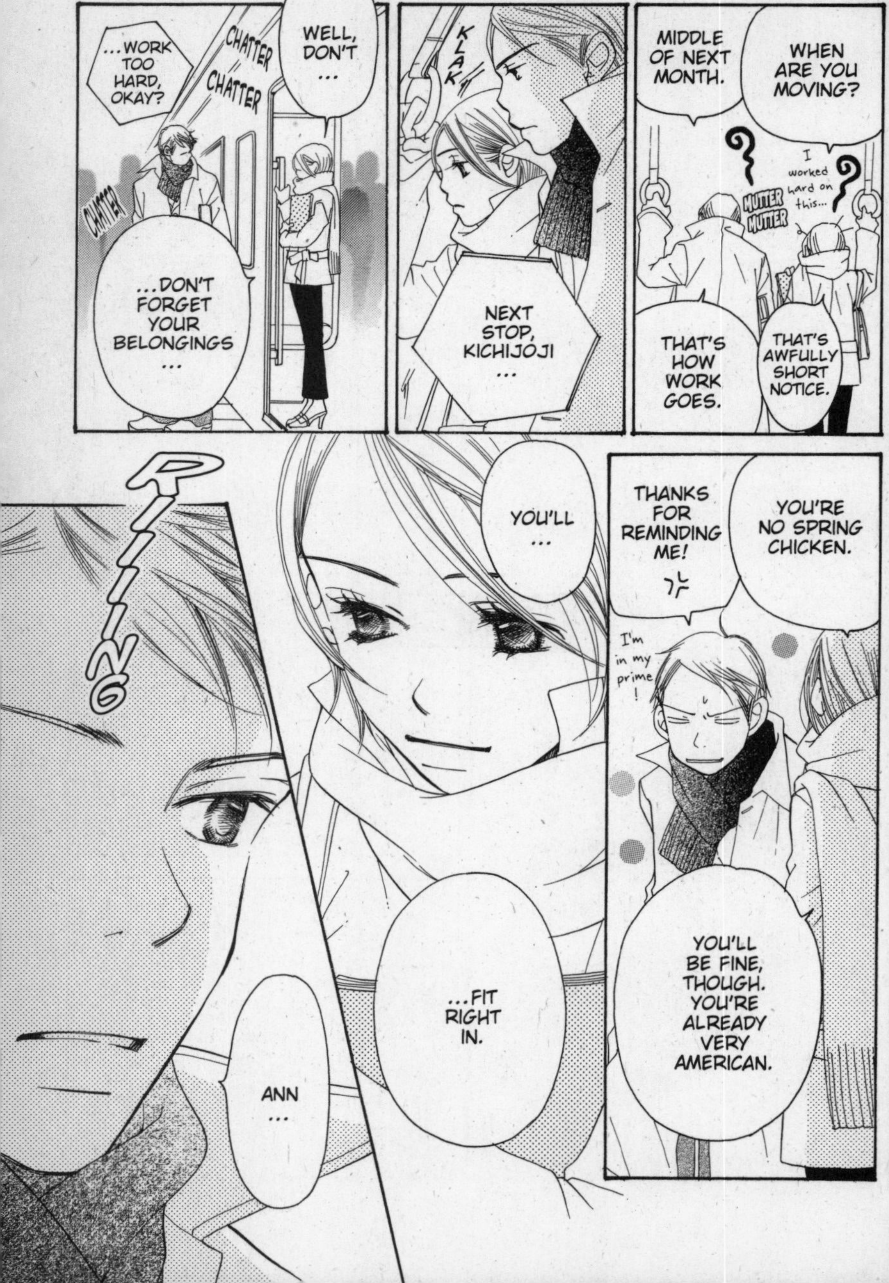
WHEN ARE YOU MOVING?
MIDDLE OF NEXT MONTH.
I worked hard on this...
MUTTER MUTTER
THAT'S AWFULLY SHORT NOTICE.
THAT'S HOW WORK GOES.
KLAK
NEXT STOP, KICHIJOJI ...
WELL, DON'T ...
CHATTER
CHATTER
...WORK TOO HARD, OKAY?
CHATTER
...DON'T FORGET YOUR BELONGINGS ...
YOU'RE NO SPRING CHICKEN.
THANKS FOR REMINDING ME!
I'm in my prime!
YOU'LL BE FINE, THOUGH. YOU'RE ALREADY VERY AMERICAN.
YOU'LL ...
...FIT RIGHT IN.
RIIING
ANN ...

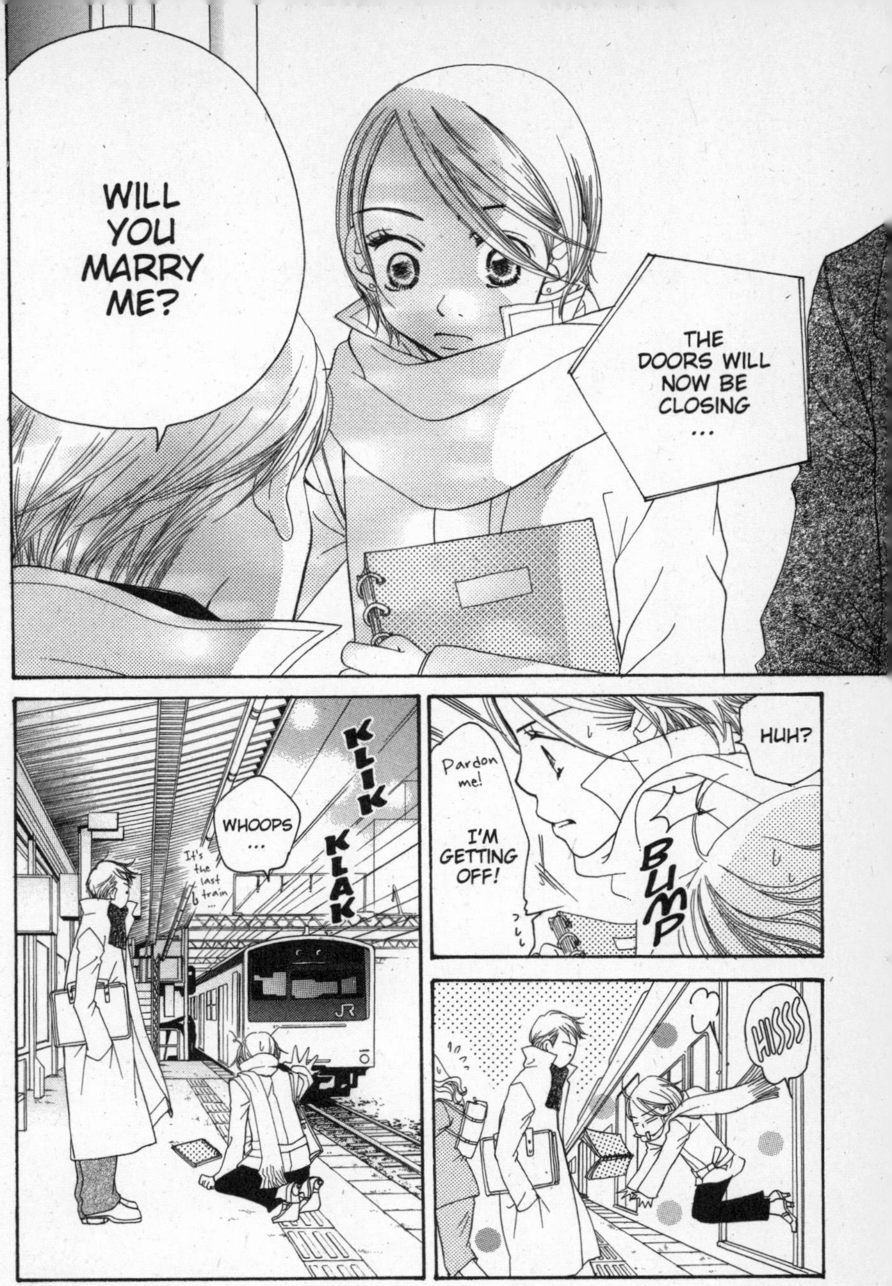
WILL YOU MARRY ME?
THE DOORS WILL NOW BE CLOSING ...
HUH?
BUMP
Pardon me!
I'M GETTING OFF!
HISSSS
KLIK
KLAK
WHOOPS ...
It's the last train ...

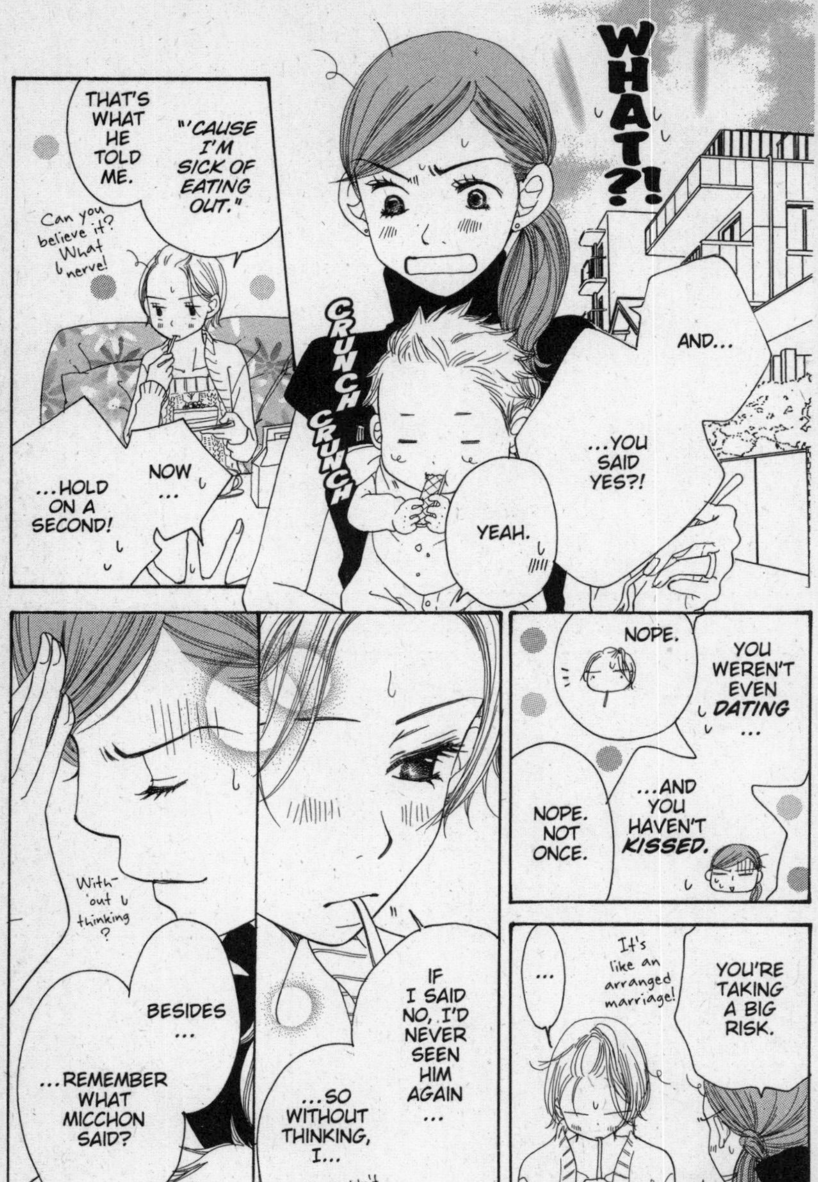
WHAT?!
AND...
...YOU SAID YES?!
YEAH.
CRUNCH CRUNCH
"'CAUSE I'M SICK OF EATING OUT."
THAT'S WHAT HE TOLD ME.
Can you believe it? What nerve!
NOW ...
...HOLD ON A SECOND!
YOU WEREN'T EVEN *DATING* ...
NOPE.
...AND YOU HAVEN'T *KISSED.*
NOPE. NOT ONCE.
YOU'RE TAKING A BIG RISK.
It's like an arranged marriage!
...
IF I SAID NO, I'D NEVER SEEN HIM AGAIN ...
...SO WITHOUT THINKING, I...
It wouldn't work long distance...
With-out thinking?
BESIDES ...
...REMEMBER WHAT MICCHON SAID?

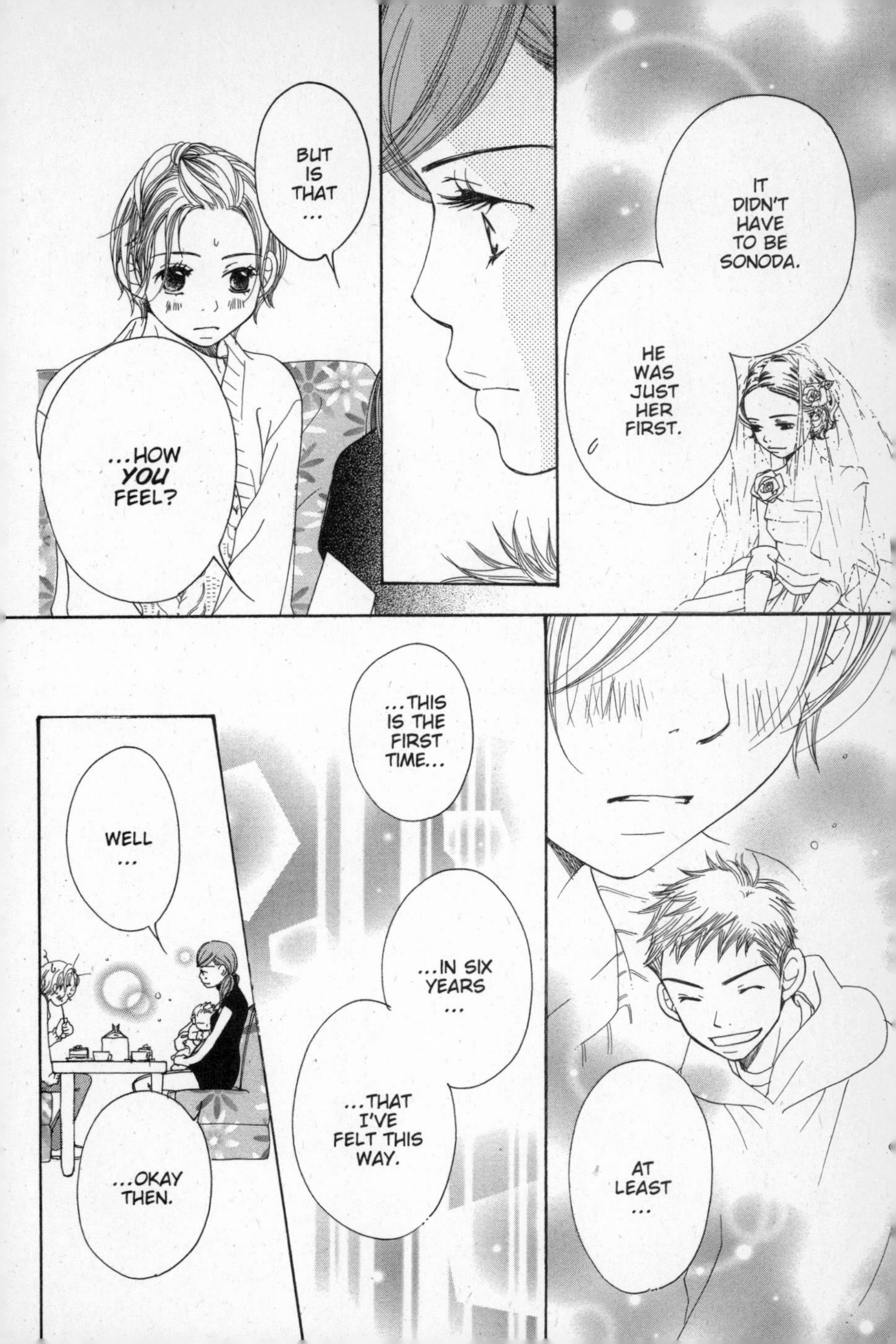
IT DIDN'T HAVE TO BE SONODA.
HE WAS JUST HER FIRST.
BUT IS THAT ...
...HOW *YOU* FEEL?
AT LEAST ...
...THIS IS THE FIRST TIME...
...IN SIX YEARS ...
...THAT I'VE FELT THIS WAY.
WELL ...
...OKAY THEN.

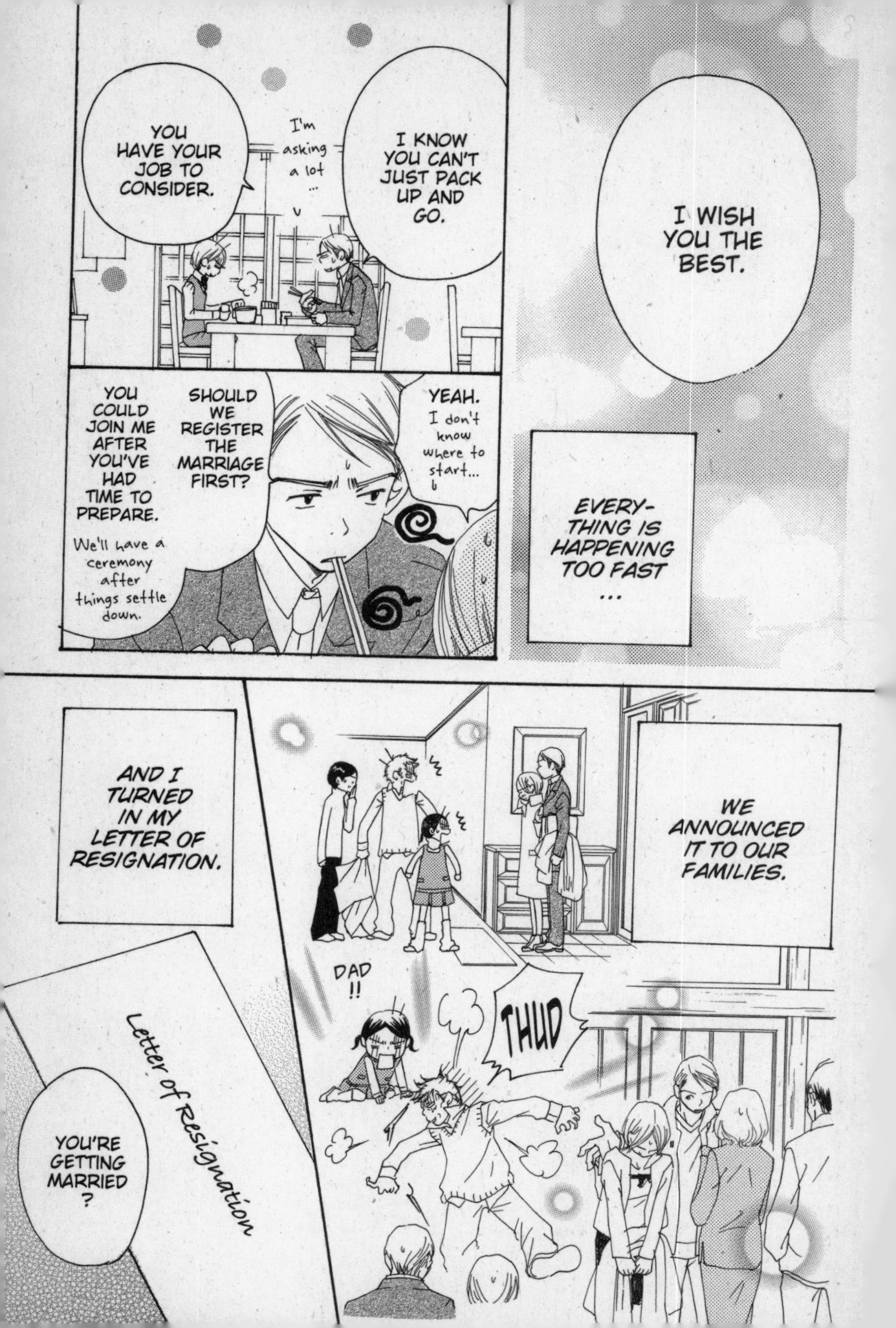
I WISH YOU THE BEST.
EVERY-THING IS HAPPENING TOO FAST ...
I KNOW YOU CAN'T JUST PACK UP AND GO.
I'm asking a lot ...
YOU HAVE YOUR JOB TO CONSIDER.
YEAH.
I don't know where to start...
SHOULD WE REGISTER THE MARRIAGE FIRST?
YOU COULD JOIN ME AFTER YOU'VE HAD TIME TO PREPARE.
We'll have a ceremony after things settle down.
WE ANNOUNCED IT TO OUR FAMILIES.
THUD
DAD !!
AND I TURNED IN MY LETTER OF RESIGNATION.
Letter of Resignation
YOU'RE GETTING MARRIED ?

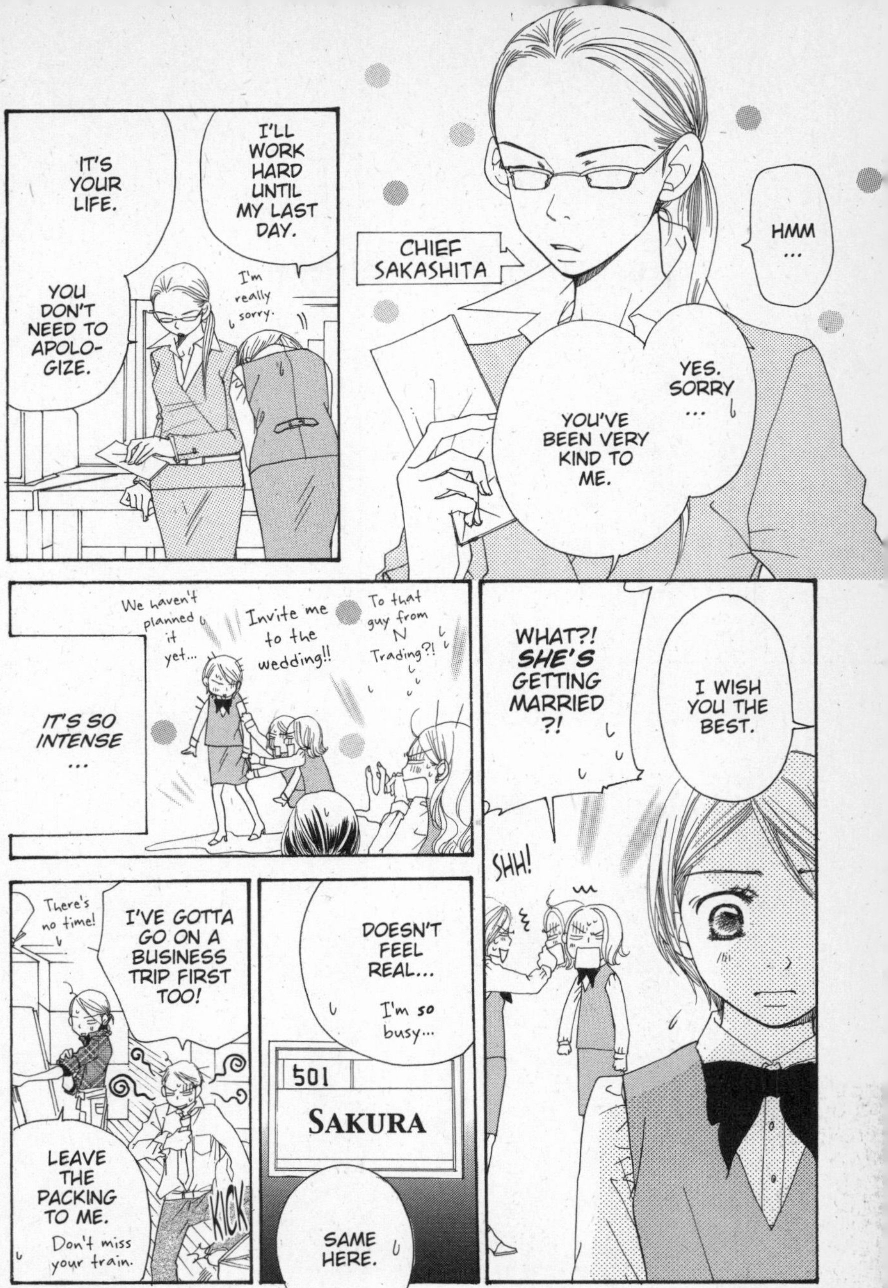
HMM...
CHIEF SAKASHITA
YES. SORRY...
YOU'VE BEEN VERY KIND TO ME.
I'LL WORK HARD UNTIL MY LAST DAY.
IT'S YOUR LIFE.
I'm really sorry.
YOU DON'T NEED TO APOLOGIZE.
I WISH YOU THE BEST.
WHAT?! SHE'S GETTING MARRIED?!
SHH!
To that guy from N Trading?!
Invite me to the wedding!!
We haven't planned it yet...
IT'S SO INTENSE...
DOESN'T FEEL REAL...
I'm so busy...
501
SAKURA
SAME HERE.
I'VE GOTTA GO ON A BUSINESS TRIP FIRST TOO!
There's no time!
LEAVE THE PACKING TO ME.
Don't miss your train.
KICK

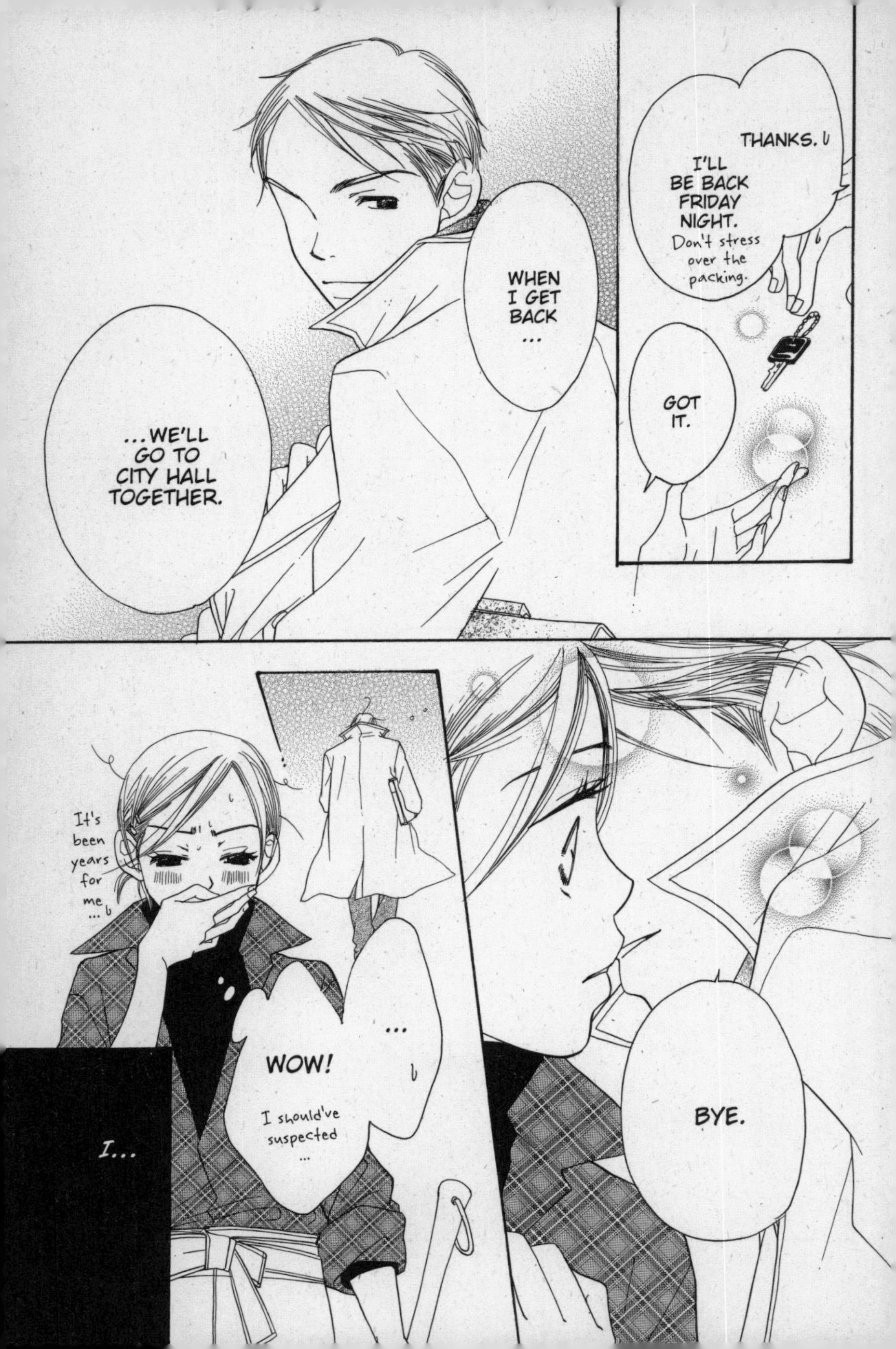
THANKS.
I'LL BE BACK FRIDAY NIGHT.
Don't stress over the packing.
GOT IT.
WHEN I GET BACK ...
...WE'LL GO TO CITY HALL TOGETHER.
BYE.
... WOW!
I should've suspected ...
It's been years for me ...
I...

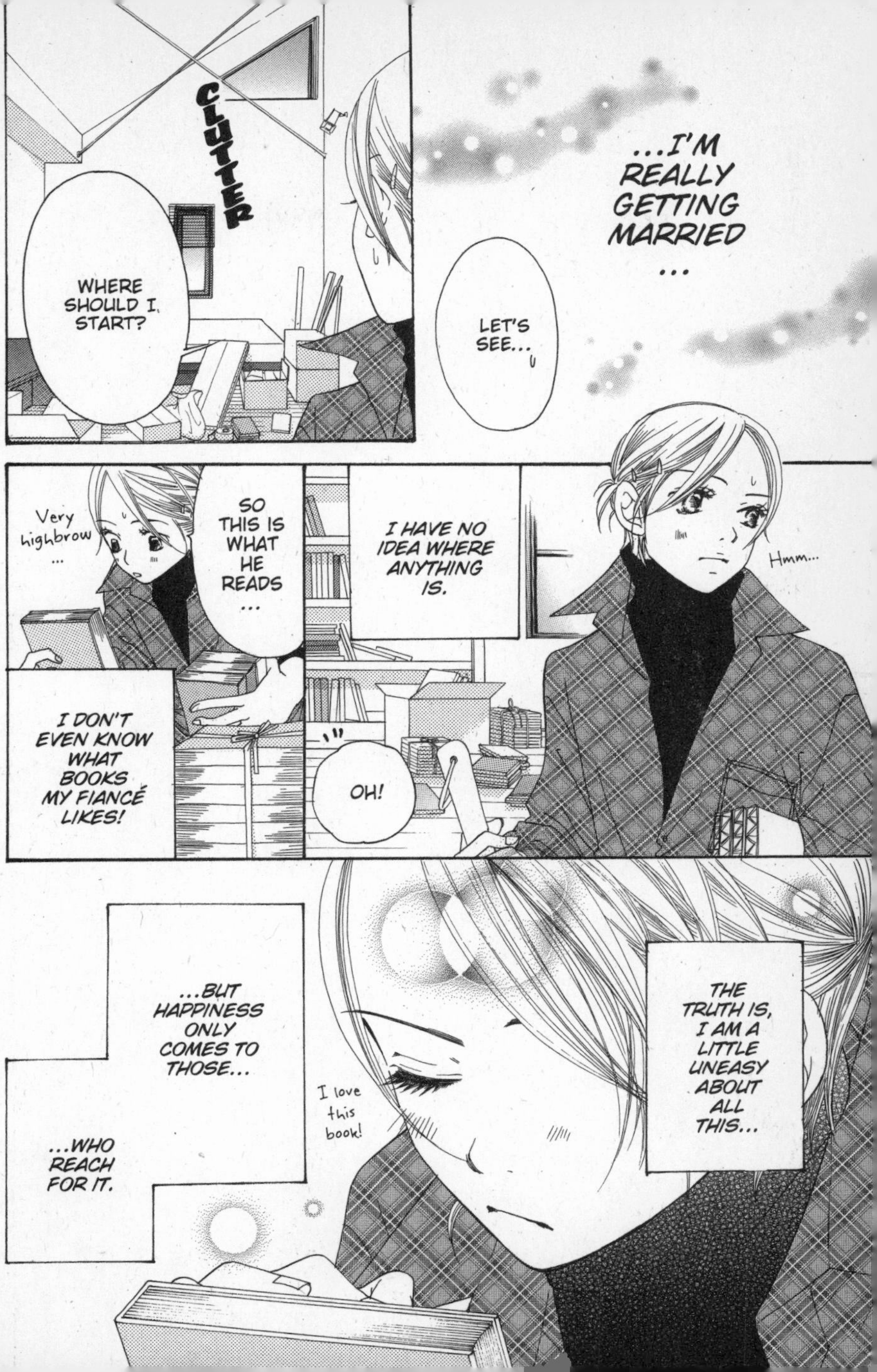
...I'M REALLY GETTING MARRIED...
LET'S SEE...
Hmm...
CLUTTER
WHERE SHOULD I START?
I HAVE NO IDEA WHERE ANYTHING IS.
OH!
SO THIS IS WHAT HE READS...
Very highbrow...
I DON'T EVEN KNOW WHAT BOOKS MY FIANCÉ LIKES!
THE TRUTH IS, I AM A LITTLE UNEASY ABOUT ALL THIS...
I love this book!
...BUT HAPPINESS ONLY COMES TO THOSE...
...WHO REACH FOR IT.

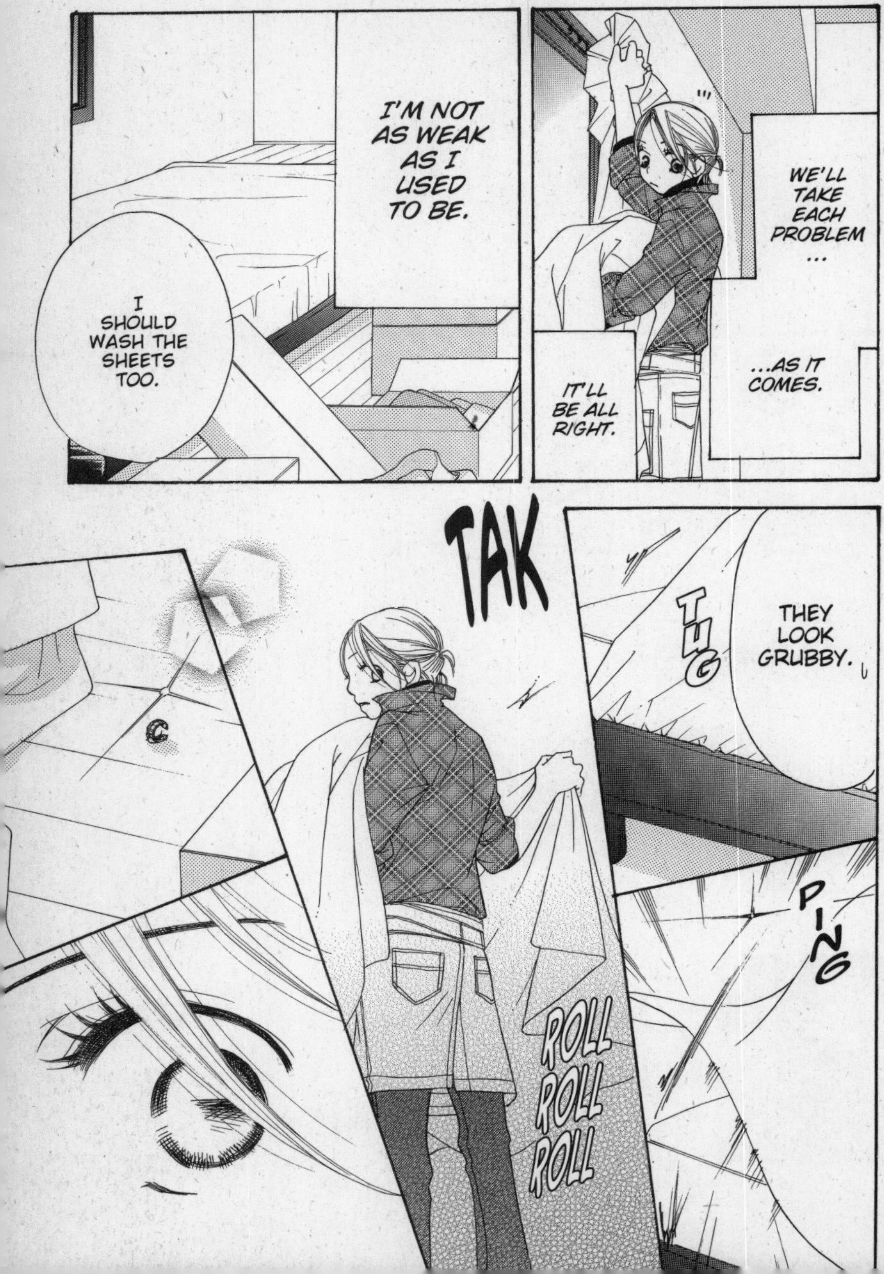
WE'LL TAKE EACH PROBLEM ...
...AS IT COMES.
IT'LL BE ALL RIGHT.
I'M NOT AS WEAK AS I USED TO BE.
I SHOULD WASH THE SHEETS TOO.
TUG
THEY LOOK GRUBBY.
PING
TAK
ROLL ROLL ROLL

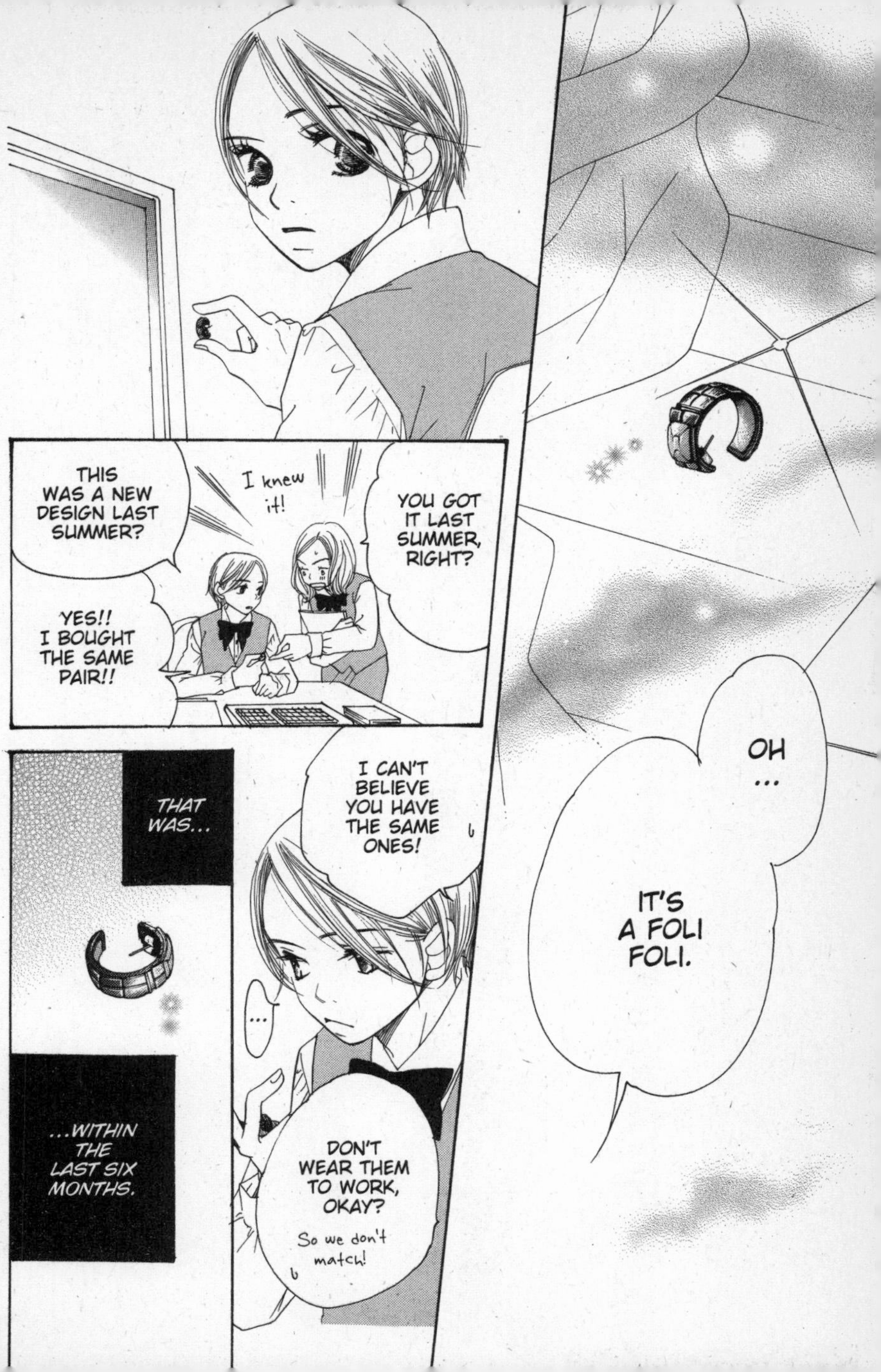
OH ...
IT'S A FOLI FOLI.
YOU GOT IT LAST SUMMER, RIGHT?
I knew it!
THIS WAS A NEW DESIGN LAST SUMMER?
YES!! I BOUGHT THE SAME PAIR!!
I CAN'T BELIEVE YOU HAVE THE SAME ONES!
...
DON'T WEAR THEM TO WORK, OKAY?
So we don't match!
THAT WAS...
...WITHIN THE LAST SIX MONTHS.

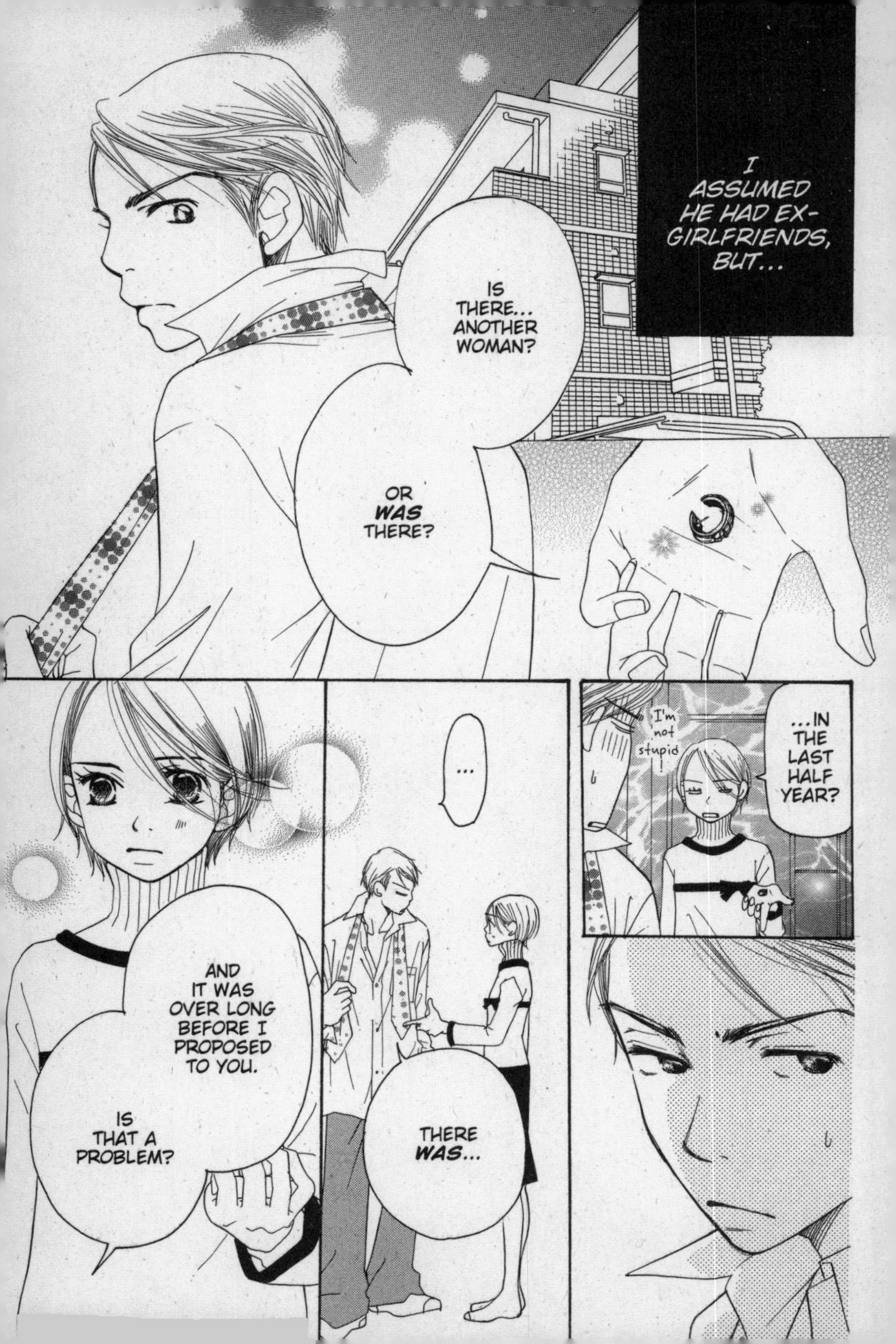
I ASSUMED HE HAD EX-GIRLFRIENDS, BUT...
IS THERE... ANOTHER WOMAN?
OR *WAS* THERE?
...IN THE LAST HALF YEAR?
I'm not stupid!
...
THERE *WAS*...
AND IT WAS OVER LONG BEFORE I PROPOSED TO YOU.
IS THAT A PROBLEM?

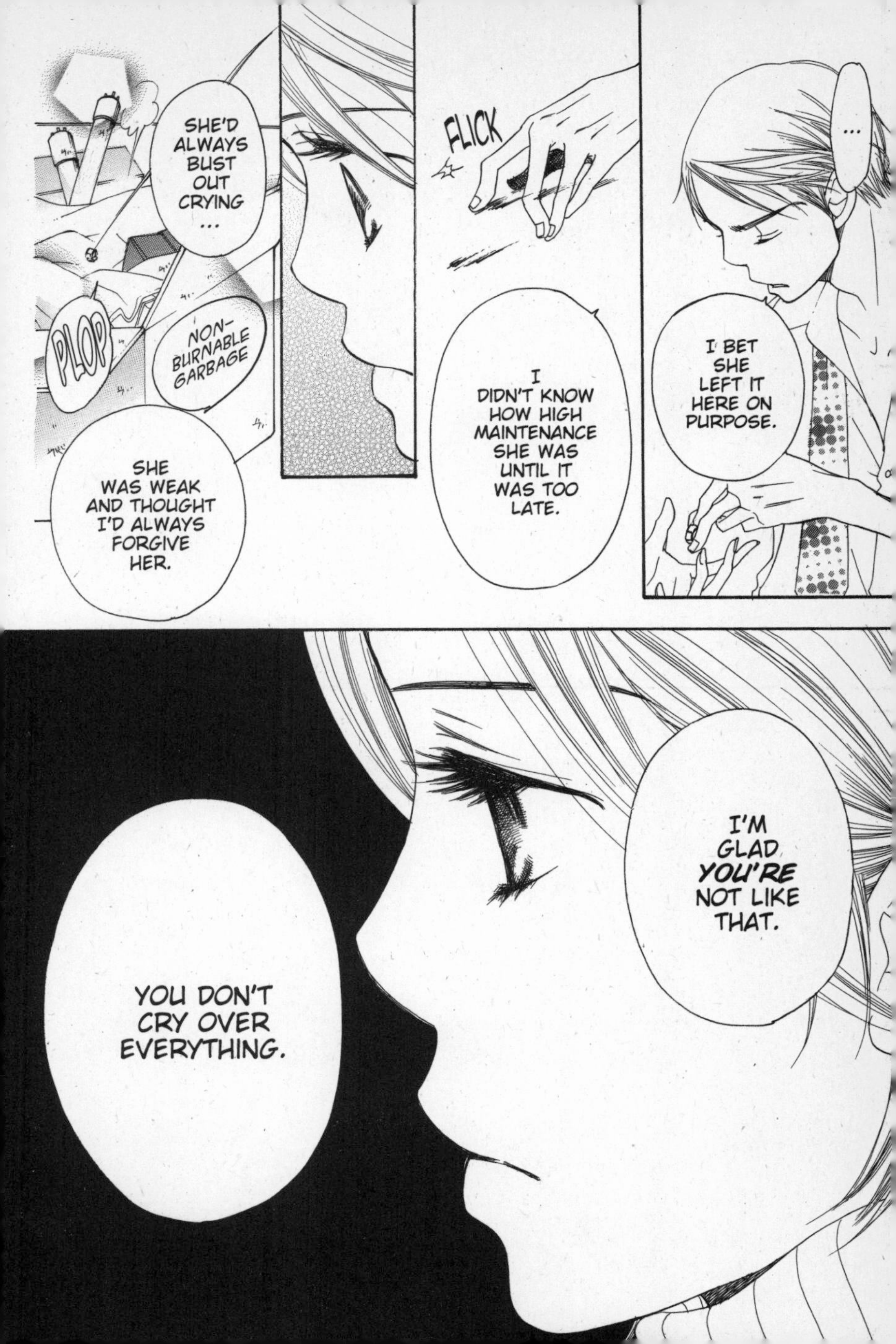
...
I BET SHE LEFT IT HERE ON PURPOSE.
FLICK
I DIDN'T KNOW HOW HIGH MAINTENANCE SHE WAS UNTIL IT WAS TOO LATE.
SHE'D ALWAYS BUST OUT CRYING ...
NON-BURNABLE GARBAGE
PLOP
SHE WAS WEAK AND THOUGHT I'D ALWAYS FORGIVE HER.
I'M GLAD *YOU'RE* NOT LIKE THAT.
YOU DON'T CRY OVER EVERYTHING.

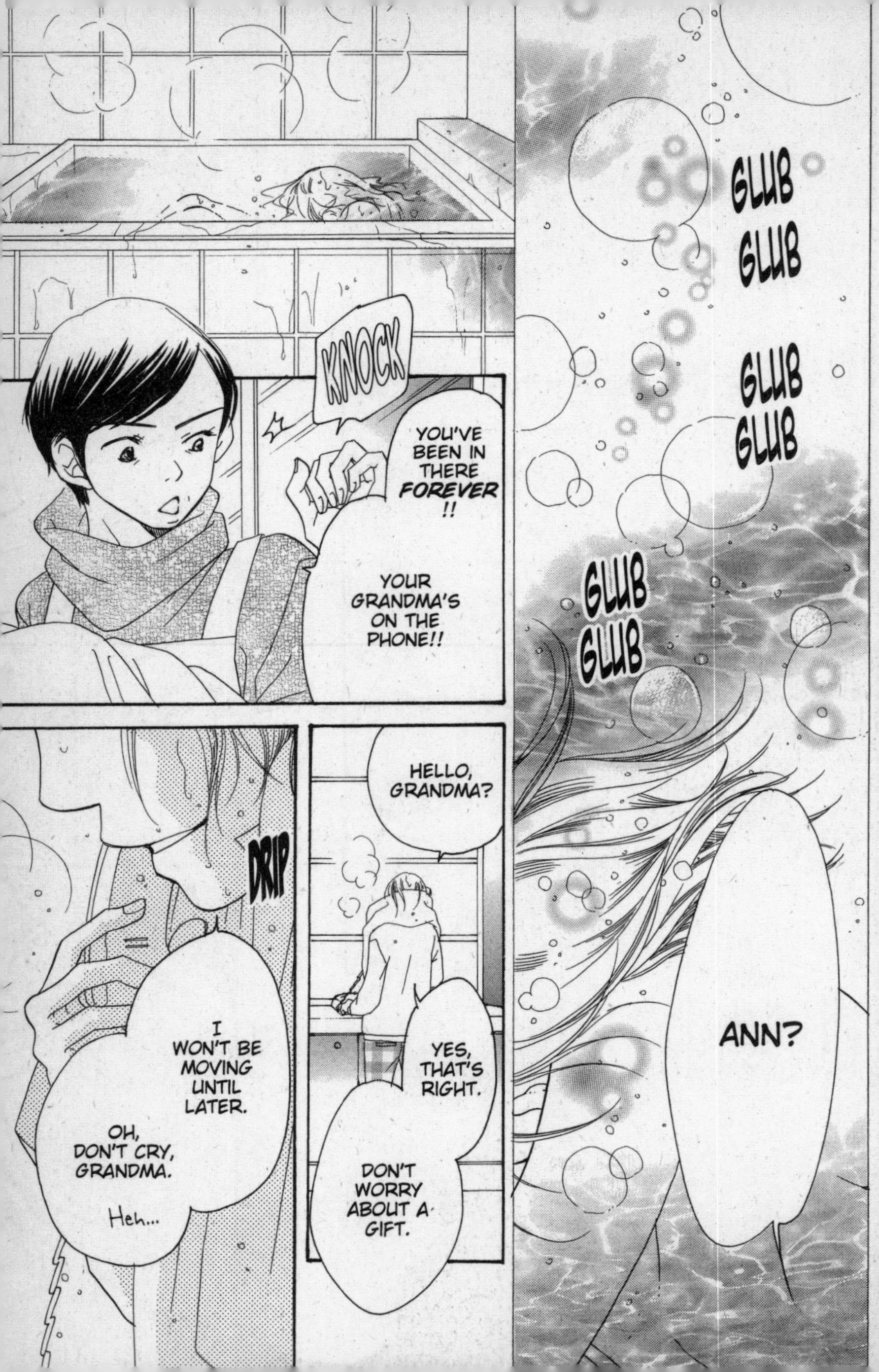
GLUB GLUB
GLUB GLUB
GLUB GLUB
ANN?
KNOCK
YOU'VE BEEN IN THERE *FOREVER*!!
YOUR GRANDMA'S ON THE PHONE!!
HELLO, GRANDMA?
YES, THAT'S RIGHT.
DON'T WORRY ABOUT A GIFT.
DRIP
I WON'T BE MOVING UNTIL LATER.
OH, DON'T CRY, GRANDMA.
Heh...

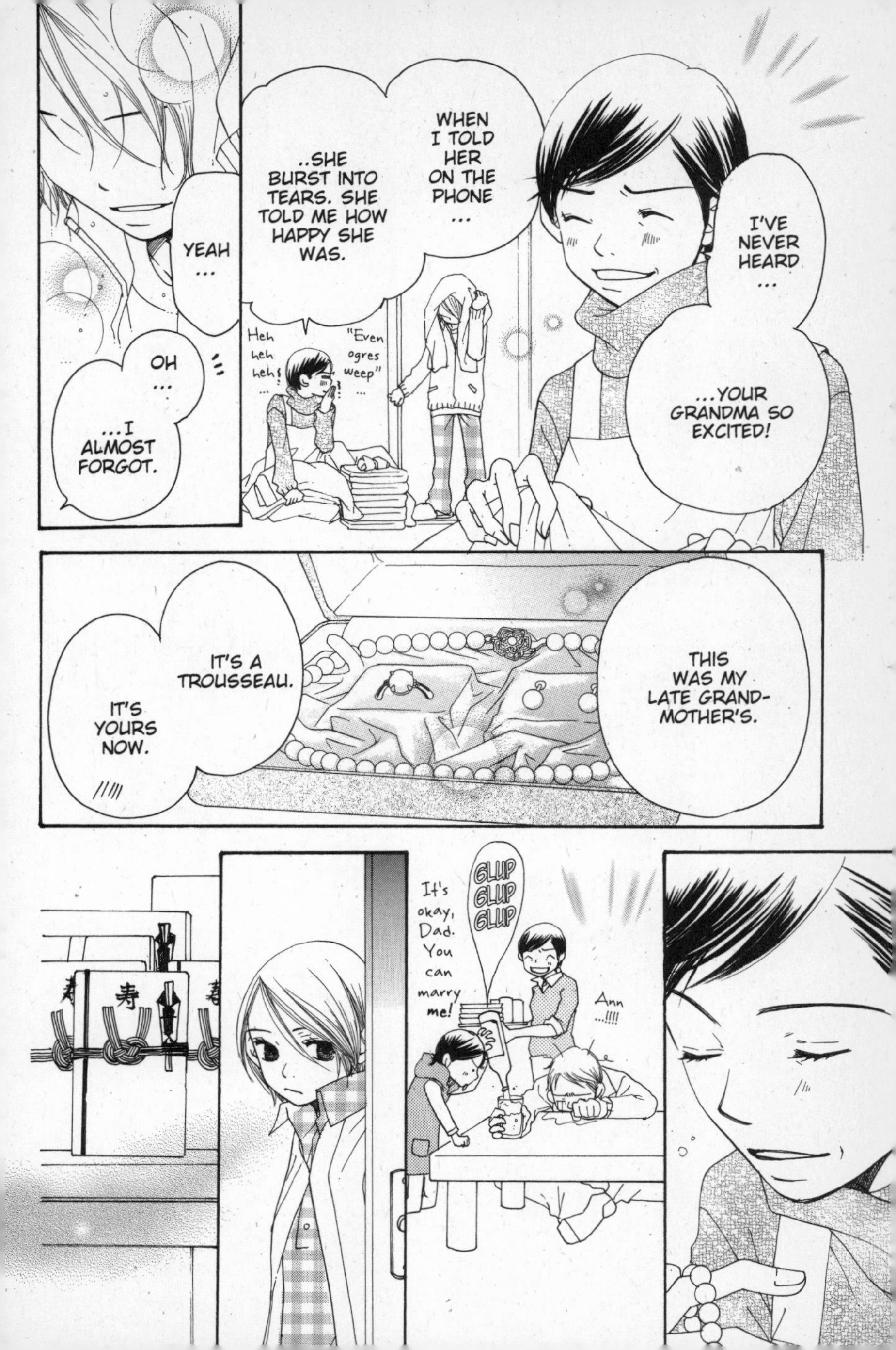
I'VE NEVER HEARD...
...YOUR GRANDMA SO EXCITED!
WHEN I TOLD HER ON THE PHONE...
..SHE BURST INTO TEARS. SHE TOLD ME HOW HAPPY SHE WAS.
"Even ogres weep"...
Heh heh heh...
YEAH...
OH...
...I ALMOST FORGOT.
THIS WAS MY LATE GRANDMOTHER'S.
IT'S A TROUSSEAU.
IT'S YOURS NOW.
Ann...!!!
GLUP GLUP GLUP
It's okay, Dad. You can marry me!
寿
寿

Winter, Age 26:
Evanescent

All of a sudden, Ann is 26! I think that's a difficult age to categorize. It depends on when you start working for a living.

I began working in manga when I was a student. I've always wondered what it would be like to work in an office... It must be nice to have lunch in a fancy place and wear a company cardigan working somewhere like, say, Marunouchi. (Obviously, I watch too many TV dramas.)

Working women always look pretty. Very nice.

The story is speeding toward the end. I hope you'll stick with me all the way!

See you next volume!

Hinako Ashihara

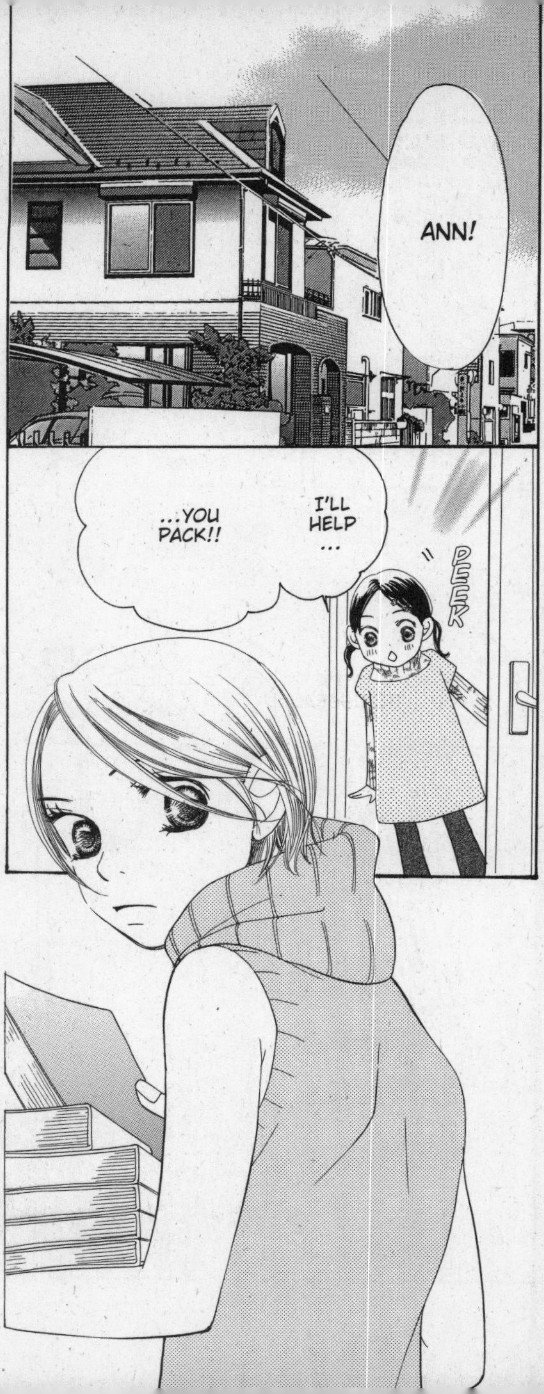
ANN!
I'LL HELP ... ...YOU PACK!!
PEEK

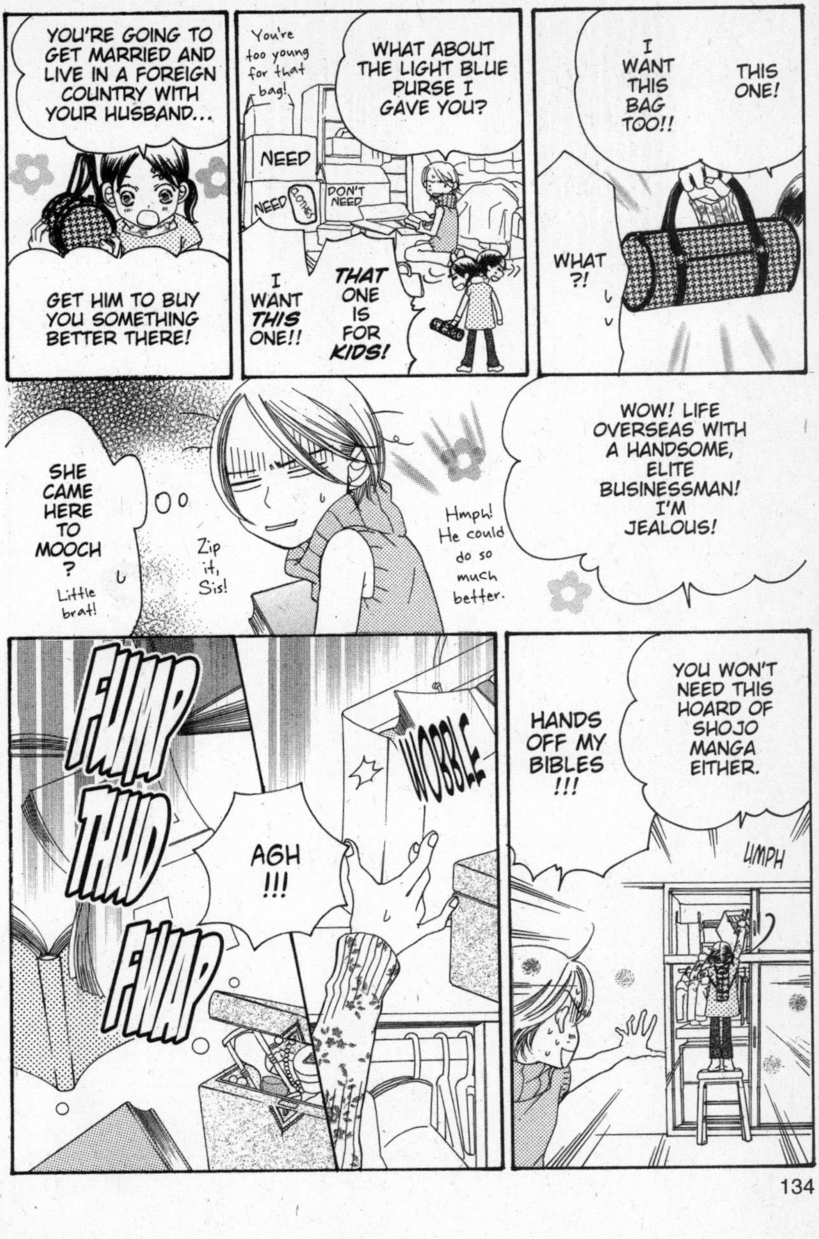
I WANT THIS BAG TOO!!
THIS ONE!
WHAT?!
WHAT ABOUT THE LIGHT BLUE PURSE I GAVE YOU?
You're too young for that bag!
NEED
NEED
CLOTHES
DON'T NEED
THAT ONE IS FOR KIDS!
I WANT THIS ONE!!
YOU'RE GOING TO GET MARRIED AND LIVE IN A FOREIGN COUNTRY WITH YOUR HUSBAND...
GET HIM TO BUY YOU SOMETHING BETTER THERE!
WOW! LIFE OVERSEAS WITH A HANDSOME, ELITE BUSINESSMAN! I'M JEALOUS!
Hmph! He could do so much better.
Zip it, Sis!
SHE CAME HERE TO MOOCH?
Little brat!
YOU WON'T NEED THIS HOARD OF SHOJO MANGA EITHER.
HANDS OFF MY BIBLES!!!
UMPH
WOBBLE
AGH!!!
FWUMP
THUD
FWAP

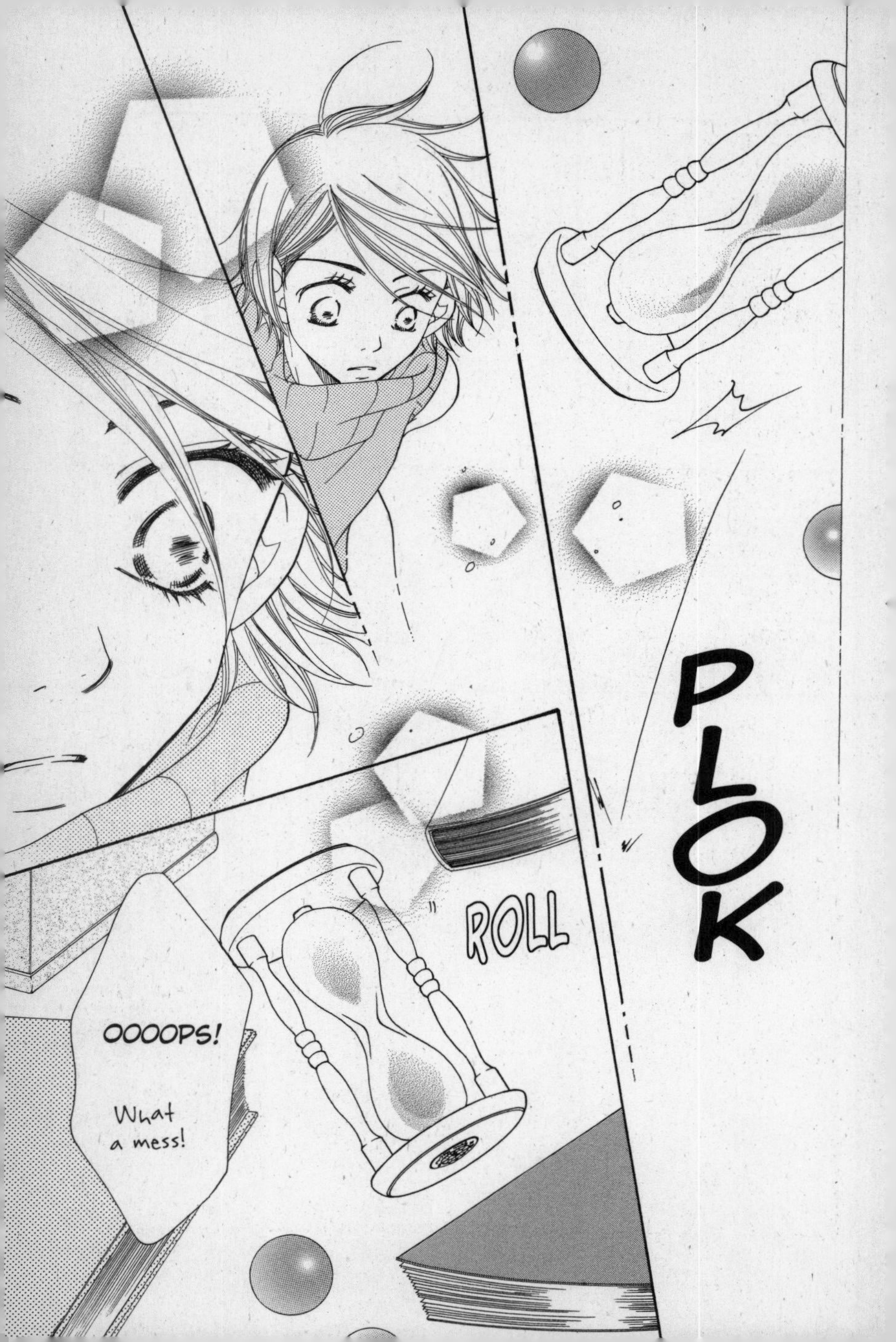
PLOK
ROLL
OOOOPS!
What a mess!

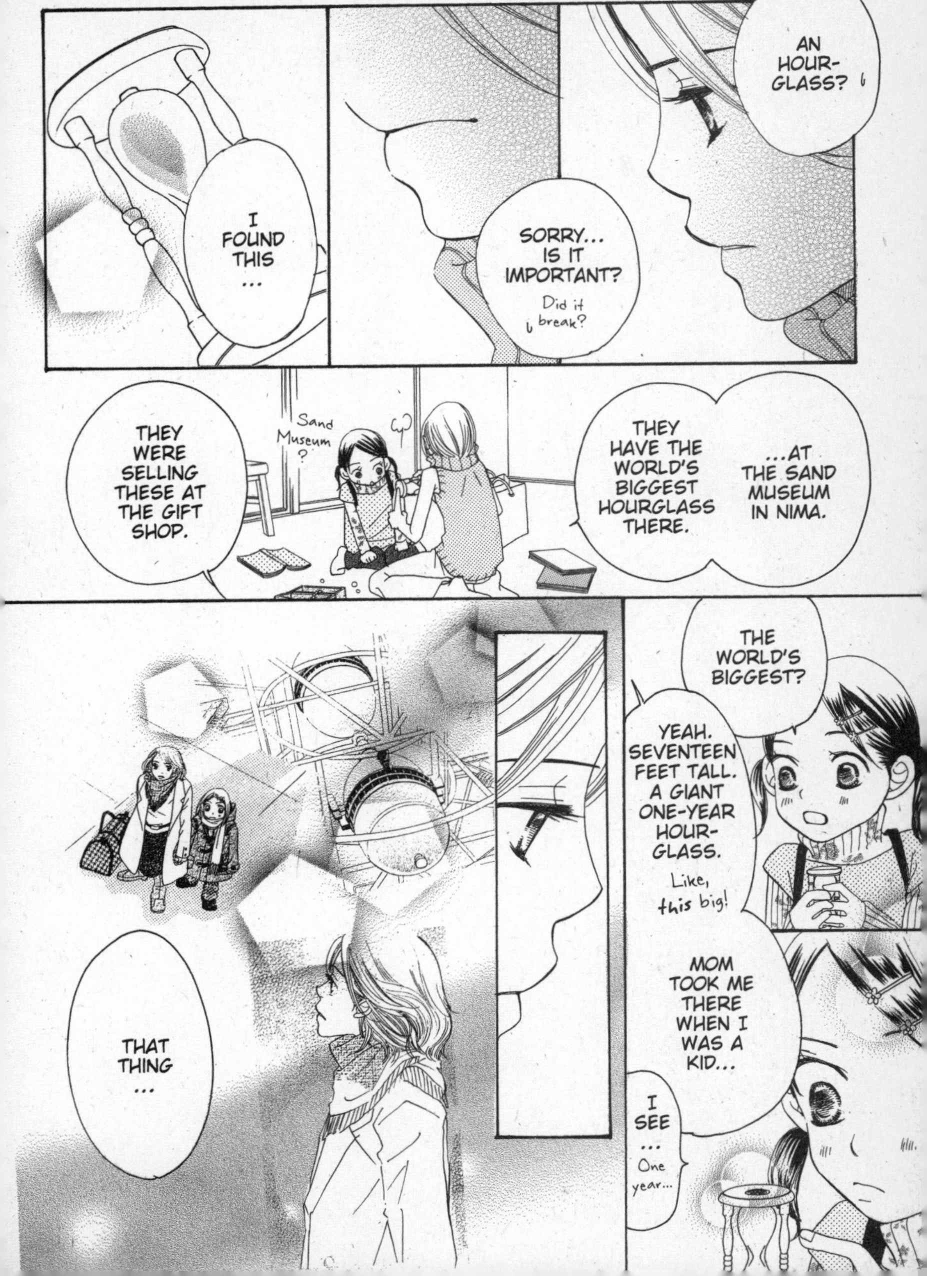
AN HOUR-GLASS?
SORRY... IS IT IMPORTANT?
Did it break?
I FOUND THIS ...
THEY HAVE THE WORLD'S BIGGEST HOURGLASS THERE.
...AT THE SAND MUSEUM IN NIMA.
Sand Museum?
THEY WERE SELLING THESE AT THE GIFT SHOP.
THE WORLD'S BIGGEST?
YEAH. SEVENTEEN FEET TALL. A GIANT ONE-YEAR HOUR-GLASS.
Like, this big!
MOM TOOK ME THERE WHEN I WAS A KID...
I SEE ...
One year...
THAT THING ...

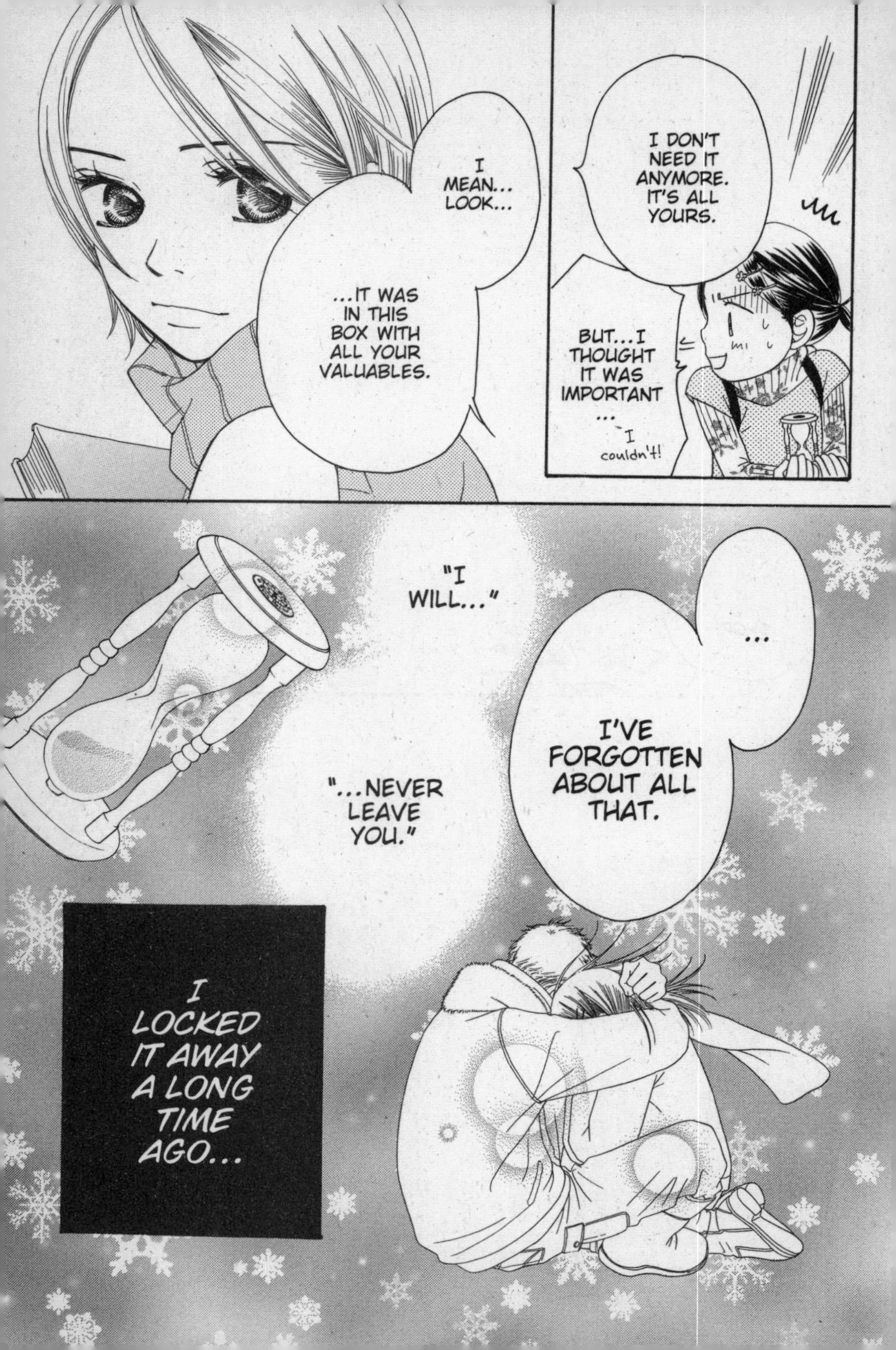
I DON'T NEED IT ANYMORE. IT'S ALL YOURS.
BUT...I THOUGHT IT WAS IMPORTANT...
I couldn't!
I MEAN... LOOK...
...IT WAS IN THIS BOX WITH ALL YOUR VALUABLES.
...
I'VE FORGOTTEN ABOUT ALL THAT.
"I WILL..."
"...NEVER LEAVE YOU."
I LOCKED IT AWAY A LONG TIME AGO...

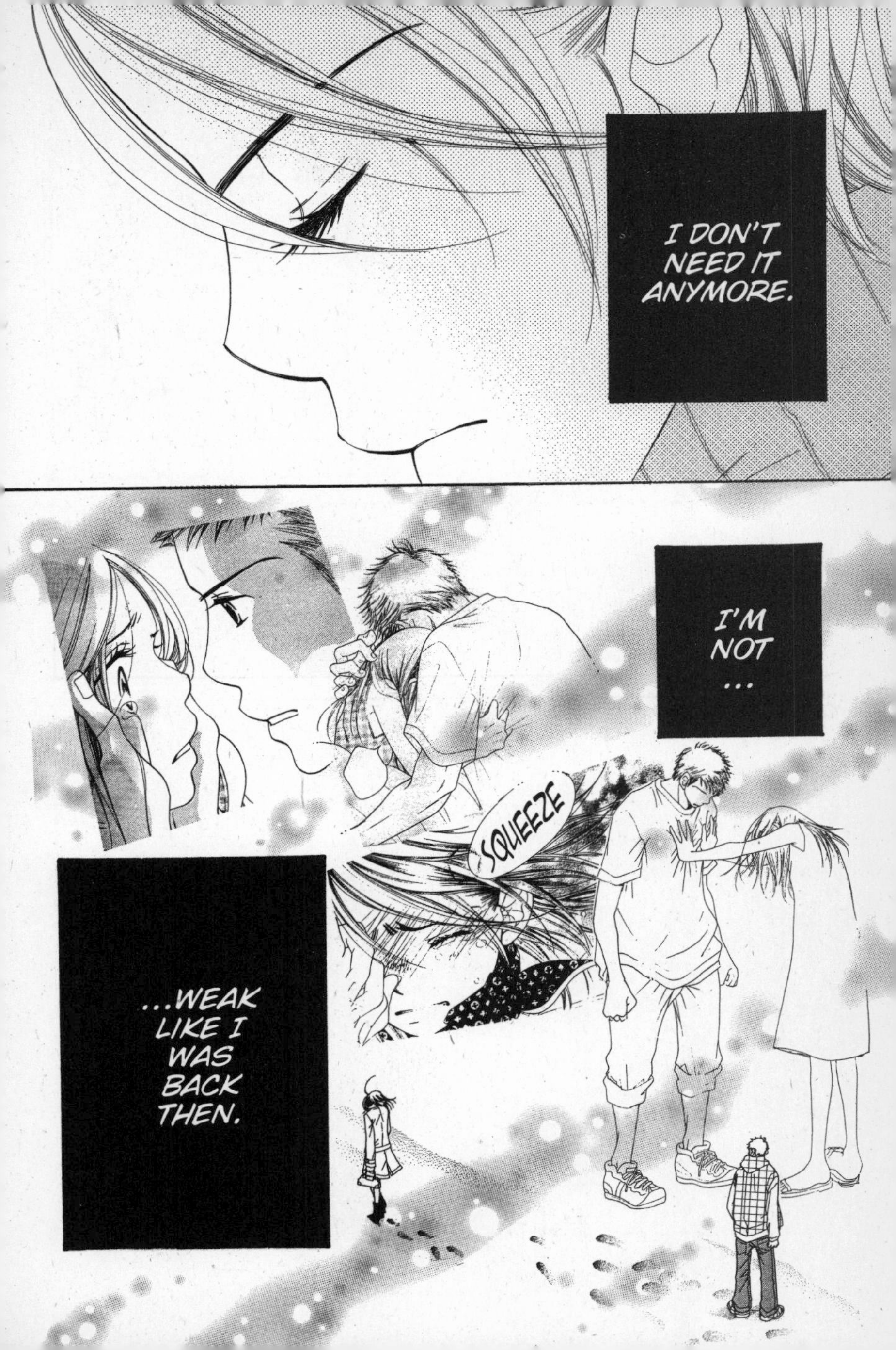
I DON'T NEED IT ANYMORE.
I'M NOT ...
SQUEEZE
...WEAK LIKE I WAS BACK THEN.

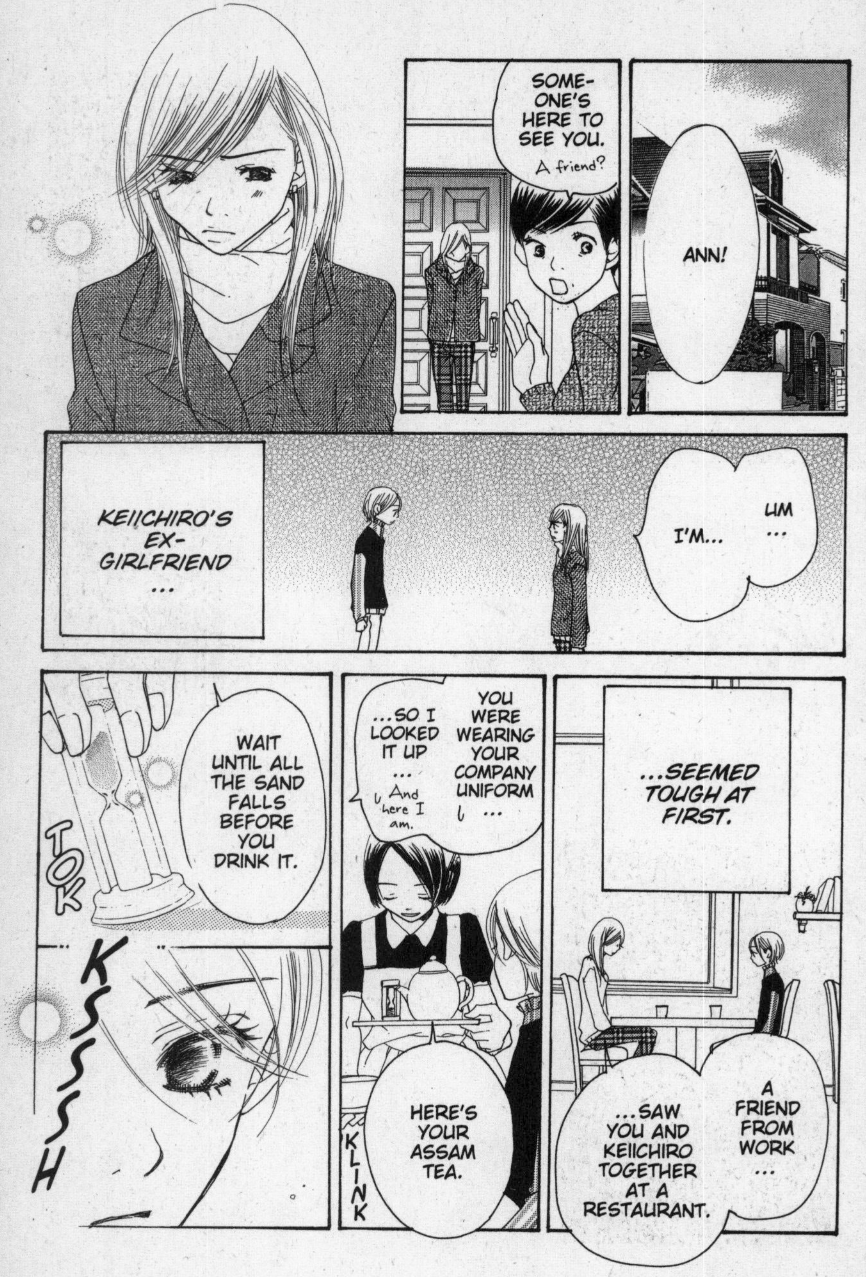
ANN!
SOME-ONE'S HERE TO SEE YOU.
A friend?
UM ... I'M...
KEIICHIRO'S EX-GIRLFRIEND ...
...SEEMED TOUGH AT FIRST.
A FRIEND FROM WORK ...
...SAW YOU AND KEIICHIRO TOGETHER AT A RESTAURANT.
YOU WERE WEARING YOUR COMPANY UNIFORM ...
...SO I LOOKED IT UP ...
And here I am.
HERE'S YOUR ASSAM TEA.
KLINK
WAIT UNTIL ALL THE SAND FALLS BEFORE YOU DRINK IT.
TOK
KSSSSH

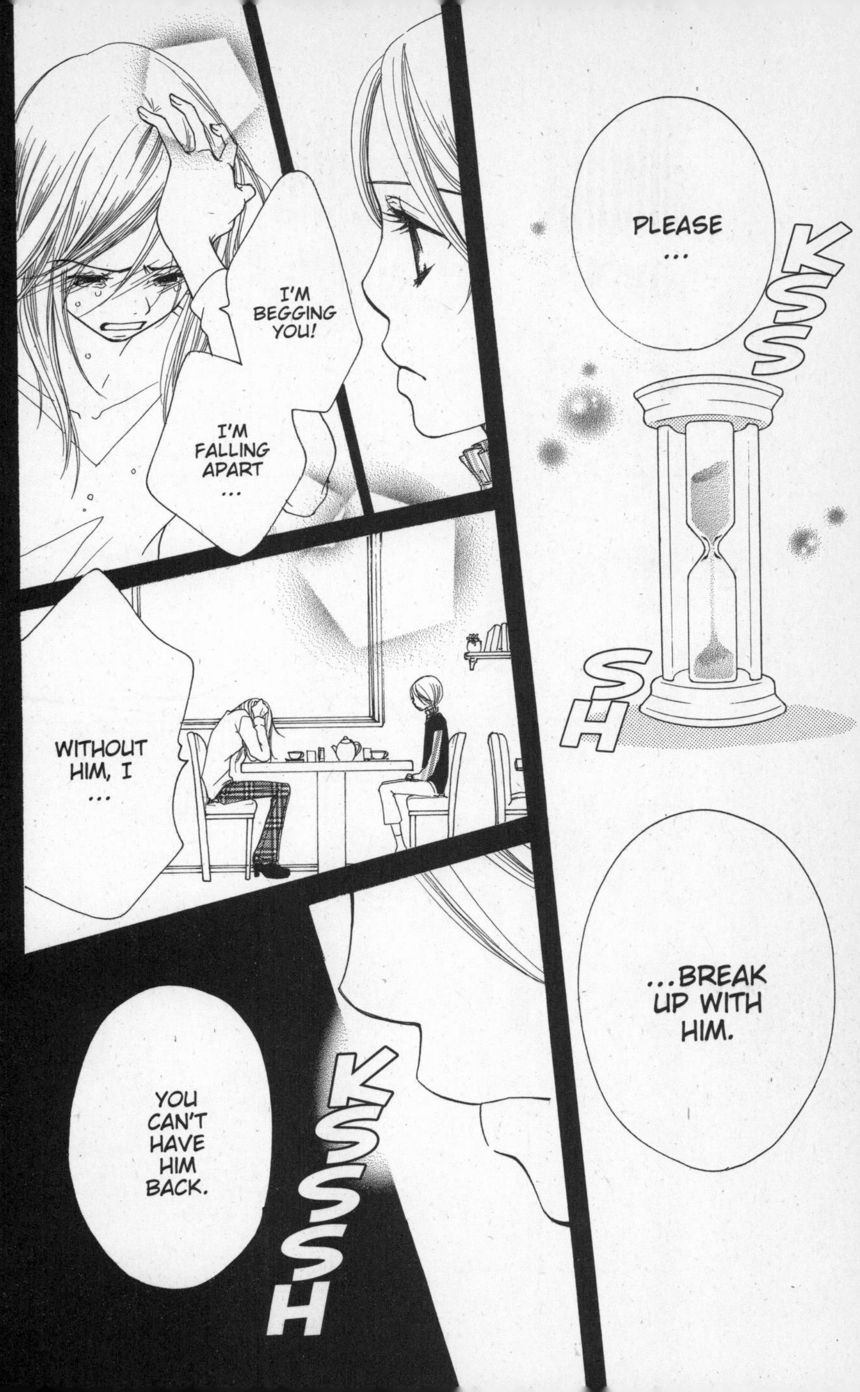
PLEASE ...
KSS
SH
...BREAK UP WITH HIM.
I'M BEGGING YOU!
I'M FALLING APART ...
WITHOUT HIM, I ...
YOU CAN'T HAVE HIM BACK.
KSSSH

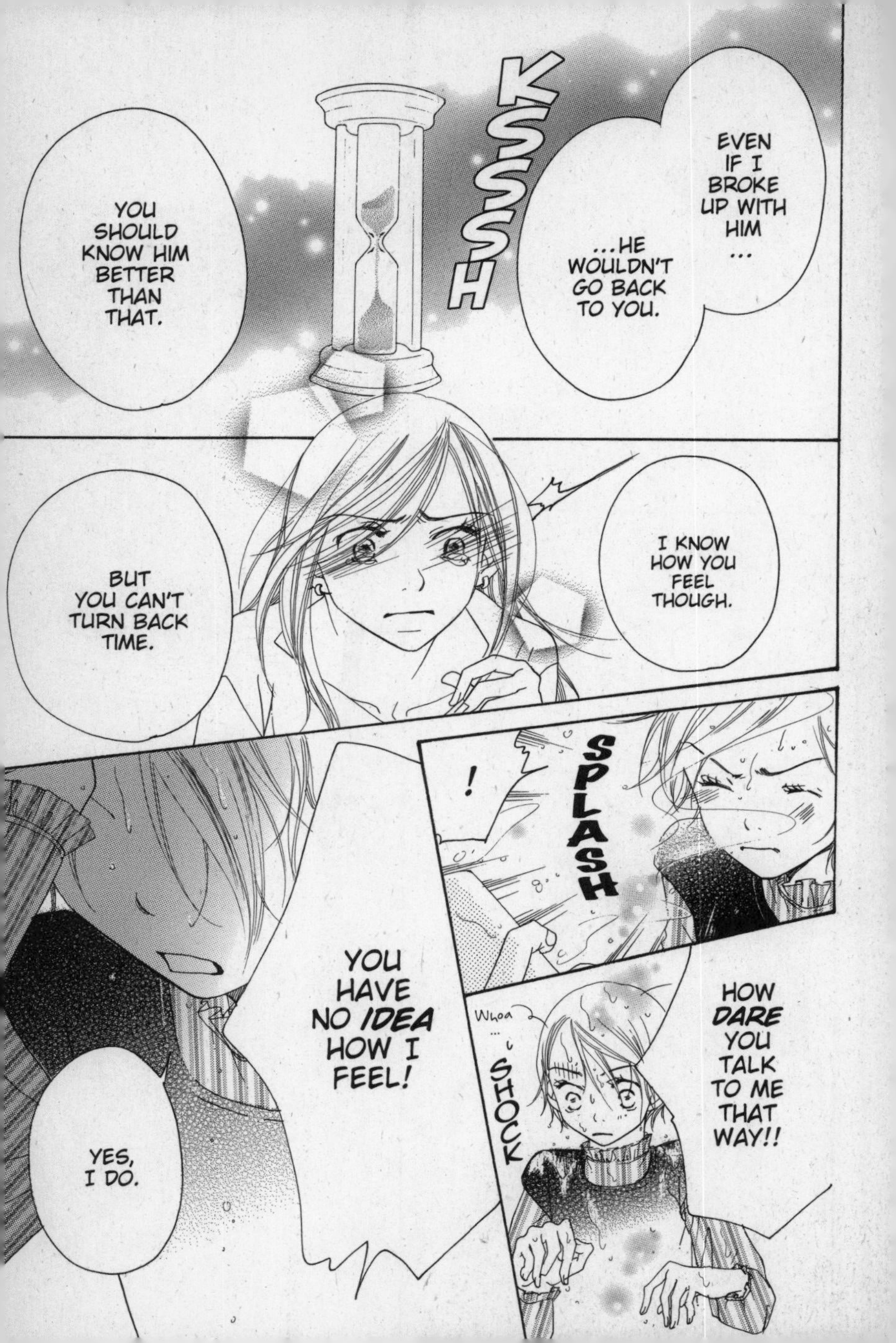
EVEN IF I BROKE UP WITH HIM...
...HE WOULDN'T GO BACK TO YOU.
KSSSH
YOU SHOULD KNOW HIM BETTER THAN THAT.
I KNOW HOW YOU FEEL THOUGH.
BUT YOU CAN'T TURN BACK TIME.
!
SPLASH
HOW DARE YOU TALK TO ME THAT WAY!!
Whoa...
SHOCK
YOU HAVE NO IDEA HOW I FEEL!
YES, I DO.

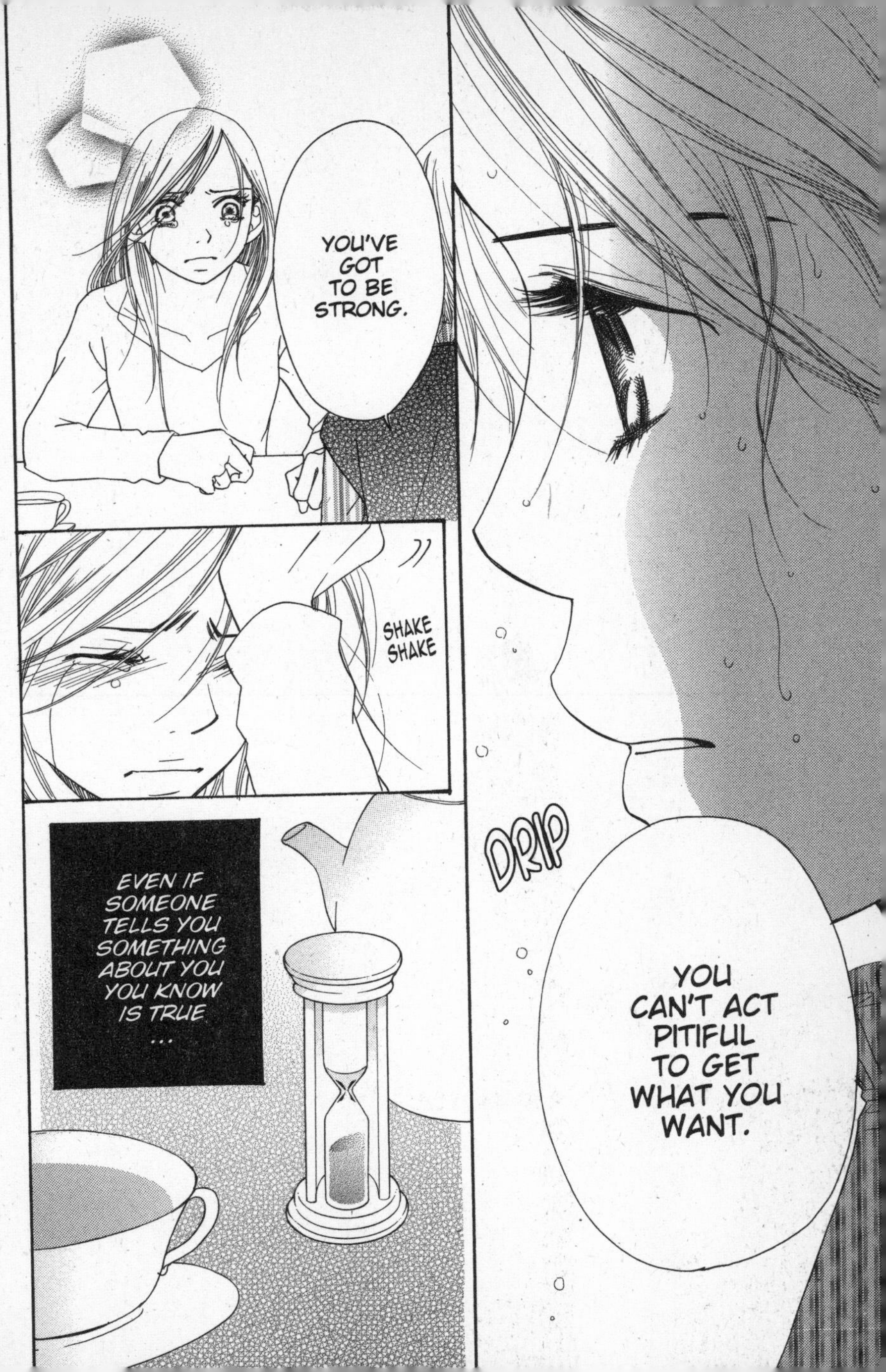
DRIP
YOU CAN'T ACT PITIFUL TO GET WHAT YOU WANT.
YOU'VE GOT TO BE STRONG.
SHAKE SHAKE
EVEN IF SOMEONE TELLS YOU SOMETHING ABOUT YOU YOU KNOW IS TRUE ...

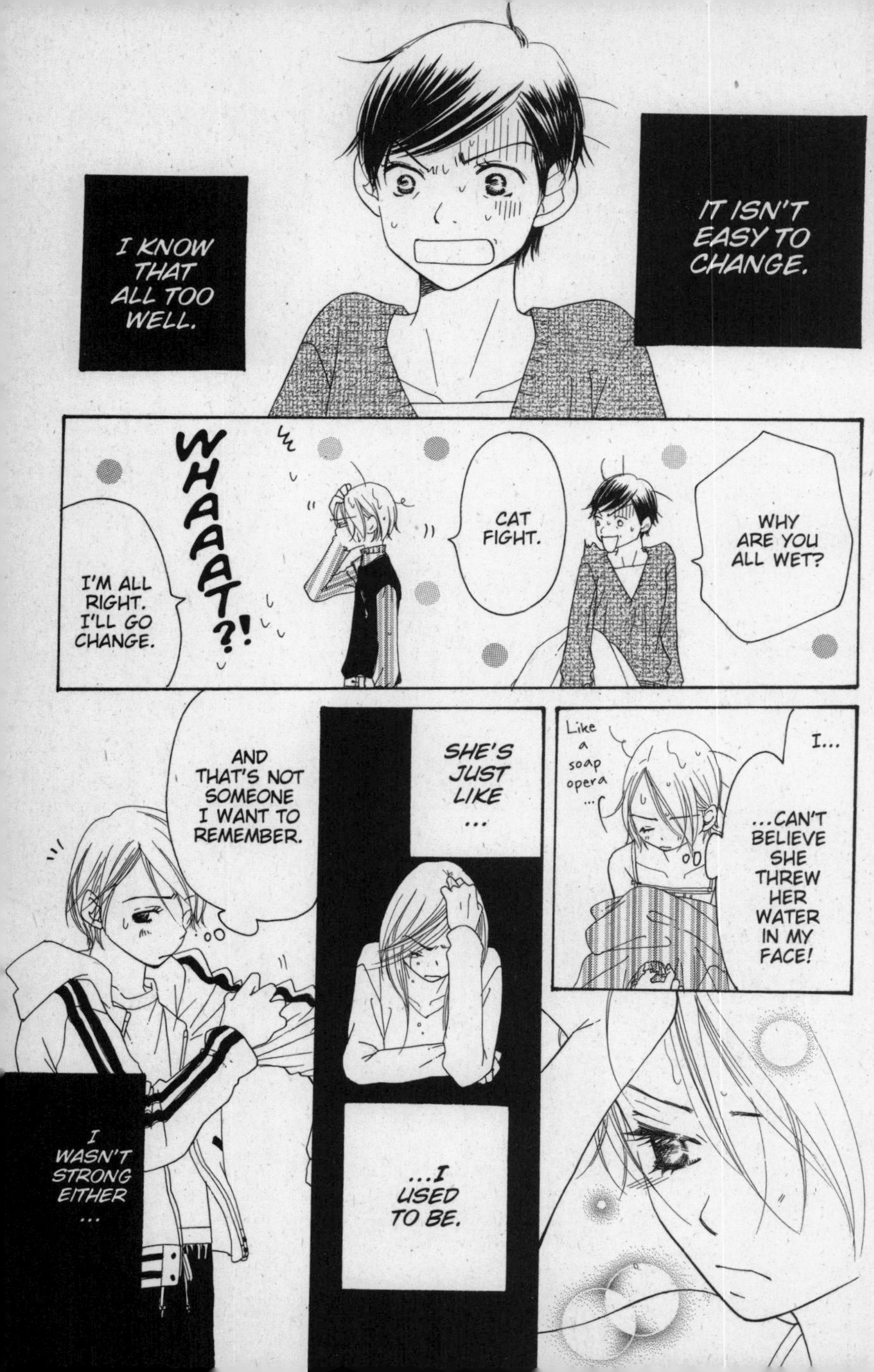
IT ISN'T EASY TO CHANGE.
I KNOW THAT ALL TOO WELL.
WHY ARE YOU ALL WET?
CAT FIGHT.
WHAAAT?!
I'M ALL RIGHT. I'LL GO CHANGE.
I...
...CAN'T BELIEVE SHE THREW HER WATER IN MY FACE!
Like a soap opera...
SHE'S JUST LIKE...
...I USED TO BE.
AND THAT'S NOT SOMEONE I WANT TO REMEMBER.
I WASN'T STRONG EITHER...

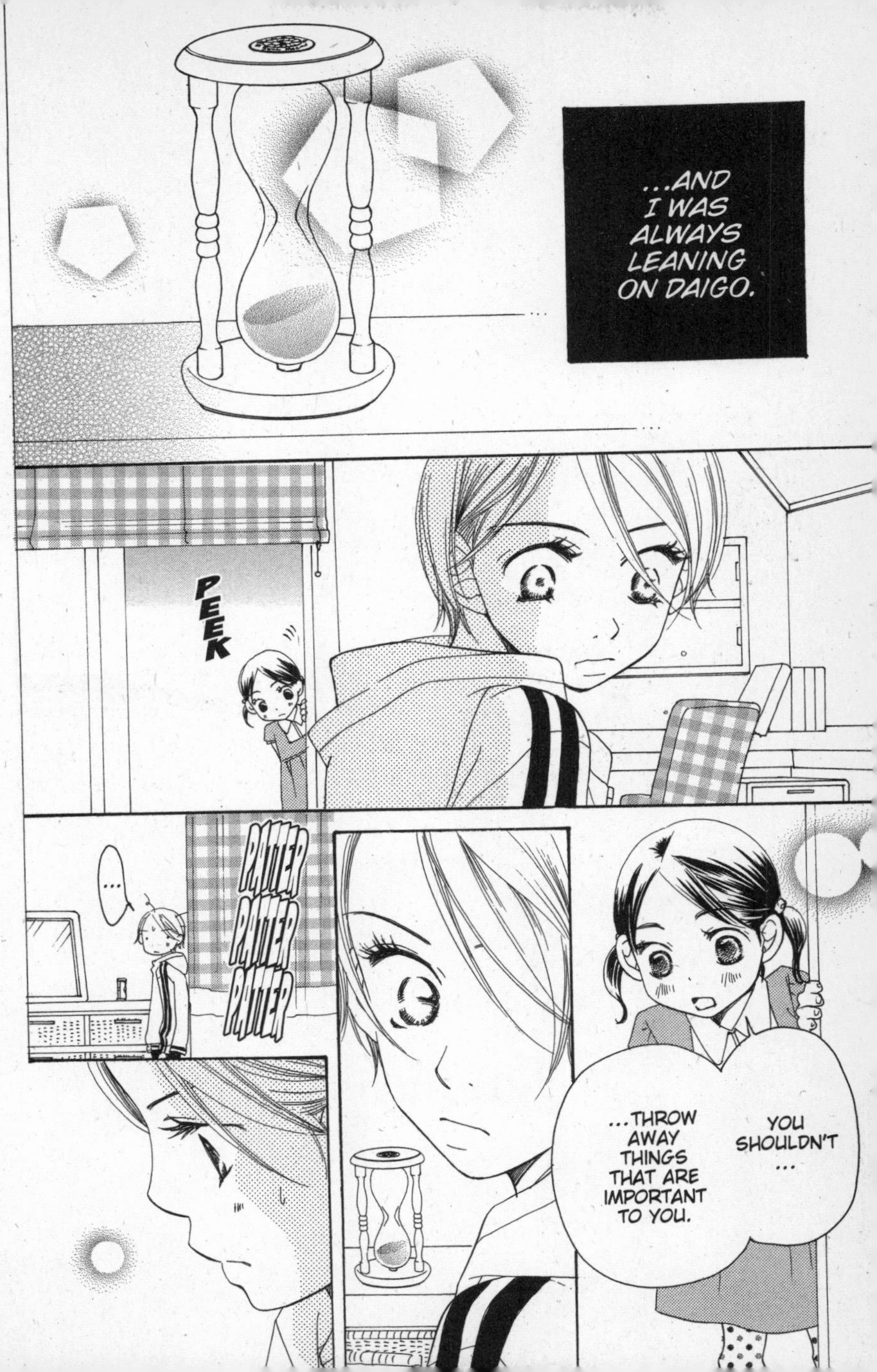
...AND I WAS ALWAYS LEANING ON DAIGO.
PEEK
YOU SHOULDN'T ...
...THROW AWAY THINGS THAT ARE IMPORTANT TO YOU.
PATTER PATTER PATTER
...

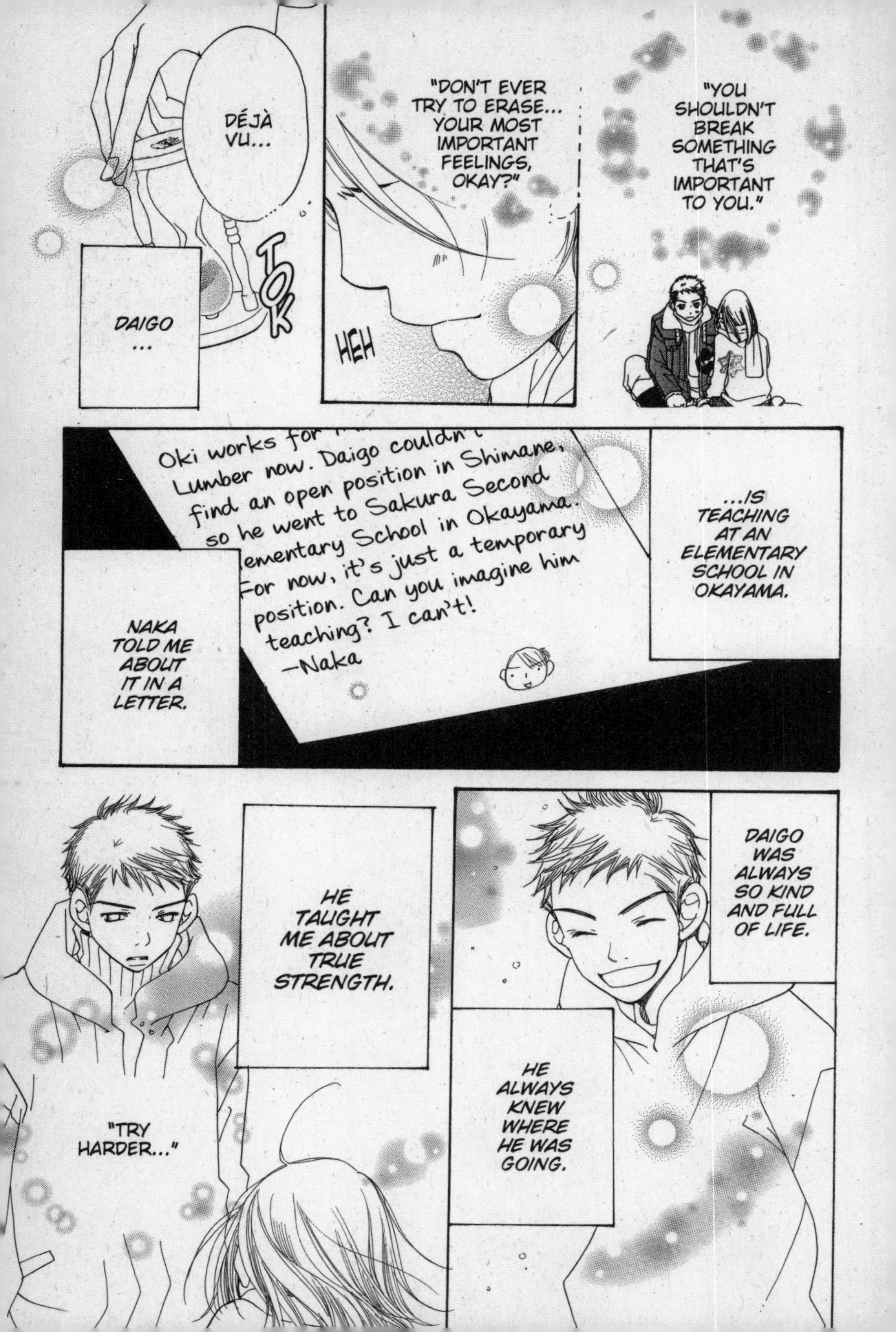
"YOU SHOULDN'T BREAK SOMETHING THAT'S IMPORTANT TO YOU."
"DON'T EVER TRY TO ERASE... YOUR MOST IMPORTANT FEELINGS, OKAY?"
HEH
DÉJÀ VU...
TOK
DAIGO ...
...IS TEACHING AT AN ELEMENTARY SCHOOL IN OKAYAMA.
Oki works for
Lumber now. Daigo couldn
find an open position in Shimane,
so he went to Sakura Second
ementary School in Okayama.
For now, it's just a temporary
position. Can you imagine him
teaching? I can't!
—Naka
NAKA TOLD ME ABOUT IT IN A LETTER.
DAIGO WAS ALWAYS SO KIND AND FULL OF LIFE.
HE ALWAYS KNEW WHERE HE WAS GOING.
HE TAUGHT ME ABOUT TRUE STRENGTH.
"TRY HARDER..."

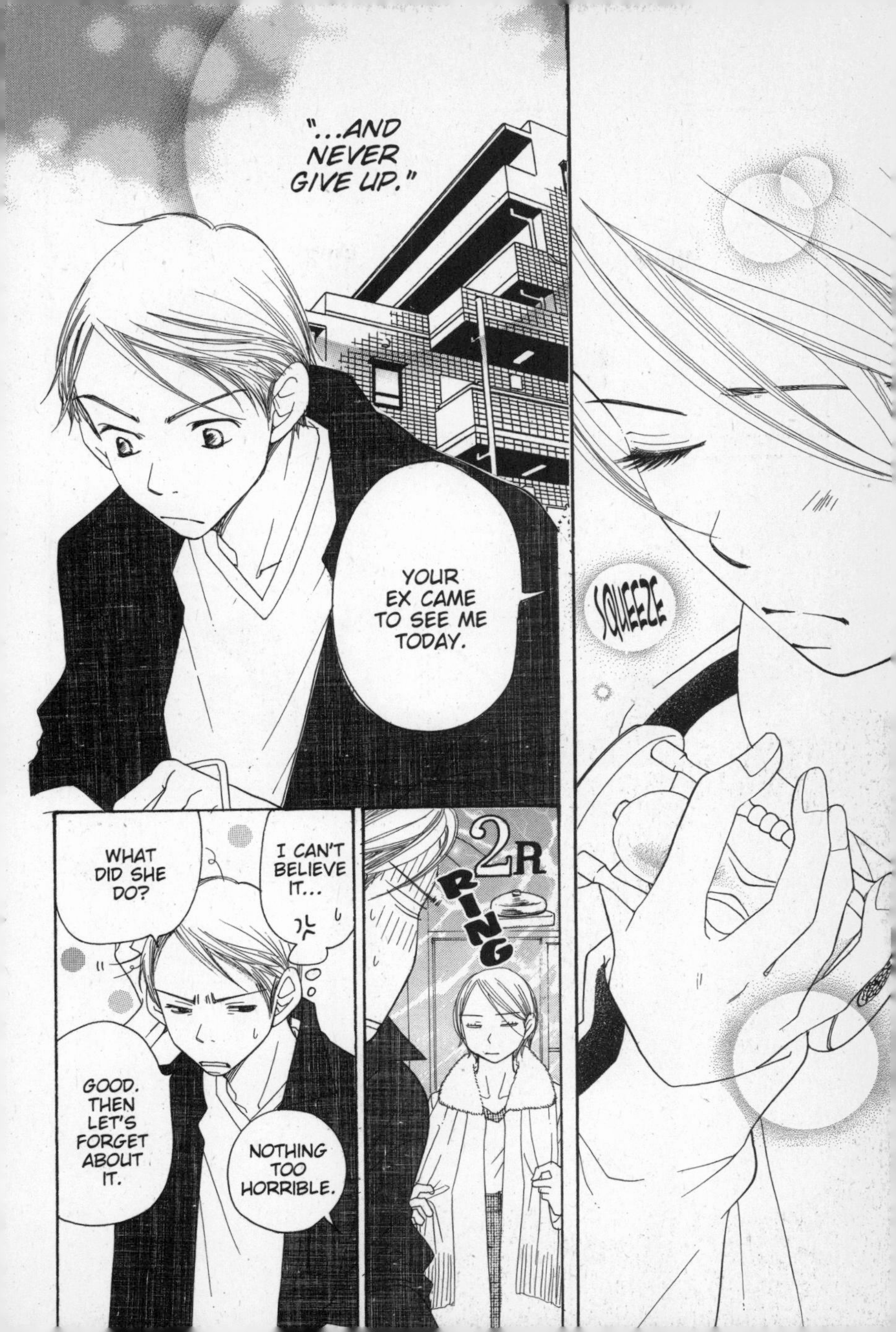
SQUEEZE
"...AND NEVER GIVE UP."
YOUR EX CAME TO SEE ME TODAY.
2R
RING
I CAN'T BELIEVE IT...
WHAT DID SHE DO?
NOTHING TOO HORRIBLE.
GOOD. THEN LET'S FORGET ABOUT IT.

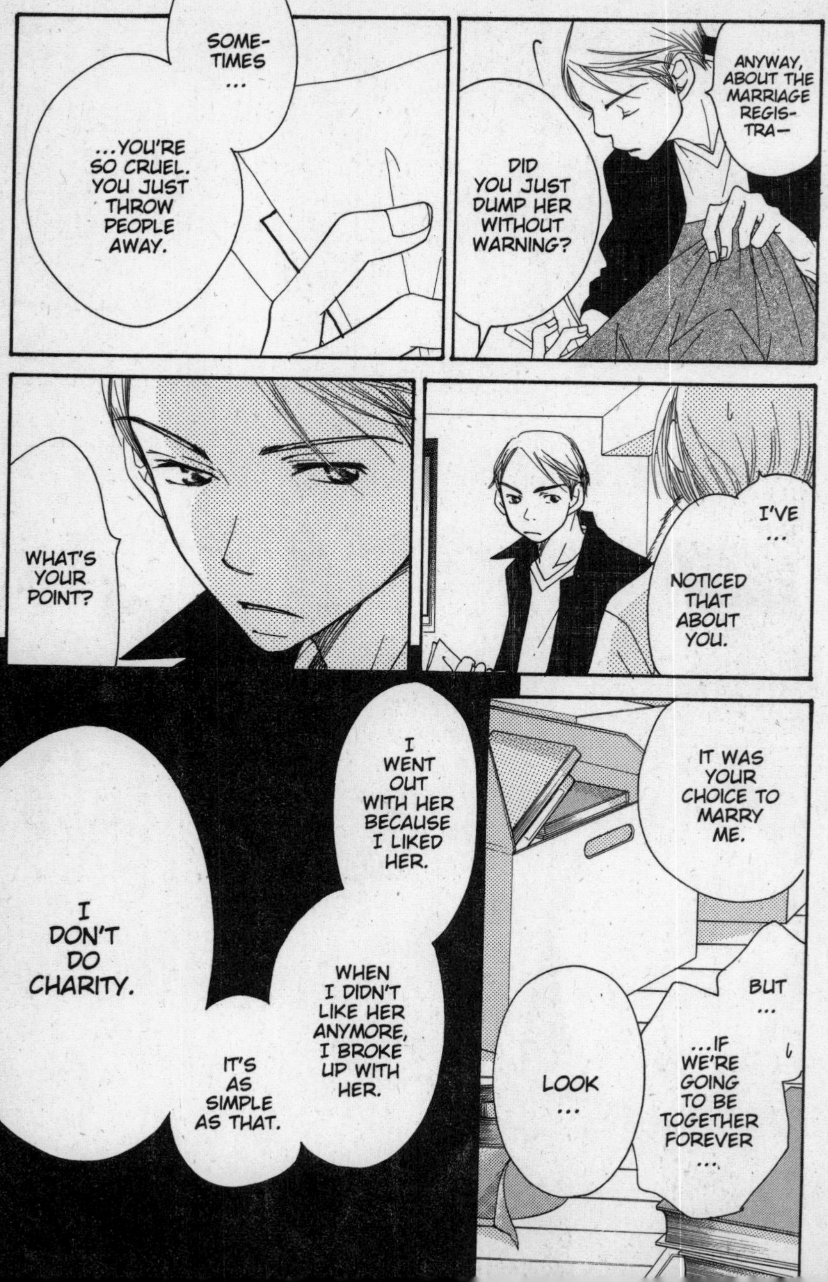
ANYWAY, ABOUT THE MARRIAGE REGIS-TRA—
DID YOU JUST DUMP HER WITHOUT WARNING?
SOME-TIMES ...
...YOU'RE SO CRUEL. YOU JUST THROW PEOPLE AWAY.
I'VE ...
NOTICED THAT ABOUT YOU.
WHAT'S YOUR POINT?
IT WAS YOUR CHOICE TO MARRY ME.
BUT ...
...IF WE'RE GOING TO BE TOGETHER FOREVER ...
LOOK ...
I WENT OUT WITH HER BECAUSE I LIKED HER.
WHEN I DIDN'T LIKE HER ANYMORE, I BROKE UP WITH HER.
IT'S AS SIMPLE AS THAT.
I DON'T DO CHARITY.

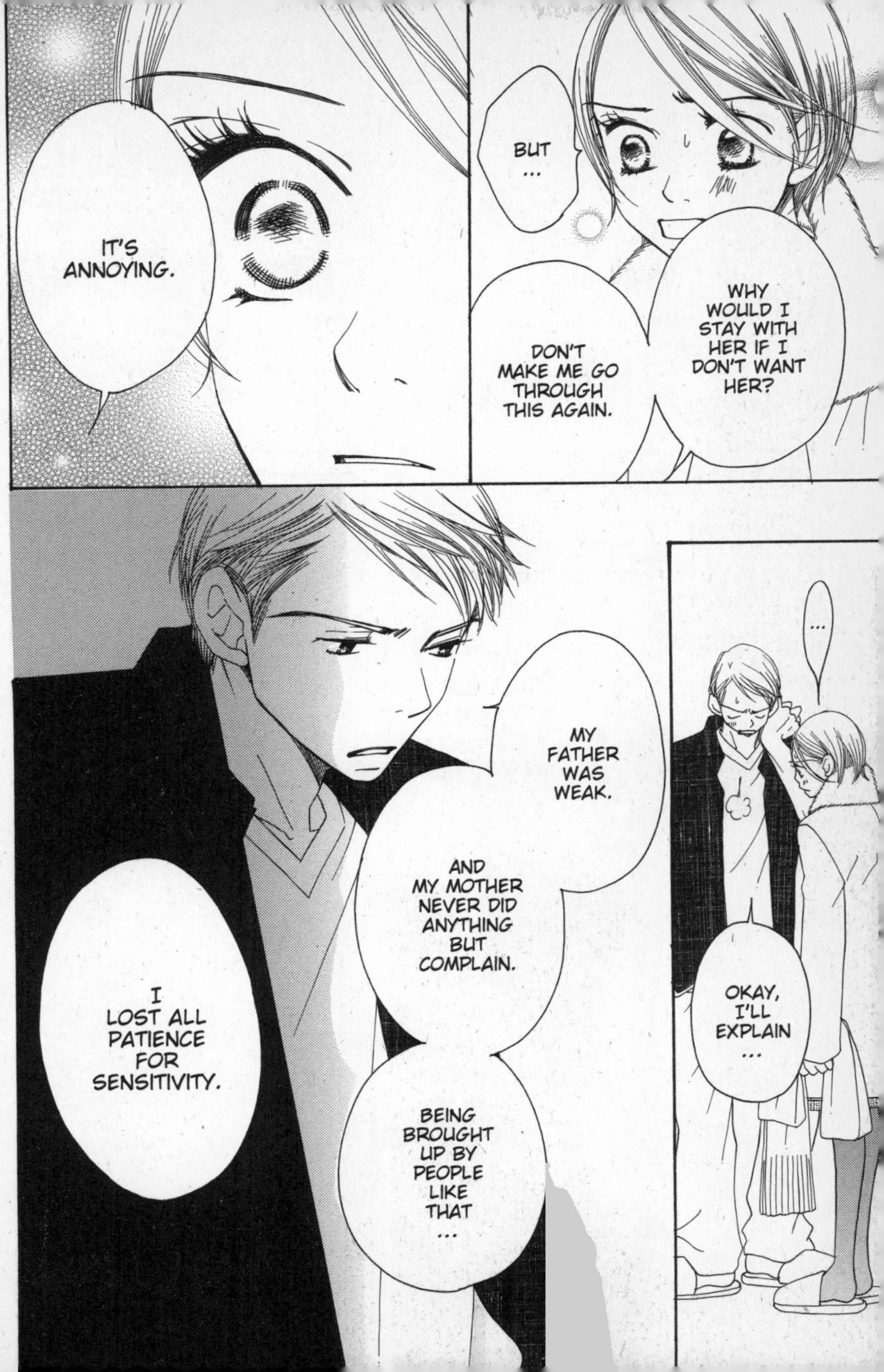
BUT ...
WHY WOULD I STAY WITH HER IF I DON'T WANT HER?
DON'T MAKE ME GO THROUGH THIS AGAIN.
IT'S ANNOYING.
...
OKAY, I'LL EXPLAIN ...
MY FATHER WAS WEAK.
AND MY MOTHER NEVER DID ANYTHING BUT COMPLAIN.
BEING BROUGHT UP BY PEOPLE LIKE THAT ...
I LOST ALL PATIENCE FOR SENSITIVITY.

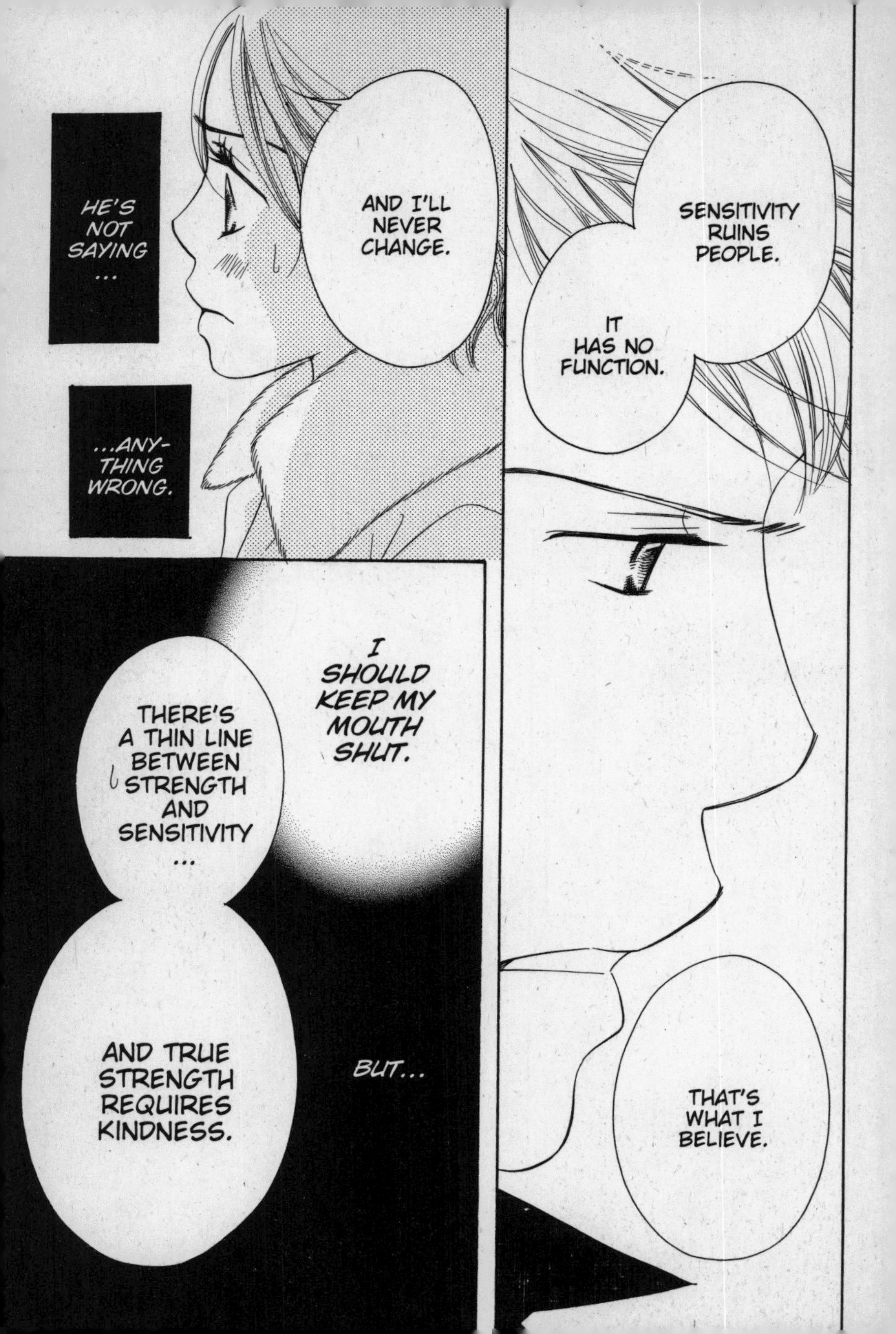
SENSITIVITY RUINS PEOPLE.
IT HAS NO FUNCTION.
THAT'S WHAT I BELIEVE.
AND I'LL NEVER CHANGE.
HE'S NOT SAYING...
...ANYTHING WRONG.
I SHOULD KEEP MY MOUTH SHUT.
BUT...
THERE'S A THIN LINE BETWEEN STRENGTH AND SENSITIVITY...
AND TRUE STRENGTH REQUIRES KINDNESS.

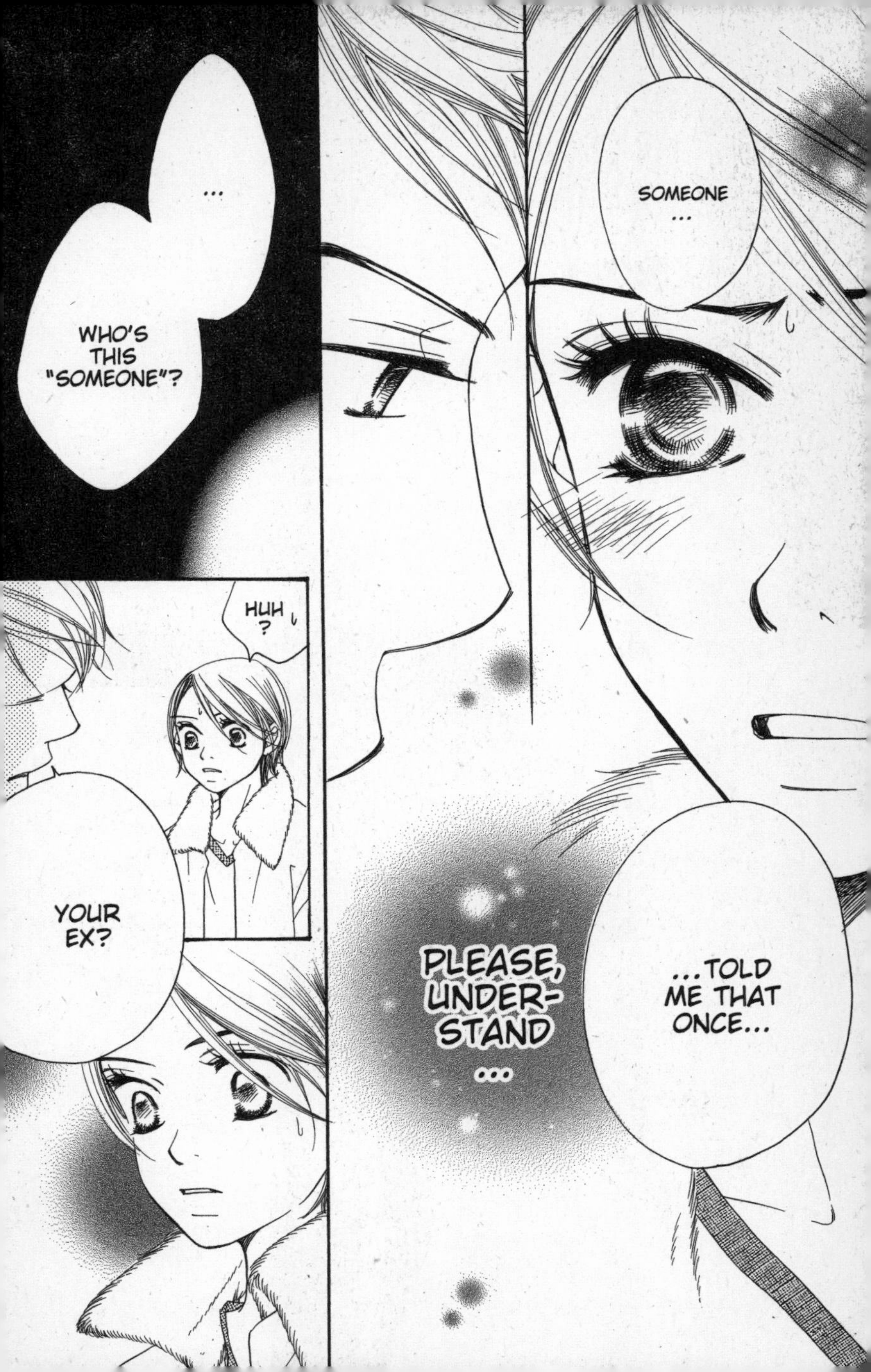
SOMEONE ...
...TOLD ME THAT ONCE...
PLEASE, UNDER-STAND ...
...
WHO'S THIS "SOMEONE"?
HUH?
YOUR EX?

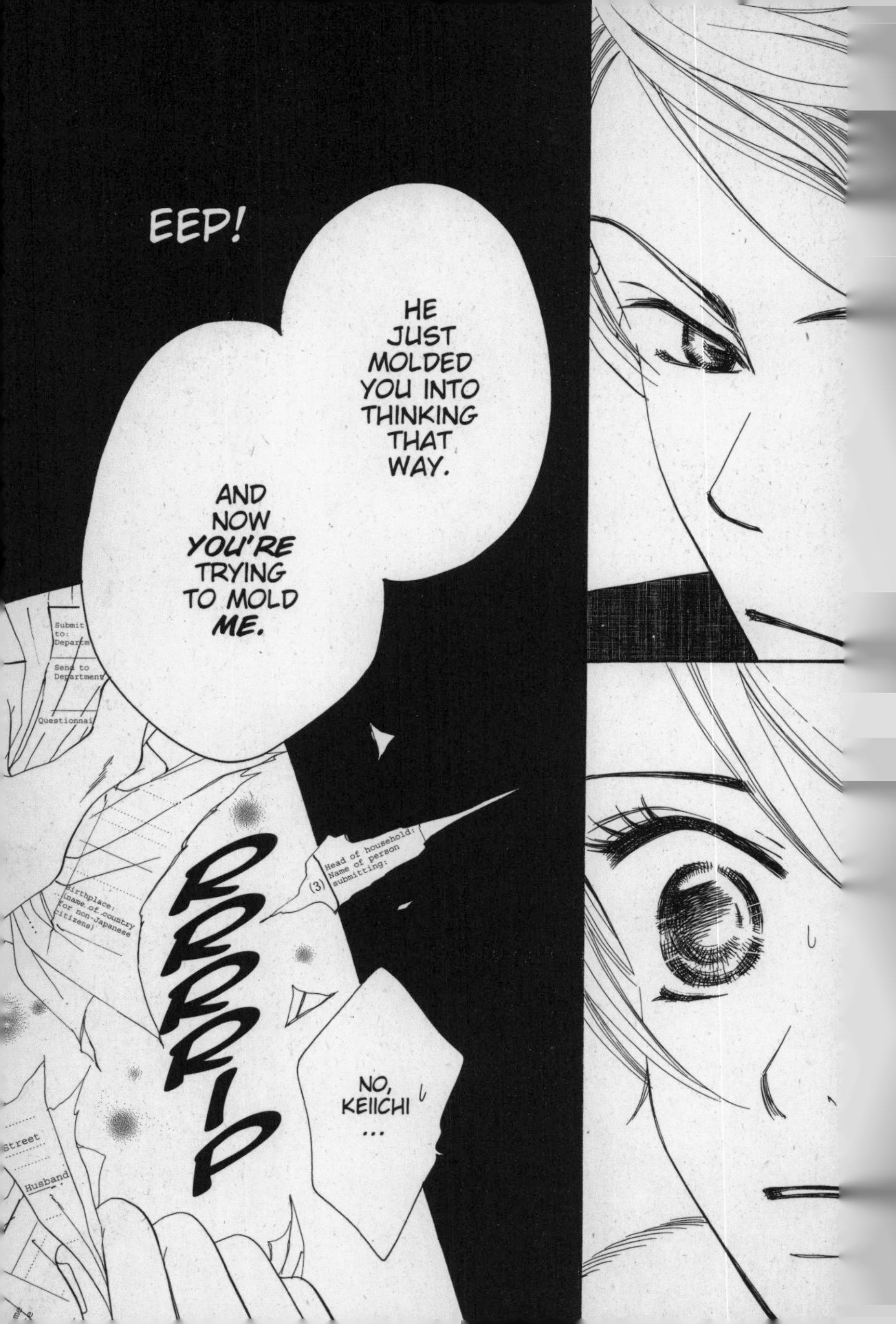
HE JUST MOLDED YOU INTO THINKING THAT WAY.
AND NOW *YOU'RE* TRYING TO MOLD *ME.*
EEP!
Submit to: Departm
Send to Department
Questionnai
Head of household: Name of person submitting:
(3)
Birthplace: (name of country for non-Japanese citizens)
Street
Husband
RRRRIP
NO, KEIICHI ...

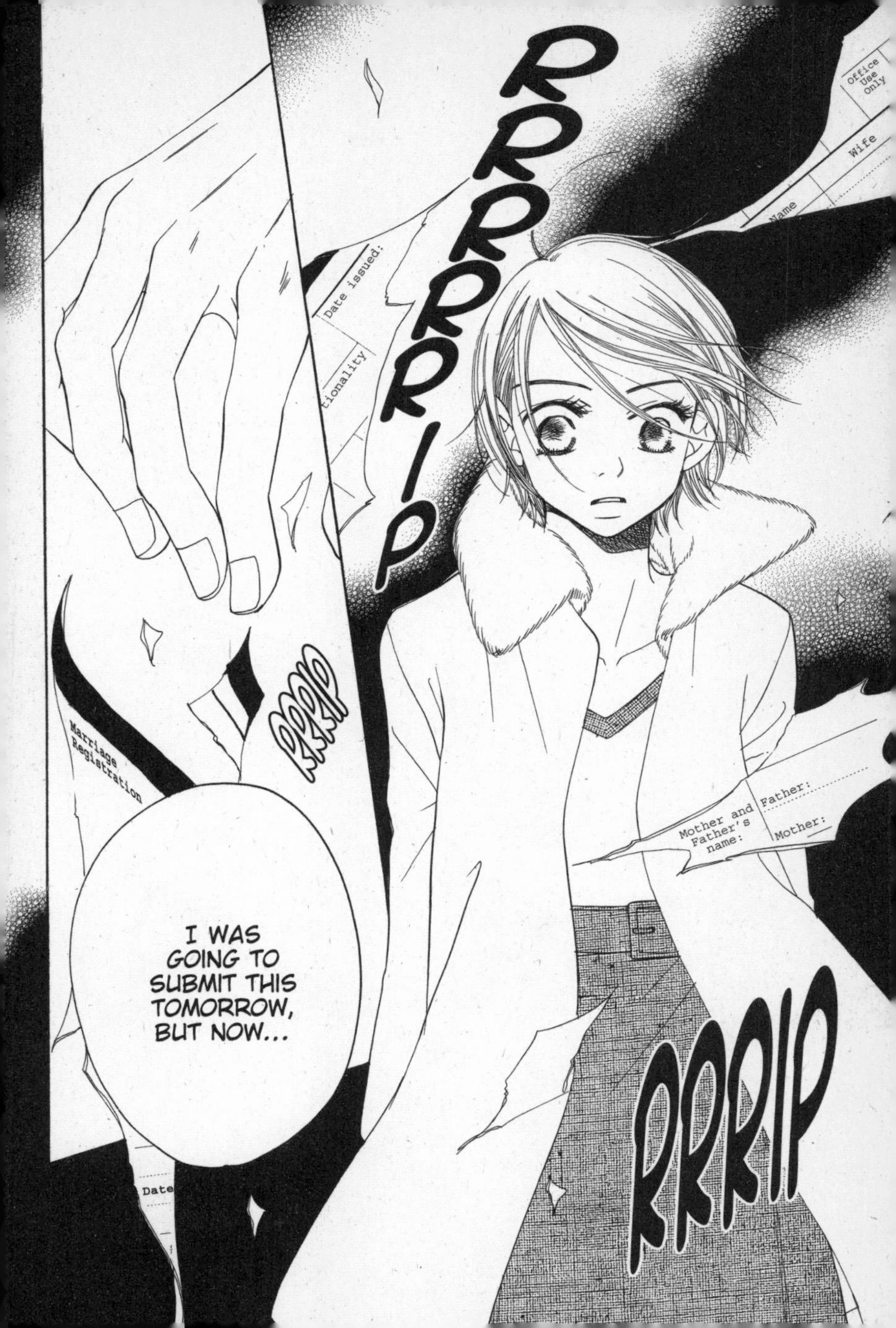
RRRRRRIP
Office Use Only
Wife
Name
Date issued:
tionality
Mother and Father:
Father's name:
Mother:
Marriage Registration
I WAS GOING TO SUBMIT THIS TOMORROW, BUT NOW...
Date
RRRIP

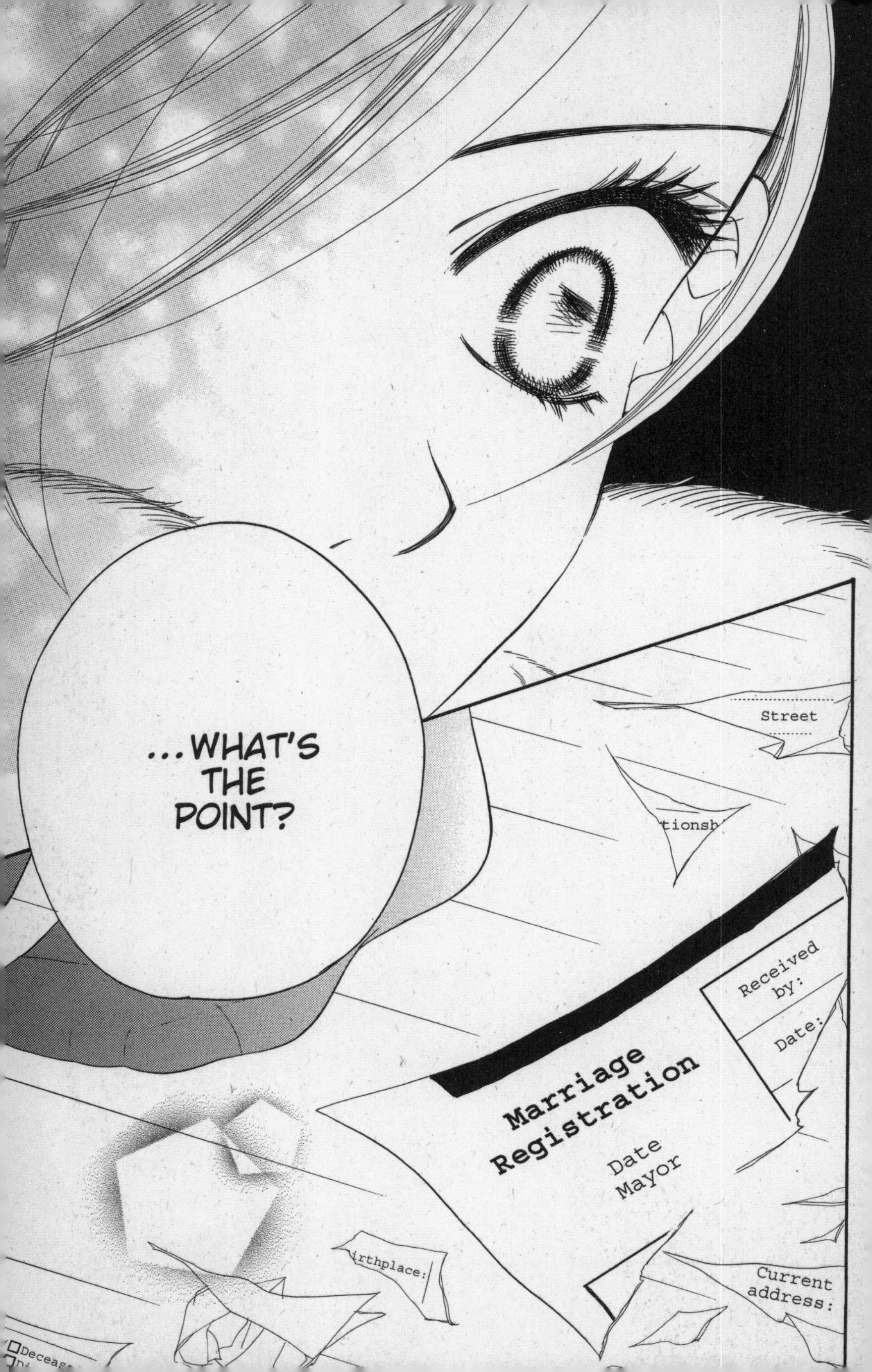
...WHAT'S THE POINT?
Street
Received by:
Date:
Marriage Registration
Date
Mayor
Current address:

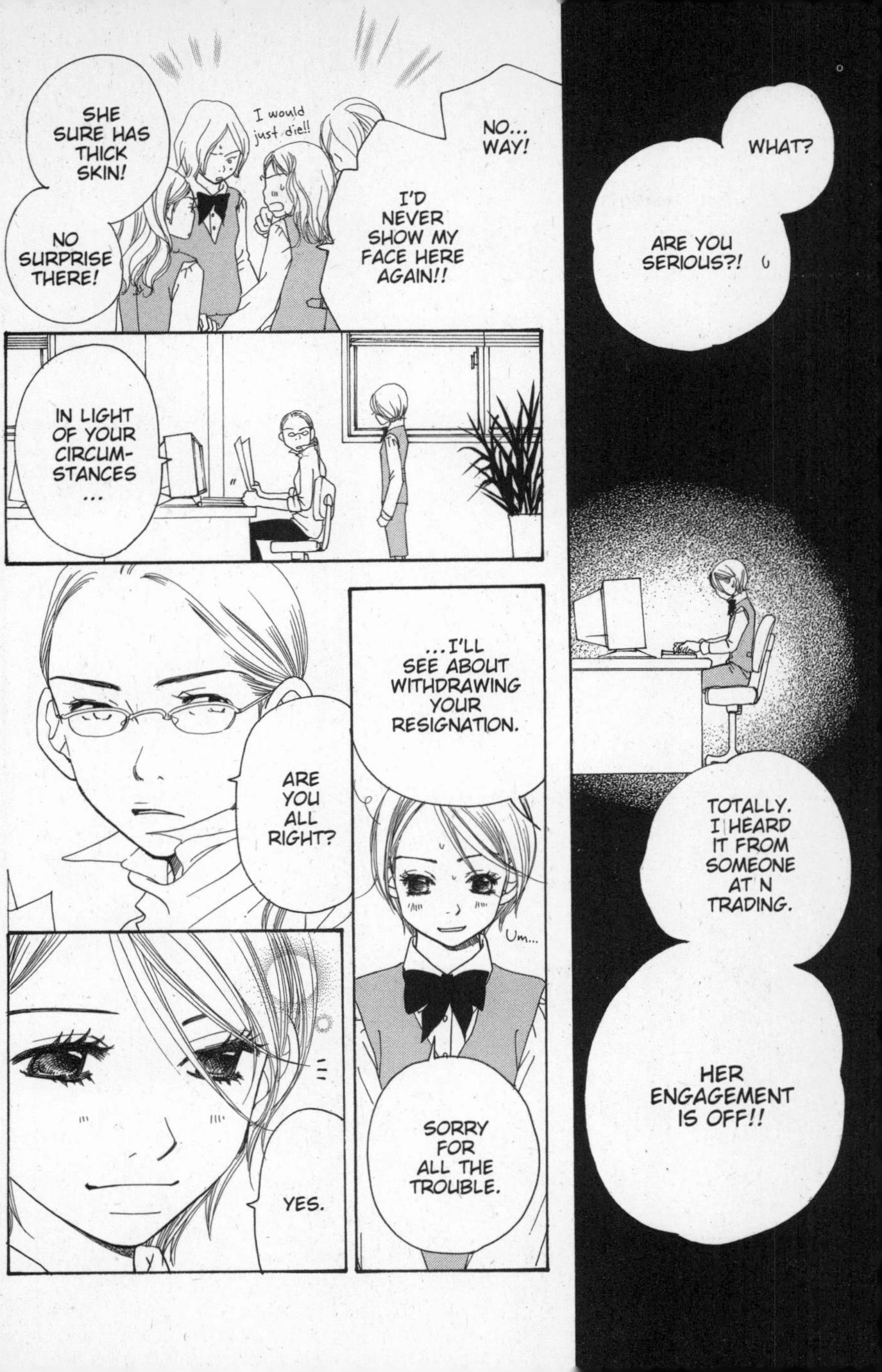
WHAT?
ARE YOU SERIOUS?!
TOTALLY. I HEARD IT FROM SOMEONE AT N TRADING.
HER ENGAGEMENT IS OFF!!
NO... WAY!
I'D NEVER SHOW MY FACE HERE AGAIN!!
I would just die!!
SHE SURE HAS THICK SKIN!
NO SURPRISE THERE!
IN LIGHT OF YOUR CIRCUM-STANCES...
...I'LL SEE ABOUT WITHDRAWING YOUR RESIGNATION.
ARE YOU ALL RIGHT?
Um...
SORRY FOR ALL THE TROUBLE.
YES.

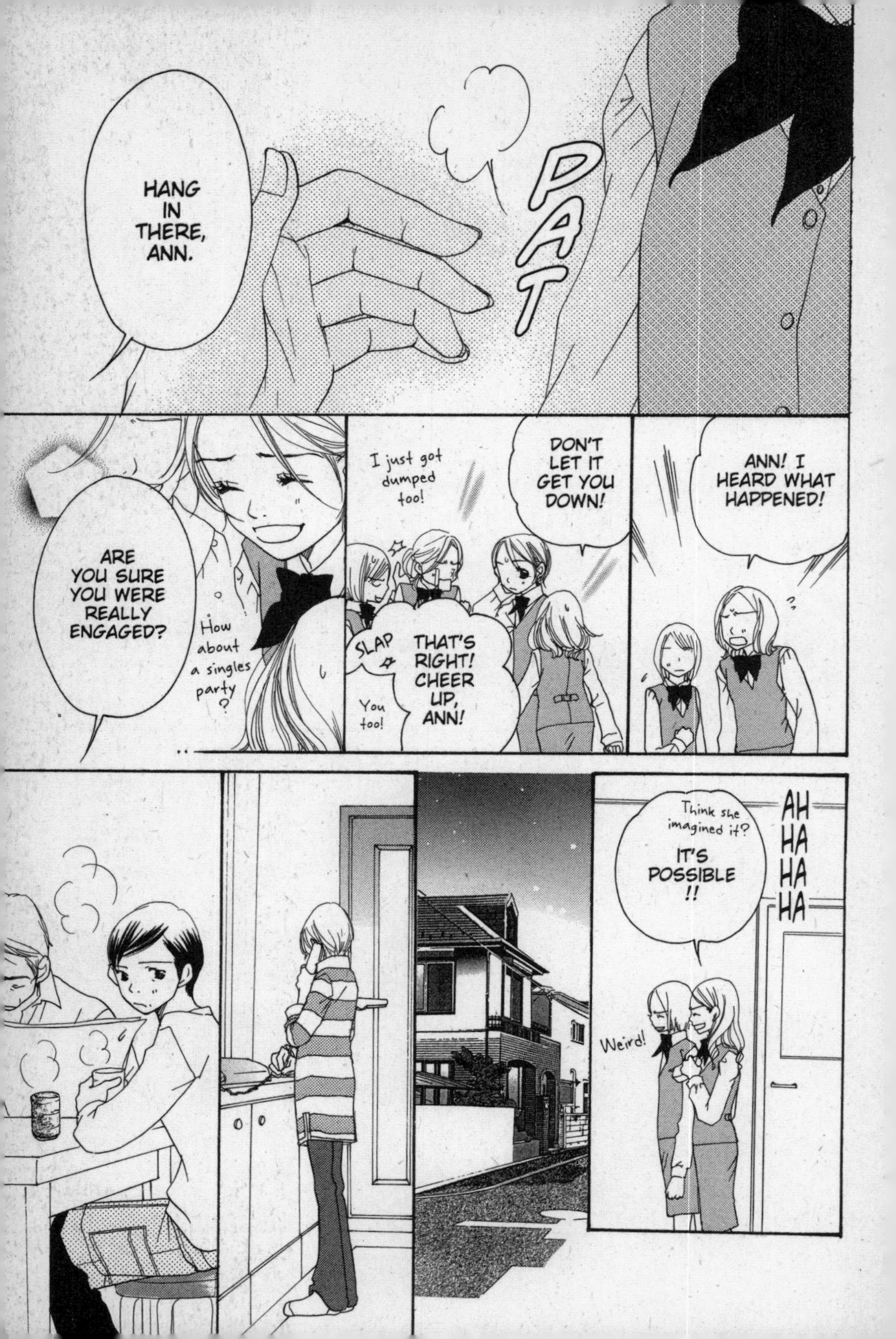
PAT
HANG IN THERE, ANN.
ANN! I HEARD WHAT HAPPENED!
DON'T LET IT GET YOU DOWN!
I just got dumped too!
THAT'S RIGHT! CHEER UP, ANN!
SLAP
You too!
ARE YOU SURE YOU WERE REALLY ENGAGED?
How about a singles party?
AH HA HA HA
Think she imagined it?
IT'S POSSIBLE!!
Weird!

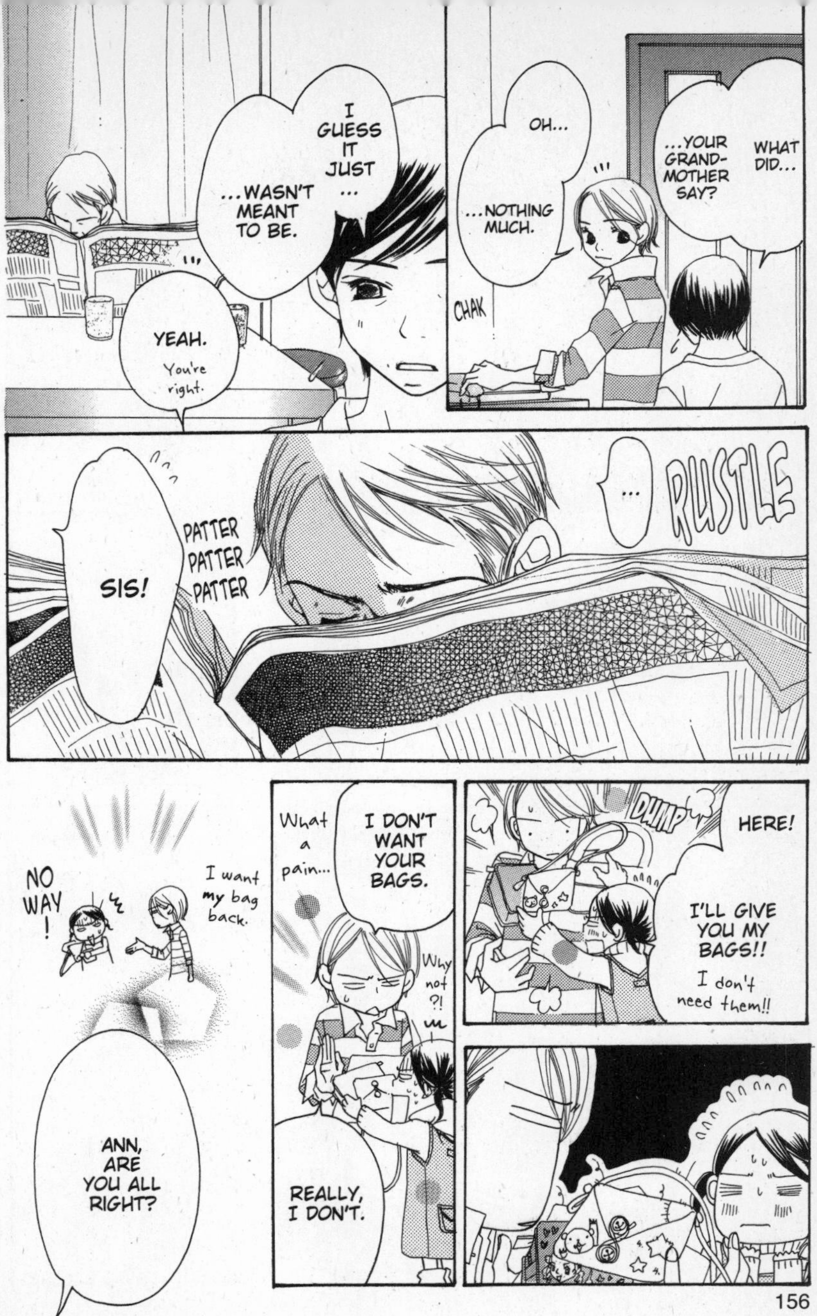

WHAT DID...
...YOUR GRAND-MOTHER SAY?
OH...
...NOTHING MUCH.
CHAK
I GUESS IT JUST ...
...WASN'T MEANT TO BE.
YEAH.
You're right.
RUSTLE
...
PATTER PATTER PATTER
SIS!
HERE!
DUMP
I'LL GIVE YOU MY BAGS!!
I don't need them!!
I DON'T WANT YOUR BAGS.
What a pain...
Why not?!
REALLY, I DON'T.
I want my bag back.
NO WAY!
ANN, ARE YOU ALL RIGHT?

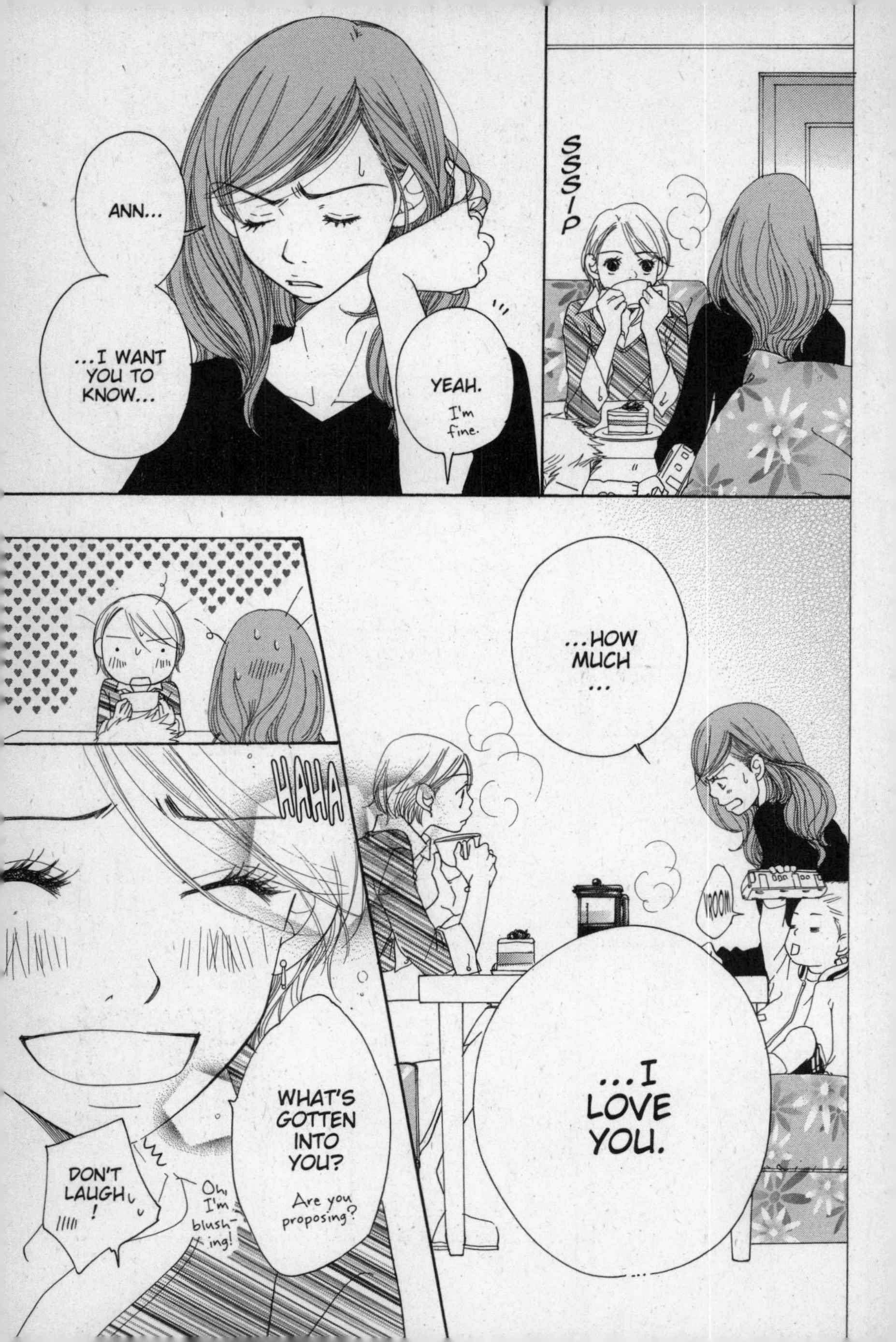
SSSIP
YEAH. I'm fine.
ANN...
...I WANT YOU TO KNOW...
...HOW MUCH ...
VROOM
...I LOVE YOU. ...
HAHA
WHAT'S GOTTEN INTO YOU? Are you proposing?
Oh, I'm blush-ing!
DON'T LAUGH!

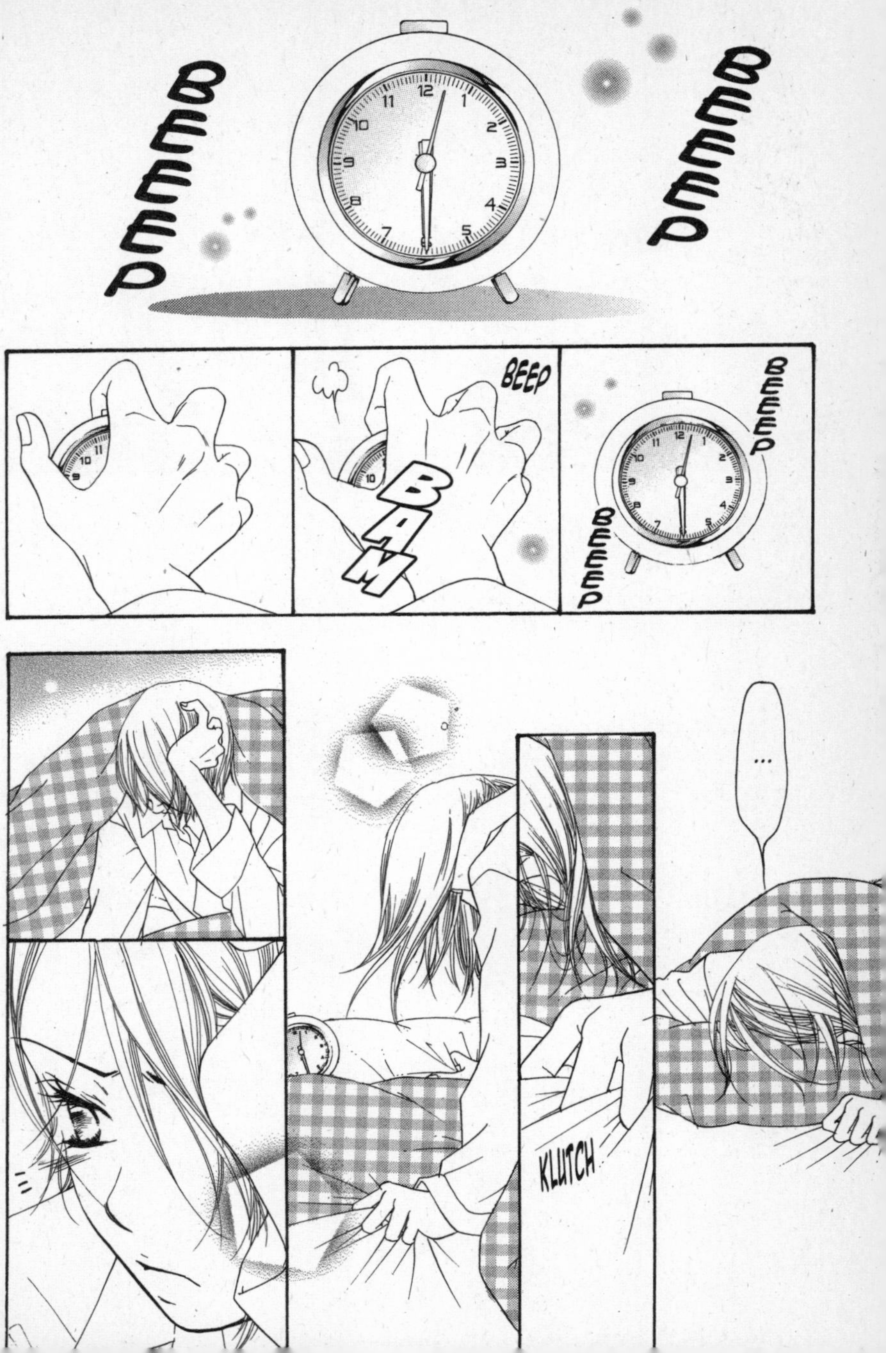
BEEEEP
BEEEEP
BEEEP
BEEEP
BEEP
BAM
...
KLUTCH

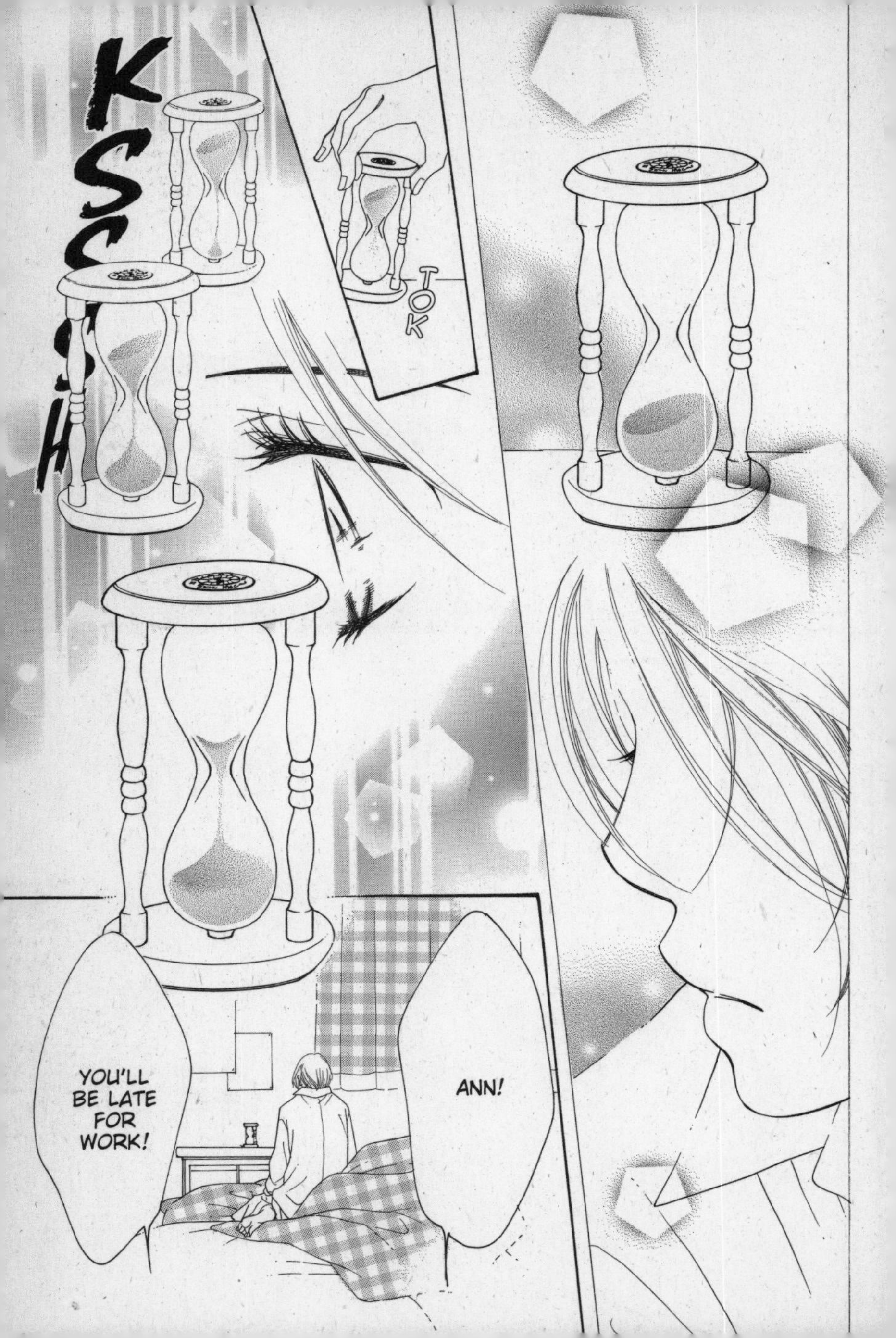
TOK
KSCSH
ANN!
YOU'LL BE LATE FOR WORK!

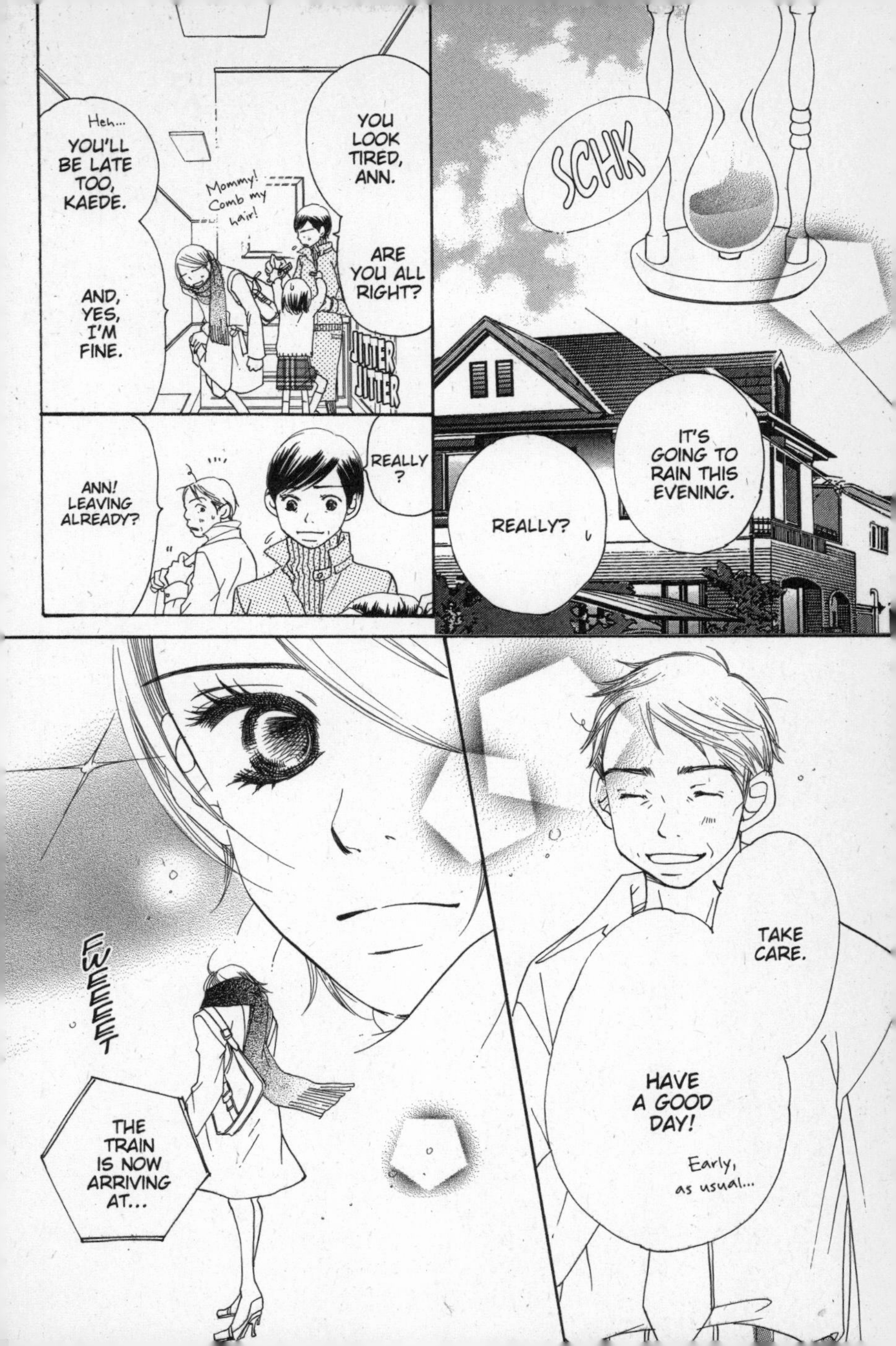
SCHK
IT'S GOING TO RAIN THIS EVENING.
REALLY?
YOU LOOK TIRED, ANN.
ARE YOU ALL RIGHT?
Mommy! Comb my hair!
JITTER JITTER
Heh... YOU'LL BE LATE TOO, KAEDE.
AND, YES, I'M FINE.
REALLY?
ANN! LEAVING ALREADY?
TAKE CARE.
HAVE A GOOD DAY!
Early, as usual...
FWEEEET
THE TRAIN IS NOW ARRIVING AT...

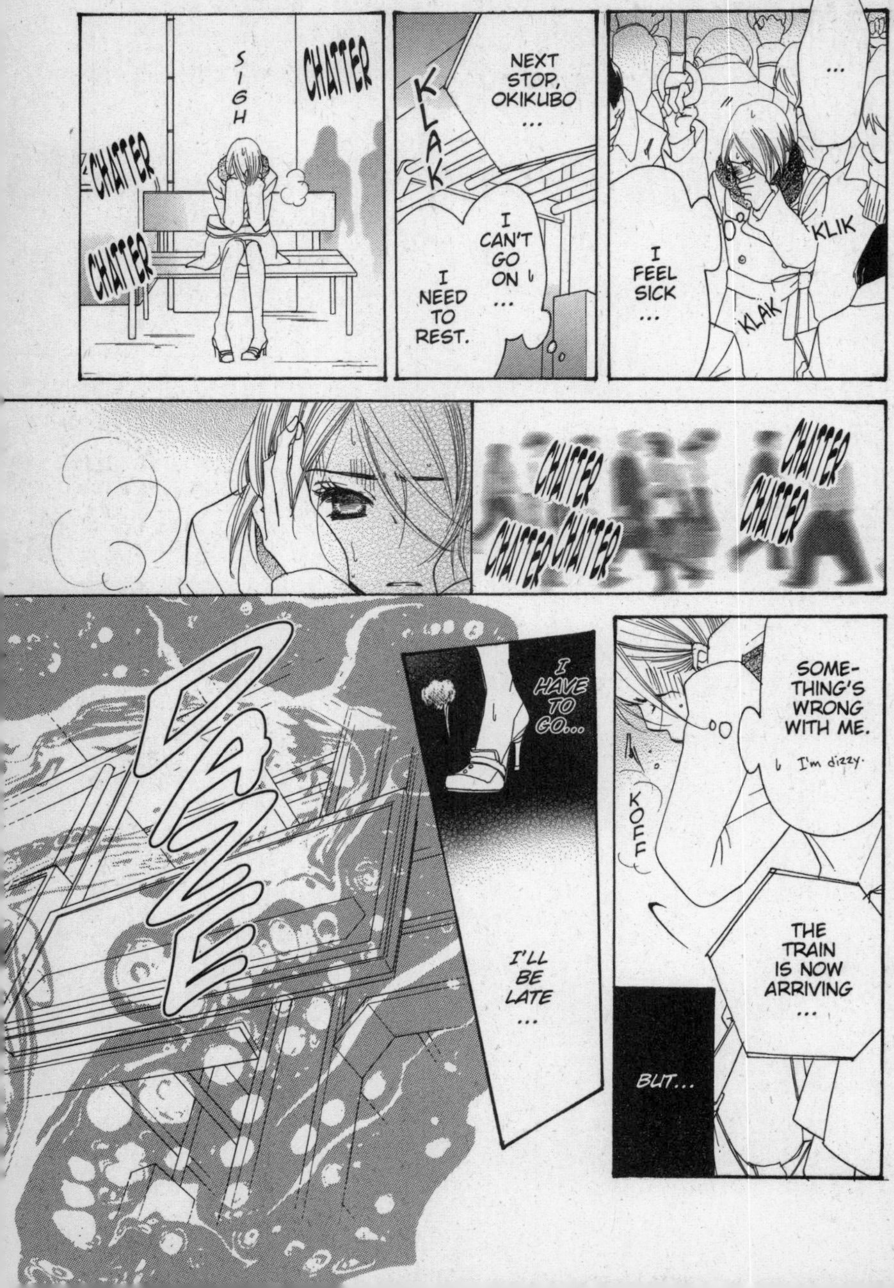
...
I FEEL SICK ...
KLIK
KLAK
NEXT STOP, OKIKUBO ...
KLAK
I CAN'T GO ON ...
I NEED TO REST.
SIGH
CHATTER
CHATTER
CHATTER
CHATTER
CHATTER
CHATTER
CHATTER
SOME-THING'S WRONG WITH ME.
I'm dizzy.
KOFF
THE TRAIN IS NOW ARRIVING ...
BUT...
I HAVE TO GO...
I'LL BE LATE ...
DASH

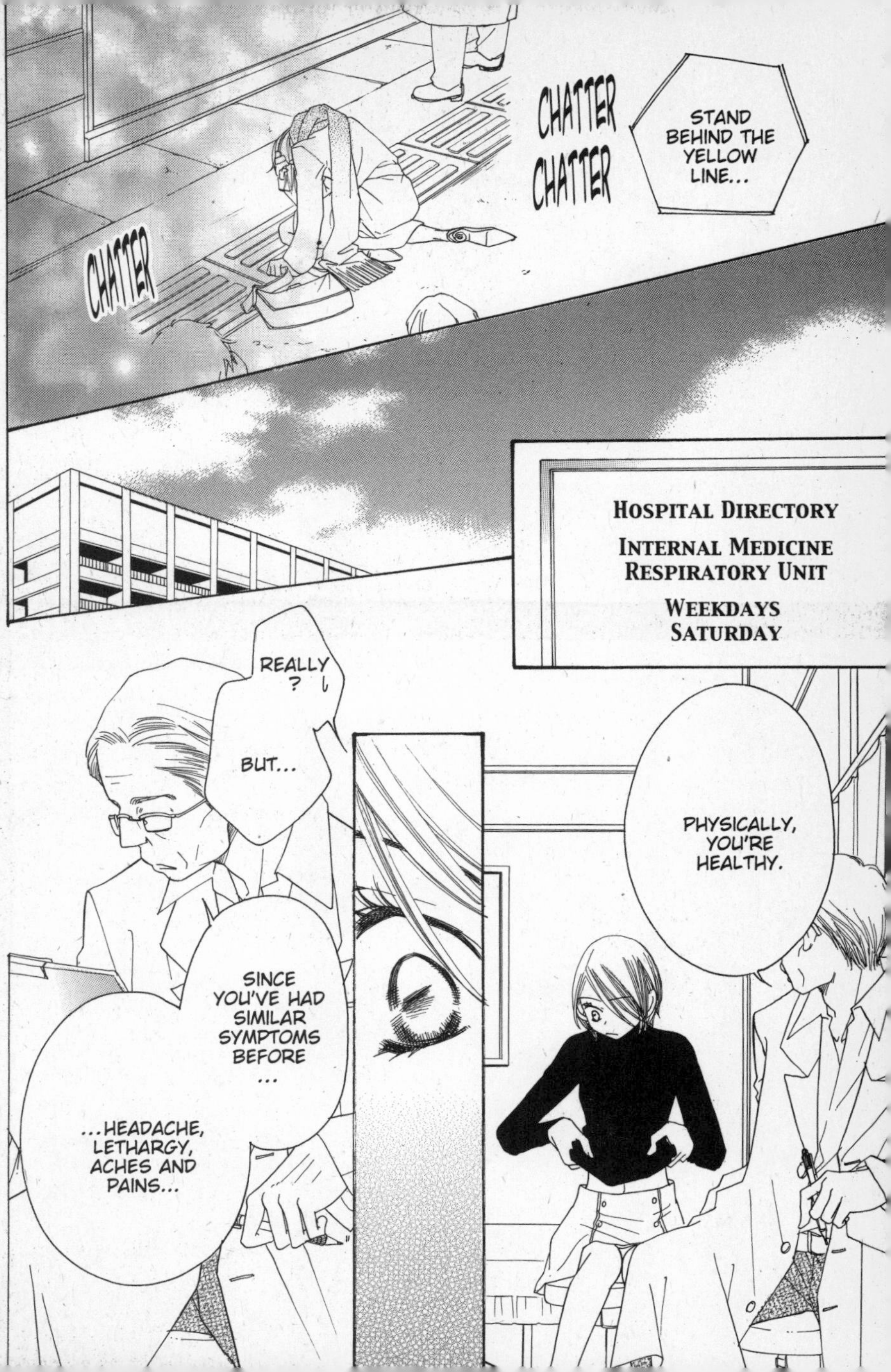
STAND BEHIND THE YELLOW LINE...
CHATTER CHATTER
CHATTER
HOSPITAL DIRECTORY
INTERNAL MEDICINE RESPIRATORY UNIT
WEEKDAYS SATURDAY
PHYSICALLY, YOU'RE HEALTHY.
REALLY?
BUT...
SINCE YOU'VE HAD SIMILAR SYMPTOMS BEFORE...
...HEADACHE, LETHARGY, ACHES AND PAINS...

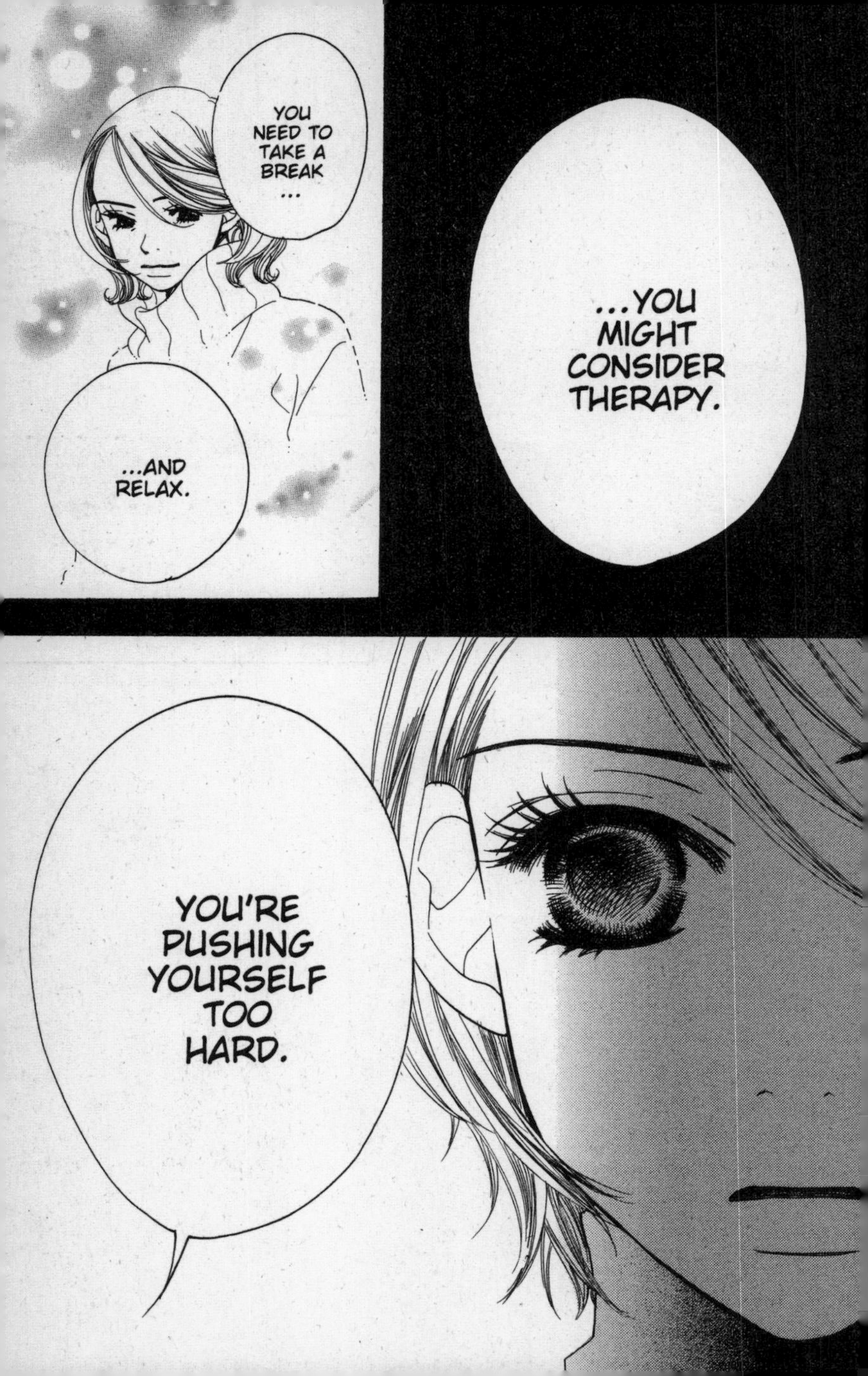
...YOU MIGHT CONSIDER THERAPY.
YOU NEED TO TAKE A BREAK ...
...AND RELAX.
YOU'RE PUSHING YOURSELF TOO HARD.

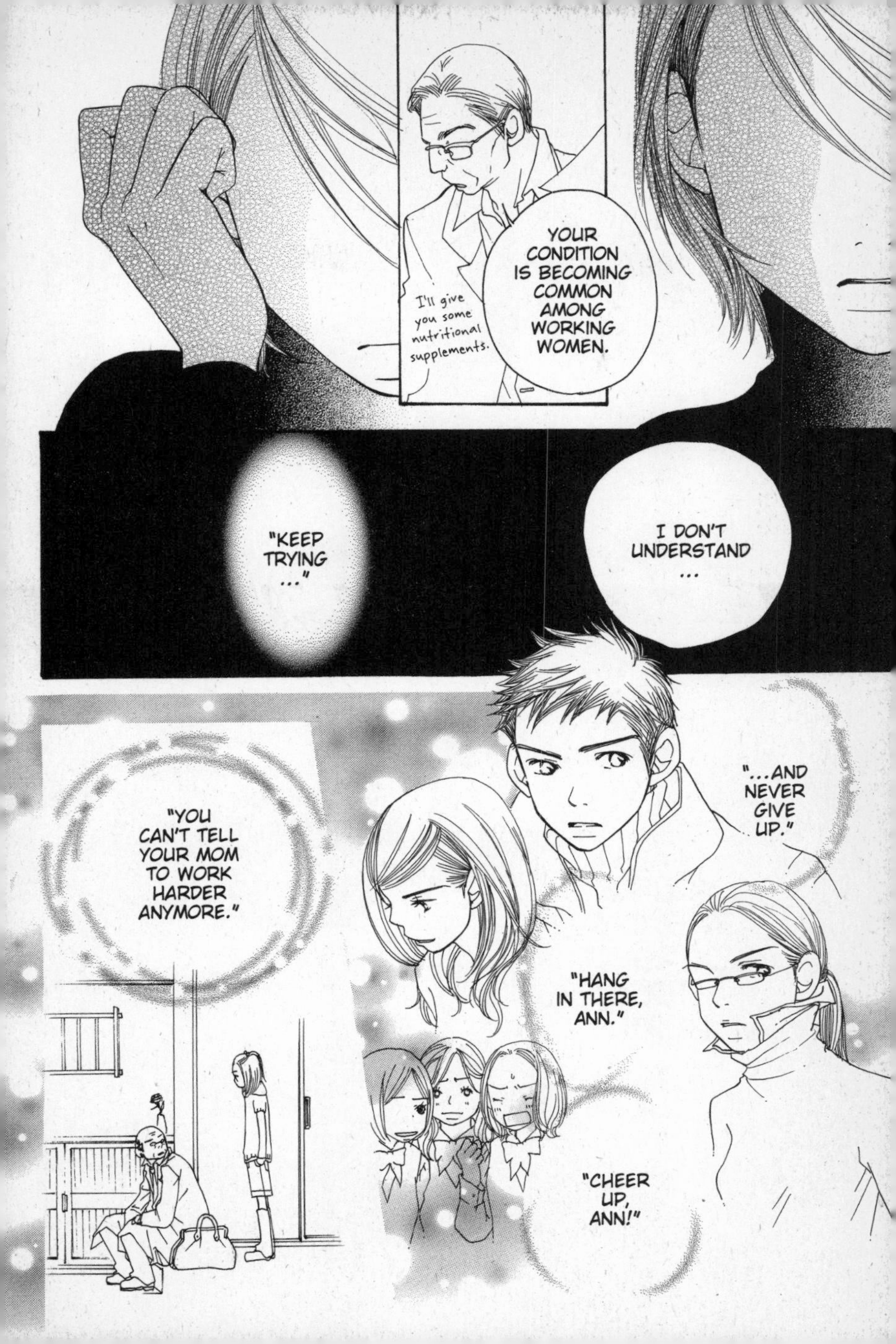
YOUR CONDITION IS BECOMING COMMON AMONG WORKING WOMEN.
I'll give you some nutritional supplements.
I DON'T UNDERSTAND ...
"KEEP TRYING ..."
"...AND NEVER GIVE UP."
"YOU CAN'T TELL YOUR MOM TO WORK HARDER ANYMORE."
"HANG IN THERE, ANN."
"CHEER UP, ANN!"

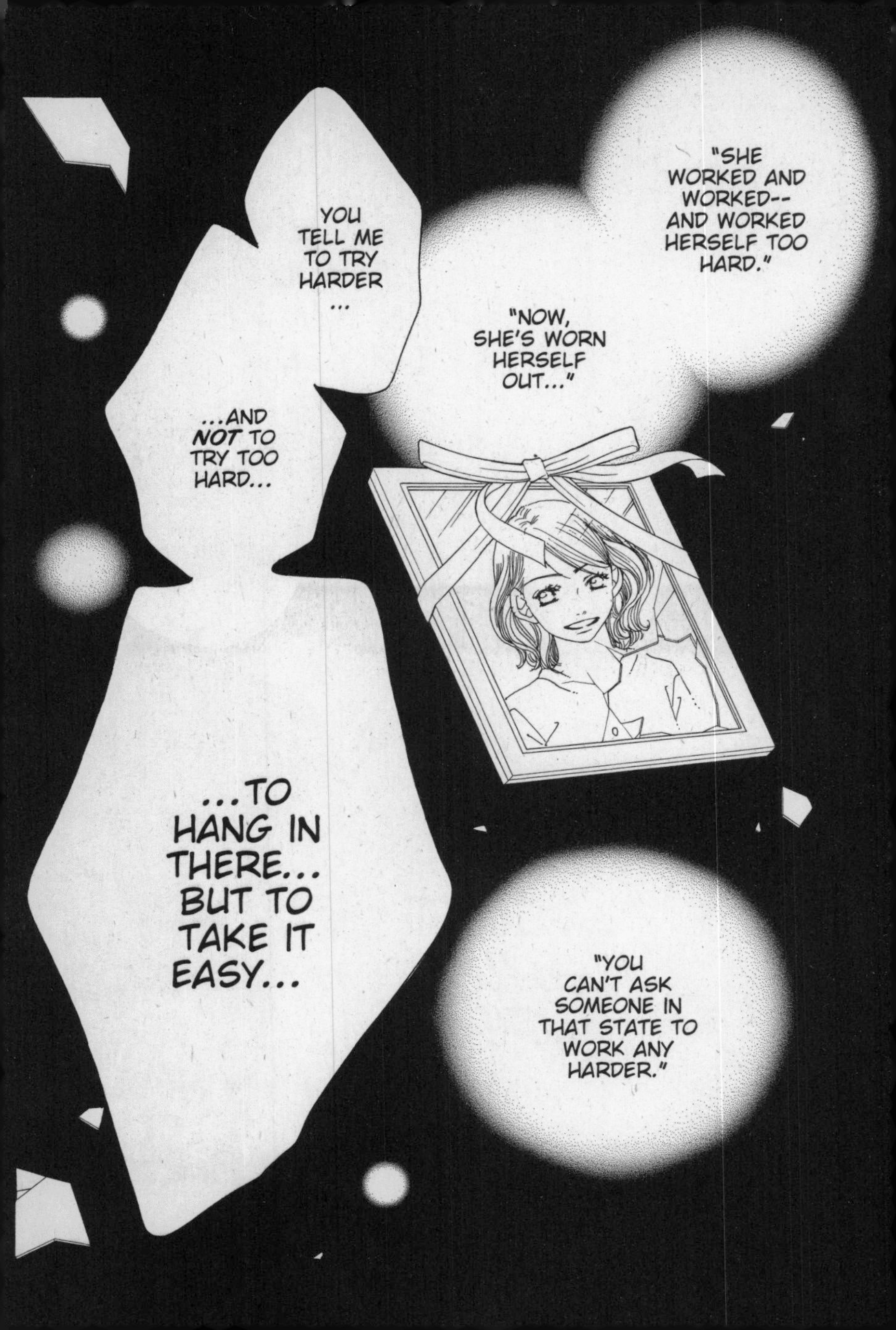
"SHE WORKED AND WORKED-- AND WORKED HERSELF TOO HARD."
"NOW, SHE'S WORN HERSELF OUT..."
"YOU CAN'T ASK SOMEONE IN THAT STATE TO WORK ANY HARDER."
YOU TELL ME TO TRY HARDER ...
...AND *NOT* TO TRY TOO HARD...
...TO HANG IN THERE... BUT TO TAKE IT EASY...

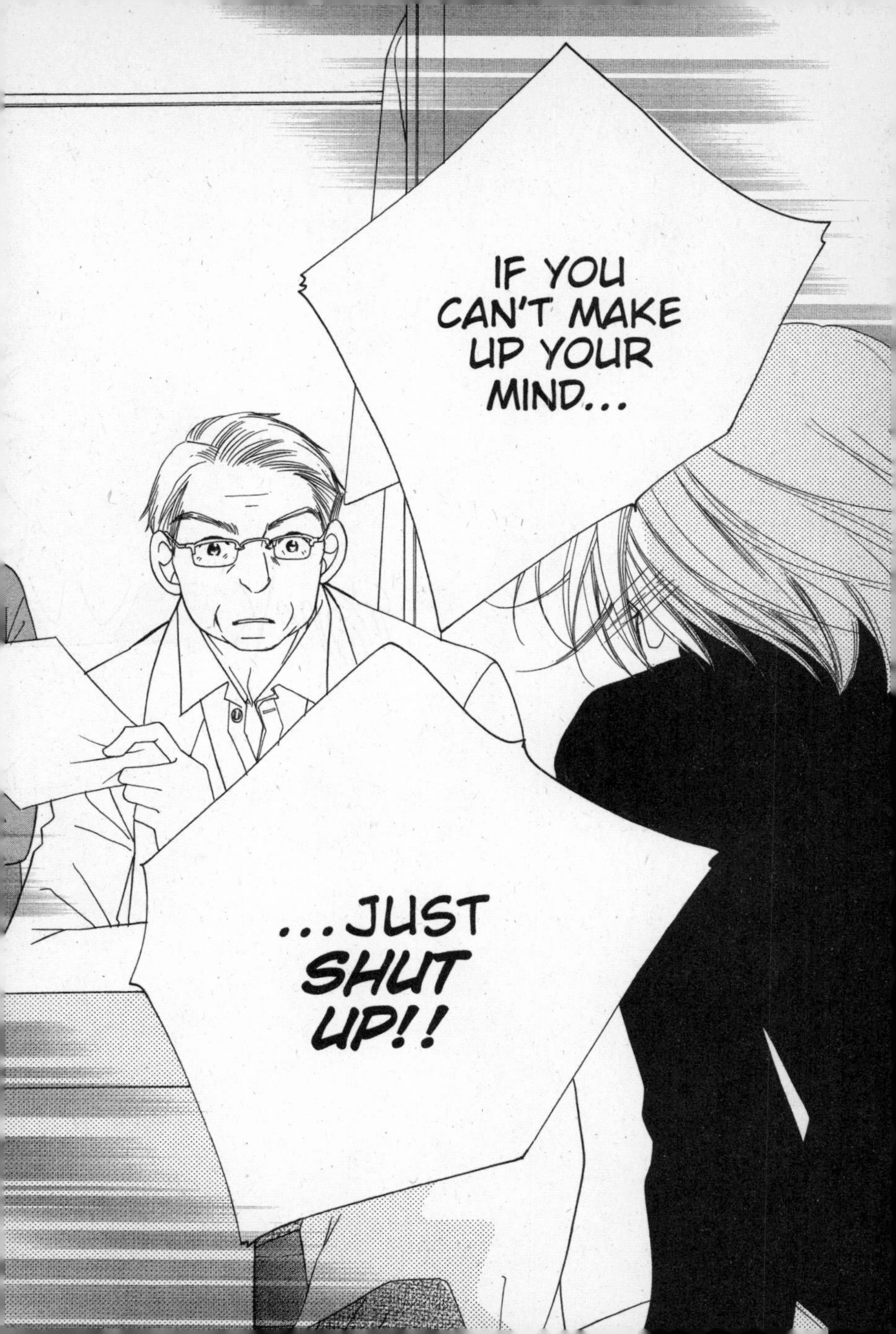
IF YOU CAN'T MAKE UP YOUR MIND...
...JUST SHUT UP!!

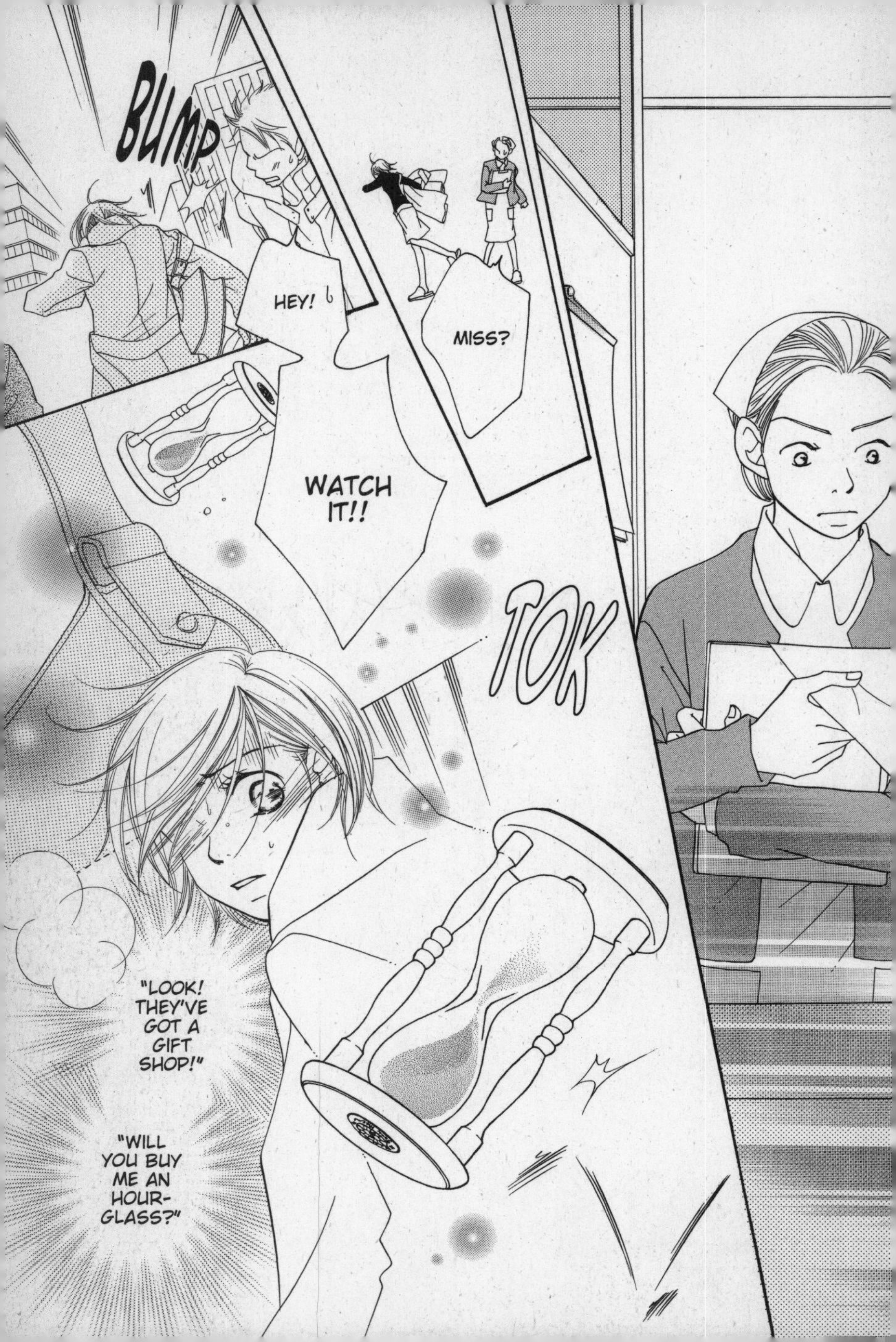
MISS?
BUMP
HEY!
WATCH IT!!
TOK
"LOOK! THEY'VE GOT A GIFT SHOP!"
"WILL YOU BUY ME AN HOUR-GLASS?"

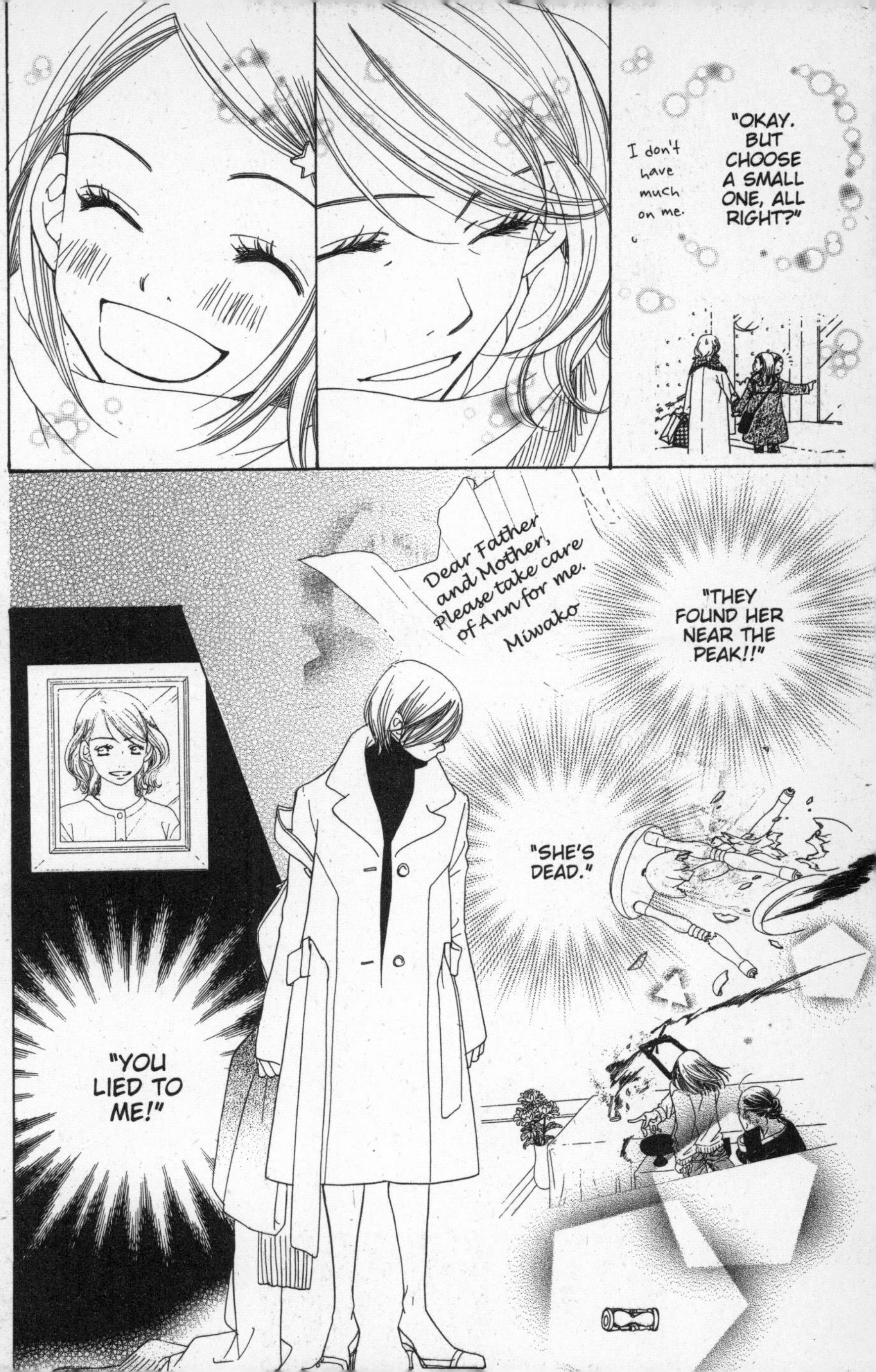
"OKAY. BUT CHOOSE A SMALL ONE, ALL RIGHT?"
I don't have much on me.
"THEY FOUND HER NEAR THE PEAK!!"
Dear Father and Mother, Please take care of Ann for me. Miwako
"SHE'S DEAD."
"YOU LIED TO ME!"

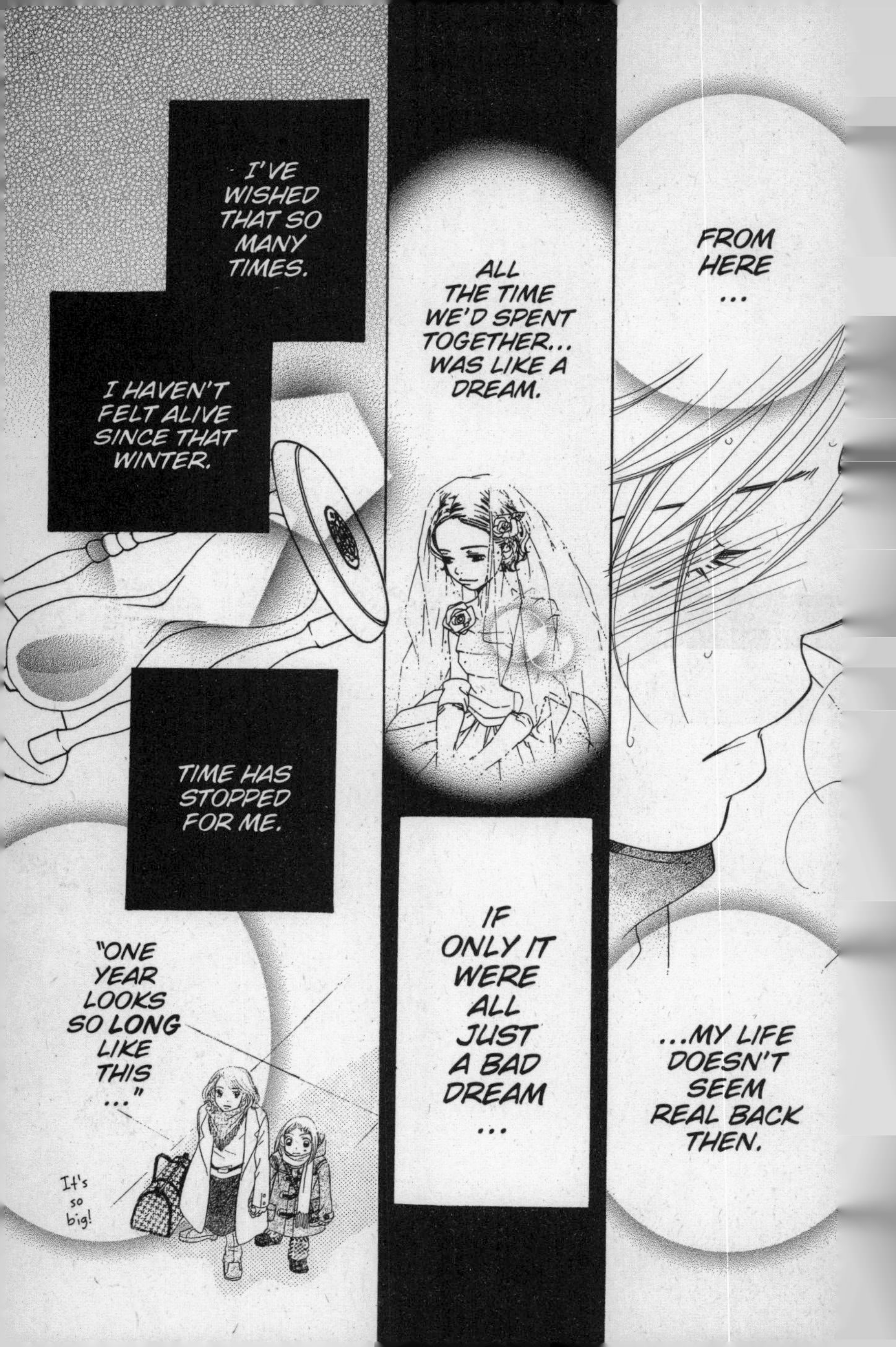
FROM HERE...
...MY LIFE DOESN'T SEEM REAL BACK THEN.
ALL THE TIME WE'D SPENT TOGETHER... WAS LIKE A DREAM.
IF ONLY IT WERE ALL JUST A BAD DREAM...
I'VE WISHED THAT SO MANY TIMES.
I HAVEN'T FELT ALIVE SINCE THAT WINTER.
TIME HAS STOPPED FOR ME.
"ONE YEAR LOOKS SO LONG LIKE THIS..."
It's so big!

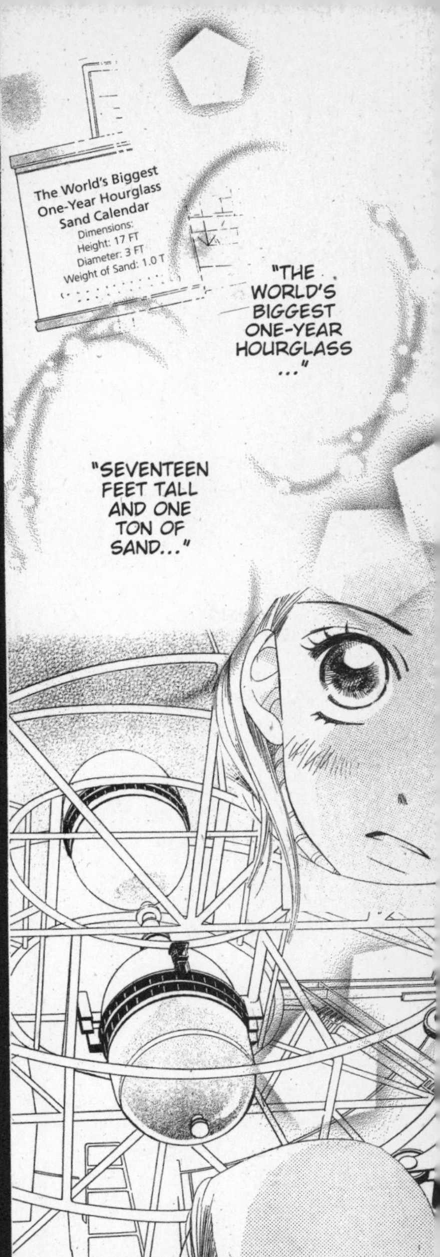
The World's Biggest One-Year Hourglass Sand Calendar
Dimensions:
Height: 17 FT
Diameter: 3 FT
Weight of Sand: 1.0 T
"THE WORLD'S BIGGEST ONE-YEAR HOURGLASS ..."
"SEVENTEEN FEET TALL AND ONE TON OF SAND..."

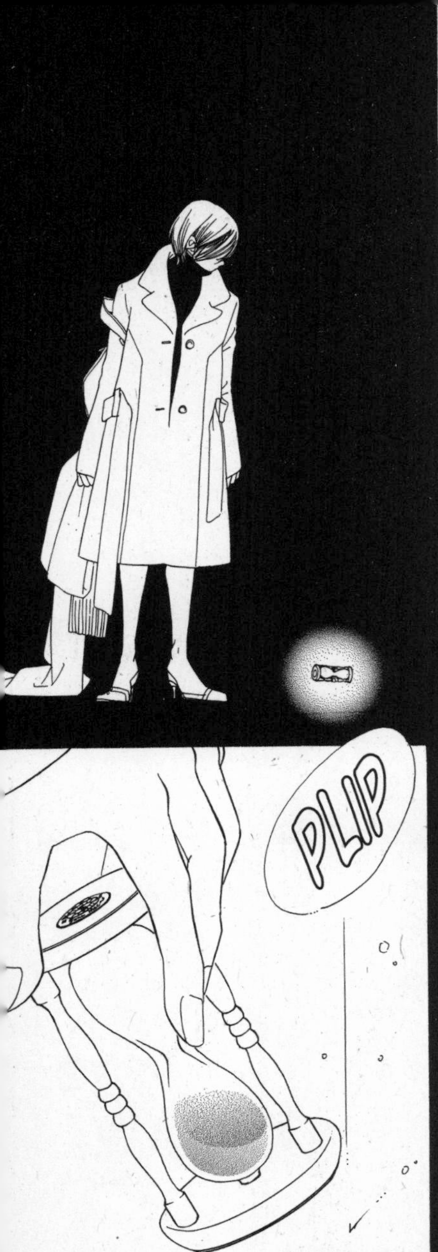
PLIP

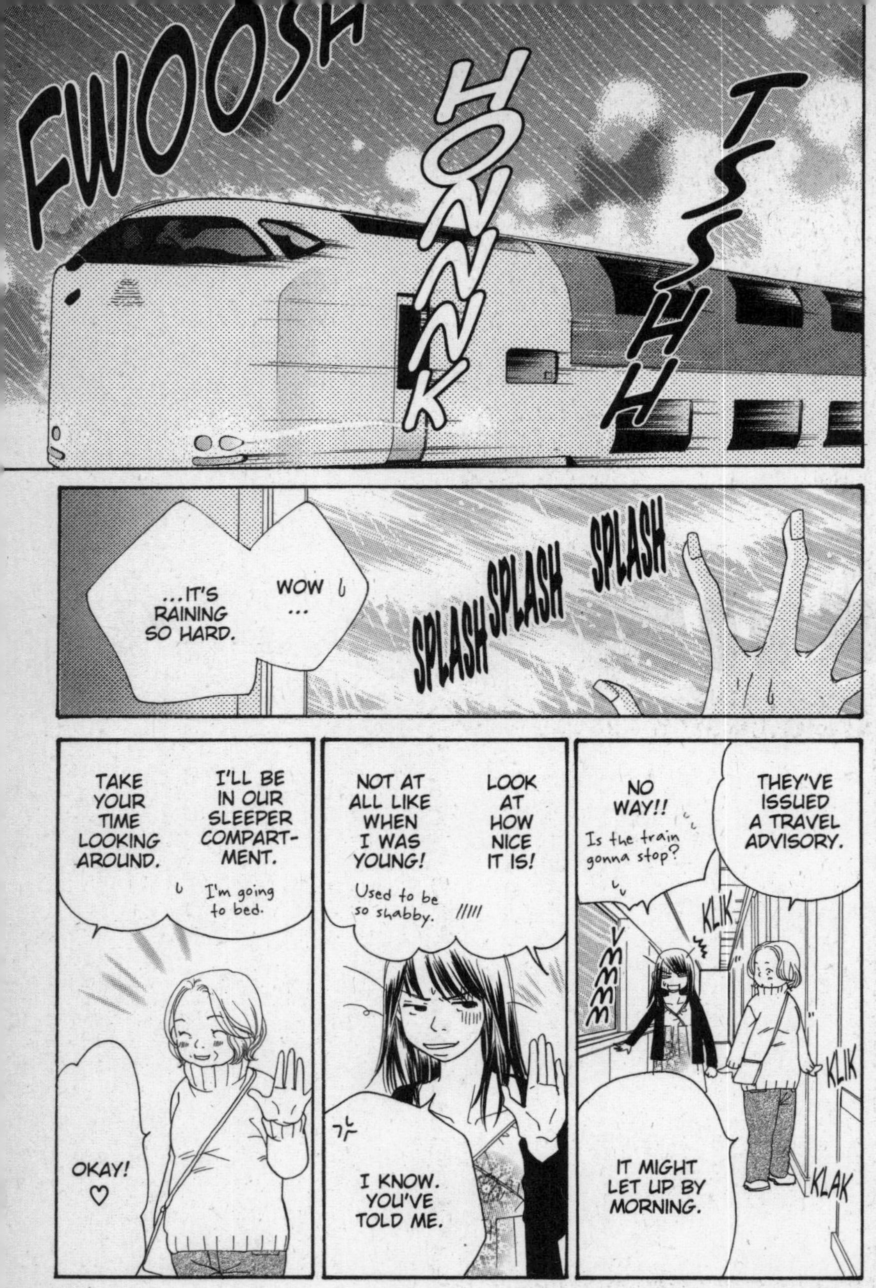
TSSHH
HONNK
FWOOSH
SPLASH
SPLASH
SPLASH
WOW ...
...IT'S RAINING SO HARD.
THEY'VE ISSUED A TRAVEL ADVISORY.
NO WAY!!
Is the train gonna stop?
KLIK
VMMM
KLIK
KLAK
IT MIGHT LET UP BY MORNING.
LOOK AT HOW NICE IT IS!
NOT AT ALL LIKE WHEN I WAS YOUNG!
Used to be so shabby.
I KNOW. YOU'VE TOLD ME.
I'LL BE IN OUR SLEEPER COMPARTMENT.
I'm going to bed.
TAKE YOUR TIME LOOKING AROUND.
OKAY! ♡

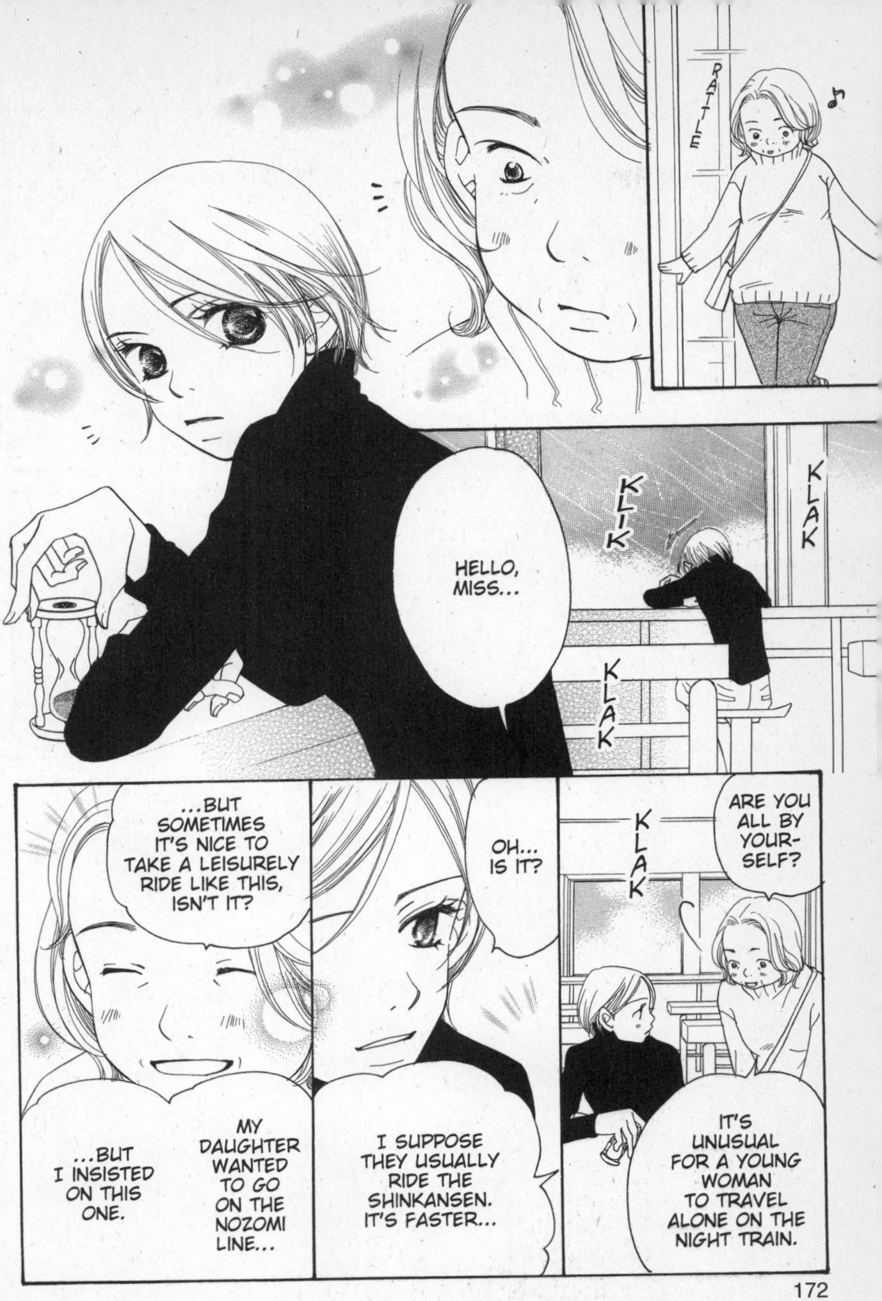
RATTLE
KLIK
KLAK
HELLO, MISS...
KLAK
KLAK
ARE YOU ALL BY YOURSELF?
IT'S UNUSUAL FOR A YOUNG WOMAN TO TRAVEL ALONE ON THE NIGHT TRAIN.
OH... IS IT?
I SUPPOSE THEY USUALLY RIDE THE SHINKANSEN. IT'S FASTER...
...BUT SOMETIMES IT'S NICE TO TAKE A LEISURELY RIDE LIKE THIS, ISN'T IT?
MY DAUGHTER WANTED TO GO ON THE NOZOMI LINE...
...BUT I INSISTED ON THIS ONE.

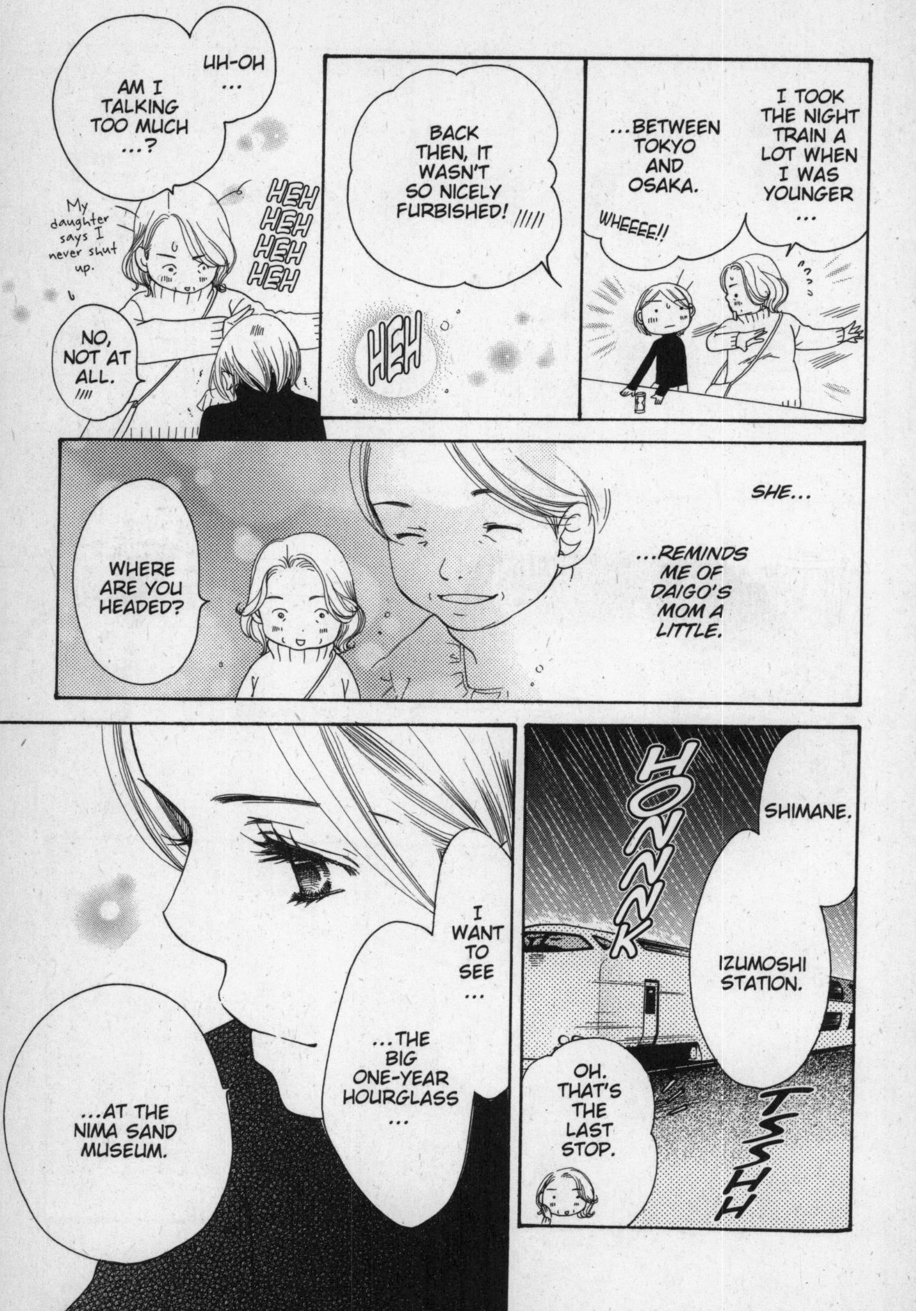
I TOOK THE NIGHT TRAIN A LOT WHEN I WAS YOUNGER...
...BETWEEN TOKYO AND OSAKA.
WHEEEEE!!
BACK THEN, IT WASN'T SO NICELY FURBISHED! ////
HEH
UH-OH ...
AM I TALKING TOO MUCH ...?
HEH HEH HEH HEH
My daughter says I never shut up.
NO, NOT AT ALL. ////
SHE...
...REMINDS ME OF DAIGO'S MOM A LITTLE.
WHERE ARE YOU HEADED?
SHIMANE.
HONNNK
IZUMOSHI STATION.
OH. THAT'S THE LAST STOP.
TSSHH
I WANT TO SEE ...
...THE BIG ONE-YEAR HOURGLASS ...
...AT THE NIMA SAND MUSEUM.

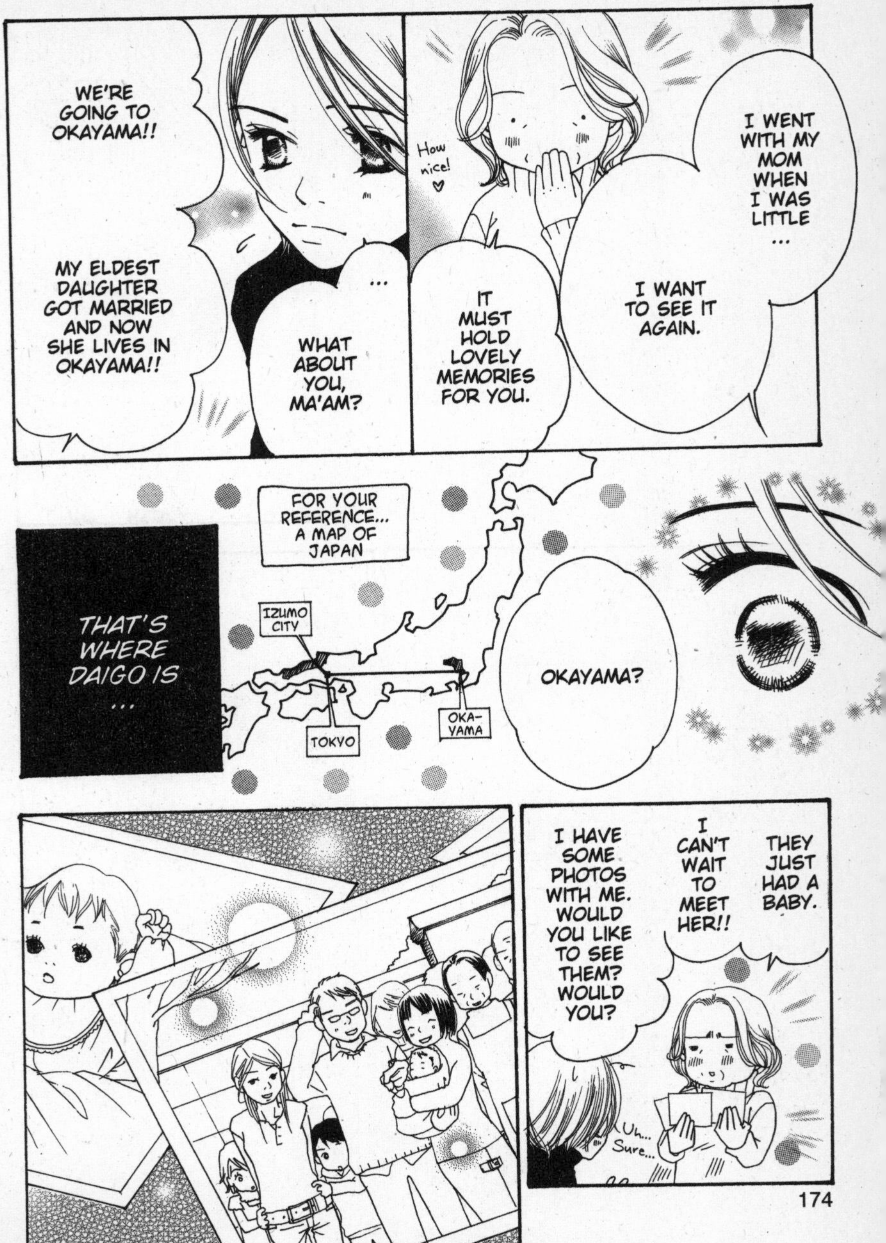
I WENT WITH MY MOM WHEN I WAS LITTLE...
I WANT TO SEE IT AGAIN.
How nice! ♥
IT MUST HOLD LOVELY MEMORIES FOR YOU.
...
WHAT ABOUT YOU, MA'AM?
WE'RE GOING TO OKAYAMA!!
MY ELDEST DAUGHTER GOT MARRIED AND NOW SHE LIVES IN OKAYAMA!!
OKAYAMA?
FOR YOUR REFERENCE... A MAP OF JAPAN
IZUMO CITY
OKA-YAMA
TOKYO
THAT'S WHERE DAIGO IS...
THEY JUST HAD A BABY.
I CAN'T WAIT TO MEET HER!!
I HAVE SOME PHOTOS WITH ME. WOULD YOU LIKE TO SEE THEM? WOULD YOU?
Uh... Sure...

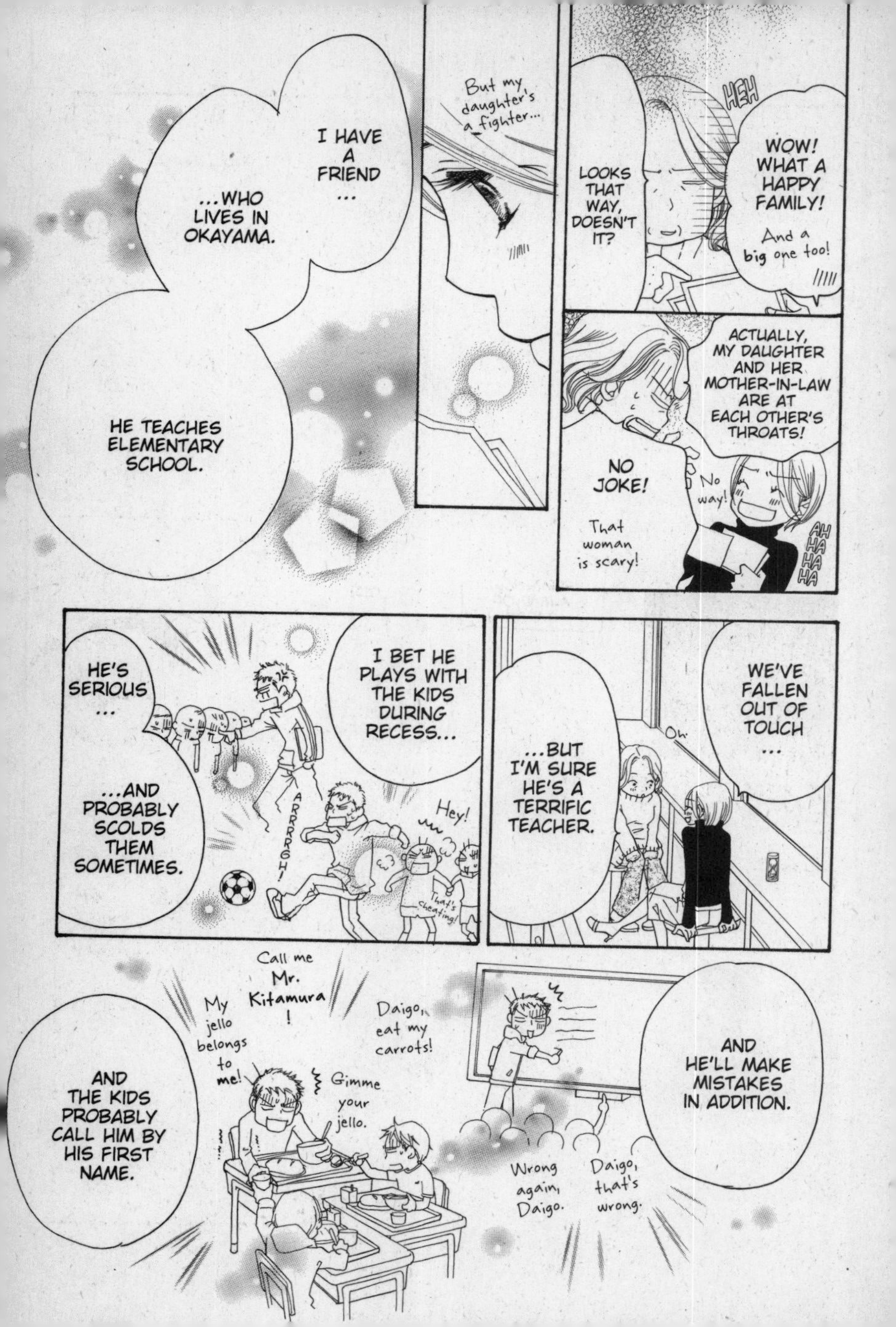
HEH
WOW! WHAT A HAPPY FAMILY!
And a big one too!
LOOKS THAT WAY, DOESN'T IT?
ACTUALLY, MY DAUGHTER AND HER MOTHER-IN-LAW ARE AT EACH OTHER'S THROATS!
AH HA HA HA
No way!
NO JOKE!
That woman is scary!
But my daughter's a fighter...
I HAVE A FRIEND...
...WHO LIVES IN OKAYAMA.
HE TEACHES ELEMENTARY SCHOOL.
WE'VE FALLEN OUT OF TOUCH...
Oh
...BUT I'M SURE HE'S A TERRIFIC TEACHER.
I BET HE PLAYS WITH THE KIDS DURING RECESS...
Hey!
HE'S SERIOUS...
ARRRRGH!
That's cheating!
...AND PROBABLY SCOLDS THEM SOMETIMES.
AND HE'LL MAKE MISTAKES IN ADDITION.
Daigo, that's wrong.
Wrong again, Daigo.
Daigo, eat my carrots!
Call me Mr. Kitamura!
My jello belongs to me!
Gimme your jello.
AND THE KIDS PROBABLY CALL HIM BY HIS FIRST NAME.

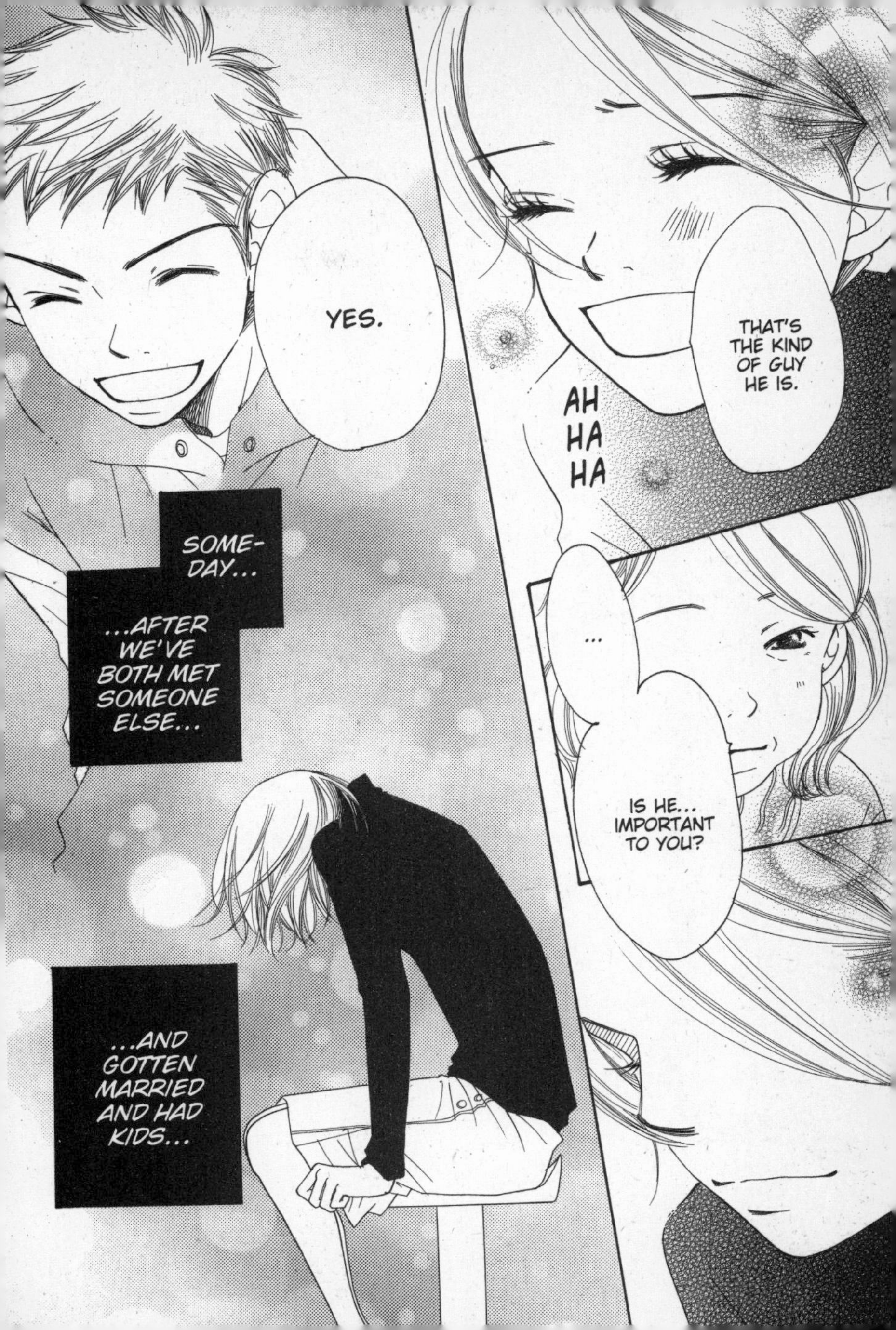
THAT'S THE KIND OF GUY HE IS.
AH HA HA
...
IS HE... IMPORTANT TO YOU?
YES.
SOME-DAY...
...AFTER WE'VE BOTH MET SOMEONE ELSE...
...AND GOTTEN MARRIED AND HAD KIDS...

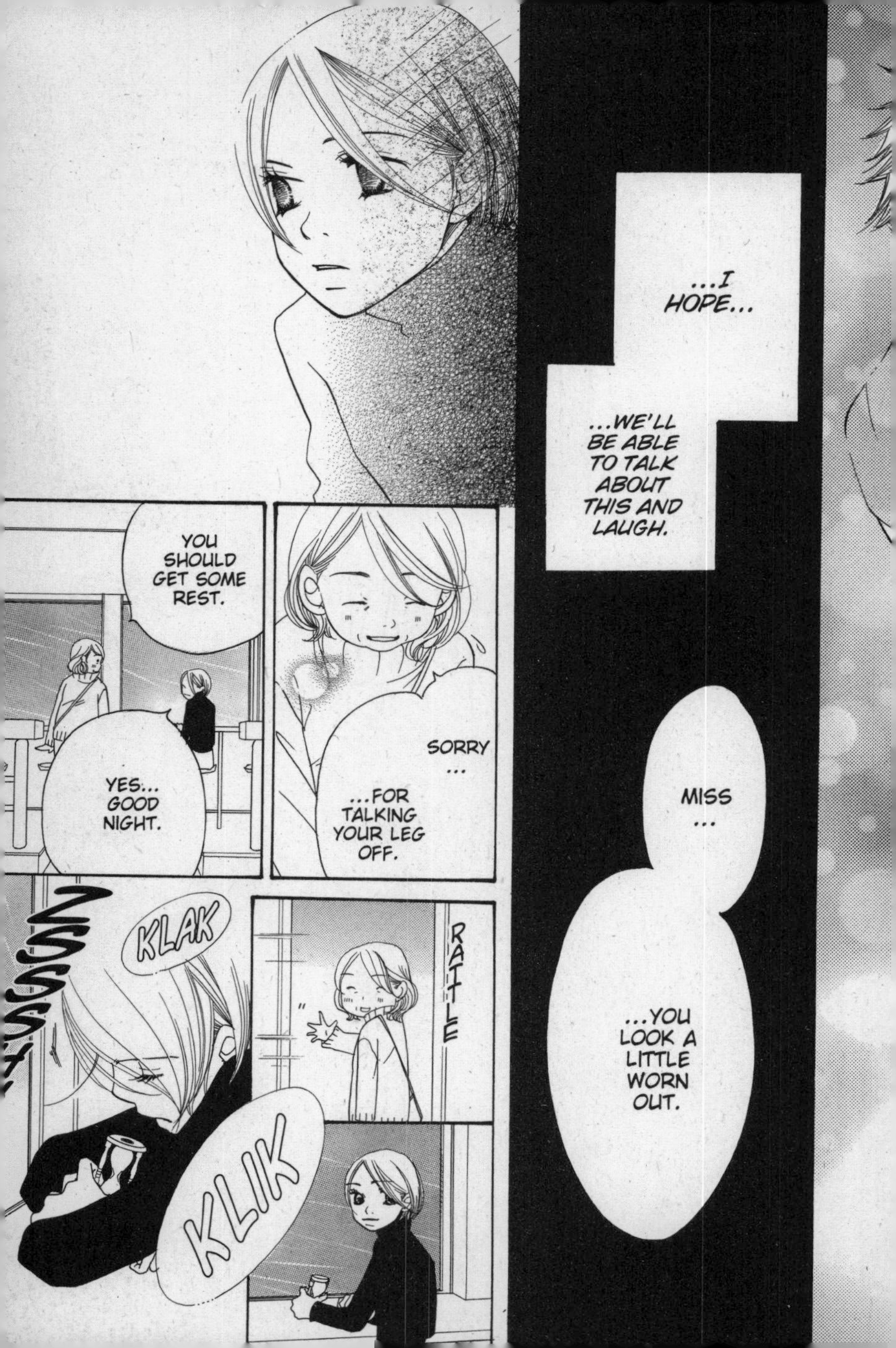
...I HOPE...
...WE'LL BE ABLE TO TALK ABOUT THIS AND LAUGH.
MISS...
...YOU LOOK A LITTLE WORN OUT.
SORRY...
...FOR TALKING YOUR LEG OFF.
YOU SHOULD GET SOME REST.
YES... GOOD NIGHT.
RATTLE
KLIK
KLAK
ZSSSS

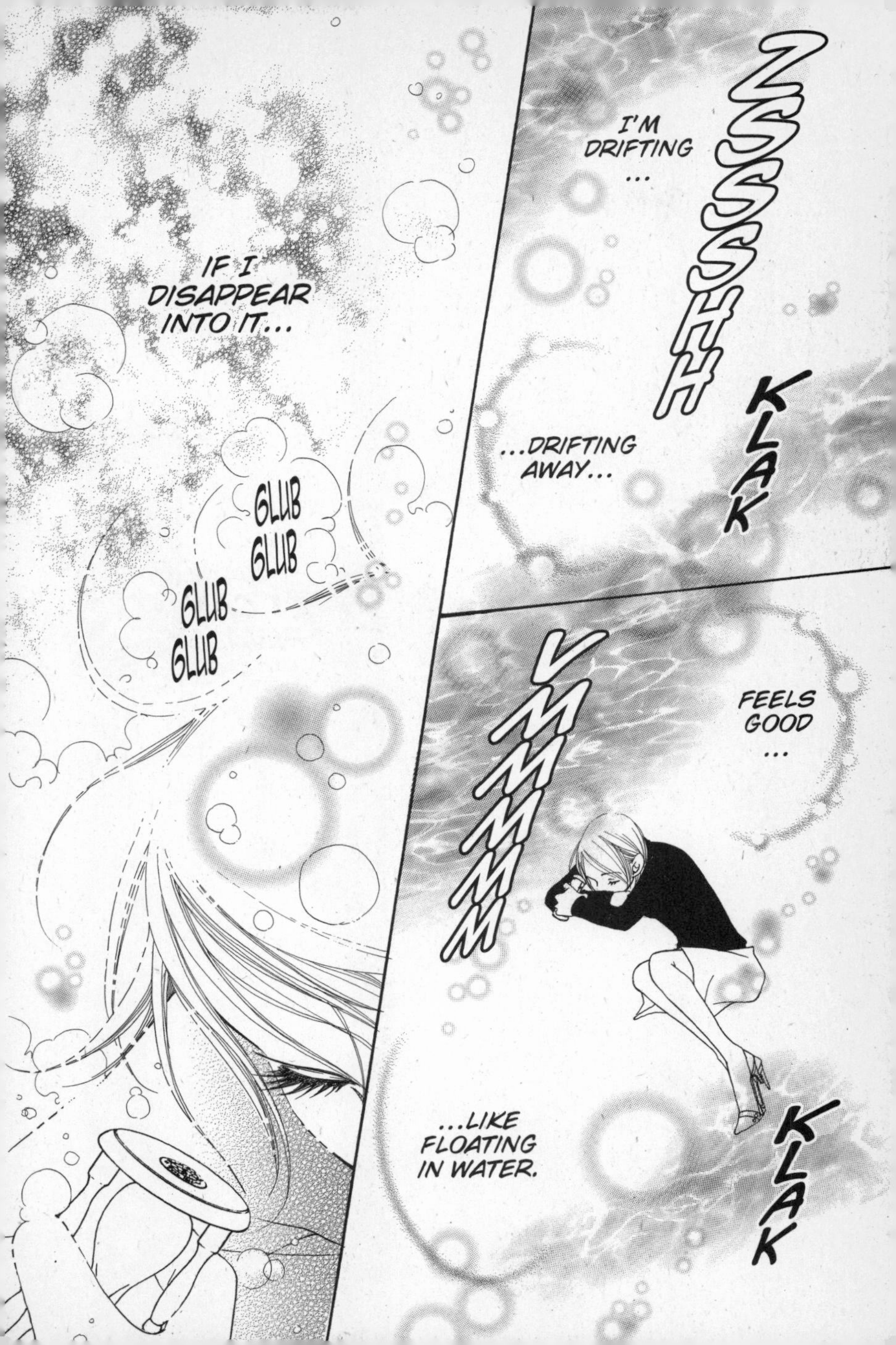
ZSSSHHH
I'M DRIFTING ...
KLAK
...DRIFTING AWAY...
FEELS GOOD ...
VMMMMMM
KLAK
...LIKE FLOATING IN WATER.
IF I DISAPPEAR INTO IT...
GLUB GLUB
GLUB GLUB GLUB

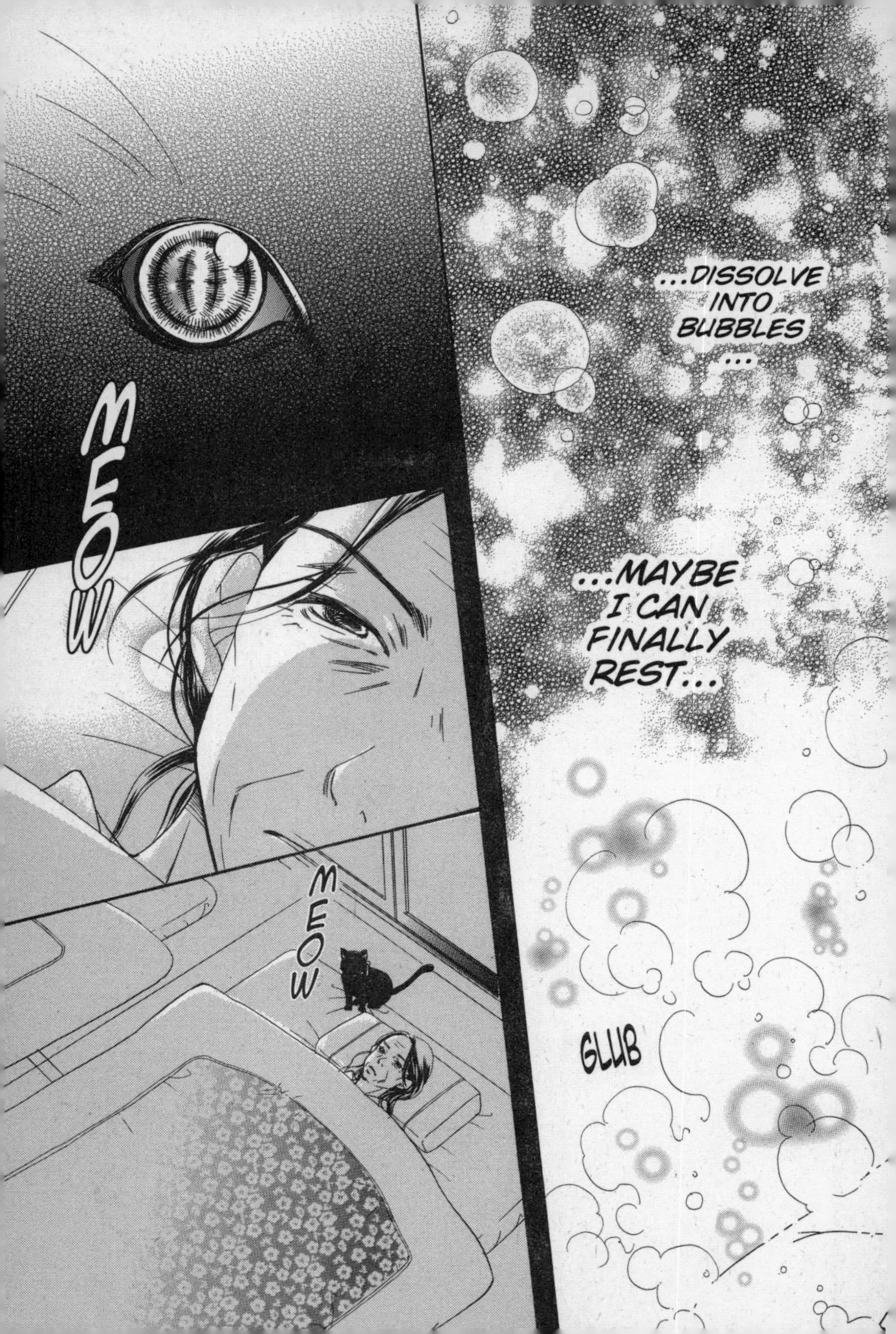
...DISSOLVE INTO BUBBLES ...
...MAYBE I CAN FINALLY REST...
GLUB
MEOW
MEOW

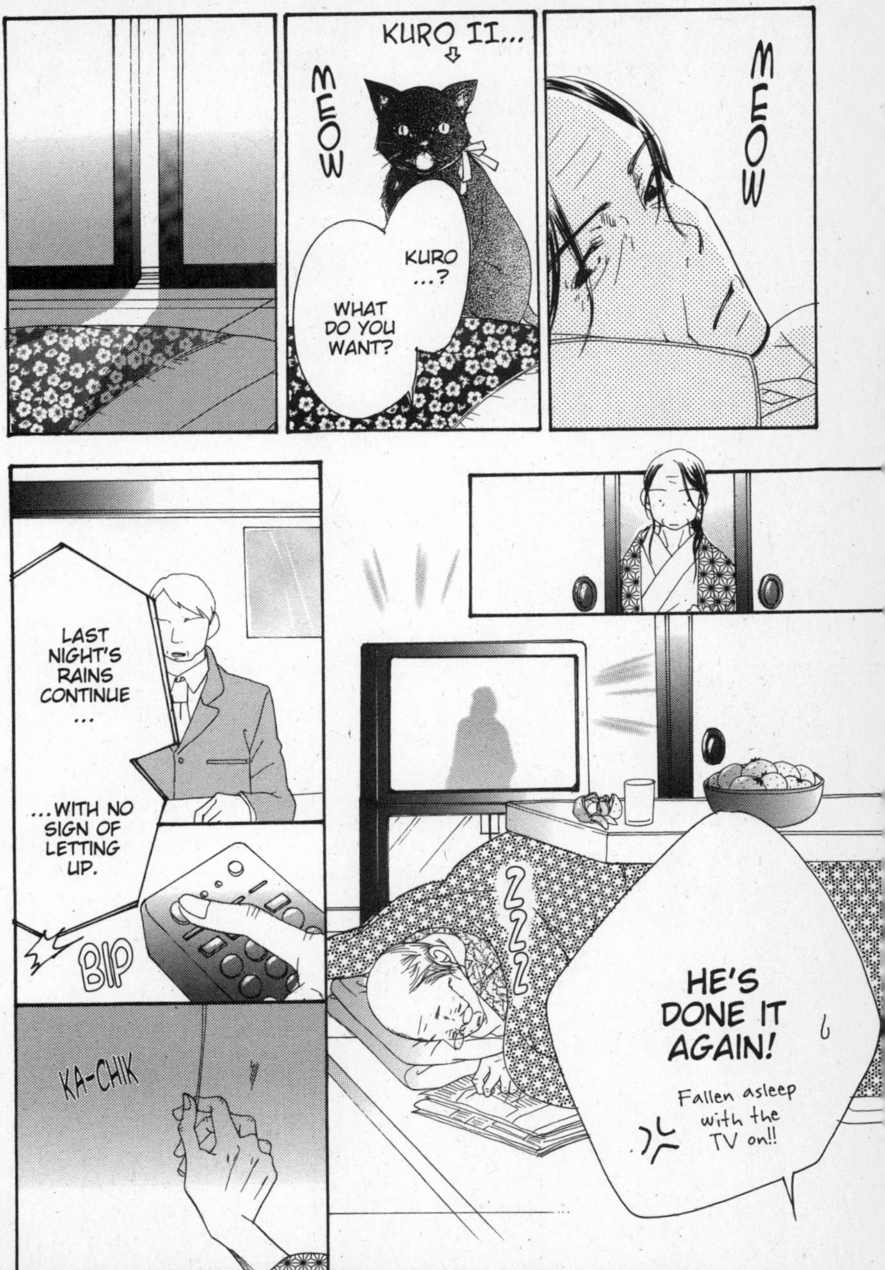
MEOW
KURO II...
MEOW
KURO ...?
WHAT DO YOU WANT?
ZZZ
HE'S DONE IT AGAIN!
Fallen asleep with the TV on!!
LAST NIGHT'S RAINS CONTINUE ...
...WITH NO SIGN OF LETTING UP.
BIP
KA-CHIK

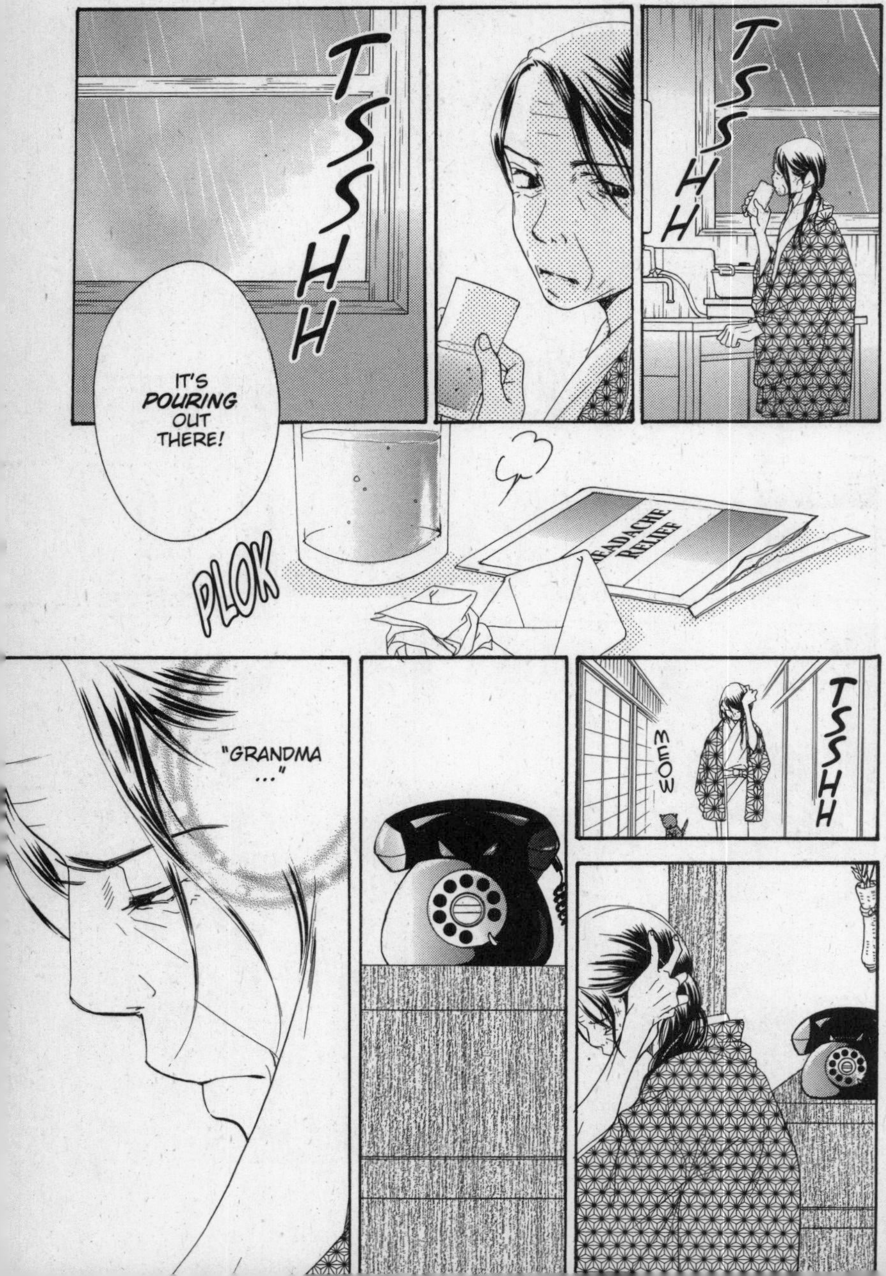
TSSHH
TSSHH
IT'S POURING OUT THERE!
EADACHE RELIEF
PLOK
TSSHH
MEOW
"GRANDMA ..."

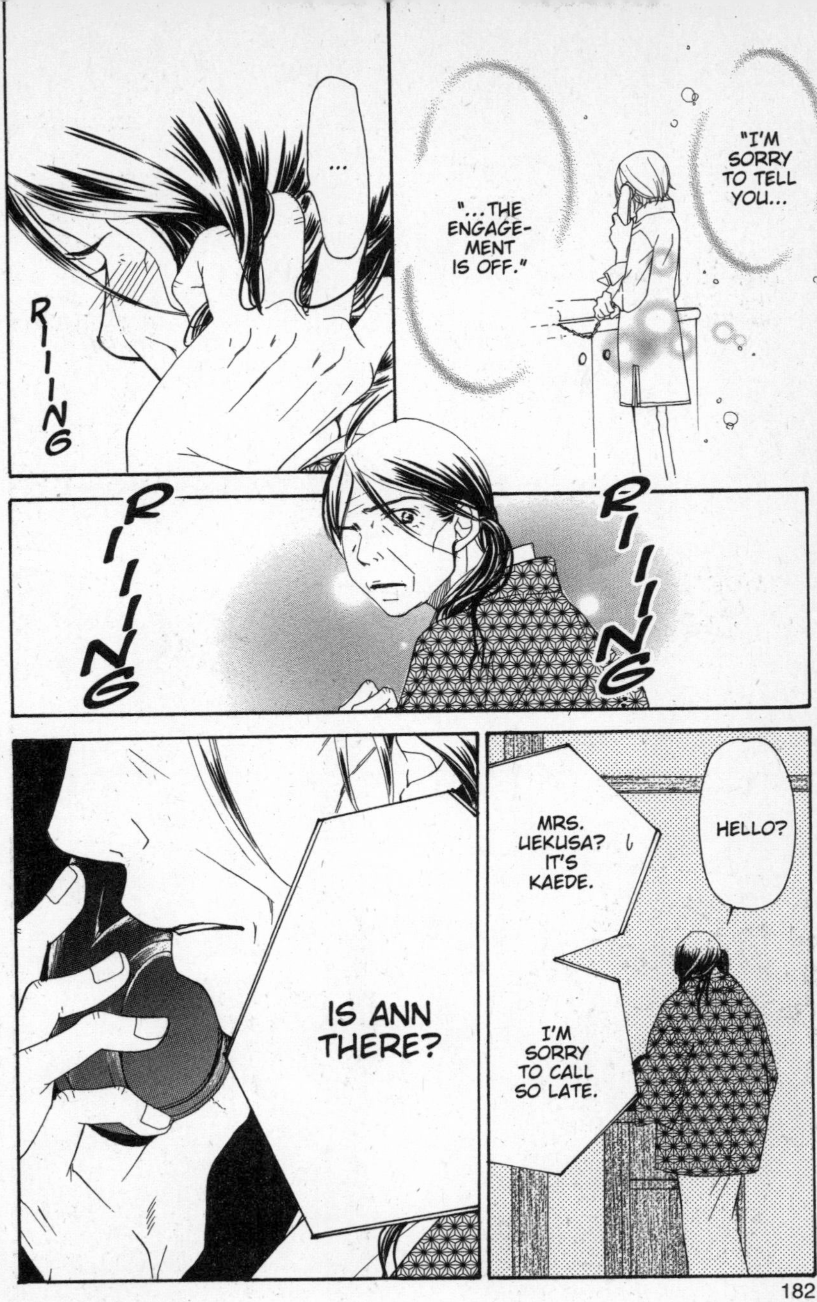
"I'M SORRY TO TELL YOU...
"...THE ENGAGEMENT IS OFF."
...
RIIING
RIIING
RIIING
HELLO?
MRS. UEKUSA? IT'S KAEDE.
I'M SORRY TO CALL SO LATE.
IS ANN THERE?

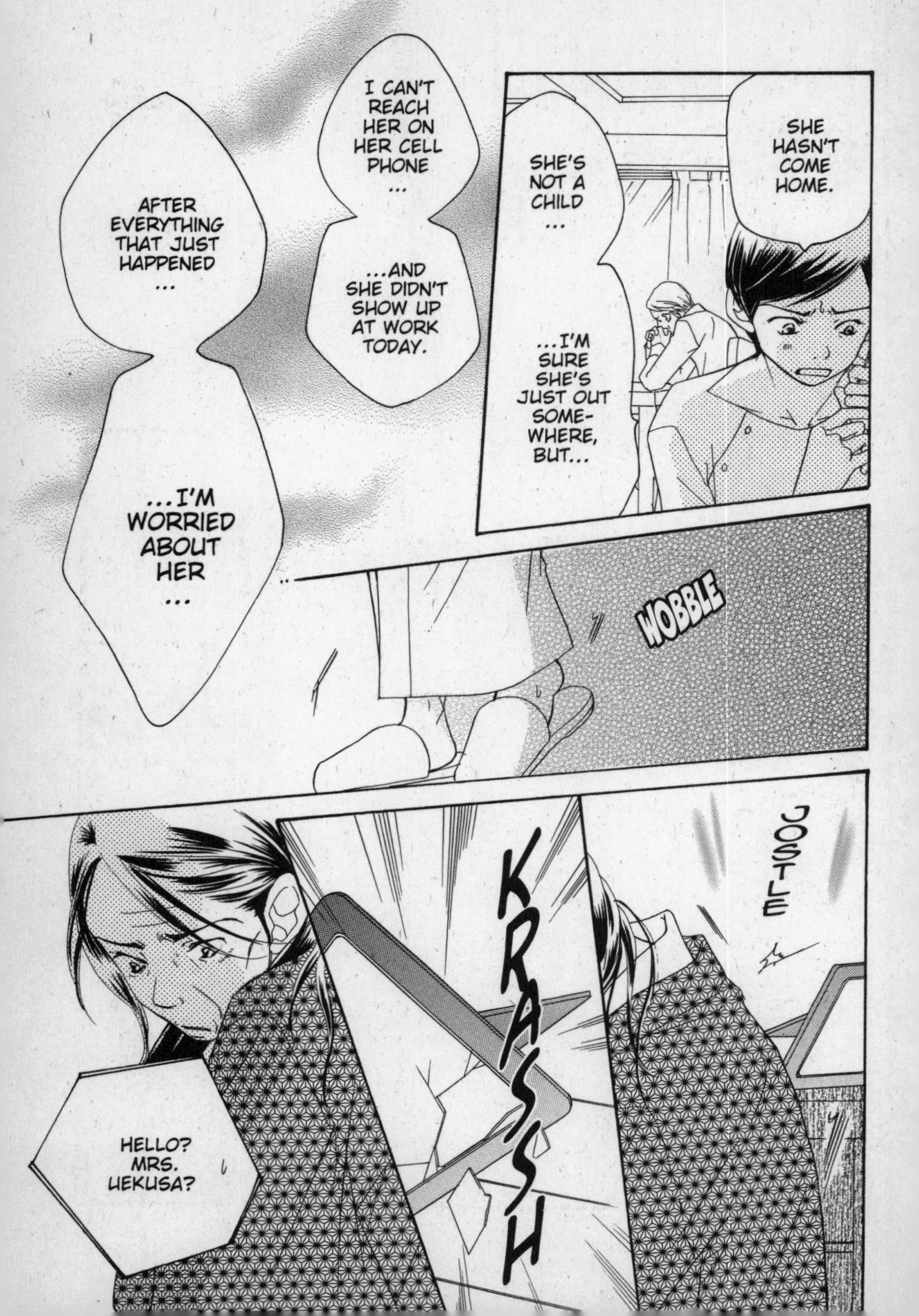
SHE HASN'T COME HOME.
SHE'S NOT A CHILD ...
...I'M SURE SHE'S JUST OUT SOME-WHERE, BUT...
I CAN'T REACH HER ON HER CELL PHONE ...
...AND SHE DIDN'T SHOW UP AT WORK TODAY.
AFTER EVERYTHING THAT JUST HAPPENED ...
...I'M WORRIED ABOUT HER ...
WOBBLE
JOSTLE
KRASSH
HELLO? MRS. UEKUSA?

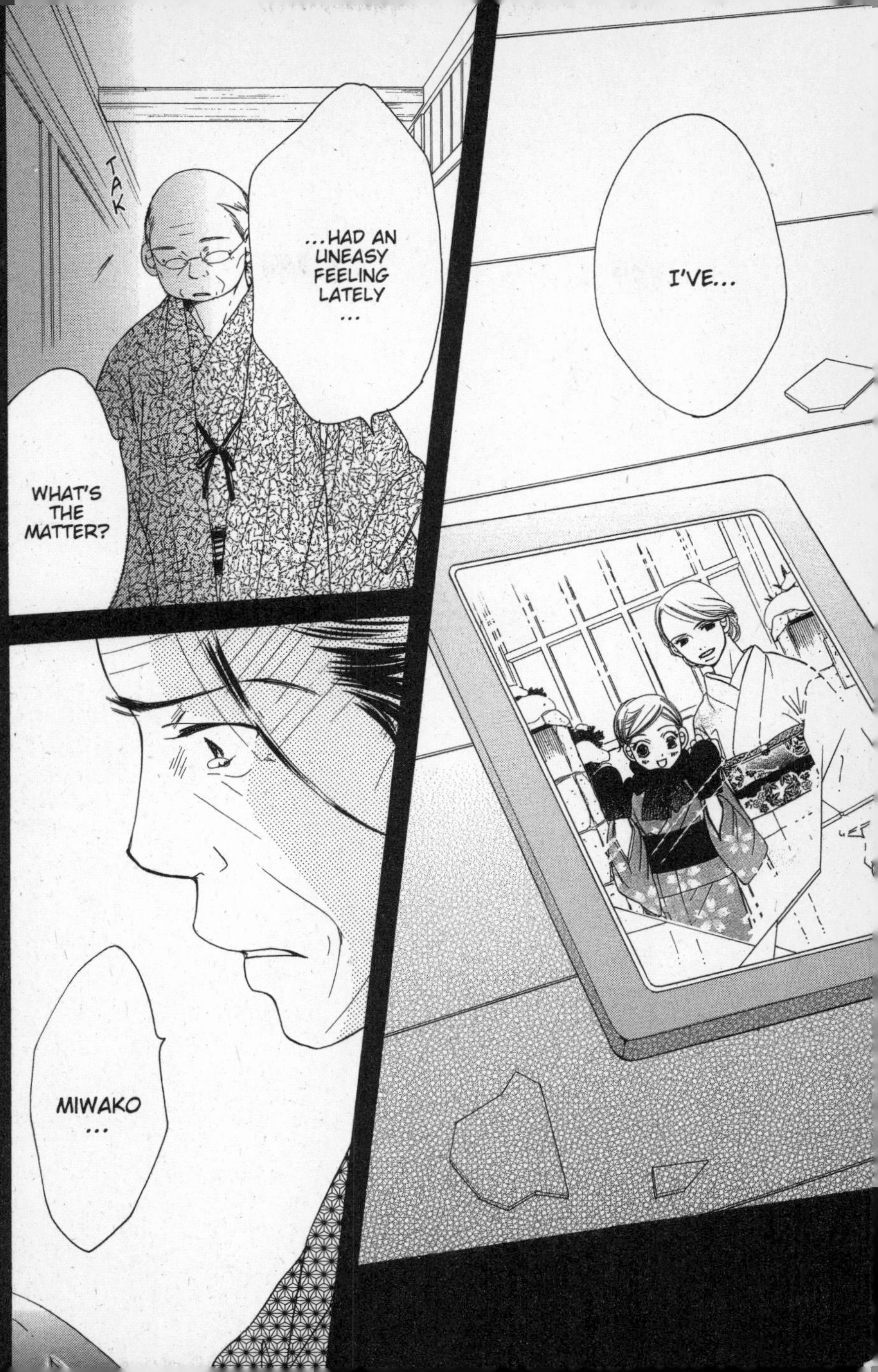

I'VE...
...HAD AN UNEASY FEELING LATELY...
TAK
WHAT'S THE MATTER?
MIWAKO...

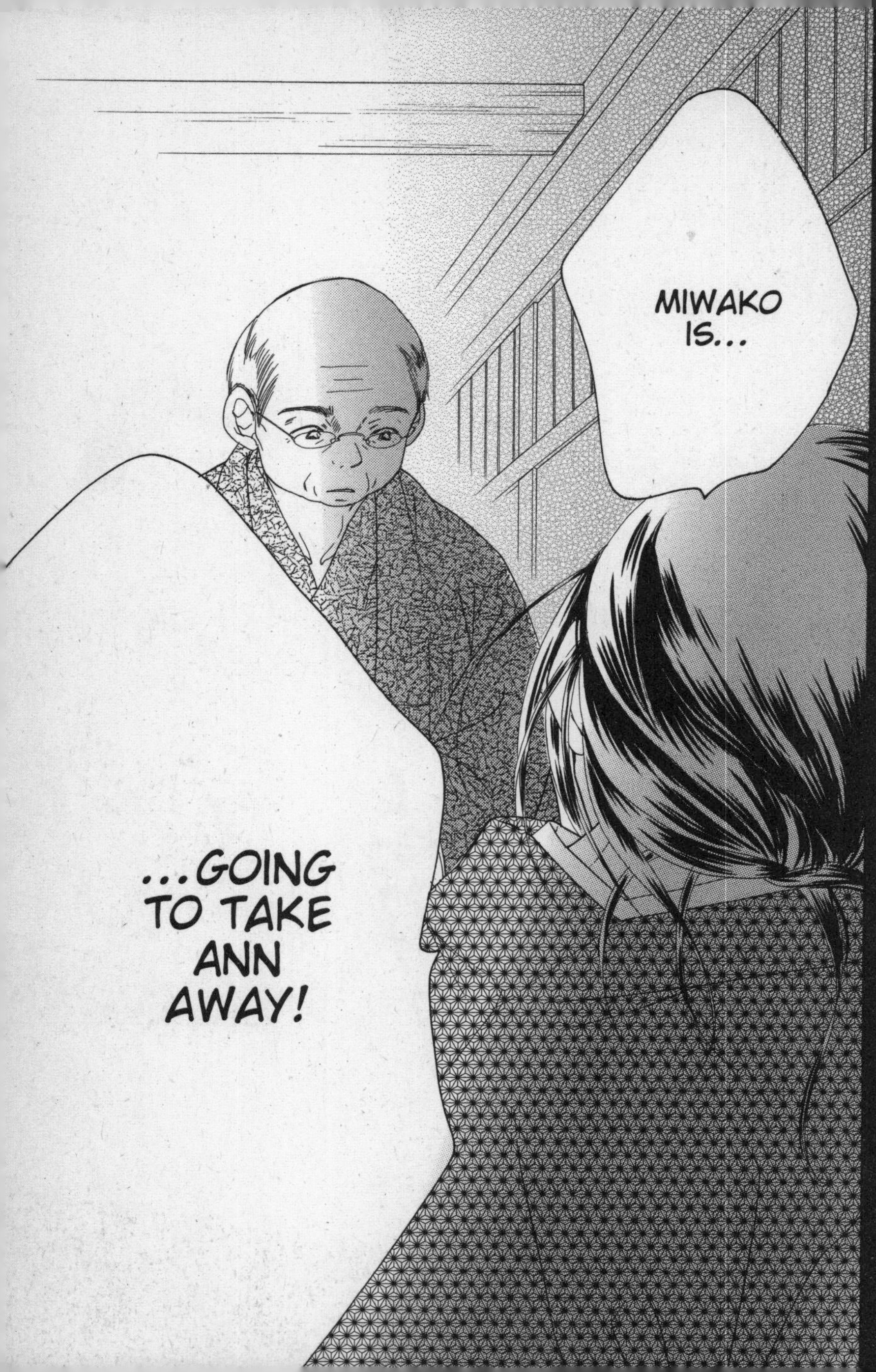
MIWAKO IS...
...GOING TO TAKE ANN AWAY!

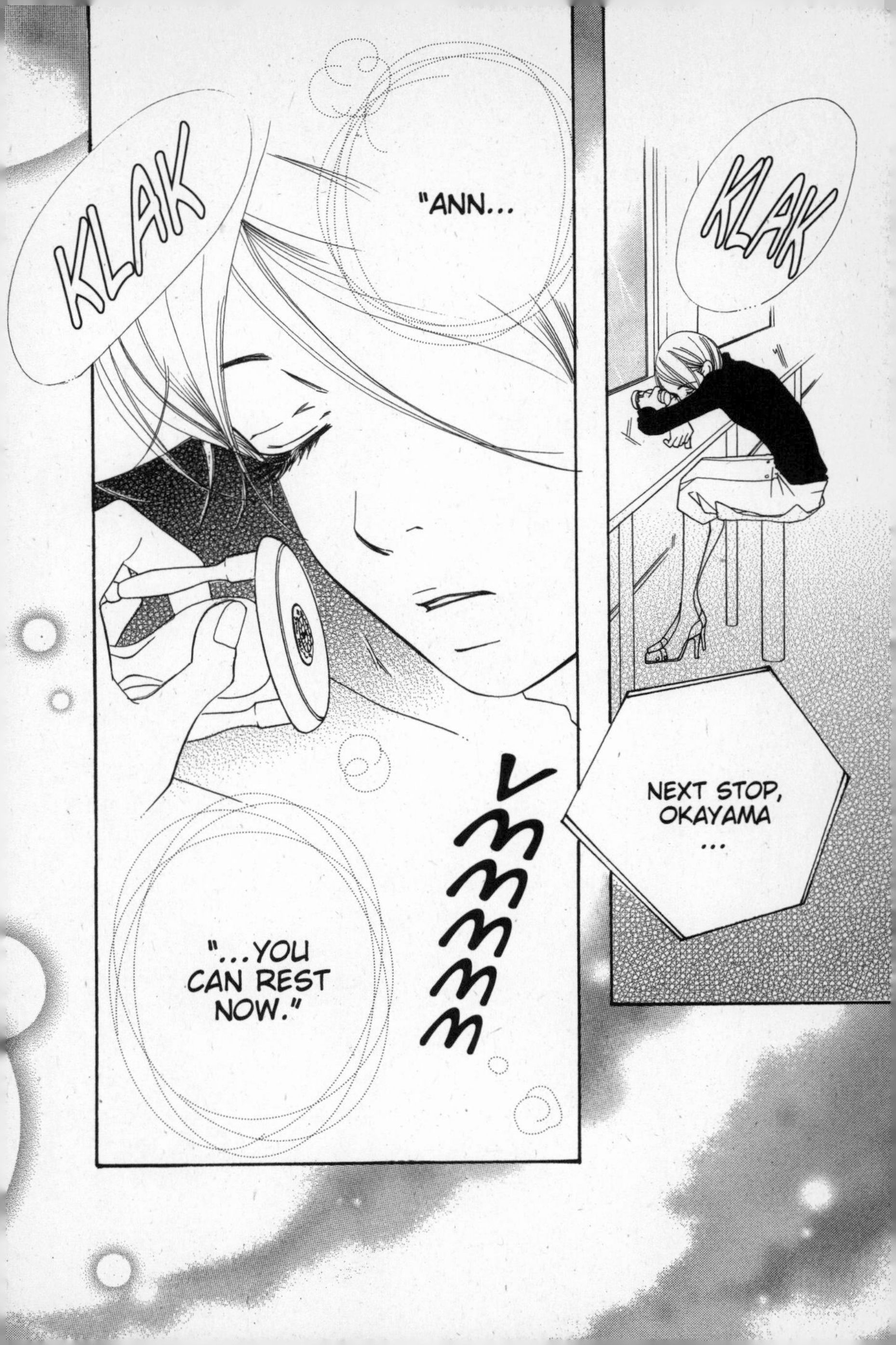
KLAK
NEXT STOP, OKAYAMA ...
KLAK
"ANN...
"...YOU CAN REST NOW."
VMMMMMM

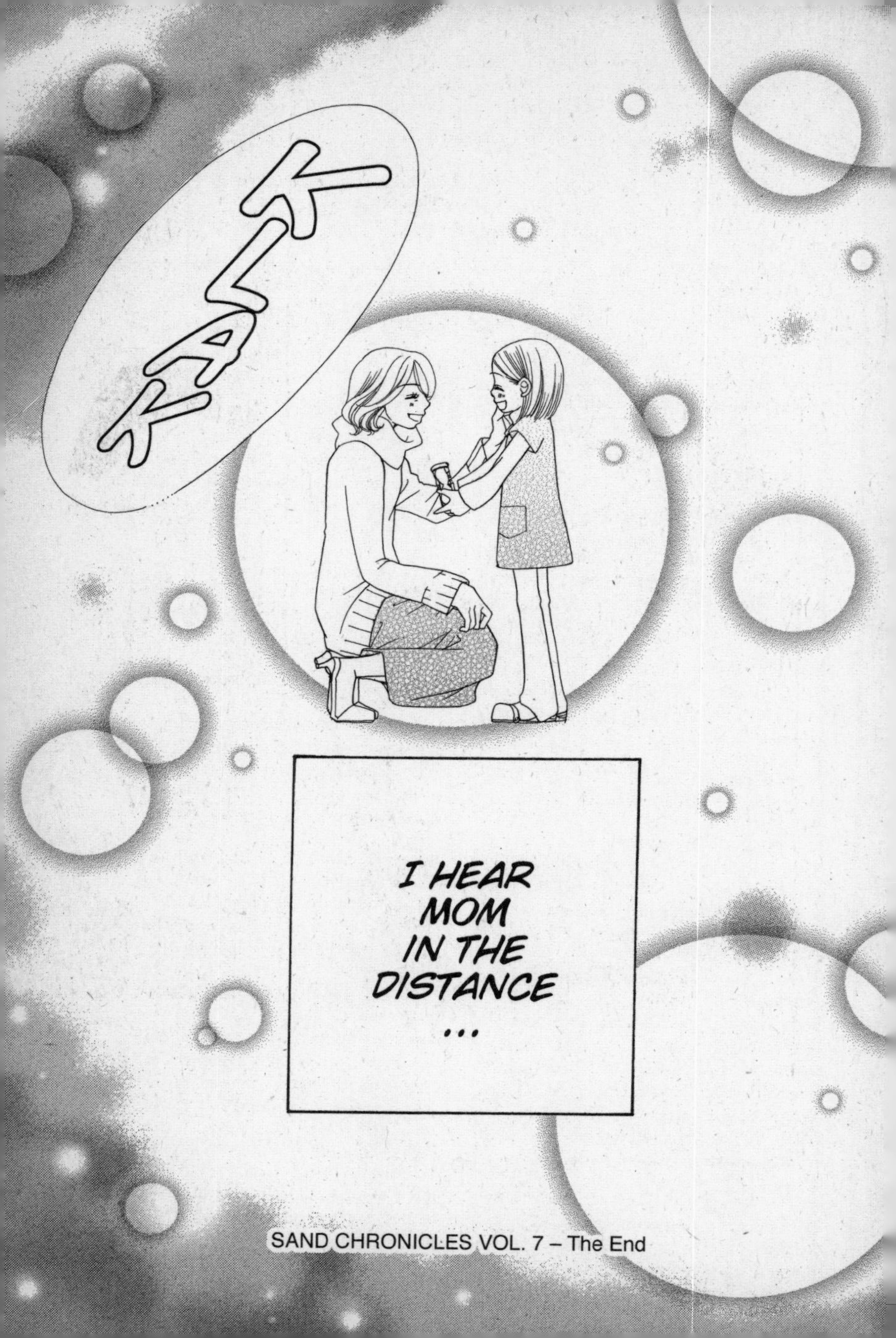
KLAK
I HEAR MOM IN THE DISTANCE...
SAND CHRONICLES VOL. 7 – The End

Glossary

If only adolescence came with an instruction manual.
We can't give you that, but this glossary of terms
might prove useful for this volume.

Page 4: evanescent
Originally the word *utakata*, which has the connotation of something vanishing like smoke. It could also be translated as "transient, fragile, bubble, foam." Indeed, one of the kanji means "bubble," and Ann talks in this chapter about turning into bubbles and disappearing into water. "Evanescent" poetically captures these various nuances.

Page 11, panel 4: Coming-of-Age ceremony
Coming-of-Age Day is usually the second Monday in January. Youth turning twenty attend ceremonies and parties to celebrate becoming an adult.

Page 16, panel 5: *shochu*
Shochu is an alcoholic beverage made from fermented rice or potatoes that is similar to vodka.

Page 16, panel 5: *ponshu*
Nihonshu, or Japanese *sake*.

Page 30, panel 5: *furisode*
A kind of kimono for young adult, unmarried women characterized by long sleeves. Often worn by girls at their Coming-of-Age ceremony.

Page 41, panel 6: "Naka looks like his daughter."
In the original, the friend said Naka and her boyfriend looked like an *enko*-couple. *Enko* is short for *enjo-kosai*, which literally means "compensated-relationship dating." As with paid escorts in the U.S., the pairing usually consists of an older person paying for the companionship of a younger person.

Page 47, panel 6: closing ceremony
Originally *ote wo haishaku*, a request to begin clapping in unison to a predetermined rhythm. A ritual people perform at the end of a gathering.

Page 52, panel 8: *Izumo soba*
Soba are buckwheat noodles. Many regions around Japan have a special local method of preparation.

Page 97, panel 2: the witch
Originally *otsubone*, a term used to denote a woman with a long professional career. Historically, an *otsubone* was a lord's high-ranking first wife.

Page 112, panel 3: *yubamaki*
Yuba is tofu skin or dried beancurd. *Yubamaki* (literally "tofu skin roll") is *yuba* around some kind of filling.

Page 123, panel 3, "Should we register the marriage first?"
In Japan, people legalize their marriage by registering at a local government office. The wedding ceremony for family and friends is merely a celebration and often occurs long after registration.

Page 132, panel 1: "Even ogres weep."
The original is a shortened version of the saying *oni no me nimo namida*. The general sense of this expression is that even cold or unemotional people cry.

Page 132, panel 7: wedding money envelopes
The kanji on these envelopes, *kotobuki*, means "longevity" and "congratulations." People usually give money enclosed in these envelopes to a marrying couple.

Page 139, panel 6: company uniform
While it isn't as prevalent as it used to be, many companies in Japan still require female employees to wear uniforms. The male employee's "uniform" is often just a Western-style suit.

Profile of Hinako Ashihara

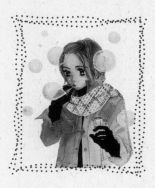

This time the story is about Ann's life at 20 and 26. I thought this was a long way off, but now Ann is all of 26! Amazing!
—Hinako Ashihara

Hinako Ashihara won the 50th Shogakukan Manga Award for *Sunadokei*. She debuted with *Sono Hanashi Okotowari Shimasu* in *Bessatsu Shojo Comics* in 1994. Her other works include *SOS*, *Forbidden Dance*, and *Tennen Bitter Chocolate*.

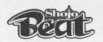

SAND CHRONICLES
Vol. 7
Shojo Beat Manga Edition

STORY AND ART BY HINAKO ASHIHARA

English Adaptation/John Werry
Translation/Kinami Watabe, HC Language Solutions Inc.
Touch-up Art & Lettering/Rina Mapa
Additional Touch-up/Rachel Lightfoot
Design/Izumi Evers
Interior/Deirdre Shiozawa
Editor/Annette Roman

VP, Production/Alvin Lu
VP, Sales & Product Marketing/Gonzalo Ferreyra
VP, Creative/Linda Espinosa
Publisher/Hyoe Narita

SUNADOKEI 7 by Hinako ASHIHARA © 2005 Hinako ASHIHARA
All rights reserved. Original Japanese edition
published in 2005 by Shogakukan Inc., Tokyo.

Printed in Canada

Published by VIZ Media, LLC
P.O. Box 77010
San Francisco, CA 94107

10 9 8 7 6 5 4 3 2 1
First printing, January 2010

www.viz.com   www.shojobeat.com

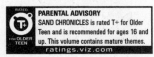

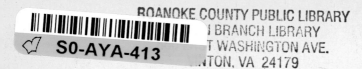

Sand
Chronicles